AF266426

# STILL HERE

# Life Unresolved

AF266426

# STILL HERE

# Life Unresolved

Andrew Ford

Copyright © 2026 by Andrew Ford
All rights reserved.

No part of this book may be reproduced, stored in a retrieval system, or transmitted in any form or by any means—electronic, mechanical, photocopying, recording, or otherwise—without prior written permission of the publisher, except for brief quotations used in reviews or other uses permitted under copyright law.

This is a work of memoir. Certain names, identifying details, and nonessential characteristics have been changed for privacy. Dialogue has been reconstructed from memory. Dates are approximate unless the timing is material to the narrative.

The opinions and experiences expressed are the author's own. This book is not intended as medical, legal, or professional advice.

First edition: January 2026

ISBN 978-1-972034-00-2 (hardcover)
ISBN 978-1-972034-01-9 (paperback)
ISBN 978-1-972034-02-6 (epub)
ISBN 978-1-972034-03-3 (audiobook)

Cover and interior design: Andrew Ford
Published by Andrew S. Ford (imprint)
Kansas City, Kansas, United States of America

Printed in the United States of America
10 9 8 7 6 5 4 3 2 1

Library of Congress Control Number: 2026903762

For those who keep going without the comfort of resolution.

*"Survival is not the same thing as healing."*

# CONTENT NOTE

This book contains material that may be difficult to read.

It includes depictions of war and its aftermath, exposure to violence, psychological distress, suicidal ideation and attempts, substance use, altered states of consciousness, family rupture, grief, spiritual struggle, and prolonged emotional numbness. Some scenes are intentionally immersive and may evoke sensations of disorientation, panic, or despair rather than describe them at a distance.

Nothing in this book is presented for shock value or instruction. It is written to reflect how these experiences were lived, not how they are typically summarized.

This is not a guide to recovery. It does not offer reassurance, coping strategies, or resolution. It does not move away from painful material once it appears.

Readers who are currently struggling with thoughts of self-harm or who know they are vulnerable to immersive depictions of psychological distress should consider whether now is the right time to read this book.

The responsibility for turning the page remains with the reader.

# Author's Note

This book is a memoir, but it is not an inventory. It is not a comprehensive record of every year, every relationship, every conversation, every wound. It is a reconstruction of the events that surfaced to memory while writing—events that carried enough charge to reshape the rest of my life, or enough weight to explain why certain parts of my mind now behave the way they do.

Memory is not a camera. It is closer to a nervous system: selective, adaptive, sometimes precise, sometimes missing entire sections. Some scenes in these pages are sharp down to smell and sound. Others are remembered as atmosphere—how a room felt, how a season moved, how a household held itself when no one spoke about what was happening. Where dialogue appears, it is reconstructed from recollection. Where dates appear, they are approximate unless the time period matters to the logic of what occurred. The sequence of events is true in the way lived experience is true, even when the mind can't provide a perfect timestamp.

For privacy and safety, identifying details have been changed. Names are omitted or replaced. Certain locations are generalized. Some characteristics of secondary people have been altered so the individuals in my life cannot be easily traced through a combination of specifics. If a detail felt both vivid and unnecessary, I chose necessity over completeness. That choice is not an attempt to manipulate perception; it is an ethical boundary. I am telling my story. Other people appear here because they were part of my environment. They do not appear here to be prosecuted.

Some portions of my military experience are described in broad terms and with intentional restraint. Parts of the work involved sensitive or classified elements. This book does not attempt to reveal those elements or to create a comprehensive operational account. It focuses on what service did to my body and mind—how the environment trained the nervous system, how threat became a baseline, how moral friction and constant vigilance migrated into civilian life and kept running even when the context changed.

This is also not a book written to prove a single cause. It would be easy to force a clean line from childhood to adulthood and claim inevitability. That kind of story reads smoothly and sells a satisfying explanation. It would also be dishonest. Early chapters are not presented as destiny. They are presented as a context—an atmosphere that shaped certain habits, certain sensitivities, certain strategies—but the major shifts in my present condition are not explained by childhood alone. Many people come from difficult beginnings and do not develop what I developed. The point here is accumulation: how different kinds of stress stacked over time, how certain experiences turned adaptation into impairment, and how later losses and family dynamics kept reactivating what my body had already learned.

There are moments in these pages that may be difficult to read. The book includes depictions of war-zone conditions, violence, and death. It includes descriptions of suicidal thinking and suicide attempts. It includes altered states and treatment experiences. I have written these sections to be honest about what occurred and what it felt like to inhabit it, without turning them into instruction. If any of those topics are unsafe for you to engage right now, it may be wise to skip those passages or put the book down. There is no moral requirement to finish a difficult story on a deadline.

My intent in writing this was not inspiration. I am wary of trauma-as-product. I am wary of the cultural demand that every injury become a lesson, and every survival become a redemption arc. Some people do heal cleanly. Some people do not. Some lives resolve into a narrative of recovery that can be framed as victory. Mine has not, at least not in the way stories are usually allowed to end.

What I can offer is documentation: a lived account of what it looks like when the mind remains on alert long after the threat environment is gone; what it looks like when grief flattens instead of releasing; what it looks like when family obligation collides with instability; what it looks like when a person can appear competent while privately managing a system that doesn't reliably cooperate. If there is value here, it is in accuracy rather than uplift—naming what many people carry quietly, and refusing to soften it into something comfortable.

The structure of the book reflects the way my life has been lived: through systems. Routine, lists, rituals, small sanctuaries, careful control of stimulus, the constant effort to keep the mind from becoming the only place I live. Those systems may appear obsessive from the outside. For me, they are scaffolding. They are not personality quirks. They are maintenance requirements.

I have used language throughout the book that can sound clinical at times—terms that describe patterns of vigilance, dissociation, depression, anxiety, impairment. I did not choose that language to reduce myself to categories. I chose it because the categories exist whether I use them or not, and because naming a pattern can reduce shame. When a system has a name, it can be managed. When it has no name, it can only be endured.

Finally, a note about the title: *Still Here* is not a triumphant declaration. It is a statement of fact. "Unresolved" is not a tease. It is the condition. Life does not always deliver closure, and the mind does not always translate suffering into wisdom. Sometimes continuing is the whole story. Sometimes endurance is not beautiful. Sometimes it is simply what happens when a person keeps taking the next step because structure is the only thing strong enough to hold the day together.

That is what these pages are. A record. A map of a mind.

A life that kept going without the comfort of resolution.

# Table of Contents


CONTENT NOTE......................................................................7

Author's Note.......................................................................9


CHAPTER 1 – The Baseline....................................................15

CHAPTER 2 – First Rooms....................................................33

CHAPTER 3 – Second Yard...................................................51

CHAPTER 4 – Between Bells.................................................69

CHAPTER 5 – The Exit Door................................................87

CHAPTER 6 – Borrowed Order...........................................107

CHAPTER 7 – After the Uniform........................................125

CHAPTER 8 – The Ring Dish..............................................143

CHAPTER 9 – Years of Vanishing.......................................161

CHAPTER 10 – The Machine Moves...................................179

CHAPTER 11 – Dust and Silence........................................197

CHAPTER 12 – The Long Debrief.......................................217

CHAPTER 13 – Wide Sky....................................................235

CHAPTER 14 – Winter Roads.............................................259

CHAPTER 15 – Frozen Time...............................................279

CHAPTER 16 – Learning Help.............................................301

CHAPTER 17 – Altered Semesters.......................................321

CHAPTER 18 – A Hitchable Home......................................367

CHAPTER 19 – Thin-Walled Quiet......................................399

CHAPTER 20 - Residue........................................................415


Afterword...........................................................................435

Author's Note On Process...................................................449

Timeline.............................................................................451

Glossary.............................................................................455

Comprehensive Discussion & Question Guide......................465

Crisis and Support Resources..............................................473

Acknowledgments...............................................................475

About the Author................................................................479

# CHAPTER 1

# *The Baseline*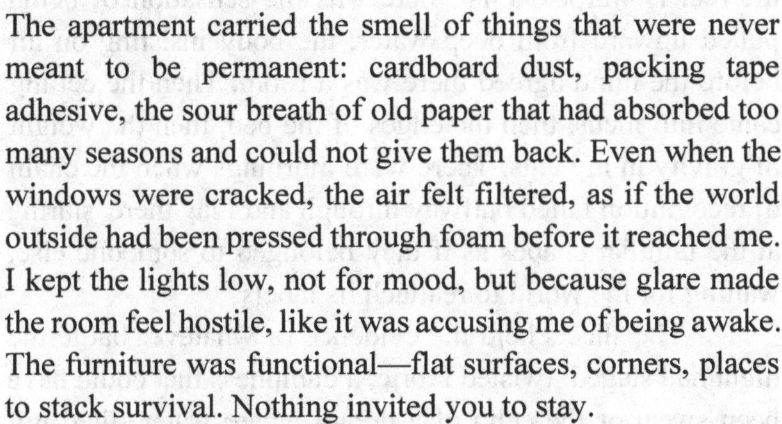

The apartment carried the smell of things that were never meant to be permanent: cardboard dust, packing tape adhesive, the sour breath of old paper that had absorbed too many seasons and could not give them back. Even when the windows were cracked, the air felt filtered, as if the world outside had been pressed through foam before it reached me. I kept the lights low, not for mood, but because glare made the room feel hostile, like it was accusing me of being awake. The furniture was functional—flat surfaces, corners, places to stack survival. Nothing invited you to stay.

Quiet should have been a gift, but it wasn't the kind of quiet people describe when they mean comfort. It was sealed quiet, a tight lid pressed down over the room until my breathing felt monitored. Under that lid lived a thin, constant tone, a sound that never belonged to any appliance and never came from any direction I could point to. Some mornings it hovered in the distance; other mornings it sat right behind the ears, bright and merciless, like a wire stretched too tight. The moment I noticed it, it grew louder, like attention fed it.

The tone was not alone. It recruited. If I turned the ceiling fan on, it harmonized with the blades until the room sounded like a distant engine. If I left the fridge humming, the hum became suspicious, too steady to be trusted, as if it were hiding a message in its frequency. I could hear electricity in the walls on the bad days, a faint buzzing like a beehive behind drywall. Auditory attention became a curse: once a sound entered my awareness, it refused to leave, looping in my head even after it stopped, replaying like a fragment of a song you can't turn off.

Waking did not arrive as a clean event. It arrived in fragments, the way a film spools through a projector when the reel is warped. First there was the sensation of being pulled upward from deep water, the body insisting on air before the mind agreed there was a room. Then the ceiling came into focus, then the edges of the bed, then the weight of gravity in my legs. There were mornings when the chain of recognition failed halfway through and I lay there, staring at the familiar shapes as if they belonged to someone else, waiting for the world to reattach its labels.

The sheets held the evidence of whatever battle the night had staged: twisted fabric, a dampness that could have been sweat or the echo of a dream where water filled my lungs. My skin tingled in patches, as if nerves were waking up at different speeds. I did a body scan the way you check a vehicle after an impact—shoulders, neck, jaw, hands. Sometimes pain announced itself late, blooming behind the eyes or drilling into a temple. Sometimes the pain never arrived, and the absence felt like a trick, like the body was hiding something it would reveal later when I had fewer defenses.

The clock on the nightstand claimed time was moving in a straight line. My body disagreed. Sleep was not rest; it was a series of ambushes, a door I had to walk through even though something waited behind it. Sometimes I snapped awake with a sound stuck in my throat, my heart trying to kick its way out of my ribs. Sometimes I woke with damp hands and no memory of a nightmare, only the aftertaste of terror, as if the fear had been injected directly into my bloodstream without bothering to show me the scene.

There was a particular cruelty to the nights when I didn't dream at all, when sleep was just a black hole that swallowed hours and spit me out unchanged. Those were the mornings when I felt most broken, because it meant even unconsciousness couldn't process anything; it could only pause it. I stared at the ceiling and bargained with time: give me one normal hour, one stretch of rest that doesn't feel like drowning, one interval where my nervous system isn't braced for impact. The bargains went unanswered. The day arrived anyway, indifferent to negotiation.

In the first minute after waking, the world looked like it had been assembled in the dark. Edges shimmered. The air itself seemed grainy, as if the room were filled with invisible static. It wasn't hallucination in the storybook sense—no ghosts, no figures perched in the corners—but it was distortion, a constant interference that made everything feel slightly unreal. When I blinked, the patterns clung to the inside of my eyelids for a moment, a faint lattice of light that refused to vanish quickly, as if the nervous system didn't know how to close a file.

Screens made everything worse, but I reached for them anyway because distraction was the closest thing to control. The glow of a phone in a dark room turned the visual grain into a storm, tiny sparks swarming at the edges of letters. If I scrolled too fast, afterimages lingered like bruises on the inside of my eyes. High-contrast images—white text on black, bright icons, sudden video cuts—felt like small assaults. I blinked hard, pressed my palms into my eye sockets, tried to reset the signal, and still the static waited, patient and persistent.

I lay still and listened for the building. Pipes, footsteps, a neighbor's door, the elevator cable. Any evidence that other people existed in the same structure and were moving through their own mornings, in their own straight lines. When nothing came, the room felt too empty, and the emptiness felt like pressure. The mind started searching for something to attach to—sound, memory, danger. It found the tone in my head and amplified it until it was the only thing that seemed unquestionably real, the one constant the day could not dispute.

Isolation didn't feel peaceful. It felt like being sealed in a room where the air supply was measured. I could go days without hearing my own voice, and when I finally spoke—testing it, a word into the sink—it sounded foreign, like an actor trying on a role. I didn't invite anyone over, not because I hated people, but because I couldn't predict what version of myself would answer the door. If someone knocked unexpectedly, my first thought was not "who is it," but "what did I do wrong." The mind assigned threat to neutrality by default, as if calm were camouflage.

Getting out of bed meant negotiating with a body that didn't trust the day. The muscles held old tension like a debt. My hands shook sometimes, not dramatically, not enough to draw attention, but enough that I noticed it while reaching for a glass or pulling on a shirt. The stomach could be calm and then suddenly fold in on itself, as if it had been surprised by its own existence. Hunger didn't show up like hunger; it showed up as nausea, as irritation, as the sense that eating was a complicated task with consequences I couldn't predict.

The body kept a ledger of old impacts. Knees complained on stairs that were not steep. Fingers stiffened for no good reason, like they had forgotten how to be loose. There were days the lower back felt like a knot that had been tightened by invisible hands while I slept. The discomfort wasn't always sharp; sometimes it was a dull insistence, a background ache that made every movement feel like it was being graded. I caught myself moving carefully, protecting parts of myself without knowing why, as if the body expected punishment for the wrong posture.

I moved through the room in a careful way, as if sudden motion could crack the fragile sense of reality that had been stitched together during the night. The floor under my feet felt solid, but my mind treated it like a suggestion. There were days when the hallway seemed longer than it should be, as if the apartment had subtly rearranged itself while I slept. I paused and stared at the doorframe, measuring it with my eyes, testing whether the world still obeyed its own dimensions, whether the rules had stayed in place while I wasn't looking.

The bathroom light was harsh, a small sun with no mercy. The mirror caught me from the side like a surveillance camera. I didn't study the face; studying led to questions I couldn't answer, and questions led to spirals. I washed because the body needed it, because the rules of being a person demanded it, but the act didn't feel like care. It felt like maintenance. Water ran over my hands and I watched it like it belonged to a stranger. The sound of the faucet became another tone competing with the one that lived behind my ears.

In the mirror, the smallest details could trigger disgust: the tired heaviness under the eyes, the way my expression seemed to default to defense. I tried not to make a story out of it. Stories were dangerous, because once the mind started narrating, it started prosecuting. I shaved or didn't shave, brushed my teeth longer than necessary, rinsed until my mouth felt numb, trying to scrub out the taste of the night. The toothbrush scraped against enamel with a sound that made my scalp tighten. I watched my own hands move, precise and automatic, and felt like I was supervising a task instead of inhabiting it.

Some mornings the body betrayed me in humiliating ways. The mind decided a task had been completed—relief, routine, the simple privacy of a closed door—and only later did evidence appear that the decision had been wrong. A damp patch on the floor where it shouldn't be. The wrong drawer opened. The wrong room. It wasn't drunkenness or carelessness; it was a brief slip of alignment, a moment when the internal map of the apartment misregistered and the body acted on the wrong coordinates. Cleaning it up was not just about mess; it was about identity. If I could not trust my own map, what else could I not trust?

After a slip—after evidence showed my brain had misfiled the simplest private act—I felt a hot wave of humiliation that had nowhere to go. The apartment became an accomplice. Every object felt like a witness: the hamper, the baseboards, the corner where a mistake had landed. I cleaned with intensity, not because cleanliness mattered, but because erasing the trace felt like erasing the fact that it happened. I opened windows even when the air outside was cold. I scrubbed until my hands stung. Shame turned physical, a heat rising in the chest, and the only counterspell was routine: wipe, rinse, repeat—because repetition was the only spell I had.

The kitchen was a collection of quiet disappointments: cabinets that opened with a sigh, plates that had to be washed before they could be used, a fridge that held more intentions than food. I stood there with the door open and felt my mind stall, as if each option demanded a level of future-planning I didn't possess. The simplest meal required decisions: what, how much, now or later, will it sit right, will it hurt, will it make the day worse. I closed the fridge and leaned on the counter, staring at the blank surface like it could offer instruction.

When I did eat, it was often the same safe rotation, the same predictable textures. Anything new felt like risk. The body had its own moods, and it punished surprise. Some days there was a sharp urgency after eating, a sprint to the bathroom that felt like the gut had turned on me out of spite. Other days there was a heaviness, as if the food had become a stone. The mind watched all of it with a detached dread, like a scientist observing an experiment that could never be replicated because the variables kept changing without warning.

I tried to build a routine the way people build fences —straight lines, repeated actions, barriers against chaos. Wake, wash, eat, move. But the mind sabotaged repetition by insisting each moment was new and dangerous. Even familiar sounds could trigger a flare of panic: a car door outside, a sudden laugh from a neighboring balcony, a distant bang that could have been anything. The body reacted before I could interpret, heart speeding, shoulders rising, breath tightening. It felt unfair to be startled by life's background noise, as if existence itself had become a threat.

Sound outside the apartment had its own hierarchy of threat. A distant siren was background. A sharp bark of a car horn could jolt my whole body upright. A sudden metallic bang—trash can, construction, someone dropping something—sent heat up my spine, a flash of readiness that felt ridiculous once my mind caught up. The body didn't care that it was ridiculous. It reacted as if the world still required that level of alertness. Even when I left the building and walked to the car, I moved like I was crossing an exposed space, head swiveling, eyes scanning for nothing in particular, braced for impact that never announced itself ahead of time.

Phones were supposed to connect you to other human beings. Mine felt like an instrument for guilt. Messages accumulated like dust. I could see the little numbers, the unanswered calls, the reminders of obligations. Some were harmless—an invitation, a check-in—but my brain treated them like traps. Replying meant entering a conversation. Conversation meant being seen. Being seen meant being asked to account for myself, to explain why I was not living like the version of me people expected to exist. I watched the notifications pile up and felt the weight of them press down on my chest.

The longer I stayed silent, the harder it became to break silence. Messages from people who cared—or who had once cared—began to feel like artifacts from a different life. I could hear their voices in my head sometimes, not as hallucination, but as memory, the way you can replay a familiar cadence. The memory carried expectations: the version of me that joked, that showed up, that participated. Facing those expectations made my chest tighten. So I postponed. I told myself I would respond later, after I was calmer, after the day was cleaner, after I had something to offer. Later became a horizon that kept moving away.

There were days I avoided leaving the apartment entirely, not out of laziness but out of fear of what the outside would do to me. Bright light made the static in my vision roar. Crowds turned the air into a swarm. Even a short drive felt like a gamble with my nervous system, because any unpredictable noise, any near-miss, any sudden brake lights could pull me into a state where the world narrowed to threat. Staying inside seemed safer, and safety became its own prison. The walls protected me, but they also trained me to fear what lived beyond them.

Inside that horizon, the mind tried to escape by going upward into theory. If the body couldn't tolerate the day, the brain tried to outthink the day. It built models of reality like scaffolding: branching timelines, overlapping worlds, the possibility that consciousness was a radio tuned to a particular frequency. If there were infinite versions of me, maybe one of them was living a clean life, waking rested, drinking something warm without dread. The thought didn't comfort me; it made me feel split, scattered across a universe I couldn't reach, like a shattered mirror reflecting lives I wasn't allowed to inhabit.

In the abstract spaces of my mind, I ran thought experiments the way other people ran errands. If consciousness could be copied, would the copy be me or just a convincing counterfeit? If time was not a line but a field, could a person step sideways into a neighboring moment the way you step from one room into another? I pictured the apartment as a node, a fixed coordinate, and myself as a traveler who kept respawning here after every collapse. The theories weren't hobbies. They were coping mechanisms: if reality was flexible, maybe suffering wasn't permanent; if reality was layered, maybe there was a layer where I could breathe.

Sometimes the theories arrived uninvited, like intrusive images. I brushed my teeth and suddenly the mind leapt: what if this moment has already happened, not once but an infinite number of times, in an infinite number of variations? What if the sensation of déjà vu is a glitch in the stitching, the seam between two nearly identical universes rubbing raw? The room tilted—not physically, but conceptually—until even the toothbrush felt like a prop. I spit, rinsed, stared at my hands dripping water into the sink, and the water looked too bright, too sharp, like it was rendered rather than real.

Sometimes the theories shifted into something darker: the suspicion that I was watching my own life through glass, that the person moving through the room was a character and I was the audience. I looked at my hands and felt a second of detachment, as if the skin were a glove. If I pinched my arm, pain arrived on schedule, but the schedule itself felt suspicious, like a programmed response. The mind whispered simulation, loop, glitch. It pointed to tiny coincidences—the same number on a clock, the same phrase overheard twice—and treated them like evidence. In that state, comfort became impossible, because even comfort would feel staged.

The problem was that my mind no longer trusted "just." Nothing was just. A shadow on the wall could be a trick of light, or it could be the shape of fear. A sound could be a neighbor, or it could be the beginning of something that would never end. Even my own thoughts felt external sometimes, like they were being played into my head from a speaker I couldn't locate. I caught myself listening to the inside of my skull the way you listen to a hallway at night, trying to identify footsteps, trying to decide whether to get up and check or pretend not to hear.

Sleep, when it came, did not reset the system. It opened a second theater, a place where the mind staged scenes with the vividness of memory but the logic of chaos. I could be in a vehicle that wasn't quite a vehicle, moving too fast over a road that wasn't quite a road. The body lurched, weightless, as if gravity had been temporarily canceled. Sometimes everything slowed and I looked up through glass at the moon, huge and close, and in that slow-motion clarity I understood—without words—that impact was inevitable, that the dream was guiding me toward something I couldn't avoid.

Then the dream switched without warning. Water rose where there hadn't been water. The vehicle sank as calmly as a stone. The cold wrapped around my chest. I tried to inhale and only took in liquid, panic blooming instantly, absolute and animal. The drowning felt real enough that waking was like being torn out of the ocean. I jerked upright, gulping air, hands clawing at sheets as if they were seaweed. The room was dark and still, and the tone in my head was waiting, unchanged, like it had been standing guard while I slept.

Other dreams had a quieter violence. I was in an enclosed space with patterned walls, colors too saturated, geometry too precise, like the inside of a machine designed by an artist. There was a chair in the center that looked ordinary until I sat in it, and then the chair became a mechanism. Straps, locks, a feeling of being plugged into something unseen. The dream flooded me with sensation— joy sharp enough to hurt, a sense of connection that felt cosmic—and at the peak of it I snapped awake, heart racing, grieving a joy that evaporated the moment consciousness returned.

The waking world carried residue from those nights. I walked through the apartment with the feeling that I had just returned from somewhere else, somewhere my body still wanted to believe in. The line between dream and day blurred in small ways. A corner of the room looked unfamiliar for a second, like the texture had been swapped. I heard a sound and didn't know whether it came from the building or from the afterimage of sleep. My brain tested reality the way you test a tooth with your tongue, pressing on it again and again to see if it would wobble.

I tried to counter that weakness with rituals: the same mug, the same chair, the same music at low volume. I kept my environment controlled because control was the closest thing to peace I could access. But control had a cost. It narrowed the world until it was a set of variables I could manage, and anything outside that set became intolerable. A knock at the door could turn my whole body to ice. The thought of unexpected visitors made my skin crawl. I did not want to be witnessed in my unguarded state, mid-collapse, mid-recalibration, looking like a person who had lost the basic skill of being okay.

There were times I had to go somewhere else— appointments, errands, obligations that did not care about my internal weather. Those trips felt like leaving a bunker. The outside air was too bright, too loud, full of motion. My eyes caught on reflective surfaces: windshields, windows, chrome. The visual static thickened, and with it came irritability, an urge to flee. People moved in groups, laughing, talking into earbuds, carrying drinks, existing with a casual confidence that felt almost obscene. I moved through them like a ghost trying to imitate a body, careful not to collide, careful not to look too strange.

After those trips, the apartment didn't feel like home. It felt like recovery. I returned and shut the door and stood with my back against it, breathing as if I had just outrun something. My hands tingled. My jaw ached from being clenched without permission. Sometimes the body crashed into exhaustion so fast it felt like a switch had been flipped. Other times it refused rest entirely, the nervous system stuck in overdrive, a motor that wouldn't shut off. I paced the room, touching surfaces as I passed, as if contact could reassure me that the apartment had not drifted away while I was gone.

The pacing wasn't purposeful. It was a form of containment. Movement was the only thing that kept the mind from collapsing inward. If I sat too still, thoughts swarmed: images I didn't ask for, sounds that weren't sounds so much as echoes of sounds, sensations that belonged to other times. The apartment filled with them until it felt crowded with invisible occupants. I stood at the sink and gripped the edge of the counter until my knuckles went pale, trying to anchor myself to something that did not shift, trying to convince my nervous system that the present was safe.

When the detachment got stronger, my name felt like a label someone else had applied. Pronouns became awkward. I thought "I" and it sounded like a lie, like using the wrong word in a language you barely spoke. In those moments, the apartment felt less like a place I inhabited and more like a set that had been built around me, walls painted with realism. I touched the doorframe, the countertop, the fabric of the couch, trying to convince myself it was real by collecting texture. Texture helped, briefly. Cold metal, rough paint, smooth ceramic—proof that matter still existed even when meaning dissolved.

Sometimes the mind offered a bargain: if I allowed it to drift far enough, if I stopped insisting on ordinary reality, it would stop hurting me in the way ordinary reality hurt. It opened a door to abstraction. In that space, the apartment became less important. The body became a shell. The self became an observer floating above a timeline. It sounded like relief on paper, but in practice it was terrifying. The moment I felt myself detaching, panic spiked, because detaching felt like disappearing, and disappearing felt too close to not coming back.

The day dragged itself forward anyway, indifferent. I lost track of time without realizing I had lost it. I looked up and discovered hours had been swallowed, as if the air had eaten them. The sun changed position. The light in the room tilted. A shadow migrated across the floor, slow and patient. I tried to reconstruct what I had done during the missing time and came up with nothing but fragments: standing in the kitchen, staring at a wall, scrolling without absorbing meaning, sitting on the edge of the bed with my hands clasped as if in prayer to nothing.

Some part of me insisted on keeping records. Not written records—those felt like evidence—but mental checklists: did I take care of the basics, did I eat, did I wash, did I answer anyone, did I leave the bed. The checklists were harsh. They treated survival as performance. Failing them triggered shame, and shame triggered withdrawal, and withdrawal made everything worse. I told myself I was a grown person and should be able to do grown-person tasks.

The telling didn't help. It only added a second layer of pain, the pain of failing at the pain.

Shame lived in the body, not as an idea but as heat. It rose in my chest when I looked at unwashed dishes, when I looked at the pile of laundry that had become a landscape. It rose when I thought about the people who used to see me as competent, reliable, dependable. It rose when I thought about how my life had narrowed to managing symptoms and avoiding triggers. The shame was not loud. It was persistent. It was the kind that convinces you that asking for help is an accusation, that needing anything makes you a burden, that your existence has become an expense no one agreed to pay.

There were physical problems that were harder to speak about even to myself. The body did not cooperate with intimacy the way it once had, and even the memory of closeness could ignite bitterness. Pain arrived like a migraine wave sometimes, a pressure behind the eyes that turned light into a weapon. Sleep cycles drifted until day and night felt like suggestions rather than rules. Weight clung to me in a way that felt unjust, as if the body had decided to store everything it couldn't process. Each issue alone would have been manageable. Together they formed a cage, each bar a separate limitation, each limitation feeding the others.

I tried to do small repairs. One shower became a victory, not because the act was difficult in a technical sense, but because it required consent from every part of my nervous system. One cleaned surface became proof that I could still alter my environment. I wiped a counter and stared at the clean strip, the way you stare at a cleared path in a forest. The victories never lasted. The mess returned. The tone returned. The dreams returned. The repairs were temporary, like putting a bandage on a wound that kept reopening. Still, I kept making them, because stopping completely felt like surrendering the right to call myself alive.

Sometimes the outside world reached in anyway. A voicemail. A letter. A notice. A reminder that systems existed—money, schedules, deadlines—and those systems did not care about dissociation or panic. My chest tightened as soon as I saw official-looking text. I held the paper and felt like it weighed more than it should. The mind started calculating consequences, and consequences multiplied until they felt infinite. In that moment, multiverse theory wasn't comforting; it was torture. If there were infinite timelines, there were infinite ways to fail, infinite realities where one missed deadline turned into a cascade of irreversible loss.

I negotiated with myself the way you negotiate with a dangerous animal. Slow movements. Soft voice. No sudden demands. If I pushed too hard, the system revolted. If I did nothing, the system collapsed. The balance was narrow. I promised myself a task and offered a reward: make the call, then sit in the dark. Walk outside, then return to the bunker. Eat something, then lie down. I hated the bargaining because it made me feel childish, but the alternative was worse. The alternative was paralysis so complete it felt like being buried under invisible weight, unable to move not because the muscles failed, but because meaning failed.

Some days a wave of anger cut through the fog. It flared with no clear target, an electrical surge that made me want to break something just to hear a different sound. The anger felt like proof that a part of me was still alive, still reacting, still refusing to accept this as normal. But it also scared me because it came with images of past explosions, moments when the body had been trained to respond to threat with force. Anger was a door that opened onto other rooms I didn't want to enter, rooms full of adrenaline and consequence. I kept the door closed as best I could, and the effort of keeping it closed became another kind of exhaustion.

At night the apartment became a sealed container again. The world outside dimmed, and with it the pressure of expectation, but the mind did not relax. Darkness invited the theater back. I lay in bed and waited for sleep like you wait for a storm you can't outrun. Sometimes I resisted it and lost anyway. Sometimes I surrendered and still got punished. The sheet against my skin felt too hot, then too cold. The tone in my head sharpened. My eyes closed and the visual static bloomed behind the lids, bright specks drifting like ash in a black sky.

There were moments, in that half-sleep threshold, when reality felt negotiable. The apartment seemed to drift, as if it were a module attached to a larger machine. I imagined the walls sliding open to reveal other rooms, other versions of the same life. In one, the bed was shared. In another, the sink was clean. In another, the mind was quiet. The images came with a grief so sharp it felt like a blade. Because if those versions could exist, it meant my current version was not inevitable. It meant something had gone wrong. It meant the gap between what could be and what was had become a canyon I couldn't cross.

The morning always returned. Light seeped in through the blinds in thin bars, cutting the room into stripes like a cage. The body surfaced from sleep with the same heaviness, the same reluctant awareness. The first breath arrived like a decision. The mind scanned: tone, static, nausea, dread. The apartment was unchanged, stubbornly itself. The world was still waiting outside, full of people living straight-line lives. And I was here, in the same contained space, trying to assemble a day out of fragments, trying to make a self hold together long enough to complete the next small task.

There was no clean ending to that cycle, only continuation. Each day was a rehearsal for the next, each night a trapdoor into the theater. The cost wasn't dramatic in a way that earned sympathy from strangers. It was slow cost. It was the erosion of confidence, the shrinking of possibilities, the quiet surrender of things most people take for granted. The apartment held the evidence in small ways: the half-finished tasks, the controlled lighting, the careful routes I walked from room to room. It held the shape of a life reduced to survival, a life that had learned to fear itself.

On the worst nights, lying awake with the tone screaming and the mind spinning through alternate universes like a roulette wheel, one thought surfaced with brutal simplicity: I was still here. Not because I had solved anything, not because I had been rescued, not because the pain had ended. I was still here because some stubborn mechanism in me refused to stop, refused to let the story end without an account. The refusal wasn't noble. It was raw. It was survival without beauty. And in that rawness, unfinished and uncomforting, the next morning waited—ready to arrive in pieces, ready to be picked up again.

# CHAPTER 2
# *First Rooms*

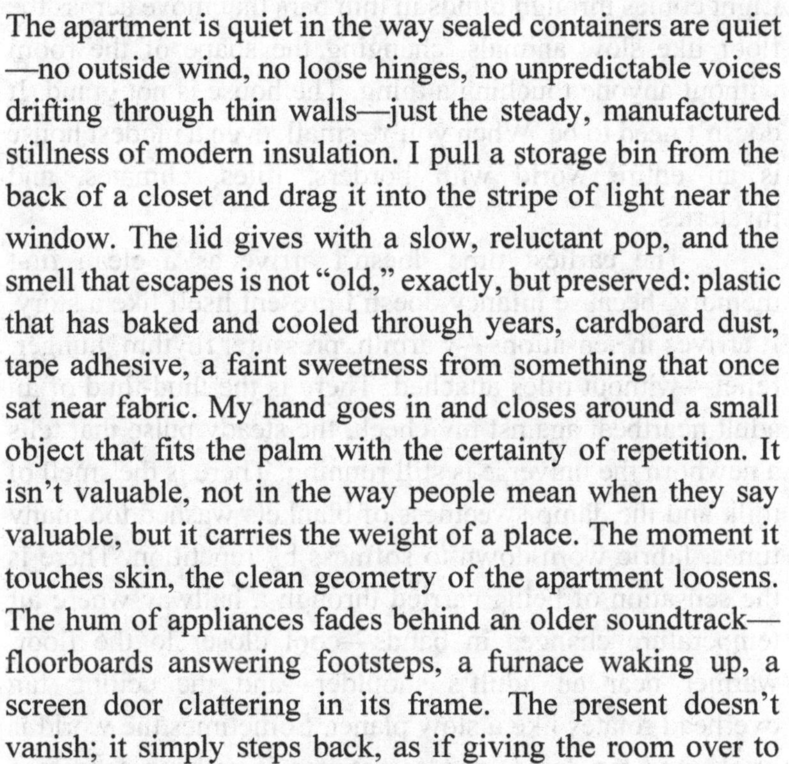

The apartment is quiet in the way sealed containers are quiet—no outside wind, no loose hinges, no unpredictable voices drifting through thin walls—just the steady, manufactured stillness of modern insulation. I pull a storage bin from the back of a closet and drag it into the stripe of light near the window. The lid gives with a slow, reluctant pop, and the smell that escapes is not "old," exactly, but preserved: plastic that has baked and cooled through years, cardboard dust, tape adhesive, a faint sweetness from something that once sat near fabric. My hand goes in and closes around a small object that fits the palm with the certainty of repetition. It isn't valuable, not in the way people mean when they say valuable, but it carries the weight of a place. The moment it touches skin, the clean geometry of the apartment loosens. The hum of appliances fades behind an older soundtrack—floorboards answering footsteps, a furnace waking up, a screen door clattering in its frame. The present doesn't vanish; it simply steps back, as if giving the room over to something that was waiting. The first house rises in front of me like a set that never stopped existing, only went dark.

The first house is modest, low, built more for function than for desire. It hugs the ground with the stubbornness of a place that expects to be stood on and endured. The exterior has the plainness of working neighborhoods—siding that dulls in summer, trim that needs paint, a porch that creaks in a familiar way. The front door sticks when it's humid and opens with a dry scrape when it isn't, and the sound becomes so normal it might as well be part of language. Inside, the air always carries a layered smell: detergent and cooking and old carpet warmed by sun, plus the quiet scent of wood and plaster holding onto years. Light comes through blinds in thin bars that move across the floor like slow animals, changing the shape of the room without anyone touching a thing. The house is not grand. It doesn't need to be. When you're small, even a modest house is an entire world with borders, rules, climates, and mysteries.

The earliest time doesn't arrive as a clean first memory, because infancy doesn't present itself like a story. It arrives in sensations—warmth, pressure, rhythm, hunger, relief—without titles attached. There is the thud-thud of an adult heartbeat against my cheek, the steady pulse that tells a newborn the universe is still running. There is the smell of milk and the damp sweetness of blankets washed too many times, fabric worn down to softness by repetition. There is the sensation of being carried through a hallway where air temperature changes in bands—cool closer to the floor, warmer near an adult's shoulder—and the ceiling fan overhead rotates like a slow planet. Sometimes the world is bright and too large, and sometimes it narrows to a face hovering close, eyes focused on me like I'm the most important thing in the room. None of it has dialogue. None of it carries a moral. It is simply the nervous system recording what it can: safe, warm, loud, quiet, again.

One of the first "events" in that time is not something I hold as a memory at all, but something I'm told later, retold enough times that it becomes a picture in my head anyway.

I'm still nursing in the story, still at an age where food and comfort are braided together so tightly they might as well be the same thing. A caregiver leaves the house to retrieve two older kids who have wandered off and gotten into trouble—kids old enough to move with their own momentum, young enough to forget consequences. The caregiver comes back, breathless and frustrated, and tries to resume the routine, tries to latch me on the way it has been done before. In the story, I refuse. Not fussy refusal, not distracted refusal—just a hard, baffling refusal, as if something has changed in a system that was supposed to be automatic. After that, in the retelling, I become "efficient," finishing quickly, refusing to continue, turning nourishment into a timed transaction. The adults attach meaning to it because adults do that. They add guilt, they add blame, they add theories. For me, it sits where it belongs: as a fact of infancy that I don't possess from the inside, one of those early-life anecdotes that says more about adult anxiety than it does about a baby.

If the house teaches anything that early, it teaches the body a map. I learn it by being carried, by being set down, by crawling from one texture to another. The living room carpet has a rough patch near a corner where people step more often. The kitchen floor is smoother and colder, the kind of surface that makes a toddler's knees sting after a while. The hallway is narrow enough that an adult brushing past can graze both walls with shoulders, and that narrowness makes sound bounce differently—voices feel closer, footsteps feel heavier. The bathroom door doesn't latch properly, so it swings open with a soft complaint if it isn't pressed shut just right, and that becomes an early lesson in privacy: there are spaces meant to be private, and privacy can fail if a hinge decides it wants to. In the first house, even the small mechanical quirks become part of life's grammar. The place teaches you how to move through it before you can explain it.

As walking arrives, the first house becomes a playground with invisible rules. Some cabinets are allowed. Some are forbidden. Certain drawers can be opened and explored, producing harmless treasures—plastic containers, mismatched lids, dull utensils. Other drawers summon an immediate voice from another room, the tone sharp enough to turn my stomach cold before I understand why. The back porch is a threshold to a different country, a place where sunlight is louder and the air tastes like grass and dust. The yard is uneven in patches, dotted with weeds and bare spots where grass refuses to thrive. A fence marks the edge of my allowed universe, and beyond it are other yards, other noises, other dogs, other lives. The fence doesn't feel like oppression when you're small; it feels like definition. It says: here is the world you can navigate, here is the world you cannot.

The house has a rhythm that runs on sound. Mornings begin with a coffee maker gurgling, a faucet running, the clink of a cup on a counter. Sometimes a radio turns on low, voices talking about weather and traffic in a tone that suggests the outside world has already started without me. Sometimes the television becomes a fireplace of moving light, filling the living room with music, laughter, cartoon violence that resets itself every episode. Adults move through tasks with practiced speed—packing lunches, finding shoes, locating missing items that always seem to vanish right when time is tight. A kid becomes a satellite in that orbit, pulled by gravity, learning to anticipate moods by the way a cabinet closes or a chair scrapes. In the first house, emotion doesn't need to be announced; it arrives through tempo. A slow morning has one kind of sound. A tense morning has another.

Faces are learned the way furniture is learned—by repetition, by the way they occupy the same spaces. There are caregivers in the house, more than one set of hands, more than one voice, and their voices carry different textures. One voice softens at the end of sentences, designed to soothe. Another voice is practical and clipped, designed to get through a list. There are other kids in the house too, bodies that run down the hallway, laughter that erupts and disappears around corners. Some of those kids are older, old enough to bring the outside world's chaos into the yard and onto the porch, old enough to make plans that don't include adult permission. Some are close enough to my age that play becomes a shared language—blocks clacking, cars rolling, stories invented with stuffed animals and action figures. In those years, "family" isn't a concept I analyze; it's simply the default population of my world, the small tribe inside the fence.

The first house contains ordinary childhood fear, the kind that blooms in empty spaces. Closets feel like mouths. Under beds feel like tunnels. Dark corners feel unfinished, like the world forgot to render them completely. At night, when the lights go out, the house doesn't disappear; it transforms. Hallways become longer. Shadows lean in. The same window that is a rectangle of sun becomes a rectangle of blackness, and the blackness feels like it contains something even if it doesn't. Bedtime rituals try to create calm—bath, towel, pajamas, teeth brushed, a story read in a softer voice—but they also highlight vulnerability. The door closes, leaving a crack of hallway light. That crack is meant to help. It also becomes a spotlight for imagination. A kid lies still and listens to the house settle, and settling sounds can resemble footsteps if you want them to.

One of the earliest medical memories that belongs to me—not retold, not borrowed from adult mouths—arrives as bright ceiling lights. I'm on my back, being rolled down a hospital hallway, the kind of hallway that smells like antiseptic and stale air-conditioning, the kind of hallway where the floors are too shiny and the sound of wheels seems amplified. The lights overhead pass in a steady rhythm, panels of brightness sliding by like frames in a film. A plastic mask comes down over my face, sealing in a scent that is part rubber, part clean chemical, and the adult voices around me sound far away as if they're speaking through water. The mask is gentle and absolute. My body resists for a moment, then loses its argument. The next moment I possess is after —procedure complete, time missing in the middle like a page torn out. Later there are stitches low on my abdomen, just above the pelvis, and gauze that has to be changed, an awkward tenderness that makes walking feel careful.

That recovery embeds itself in small, practical scenes rather than in drama. There is a bathroom in a church building—tile floor, paper towels, the smell of disinfectant mixed with old air—and a caregiver helps me manage the gauze after using the restroom. The caregiver's hands move with that blend of gentleness and efficiency adults use when they're trying to be kind while also trying to get through a task. I feel exposed, embarrassed in the way a child is embarrassed by any attention on the body. The world is full of people wearing Sunday clothes and speaking in hushed voices, and I'm in a bathroom dealing with stitches. It isn't traumatic in the cinematic sense. It's simply strange: the first time I understand that bodies can be altered, that something can be "fixed" by strangers in bright rooms, and that the proof of it stays on you for days. The house receives me back afterward with the relief of familiarity—my own bed, my own hallway, my own known sounds.

Around five, the world changes again through lenses. Prescription glasses arrive, and they're not an accessory so much as a permanent attachment. The frames sit on my face with the clumsy insistence of something new, and suddenly edges sharpen—doorframes become clean lines, leaves on trees separate into individual shapes instead of green blur. The improvement is immediate enough to feel like a trick: how long had the world been smeared and I didn't know it was smeared? I wear the glasses constantly, day and night, even to sleep, because taking them off feels like going blind on purpose. I wake with the frames still on, a little crooked, the lenses fogged at the edges from breath and sweat. There's a ritual of cleaning them with the corner of a shirt, smudges turning into streaks, streaks turning into clarity. In childhood, the glasses become part of the body's definition of normal, and the idea of being without them feels wrong, like stepping outside without skin.

The years between four and seven are peppered with injuries that don't form a single narrative but do form a catalog of being a kid in a yard full of hazards. Bare feet in summer, sprinting across grass and dirt and whatever else is hidden in the ground, and then the sudden, electric shock of pain as a rusty nail drives into the foot. The pain is sharp enough to turn the world white for a moment, and then it becomes heat that pulses with every heartbeat. Adults rush in, voices rising, hands lifting me, the house briefly converting into emergency mode. There's a tetanus shot later

—needle, sting, the indignity of being held still—and the body learns another rule: the ground can hurt you in ways you can't predict, and the consequences come in the form of strangers in clinics and chemicals in your blood.

There's a treehouse—more ambition than architecture—and the kind of climbing that feels heroic until gravity interrupts. I'm climbing in, the wood rough under my hands, the smell of sun-warmed boards and dirt below, and then something slips. For a moment my head is going toward the ground in a way that feels final, the world tilting too fast. I don't remember impact as a clean picture; I remember the sickening lurch of falling and the way adults' voices sharpen afterward, fear trying to disguise itself as scolding. The body carries these moments as sensations: the sudden absence of control, the realization that you can be airborne without wanting to be. It isn't destiny. It's childhood physics. Still, the nervous system files it away because the nervous system is built to remember what could kill you.

Another injury arrives through a door. I'm coming in through the front entrance with an adult, and the door closes in the wrong way at the wrong time. My finger catches in the jamb, and the pain is immediate and nauseating, the kind that makes sound leave your throat before you decide to cry. There's a rush to a hospital again, the cold brightness, the smell of antiseptic, and later a finger splint that turns my hand into something partly artificial. The splint is annoying and fascinating, a visible badge that draws attention I both want and hate. It makes ordinary tasks—holding a toy, grabbing a spoon—feel clumsy. It also makes me conscious of fragility in a new way: the body is not a single solid thing, but a collection of delicate parts that can be trapped, pinched, broken.

Discipline exists in the first house the way it exists in many houses—sometimes fair, sometimes reactive, sometimes arriving in the middle of the night when a kid can't even fully locate what they're being punished for. There are nights I'm woken up to spankings because the adults believe I was awake with older kids who were misbehaving. The scene isn't theatrical; it's confusing. Sleep is ripped open, light suddenly on, voices tight with fatigue and anger, and I'm forced into a waking state where I have to account for actions I don't fully understand. The body registers it as shock more than pain: the disorientation, the sense that the house can turn hostile without warning. In the morning, the house goes back to being a house. Breakfast happens. Shoes get found. Life continues. Childhood contains these contradictions easily because a child has no choice but to contain them.

The older kids in the house sometimes treat me like an accessory, a tool, a witness, and those roles come with their own kind of danger—less physical, more moral, the first taste of being pulled into someone else's mischief. There's a cruel prank that unfolds not with violence but with manipulation: an older kid convinces me to do something humiliating to another kid's drink, then convinces that kid to drink it. I don't frame it as "sexual" or "abuse" in the mind of a child; it's nastiness, a gross trick performed for laughter, the kind of thing older kids do when they want to prove they're powerful. The aftermath is immediate disgust, crying, adults furious and loud, the air in the kitchen turning sharp. I'm swept into guilt because my hands were used, because I was present, because I'm part of the chain even if

I don't fully understand the chain. It becomes an early lesson that "I was told to" doesn't erase consequence, and that shame can stick even when the act was borrowed.

There's also the mischief that steps outside the yard and into the neighborhood, where consequences are less contained by fences. One older kid takes me along like an accomplice—small enough to be ignored by adults, young enough to be trusted by the wrong person. We move through the neighborhood with the sense of being on an adventure, the air bright, the world wide, the thrill of not being supervised. A lighter is stolen from someone's car—quick hands, quick breath, the sudden spike of adrenaline—and the lighter becomes a trophy, a dangerous object in a small hand. Later, that same lighter is used to set a neighbor's grass field on fire. Fire is mesmerizing when you're a kid: the way it eats, the way it crackles, the way it turns something ordinary into something alive. In the moment, it can feel like power. Later, it becomes fear as adults discover what happened, voices rising, consequences landing, the house once again converting into emergency mode.

That same era contains an animal loss that arrives sideways. A dog is hit by a car, and I don't hold the scene as a clean memory of impact; I hold it as the knowledge arriving afterward, the adults speaking in careful tones, the heaviness that drifts into the house like smoke. Later I learn a caregiver took the dog to be euthanized. The word itself carries finality even if a child doesn't fully grasp it. Animals in childhood are often symbols of warmth and uncomplicated love, and losing one introduces an early kind of grief that doesn't need tragedy around it to be real. The yard looks the same after. The fence stands where it always stood. The porch creaks. The absence is what changes the shape of the place—an empty spot where a body used to be, a silence where there used to be panting, a routine missing its participant.

Some memories from the first house arrive as single images, vivid and isolated, not because they are world-defining but because the brain chooses strange snapshots to keep. One of those snapshots: coming home from church in Sunday clothes, the air outside tasting like late morning, and seeing another kid from the house—kid-sized, not adult— eating dog food off the ground where it's been scattered across the back porch. The scene is baffling. It has the surreal wrongness of something that doesn't belong in the script of "normal family life," and that wrongness makes it stick. I don't interpret it as a symbol. I don't build a theory about it. It lands in the mind as a question that never gets answered: why would someone do that, what hunger is that, what dare, what game, what punishment, what impulse. Adults respond in the way adults respond to sudden shame: a rush, a shout, a cleanup, a denial that this is the kind of thing that happens in their world. The porch goes back to being a porch, but the image remains, a small glitch in the memory reel.

The first house is not only chaos; it is also ordinary joy, the kind that builds itself out of cheap materials and sunlight. Summer brings a stock tank—rough metal, maybe ten feet across—filled with water until it becomes a backyard pool. Kids climb in and splash and shriek, and the water is cold enough to steal breath at first. We run in circles along the inside edge to create a current, a crude little man-made river, and then we let that current carry us, bodies turning into debris in our own creation. The hose lies in the yard like a sleeping snake, rubber warmed by sun, and the water that comes out tastes like metal and heat. In those moments, the house fades into the background and the yard becomes everything: grass underfoot, sun on shoulders, laughter sharp enough to echo off the fence.

There is work too, the kind of work that is given to kids as a way of making them feel useful, included in the machine of home. A garden grows in the yard, rows of plants that look unimpressive until they start producing. The soil smells dark and alive. Leaves brush against my legs. A caregiver shows me what to pick and what to leave, how to twist a vegetable free without tearing the whole plant, how to carry a small harvest in my hands like it's treasure. Inside, the kitchen becomes a factory for preservation: jars lined up, lids clinking, the smell of vinegar or brine, steam fogging windows. The act of jarring food feels like magic—summer being trapped in glass so it can be opened later when the world is cold. As a kid, I don't frame it as self-sufficiency or tradition. I frame it as ritual: the house doing something purposeful, adults focused, the air thick with the sense that we're preparing for a future we assume will arrive.

Downstairs—in a basement space that feels like a different climate—technology arrives in a way that feels like science fiction. A caregiver trades gardening equipment for a Macintosh computer, and the machine sits there like an artifact from another universe: beige casing, heavy monitor, a keyboard that clacks with authority. The basement smells like concrete and stored boxes, cooler than the rest of the house, and the computer's screen glows with a contained, private light. I play "Dark Castle," and the game's imagery burrows into the mind: pixelated danger, eerie corridors, the sense of being trapped in a place where you have to keep moving or lose. It isn't that the game "causes" anything later; it's simply part of the first house's strange collage—farmlike chores upstairs, digital castle downstairs. Childhood can hold those contrasts easily. A kid can go from picking vegetables to fighting monsters on a screen without needing the world to make philosophical sense.

Toys build whole economies in the first house. LEGO sets spill across carpet like a controlled disaster, plastic pieces becoming airplanes if you have the patience to follow instructions or the audacity to ignore them. Lincoln Logs stack into crude cabins, little forts that collapse and get rebuilt, the sound of wood-on-wood clicks becoming its own comfort. A toy Tonka truck becomes a vehicle for experiments. The backyard has a hill, and the hill becomes an amusement park ride. I climb into the bed of the truck and let gravity do the rest, rolling down the slope, the world vibrating, the air rushing, the fence rushing past, the thrill of speed contained by the knowledge that the hill ends before danger turns real. Dirt and grass blur. Laughter erupts. Then I drag the truck back up again and repeat, not because the ride is new, but because repetition is joy when you're seven.

The house has its encounters with animals that don't belong, and each encounter feels like the boundary between "home" and "wild" briefly dissolves. A stray dog is trapped in a cage—covered and left next to the house until animal control can retrieve it—and the cage sits there like a moral problem. The animal inside is frightened, confused, a bundle of ribs and breath. The covering over the cage makes it feel hidden and exposed at the same time. I hover near it, curious and uneasy, feeling the pull to comfort and the fear of being bitten. Adults treat it practically, the way adults treat problems: contain, wait, hand off to a system designed for it. The presence of the cage changes the sound of the yard. Every rustle becomes a reminder that not everything living belongs to you, and not everything can be saved by wanting it.

Another animal snapshot: an opossum perched on a tree branch, looking down with teeth bared in a grin that isn't a grin at all. The creature's face is a mask of threat, a tiny prehistoric thing that seems offended by our existence. It doesn't chase. It doesn't attack. It simply watches, mouth open, and the sight is enough to send a kid's imagination into overdrive. The yard feels less safe for an hour. The fence feels thinner. Night feels closer. In childhood, these moments don't need violence to be terrifying; the mere fact of wildness appearing in your familiar environment is enough. Then the opossum disappears, and the yard returns to being just grass and trees, as if the universe didn't briefly show its teeth.

Food in the first house is not a constant feast, but it is sensory and specific. A caregiver makes pasta from scratch, rolling dough on a counter dusted with flour, the air filling with that raw, wheaty smell that doesn't exist in boxed meals. The flour gets everywhere—on hands, on sleeves, in the corners of mouths when kids get too close. I watch the transformation: powder and eggs becoming something elastic and alive, something that can be cut into strips and boiled and turned into dinner. The act carries a kind of gravity because it takes time, and time spent on food feels like time spent on care. When the pasta hits boiling water, the kitchen fogs slightly, heat blooming, and the house feels briefly like the center of a warm universe.

Outside, there are mulberry trees along a back property line, and the berries stain fingers purple. Picking them is a small act of rebellion because it feels like stealing sweetness from the world without paying for it. The berries are warm from sun, soft enough to burst if squeezed, and they taste like summer turned into pulp. I eat them too fast and regret it when my stomach complains, but the regret doesn't stop me from doing it again later. There's a stump in the yard too, and it becomes a platform for little experiments with courage. I jump from that stump toward a car parked nearby, and in one of those childhood perception glitches, time slows while I'm airborne. The space between stump and car stretches. The air becomes thick. My body rotates in a way that feels both controlled and out of control, and the moment hangs long enough that I can notice details—the shine of paint, the texture of bark, the bright slice of sky. Then I land, gravity reasserting itself, and the world snaps back to normal speed as if nothing happened.

Not everything I know about the first house comes from my own eyes. There's an incident in family lore—told and retold—that involves someone pouring a glass of water into the back of a television while others are watching. I don't carry the scene as a memory of action; I carry it as a mental reconstruction built from adult voices, laughter, disbelief, irritation. In my imagination, it becomes vivid anyway: the sudden splash, the crackle of electricity, the screen flickering, the smell of hot circuitry, adults lunging forward with hands out as if hands can stop water once it's already inside. Childhood is full of these "adult-told" moments that function like myths. You inherit them as part of the house's history, even if you weren't fully present for the original sin.

The first house also teaches performance, though no one calls it that. Visitors arrive—relatives, neighbors, people from church—and the atmosphere shifts. The living room becomes a stage. Adults smile differently. Jokes get told with extra charm. Voices soften or sharpen depending on who is in the room. A kid watches these transformations and learns quietly: there is a private version of home and a public version of home, and the house can switch between them like a light. Sometimes the switch feels warm—more laughter, more food, more attention. Sometimes it feels tense—adults trying too hard, politeness stretched thin, old grudges hidden under conversation like knives under napkins. I don't interpret it as "trauma." I interpret it as weather. The house has sunny days and stormy days. You learn to read the sky.

School begins during the span of this house, and it expands my map beyond fences. A backpack smells like new fabric. Shoes feel too stiff. The classroom is a bright room filled with other kids, a place where the adult at the front has a different kind of authority than the adults at home. The rules are simple and relentless: sit still, raise your hand, wait your turn. Some days I talk. Some days I watch. Some days I come home energized. Some days I come home exhausted in a way I can't explain. The relief of returning to the first house after school is physical—familiar air, familiar smells, furniture exactly where it should be. I drop the backpack, kick off shoes, drift toward the kitchen because kitchens are where care tends to happen. Someone asks how my day was. My answers are short because a child doesn't always know how to translate experience into language. "Fine" becomes a shield. "Good" becomes a shortcut.

As seven approaches, the first house begins to feel smaller—not because it changes, but because I do. The hallway that once felt like a long corridor becomes a short passage. The ceiling that once felt far away becomes reachable in imagination. The yard fence stops feeling like a boundary and starts feeling like a suggestion. I notice details

I never cared about before: a stain in the carpet that has always been there, a dent in the wall from an old bump, a window latch that sticks. The house feels worn in, shaped by years of footsteps and routines. It doesn't feel cursed. It doesn't feel sacred. It feels like what it is: the first container that held me while I learned basic rules about bodies, people, and consequence. Whatever the present-day body and mind become later will have their own storms, their own sources, their own load-bearing events. This house is not the single cause of anything. It is simply the beginning place.

The last snapshot of the first house that belongs entirely to me is not a dramatic farewell. It is the sight of a truck packed with belongings, boxes stacked, furniture wrapped, the house briefly looking unfamiliar because it has been partially emptied of itself. Cardboard fills corners. Tape squeaks as it's pulled. The rooms echo in a way they never used to because soft objects have been removed. I stand in a living room that feels too exposed, light bouncing off bare walls, and I realize without fully naming it that the place is about to become a memory. The porch still creaks. The door still sticks. The blinds still cast bars of light across the floor. The house keeps doing its job right up until the moment it doesn't belong to us anymore. I don't have the words for grief then, not the adult kind. I only have a tightness in the chest and the strange sense that something stable is being lifted out of the ground. The first house doesn't collapse; it simply releases me, and the world beyond the fence waits.

# CHAPTER 3

## *Second Yard*

The apartment's quiet does its usual thing—turns inward, thickens, becomes a pressure rather than a relief. A box fan in the corner pushes air without moving heat, and the steady rush of it should be neutral, should be nothing, but my attention catches on the sound and won't let go. I keep my eyes on the floor where a strip of light slides under the blinds, a pale bar cutting across the carpet, and I try to let the day be only the day. The storage bin is still open beside me, lid leaned against the wall like a shield. Inside are school leftovers: a cheap plastic ruler, an old pencil with the eraser gnawed down, a flattened name tag from a long-forgotten event. When I lift the ruler, dust clings to my fingers, and the smell that rises is unmistakable—graphite and paper and cafeteria disinfectant, that lemon-bleach scent schools use to convince you cleanliness is the same thing as safety. My throat tightens the way it does when the body recognizes a place before the mind names it. The apartment stays put, but something behind my eyes shifts, and the quiet rewinds into another kind of quiet: the hush of a neighborhood morning before the buses arrive, before doors open, before the line forms at the front of the school.

The next house comes with a move that feels less like an ending than a re-centering. The truck is packed, cardboard stacked in uneven towers, furniture wrapped in blankets that make it look like the whole life has been bandaged. In the back seat, the world outside the window slides by in long strips—trees, fences, intersections—and the sensation is both dull and electric. Adults talk in the front with that clipped, practical tone people use when they're steering logistics, and every so often a word lands heavy—rent, deposit, new, closer, school—and then keeps going as if it didn't matter. The kid part of me watches the road and measures distance in feelings instead of miles. The old place drops away behind us without ceremony, and the new place rises up ahead like a blank page that still smells like ink.

The next house is sturdier in my mind than the first because I spend my grade-school years inside it, and grade school has the kind of repetition that stamps itself into memory. The house sits in a neighborhood where the streets are arranged like rules: blocks you can walk, corners you learn to look both ways at, yards with swing sets, yards with barking dogs, yards with nothing but grass and a "keep out" feeling. The house itself is ordinary—nothing that would make someone slow down to stare—but to a kid it's a universe with new boundaries. The front door sounds different than the first house's door. The hallway carries sound in a new way. The windows throw light at different angles. Even the smell is different: less old carpet, more paint and sun-warmed drywall, the faint scent of a garage or storage area where the air is always a little sharper.

The first weeks are made of small discoveries that feel like secrets. Which floorboard creaks in the hallway. Which cabinet door sticks. How the bathroom fan sounds when it's turned on, that hollow airplane roar that makes your voice echo if you talk over it. The backyard has its own geography—patches of shade, a fence line, maybe a tree that becomes a landmark the way mountains become landmarks in places that have them. There's a swing set in the yard at one point, and it becomes a machine for testing gravity: the chain squeak, the arc up and back, the split-second at the top where the body goes weightless and the world pauses before dropping again. The house is not a mythic place. It doesn't glow with meaning. It simply becomes the base from which everything else expands: school, neighborhood, other kids, the slow discovery that the world is larger than the rooms you sleep in.

Walking to school becomes one of the defining rituals of those years. Mornings have a specific bite depending on the season. In winter the air feels like it cracks inside the nose, and breath comes out in white puffs that vanish as soon as you notice them. In warmer months the walk smells like cut grass and sun-warmed pavement. Shoes scuff along sidewalks, and the cracks in the concrete become predictable hazards you either step over or step into on purpose because stepping on cracks feels like a game with invisible consequences. The backpack straps pull on shoulders in a way that makes the body feel older than it is, and the straps carry the smell of school: paper dust, cheap plastic, the faint sourness of a lunch kept too long.

At the school, lines form outside the front entrance before the doors are opened. Kids gather in knots, shifting weight from foot to foot, talking too loudly or not at all, all of us held in place by the rule that we wait until an adult decides it's time. The building itself is a brick shape that smells like floor wax and chalk and that same disinfectant that never quite covers what it's trying to cover. The line has its own hierarchy—certain kids drift to the front, certain kids hang back, some kids move between groups like they're testing where they belong. Adults stand near the doors with clipboards or keys or coffee cups, and the adults' faces look like weather: tired, neutral, impatient, amused. When the doors finally open, the line compresses and surges, and the whole body of children pours into the hallway like a river finally released.

School has routines that are both comforting and humiliating, because comfort comes from predictability and humiliation comes from being measured. The cafeteria trays are that particular beige plastic that never looks clean no matter how many times it's washed. The food comes in shapes designed for efficiency rather than joy—rectangles of pizza that taste like salt and melted plastic, chicken nuggets that are more breading than chicken, vegetables boiled until they surrender. Milk is served in small cartons that sweat when they sit too long, and peeling the carton open leaves a little strip of paper that sometimes sticks to your finger. Lunch is loud. It's a roar of voices bouncing off hard surfaces, a sound that feels like it fills the skull. The body learns to eat fast, to guard space, to keep your eyes moving because something is always happening somewhere in the room.

Even gym class takes place in the cafeteria at times, which means physical effort happens under fluorescent lights and the smell of yesterday's lunch. Folding tables get pushed aside. Lines are drawn on the floor that only make sense if you've been told the rules. Dodgeball becomes a game of survival economics: who's quick, who's targeted, who takes pleasure in throwing too hard, who flinches before the ball even arrives. Jump rope turns into rhythm and failure, the rope slapping the ground with a sound like applause that mocks you when you miss. Tetherball is a war disguised as a playground toy—hands stinging, knuckles scraped, the pole vibrating with each hit. Monkey bars are a test of grip and courage, and falling is never just falling; it's laughter from someone else, the sting of bark chips in your palms, the sudden awareness that bodies are observed.

Recess is where the real education happens, because outside, rules are negotiated rather than assigned. Groups form and dissolve. Alliances shift over the smallest things: who got picked first, who cut in line, who said something that landed wrong. Hopscotch squares get claimed like territory. Kids invent rules, then enforce them with the seriousness of judges. There are days when play is simple—running until lungs burn, laughing because the body feels like it can fly. There are days when play is a minefield—one wrong joke, one wrong look, and you can feel yourself slide toward the edge of a group. In those years, social consequence isn't permanent yet, but it feels permanent in the moment because the world is small enough that a single lunch table can feel like the whole universe.

The neighborhood around the next house widens the social map. There's a neighbor's place—close enough that it becomes an extension of the street—where a crowd of kids always seems to exist. The house feels loud from the outside, full of motion, doors opening and closing, bodies running in and out like it's a summer camp that never ends. The backyard is a constant churn of games: tag, hide-and-seek, improvised sports with rules that change mid-play. Being there is exciting in the way crowded places are exciting when you're young—more laughter, more chances, more noise, more attention to win or lose. It's also exhausting, because in a crowd you're always being watched by someone, and being watched means being judged even when no one is intentionally judging you.

Summer stretches long in grade school, long enough that it feels like the year has two lives: the school life and the summer life. The summer public swimming pool becomes a recurring landmark, a place where chlorine sharpens the air and the sun reflects off water so brightly it hurts to look at. The concrete around the pool burns feet, and running across it becomes a dance of pain and speed. The sound of the place is constant—splashes, whistles, kids yelling, lifeguards calling out warnings nobody wants to hear. Water turns bodies into something else. In the pool you can be fast or slow, brave or cautious, but you're always visible. You climb the ladder, step to the edge, and the moment before you jump is a small private battle between fear and pride. When you surface, sputtering and laughing, it feels like winning, even if nobody else notices.

Not every gap in these years contains a named event. A lot of childhood is simply time passing while the brain is absorbing. There are afternoons that blur together: cartoons on the television, snacks eaten standing at the counter, the dull comfort of being inside with the air still and the world held at bay. There are evenings when streetlights come on and the neighborhood shifts into a softer mode—parents calling kids home by name, sprinklers hissing, the smell of someone grilling drifting through open windows. There are nights when the house settles and the rooms feel too quiet, and a kid lies in bed listening to distant traffic, trying to decide whether that distant sound means freedom or danger or nothing at all. The body grows in small, unannounced increments; shoes fit and then don't; sleeves get shorter; the mirror returns a face that keeps changing without permission.

Second grade brings a spelling bee, and the spelling bee carries its own strange blend of pride and panic. Words become obstacles you either clear or crash into. Standing in front of a room of kids and adults makes the mouth feel dry, and the letters in a word feel heavier than they should. The room goes quiet in that specific way crowds go quiet when they're waiting for someone to fail. Some kids spell quickly, confident, and the confidence itself feels like power. Some kids stumble and laugh awkwardly, trying to pretend the stumble doesn't matter. When it's my turn, the word arrives and I can feel the machinery in my head turn on—sound it out, picture it, test it—while my body tries to pretend it isn't shaking. The result matters less than the sensation: the first time "thinking" feels like a visible performance rather than a private act.

By third grade, adults start treating my mind like an object they can measure. There's a day when I'm pulled from class for testing, guided down a hallway into a smaller room with different light and different air, the kind of room schools reserve for things they want to label. The tests are puzzles disguised as questions. Patterns. Shapes. Words that require you to hold multiple ideas at once. The experience is not intimidating in the way a fight is intimidating; it's strange in a quieter way, because an adult is watching how I think rather than what I know. I can feel myself moving faster than the questions, finishing and waiting, then being handed another task as if speed itself is evidence of something. When it's over, the adult's tone changes. The adults don't say a number like it's a lottery ticket; they say it like a verdict—capable, advanced, above, potential—and the verdict lands with weight.

The meaning of that verdict spreads through the year in ways that are both flattering and isolating. Teachers start expecting that I'll "get it" even when instructions are vague. Adults praise me for being "smart," which sounds like a compliment until it becomes an expectation you're responsible for maintaining. Other kids notice that adults treat you differently, and difference is dangerous in school because it makes you a target for teasing or for being used. Being seen as bright doesn't automatically make you successful; it just changes the shape of your failures. When I do well, it's treated as normal. When I don't, the question becomes why—why aren't you trying, why aren't you focused, why is someone with your mind making a mistake. The praise builds a pedestal that looks good from the outside but feels narrow to stand on, because there's less room to be ordinary.

Third grade also introduces the experience of disliking a teacher in a way that isn't petty. The teacher's presence fills the room like a smell you can't escape. Their voice has a rhythm that grates, their rules feel inconsistent, their punishments feel personal even when they aren't. The classroom becomes a place where time slows, where the clock seems to resist moving, where sitting still feels like an endurance test. I find myself watching the teacher's mood the way you watch weather, trying to predict what kind of day it will be before it hits. The teacher's disapproval, when it lands, feels like being singled out under a spotlight you didn't ask for. The body carries that discomfort even after school ends, like a film on the skin you can't wash off until the weekend arrives.

One day, the teacher drags another student out of the room, and the lesson changes from math or reading to something colder: authority is physical when it wants to be. The student is taken into a glass-walled space where other adults are present, and even from the hallway the scene is visible enough that nobody can pretend it's not happening. The adult voices are sharp. The student's posture is defensive. The air in the hallway tightens as kids watch without knowing where to put their eyes. When the punishment happens, the sound of it is less important than the fact of it—an adult choosing to make discipline public, choosing to make pain a demonstration. The classroom afterward feels different. Even kids who act tough go quiet. The lesson isn't that school is dangerous every day; it's that safety depends on who has power and what mood they're in, and those variables are out of a kid's control.

Fourth grade shifts tone. A teacher arrives who feels steadier, more humane, the kind of adult who can correct you without making you feel small. The room itself doesn't change—the same desks, the same fluorescent lights—but the air does. Instructions make sense. Praise arrives when it's earned without turning into a trap. When correction happens, it lands like guidance rather than accusation. In that year, the days feel more navigable. The mind is still quick, still restless, still prone to drifting into its own private worlds when tasks feel repetitive, but the drifting doesn't immediately turn into punishment. There's room to be curious without being labeled as disruptive. There's room to ask questions without being treated as a challenge. It's a reminder that school isn't one thing; it depends on the adult at the front and the culture they build around themselves.

Even with a better teacher, there are stretches where school becomes a grind. Busywork piles up like sandbags. Worksheets get assigned that feel like they were designed to occupy hands rather than teach anything. The mind finishes quickly and then sits in its own boredom, and boredom becomes mischief if it has nowhere to go. I draw in margins. I tap a pencil. I look out the window and watch clouds move like slow animals across the sky. Sometimes the teacher catches it and redirects me gently. Sometimes the redirection is sharp and public, and my face heats with embarrassment. The pattern repeats: speed, boredom, correction. The adults interpret it as attitude. The kid part of me interprets it as a mismatch between the pace of my head and the pace of the room.

Sometime in these years, summer school enters the picture. Summer school carries a particular humiliation because it means the summer is not fully yours. The building smells the same, but the halls are emptier, the voices echo more, the sunlight outside looks like it's mocking you through the windows. Being there doesn't always mean I failed everything; it means there's a gap someone decided needed closing, a subject that didn't stick, a requirement that has to be met. The days are shorter but feel longer because the rest of the world seems to be playing while you're sitting at a desk. Still, summer school has its own strange relief: fewer kids, less chaos, teachers who sometimes speak more softly because the crowd is smaller. The work gets done. The requirement is satisfied. The summer reopens, though it feels slightly dented.

Fifth grade sits at the edge of a cliff without announcing itself as a cliff. The body starts to change in small ways—voice cracks, limbs feel longer, appetite becomes unpredictable. Social hierarchies harden. Kids who were just kids a year ago start trying on identities like costumes: tough, funny, mean, popular, invisible. Jokes get sharper. Teasing gets more targeted. Rumors begin to carry weight, even if they're ridiculous. The playground doesn't disappear yet, but it starts to feel childish, and the kids who still want to play have to pretend they don't care what anyone thinks. I watch those shifts with a kind of cautious curiosity, as if the whole school is being slowly rewired in preparation for the next stage.

In the middle of those years—close enough to remember the shape of it, far enough that the details blur—there's an incident connected to that neighbor's house, the one full of kids, the one that always seemed to have motion spilling out of it. It happens in the basement, in a space that smells like concrete and damp storage, a cooler air that has its own heaviness. The lighting is dimmer, more yellow, and sound behaves differently down there, swallowed by walls and low ceilings. The moment begins like ordinary childhood wandering: kids drifting into a space adults aren't supervising closely, curiosity pulling bodies downward, the thrill of being somewhere that feels private. Then the atmosphere tilts. Someone older sets the terms. The energy shifts from play to something else—something secretive, pressuring, wrong in a way that a child can feel before a child can name.

The event itself doesn't live in my memory as a clear linear scene. It lives as fragments—proximity, a voice too close, the sensation of being cornered by expectation, the body's sudden stiffness, the mind's blanking to survive the moment. There's a blur where time doesn't feel like it moved normally, where the nervous system chose distance as a defense. Whether it lasted seconds or minutes is impossible to tell from the inside of a kid's perception. What does remain is the aftertaste: a thick shame that arrives too quickly to have been earned, a sense that something private was taken or forced open, and the immediate instinct to seal it shut. When I leave the basement, the upstairs light looks too bright. The ordinary noise of the house sounds too loud. The world continues as if nothing happened, which makes the wrongness feel even more isolated.

The after effects show up in ways that don't announce themselves to adults. The basement becomes a place my body resists without explanation. If someone suggests going down there for a game, I find an excuse to stay upstairs. If I have to go near the basement door, my stomach tightens and my skin turns alert, as if the air itself carries warning. Sleep shifts for a while—dreams that don't replay the event exactly, but carry the same trapped feeling, the same pressure, the same sense that saying "no" doesn't matter. I wake with a sour panic I can't explain. During the day, certain sounds—footsteps on stairs, a door closing, a voice calling from another room—can spike my attention in a way that feels outsized for a kid. The mind tries to file the incident away as "maybe it wasn't real," because denying it would be easier than holding it. The body doesn't fully cooperate with denial.

It doesn't turn me into a different person overnight. I still go to school. I still play outside. I still laugh at stupid jokes. Childhood is resilient like that; it can carry a dark pocket and still keep running. But the pocket exists, and it changes the way I guard myself in small, unconscious ways. I become more cautious about being alone with certain people. I become more aware of doors and closed spaces. I become more sensitive to the feeling of being pressured, even in harmless contexts. If someone tries to push me into a game I don't want to play, irritation flares faster than it used to, like the nervous system has learned that "minor pressure" can suddenly become something bigger. The changes are subtle enough that adults might interpret them as moodiness or stubbornness. From the inside, it feels like learning to keep a hand on the latch.

The most confusing part is the way the memory behaves. It doesn't sit still like other memories. It drifts in and out of certainty. Sometimes it feels like something that definitely happened and I was there in my body for it. Other times it feels dreamlike, as if the mind tried to soften it by putting a fog over it. That uncertainty becomes its own problem because it makes the shame harder to place. A kid doesn't have the language for coercion, boundaries, consent. A kid has only the instinct that something was wrong and the fear that speaking about it will make it worse. So it stays sealed. It becomes a private bruise. It gets carried forward quietly, resurfacing at odd moments—an intrusive image while brushing teeth, a sudden discomfort when someone stands too close—then sinking again when the day demands attention elsewhere.

Academically, the "bright mind" label continues to follow me like a shadow that's sometimes flattering and sometimes irritating. I can solve puzzles quickly, see patterns before other kids see them, connect ideas in ways that surprise teachers. But the same quickness makes the slow pace of class feel like being trapped behind glass while time crawls. I learn to entertain myself inside my own head, to build small mental games while the teacher repeats instructions. Sometimes that private world is harmless— imagining stories, planning what I'll do after school, rehearsing jokes. Sometimes it turns into a strange habit of dissociating in miniature: being physically present while mentally elsewhere, returning only when my name is called. It's not a dramatic fracture; it's a kid's adaptation to boredom and expectation. Still, it teaches the mind that "leaving" can be a tool, and tools tend to get reused later in life for reasons the kid can't predict.

Socially, I move through those years without a single defining identity. I'm not the permanent class clown. I'm not the permanent target. I'm not the permanent leader. I drift between groups, sometimes included, sometimes peripheral, sometimes invisible by choice. There's a neighbor girl I kiss once under my bed, a brief secret moment that feels both thrilling and awkward, the kind of childhood experiment that carries more curiosity than consequence. It's not romance in an adult sense; it's discovery—the fact that closeness can be chosen, that bodies can share space in a way that feels warm and slightly dangerous because it's private. The moment doesn't set a direction for the future. It simply becomes one of the small human scenes that prove childhood wasn't only fear and rules; it was also tenderness and curiosity and the impulse to connect.

At home, the next house continues to be a container rather than a cause. It holds ordinary family noise—voices from other rooms, televisions playing, dishes clinking, someone laughing at something you can't hear clearly. It holds the quiet economics of shared space: who gets the bathroom first, who leaves shoes in the hallway, who forgets to shut a door all the way. It holds small arguments between adults that flare and fade, like summer storms that don't last long enough to change the landscape. It holds the comfort of predictable routines: dinner smells, bedtime rituals, weekend mornings that feel looser because school isn't looming. The house becomes the baseline for "normal," not because it's perfect, but because it's repeated enough to feel like a fact.

Over time, the neighbor basement incident doesn't stay at the surface of daily thought, but it leaves an outline in behavior. The outline shows up as caution around certain older kids. It shows up as a preference for being near exits. It shows up as a complicated relationship with secrecy— wanting private spaces to feel safe, yet feeling uneasy when privacy is enforced by someone else. There are moments when I sense something "off" in an interaction before I can articulate why, and I step away. Adults might call it intuition or shyness. It's neither mystical nor dramatic. It's the nervous system doing what it's designed to do: flagging similarity, scanning for risk, trying to keep the body out of situations that feel like traps.

These years also carry a slow accumulation of small competencies. I learn how to navigate the school day without getting lost. I learn how to read adults—who can be joked with, who can't, who is safe, who is unpredictable. I learn how to be quiet when quiet is rewarded and loud when loud wins social points. I learn how to stand in line without fighting, how to wait until the bussed kids clear out before being allowed to walk home, how to time my pace so I don't arrive too early and have to stand alone outside the house. These are not glamorous skills, but they are foundational. They teach the body how to move through systems, how to endure boredom, how to manage small humiliations without collapsing.

The walk home after school becomes its own kind of decompression. The building releases you, and the outside air feels like freedom even when it's cold. Kids peel off toward their streets. Some run. Some linger, dragging feet because home means chores or tension or loneliness. I usually move with a steady pace, backpack shifting, shoes scuffing, mind replaying pieces of the day—something a teacher said, something a kid laughed at, a moment of embarrassment that feels larger than it should. Crossing certain intersections becomes automatic. Passing certain houses becomes familiar. The neighborhood has its own soundtrack: dogs barking behind fences, lawnmowers in summer, the distant whine of traffic from a larger road. By the time I reach my street, the school day has already started to feel like something that happened to someone else, sealed behind me until tomorrow.

The summer after fifth grade arrives with the particular feeling of being almost done with something you don't yet understand. The pool is still the pool, bright and loud and chlorinated. The sidewalk is still cracked in the same places. The swing set still squeaks. But there's a sense of being on the edge of a shift. Middle school sits ahead like a new country with rumors attached to it—older kids, harder rules, different hallways, different dangers. The body feels both eager and uneasy. Eager because growth always comes with the promise of escape from whatever bored you. Uneasy because growth also means you're about to be measured in new ways. The "smart kid" label is still there. The social games are sharpening. The private dark pocket from the basement is still sealed but not gone. And the world, even in its ordinary suburban shape, is beginning to feel less like a playground and more like a system with consequences.

None of this needs to be framed as the origin of the person I become later. The heavy load-bearing events that shape adulthood have their own eras, their own intensities, their own undeniable weight. These grade-school years are something else: a stretch of repetition where personality takes form through routine, where the mind is labeled and managed by adults, where social hierarchies begin to harden, where an isolated wrongness occurs and is carried forward without language. The next house holds all of it the way a container holds water. It doesn't decide the ocean. It simply keeps what is poured into it until the day it's time to move again.

# CHAPTER 4
# *Between Bells*

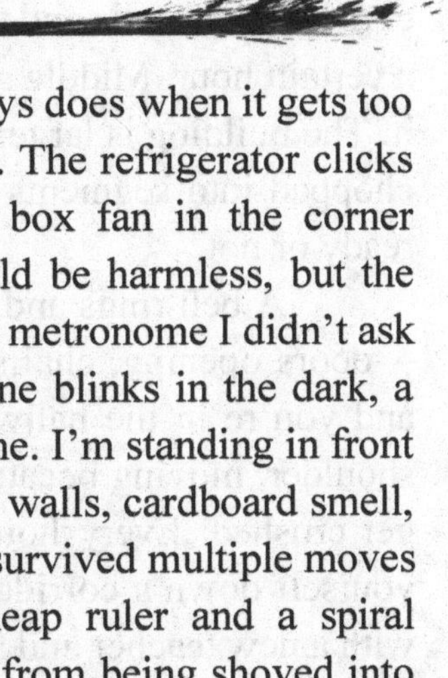

The apartment is doing what it always does when it gets too quiet: it starts manufacturing sound. The refrigerator clicks and settles like an old joint. The box fan in the corner breathes in a steady rush that should be harmless, but the longer it runs the more it feels like a metronome I didn't ask for. A notification light on my phone blinks in the dark, a tiny pulse that keeps insisting on time. I'm standing in front of an open bin on the floor—plastic walls, cardboard smell, a scatter of old school artifacts that survived multiple moves—when my fingers land on a cheap ruler and a spiral notebook with the corners rounded from being shoved into backpacks. The paper smell rises immediately: graphite, dust, that faint sour note of cafeteria disinfectant that never fully leaves school things. I slide the ruler between my hands and the fan's rush stops being a fan. It becomes a hallway. It becomes hundreds of bodies moving at once. It becomes the bell that doesn't care whether your nervous system can keep up. The apartment stays where it is, but the inside of my skull fills with fluorescent light, and the past opens like a door that was never locked—just ignored.

Middle school does not feel like a continuation of grade school. It feels like being dropped into a machine that is already running. In elementary school, the day belongs to one room, one teacher, one set of walls you learn the way you learn the shape of your own bedroom in the dark. You can disappear into routine if you're quiet enough. You can sit at a desk and let the minutes slide in a straight line from morning to afternoon. Even when a day is unfair, even when something happens that makes your stomach tighten, the structure itself is stable. The room stays put. You learn its corners and smells and the way sunlight lands on the floor at a certain hour. Middle school takes that stability and shreds it. The building is larger, the hallways louder, and the day is chopped into segments by bells that arrive whether you're ready or not.

A bell rings and the entire population surges at once —doors opening, chairs scraping, binders snapping shut— and you're in the hallway with everyone else, shoulder to shoulder, moving because movement is the only way not to get crushed. Every hour you pack up who you are, carry yourself down a corridor, and unpack again in a new room with a new teacher and a new set of eyes. The hallway is not neutral space. It's a river, and you either move with it or you're knocked aside. Even the clocks feel sharper. Time becomes pressure. Thirty seconds late is treated like a moral failure. You learn to read the bell like a warning: whatever you are, stop. Whatever you are doing, move. The day isn't a line anymore; it's a series of collisions.

The first week, I keep getting startled by how little belongs to me. No desk stays mine long enough to become safe. No routine holds long enough to become soothing. If a teacher dislikes you, you don't have the comfort of counting days and telling yourself the year will eventually end; the bell throws you into a different room in fifty minutes anyway. That should feel like mercy. Instead it feels like never getting settled, like living inside constant auditions. The moment I start understanding the rules of one room, the bell knocks me into another. My backpack tugs at my shoulders, the crowd shoves at my sides, and my mind keeps an anxious list of where I'm supposed to be next so I don't walk into the wrong door and become a joke.

There is one hour in the schedule that is treated differently by adults, the hour that comes with a label. The label is spoken like a compliment and a prophecy at the same time. A designated classroom, a designated group of kids pulled out and tested and sorted. The adults talk about it like they've found something rare and valuable, like the category itself is a gift that should make you grateful. I step into that room for the first time expecting it to feel like a refuge, expecting the air to be softer, expecting the work to finally meet me where my mind naturally sits. Instead it feels like any other room—different chairs, different posters, a teacher's voice—and the label doesn't behave like a badge. It behaves like another expectation I'm supposed to wear correctly.

The kids in that room are not all the same, even though the adults act like we've been grouped by essence. Some are loud-smart, answering before questions finish and laughing at their own cleverness. Some are competitive-smart, keeping an invisible scoreboard and caring deeply about winning even when the assignment isn't a game. Some already practice social dominance in ways adults don't see because it comes wrapped in confidence and charm. Their jokes land. Their voices fill space. They know how to stand in the center of attention without flinching. My mind can keep up with the work. It can even outrun it. But finishing quickly doesn't give me a place to stand. It gives me extra time—empty minutes at a desk while everyone else is still working—empty minutes where I can feel my difference like an itch.

The worst part is that the work rarely feels hard. It isn't insulting exactly. It just isn't deep. The adults think challenge means novelty, not intensity. We do puzzles and logic games, enrichment projects designed to be fun, and sometimes they are interesting, but most of the time they land like decorative effort. I finish and wait. Waiting in that room isn't patience; it's exposure. It's being left alone with the awareness that the label gathered us together but didn't build belonging. My brain moves fast enough to hold several layers of a problem at once, to see patterns before the steps are fully explained, but that speed doesn't translate into social ease. It just means I have more time to notice everything I don't know how to do.

Outside that hour, the building treats everyone the same: move, comply, keep up. Efficiency becomes a survival skill. The faster I move through transitions, the less I stand out in the hallway crush. The more I keep my needs compact, the less attention I attract from kids who are scanning for someone to test. That kind of efficiency does not create comfort. It creates minimization. I learn to become small on purpose, to take up less space, to keep my face neutral, to keep my hands occupied with books so my posture reads as "busy" rather than "available." The day becomes something I pass through rather than inhabit.

There are parts of those years that should be clean and stabilizing, parts where the world offers rules that make sense. I run cross-country in sixth grade. Running is supposed to be a team sport, but most of it is you and your lungs and the sound of your own feet. After school we line up, jog as a pack at first, listen to a coach shout instructions, and then run until chests burn and legs go numb in that particular way that feels both painful and pure. There is something honest about it. Nobody can argue with the clock. Nobody can humiliate you with a joke that lands harder than your effort. You finish a run knowing you did it, knowing your body carried you through, and the proof is private—breath, sweat, the steady ache in your calves.

But even running doesn't exist in a vacuum. Practice happens after a day that has already scraped you down. It happens in that loosened zone after school where supervision thins and kids become themselves more aggressively. Sometimes practice is a buffer, a way of staying in adult space longer so you don't have to cross the open field behind the school where kids gather for trouble. Sometimes it simply means you're on campus longer, exposed longer. Even the good parts of middle school are threaded through the same environment: bells, crowds, shifting hierarchies, the constant feeling that your peace is conditional on who decides to spend their boredom on you.

Music offers a different kind of structure, one that feels fairer than hallways. I play piano. I play clarinet. Band has its own discipline, a discipline that feels cleaner than most of what happens between kids. In music, expectations are clear: this note, then that note, on this beat, then the next. If you practice, you improve. If you improve, the sound changes. Cause and effect operate like a law rather than a suggestion. The room smells like instrument cases and brass polish, reeds drying on paper towels, warm breath trapped inside mouthpieces. Adults praise accuracy instead of charisma. The praise, when it comes, feels specific. It isn't a vague compliment about potential; it's approval of execution. You kept time. You listened. You belonged in the sound.

There are recognitions that arrive in that world—honor groups, small awards, adults nodding with the satisfied look they reserve for measurable talent—and those recognitions are real. They prove there is a part of me that translates cleanly into something outside my skull. But the hallways don't care. The field behind the school doesn't care. Being good at something doesn't stop other boys from deciding you are a target. Sometimes it makes you more visible, and visibility is not always a gift. Middle school runs multiple economies at once: the economy of grades and performances and adult praise, and the economy of dominance and humiliation that lives between kids. You can be rich in one and broke in the other, and the second one can hurt you in ways the first one can't prevent.

The fights start in middle school. Not in grade school, not in the first neighborhood where childhood bruises come from accidents and play. Middle school is where aggression turns physical, where the social hierarchy stops being mostly jokes and becomes something that can leave marks on your face. After school, still on school grounds, there is an open field where supervision thins and rules blur. Teachers are inside. Adults are gone. Kids cluster in shifting circles that pretend to be casual—just waiting, just hanging out—until someone decides to turn the moment into a test. I am not looking for fights. I am trying to get home. I am trying to walk the route, carry my books, and not give anyone a reason. Reasons are invented anyway.

A look held too long. A glance interpreted as disrespect. A rumor. The simple fact of being quiet without a crowd around you. Not having protection can count as provocation. Sometimes you don't need to do anything; a boy can decide you are the right size and the right kind of alone. One of them becomes the main one in my memory, the one the open field keeps returning to. He comes at me like it's his right, like my body exists as an instrument for him to prove himself in front of whoever is watching. The first time it happens my body reacts before my mind assembles a plan. I grab him and put him in a headlock and squeeze until his voice changes into bargaining.

The headlock is containment, not spectacle. It is a way of controlling someone without swinging wildly, a way of turning chaos into a shape you can hold. I feel his skull against my forearm, the tightness in my bicep, my own breathing too loud in my ears. Grass smells sweet under the sun and sharp when it's been crushed. Sweat and dirt and the metallic edge of fear mix in my mouth. His begging is raw and undignified. It startles me because it makes him human for a second. One moment he is a force, a boy convinced he can do whatever he wants. The next moment he is a boy with panic in his throat asking for mercy like he never expected to need it.

I make an offer the way a child makes an offer when he believes logic can solve people. If he leaves me alone, I will release him. It is a deal, not a threat. I am not trying to punish him. I am trying to end it. When he agrees, I let him go, and relief moves through my body like a wave. There is a foolish hope that a clear boundary can carry forward into tomorrow. Then he comes at me again. That is the lesson. Defending yourself once is not always enough. Showing you can hurt someone back is not always enough. The fight is not a misunderstanding; it is a test. He wants to see if he can make me lose control, make me look like the violent one, the unstable one, the kid adults should watch.

When he comes the second time, I put him back in the headlock. Again he begs. Again I offer the same deal. Again I let him go. This time someone else drags him away, not out of concern for me, but because the scene has stopped being entertaining in the way they want. The crowd absorbs the moment and keeps moving. My body shakes, not from fear exactly, but from adrenaline and the realization that I have done something violent and precise and it did not solve the deeper problem. The field does not become safe. The hallway does not become kind. The machine keeps running.

Not all fights go well. There are bloody noses. A split lip. At least one walk home with a black eye. Nothing breaks. Nothing leaves permanent damage in bone, but the accumulation matters. A bodily knowledge forms: school does not end when the bell rings. The building might stop owning your time at dismissal, but the social world follows you onto grass and into streets and sometimes all the way to your front yard. One bully lives in the neighborhood up the street. He follows me home. The proximity makes it feel inescapable, like my own street has been colonized by someone else's anger. I stand in the yard with the house behind me—the place that should be safe by definition—and a boy in front of me determined to prove something. Home gets stained by the fact that a boundary does not protect you if another person decides it doesn't count.

It happens inside school too, in scenes that sound ridiculous on paper because middle school can turn anything into a pretext. A chair becomes an excuse. I sit where a boy believes he owns the space, and he stands behind me and antagonizes me with a steady drip of words meant to provoke. Ignoring him does not stop him; it feeds him, because now he has an audience and a mission: make the quiet kid react. Each minute he stays behind me is a minute he is proving power. Eventually I stand and pull him into a headlock in the middle of the classroom, and the air changes instantly, the way it does when violence enters like weather. I don't release until an adult physically pulls me off, and in that separation there is shame and relief—shame because everyone has watched me become a thing I do not want to be, relief because adult authority ends it before I have to decide how far it goes.

Around that time I've been going to wrestling classes after school for only a couple of weeks. I'm not trained in any deep sense, not the way real wrestlers are trained, but the adults decide the technique came from there and remove me from the program as punishment. The logic is blunt: remove the kid from the thing that looks like fighting. Nobody wants to deal with harassment or provocation or the social cruelty that leads to a headlock. They want the visible violence to stop. They punish the tool they can identify, not the context they don't want to face. It teaches another cold lesson: systems simplify complicated problems by cutting out what they can name. The rest—the invisible pressure that creates the moment—gets ignored because ignoring it is easier than fixing it.

At home, the story of me starts to include those headlocks. It becomes a family anecdote, something that can be mentioned with a half-laugh, because adults like to turn discomfort into story. But being known for it means something deeper. It means my identity becomes physical. It means I'm being shaped into someone who solves problems by squeezing until the other person surrenders. I don't feel proud. I feel dirty. Every fight ends with exhaustion and embarrassment and the knowledge that tomorrow the hallway will still exist. There is no catharsis. There is no moment where the bullies decide to respect me forever. Winning a fight does not buy lasting safety, because the targeting isn't about the fight. It's about whether you fit.

I try fitting in through other means, and those attempts create their own consequences. For a while my body does something strange—sulfur-smelling sour burps that appear out of nowhere like a temporary chemical rebellion. It's gross and childish, but middle school is an ecosystem where attention is oxygen, and if you can produce a reaction you can briefly matter. I lean into it. I blow one toward another student. The reaction is immediate and dramatic—faces recoiling, voices rising, disgust turning into performance. Their exaggeration feels like comedy, and that comedy feels like control. For a moment I am the cause instead of the effect. I am directing energy instead of absorbing it. The relief of that control is intoxicating in the shallow way a kid will accept anything that makes him feel powerful.

The system does not find it funny. I get sent to the nurse. I get sent home. The message is clear: you can't be disgusting in a way that disrupts the machine. The machine can tolerate bullying in hallways as long as it stays under a certain volume. It can tolerate cruelty disguised as teasing because that cruelty is quiet and hard to document. It can tolerate the slow erosion of a kid's dignity because the erosion doesn't force adults to confront it. But it cannot tolerate a kid weaponizing his own body in a way that is too visible, too absurd, too hard to ignore. That becomes another pattern to notice: what gets punished is not always what is worst; it's what is loudest.

Then there is an incident where I learn the system punishes words differently than intent, and that lesson lands hard because it is my own fault. A fire happens in the community—something I have nothing to do with—and I tell another student I'm responsible for it because I think it will make me look dangerous, make me look like the kind of boy whose name carries weight. The truth underneath the lie is simple and ugly: I want attention. I want a reputation that makes people treat me like I matter. It's a fantasy of power built out of insecurity and loneliness, and it lasts only as long as it takes for adults to take it seriously.

Authorities question me. They ask details, and my answers lead them to believe I did it. The tone shifts from curiosity to suspicion. The questions go on long enough that I can feel walls closing in. In the middle of a sentence, I realize I've created a reality that can trap me. Lying to a peer is one thing. Lying into the face of authority is another. Authority builds files. Authority turns words into paperwork and consequences. I try to back out. I insist I wasn't involved. Eventually I convince them I didn't do it, but I'm suspended anyway. Suspended anyway. The punishment sticks because the system has already invested time and certainty, and it needs consequences to justify the process. The lesson lodges in my body: words can build cages, and once you're in one, the truth doesn't always open the door.

While all of this is happening—fights, suspensions, being sent home for being disgusting—I am still doing things that should make me feel steady. I am still practicing piano, the repetitive discipline of scales and pieces until patterns become muscle memory. I am still sitting in band with the clarinet cold against my hands, adjusting a reed, listening for tuning, counting rests. I am still receiving adult approval for things that make sense to adults: effort, talent, achievement. That creates a split in the middle school experience. In one world, I am rewarded for discipline. In the other, I am punished or tested by peers and systems that don't care about discipline at all. Both worlds are real, and learning to move between them without tearing feels like its own kind of labor.

Performance enters those years as a different kind of discipline, one that comes with its own brutality but also its own fairness. Rehearsal is repetition, correction, adults adjusting your posture like you're equipment. The body learns to move on cue, to hold positions, to take direction without arguing. I end up in a ballet-and-theater production in seventh grade, a holiday show with costumes and music and that specific backstage smell of makeup and sweat and dust caught in stage curtains. On stage, the world becomes measured. Marks on the floor. Counts in the music. A place to stand, a place to turn, a way to hold your arms and your face. Being watched is the point, and being watched doesn't automatically mean being hunted.

There is a feeling in rehearsal that I don't get in hallways: conditional safety. If you do what is required—if you hit your mark, remember steps, keep timing—you belong for that moment. Applause, when it comes, does not require you to be socially dominant. It requires you to be accurate. The approval is tied to execution, not to charisma. For a kid who often feels misread, that kind of clean feedback feels like water. But the safety is still conditional. When rehearsal ends and the costume is hung up, the hallway is waiting. The field is waiting. Middle school teaches a cruel contrast: you can be celebrated at night under stage lights and still be tested the next afternoon behind the school. You can be "gifted" in one room and still be the wrong kind of boy in another.

I try to add other skills the way adults encourage you to—collect achievements like armor. I take Spanish, hoping another language will become another proof of value, another thing that makes me impressive. It doesn't stick the way music sticks. Vocabulary slips away. Grammar feels like trying to hold water in my hands. I can do enough to pass through the class, but not enough to feel ownership. The failure is quiet but irritating because the label of being "bright" carries an implication that effort always translates into mastery. Middle school complicates that implication. The mind can be fast and still refuse certain kinds of learning. The mind can be capable and still get lost. That doesn't feel tragic. It feels embarrassing in a private way, like a small crack in the story adults have been telling about what I'm supposed to be.

Time in middle school is not only major incidents. It is also weather, drift, repetition that forms the background the way a hum forms the background of a room. There are mornings where the sky is gray and the bus windows fog and the building smells like wet coats. There are afternoons where spring makes the air feel electric and everyone is restless in their desks, legs bouncing, eyes going to the clock. There are days where the cafeteria is so loud it feels like the sound is rubbing the inside of your skull raw. There are nights where homework is done at a kitchen table under harsh light, pencil scraping paper, the temptation to stare off into space because staring off is easier than holding focus. There are weekends where the neighborhood feels calmer, where walking a few blocks feels like freedom because the bell isn't driving you. Those gaps matter because they are where the nervous system decides what it considers normal.

As eighth grade arrives, social life sharpens. The hierarchies harden. Kids start trying on identities like costumes: tough, funny, cruel, popular, invisible. Humor becomes sharper. Teasing becomes more targeted. Gossip gains weight even when it's ridiculous. Bodies begin to change in small ways that make everyone hypersensitive— voices cracking, limbs getting longer, the sudden self-consciousness of being watched not just socially but physically. In that environment, attention becomes a kind of currency, and the hunger for it can make you do dumb things, cruel things, desperate things. I want to belong somewhere without having to perform perfectly or fight. I want warmth that doesn't have to be earned by entertaining a crowd. I don't have a clean map for how to get it.

That hunger bleeds into the way I approach girls, and it creates mistakes that are not violent in the way fights are violent, but leave a different kind of bruise. I pursue a girl in eighth grade with the clumsy intensity of someone who wants closeness but doesn't know how to ask for it without turning it into pressure. In my head, attention feels like a door that might close if I hesitate, so I push. I confuse desire with entitlement without naming it that way. On a porch under a bright light, I lean in and try to force a kiss. The hope is that the action will create the feeling, that closeness can be manufactured, that the world will align if I'm bold enough. She resists. The visibility of it—the porch light, the open air, the sense that the whole neighborhood could see—makes shame arrive instantly, like stepping off a curb you didn't see.

Afterward, I scramble for a different kind of connection because I don't know how to sit with the fact that I've crossed a line. I talk about church and righteousness as if offering "goodness" can erase awkwardness, as if a clean story can overwrite a messy moment. Someone in her household later claims a restraining order has been filed. Whether it is official or not is less important than what the claim does to my internal world: it makes the whole situation feel adult, dangerous, permanent. It makes me feel like I have stepped into a category of person I don't want to be. The shame isn't clean. It doesn't become growth in a neat sequence. It becomes confusion and self-distrust, a new wariness of my own impulses.

Between eighth and ninth grade, that wariness collides with something else: fear that is not social, not metaphorical. I meet an older girl near the middle school soccer field, and the difference in age matters in the way it always matters when you're young. She feels more certain, more practiced, like she's already unlocked doors I'm still searching for. She talks to me. She invites me to her house. The invitation feels like being chosen out of a crowd, like a sudden promotion into a world I've been staring at from the outside. At her house she changes clothes in front of me as if modesty is optional, as if my discomfort is childish and should be outgrown on command. She insists it's fine, and that insistence has a gravitational pull. A reality gets created around me and I don't have the skills to negotiate; I have only the fear of ruining the moment by being awkward.

Then someone else from her household arrives, and the air changes instantly. Footsteps. A door. A voice carrying threat without needing to explain itself. The chase that follows is not a game. It is real panic, the body moving because it knows what it means to be hunted by someone older and stronger. A rifle appears in the equation, not as a story element but as a fact of physics and consequence. It is aimed in my direction. A threat is made that draws a boundary with a certainty my middle school world has not trained me for. In that moment, I understand in my bones that a person can end you. Not socially. Not emotionally. Physically. A gun is a different kind of sentence. It doesn't negotiate. It doesn't care what you meant. It doesn't care whether you were invited. It defines a line and assigns a consequence you cannot talk your way out of.

I leave. I do not return. I do not see her again. The episode collapses into a single message that doesn't feel like wisdom so much as shrinkage: you can misread a situation and the world can respond with lethal certainty. That message does not cleanly mature me. It makes me smaller and more cautious. It makes the adult world feel closer than it should at that age, and the closeness is not comforting. The boundary is not taught; it is enforced after the fact. The nervous system takes that enforcement seriously. It files it away as a warning about how quickly a moment can turn, how little your internal narrative protects you when consequences arrive in metal.

Looking at the middle school years as a whole, there is no straight line. There are collisions. The bell-driven shuffle between classrooms. The gifted hour that gathers "people like me" and still leaves me slightly off to the side. The discipline of music and performance offering brief islands of correctness. The field offering bruises and adrenaline and the knowledge that walking home can turn into a fight. The headlocks that make me known for a violence I don't want. The humiliation of being punished for being visible in the wrong ways—too loud, too clumsy, too stupid with words—while other, quieter cruelties are tolerated because they don't disrupt the machine. The years are not an origin myth for what I become later. They are practice in living inside systems that don't always match fairness with consequence, practice in reading rooms quickly, practice in keeping myself compact.

By the end of eighth grade, my body learns anticipation. It tenses before the last bell because the last bell isn't only freedom; it is exposure. It is the moment when the river of kids pours outside and the rules thin. My mind learns to watch adults for fairness and rarely find it in the ways that matter. It learns that labels can be true and still useless: being "bright" doesn't keep you safe, being talented doesn't buy peace, being praised doesn't stop someone from deciding you're prey. Underneath all of that, the hunger remains—the same hunger for belonging without performance, for warmth without negotiation, for a place where I don't have to squeeze someone's head until he begs just to earn a few minutes of calm. Middle school doesn't answer that hunger. It teaches what the hunger can cost, and then the bell rings again, and the machine keeps running.

# CHAPTER 5

# *The Exit Door*

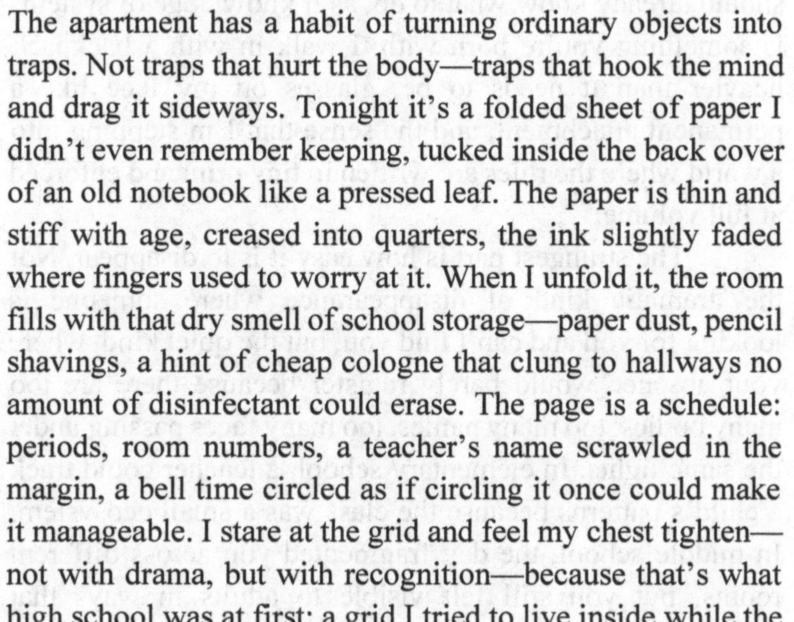

The apartment has a habit of turning ordinary objects into traps. Not traps that hurt the body—traps that hook the mind and drag it sideways. Tonight it's a folded sheet of paper I didn't even remember keeping, tucked inside the back cover of an old notebook like a pressed leaf. The paper is thin and stiff with age, creased into quarters, the ink slightly faded where fingers used to worry at it. When I unfold it, the room fills with that dry smell of school storage—paper dust, pencil shavings, a hint of cheap cologne that clung to hallways no amount of disinfectant could erase. The page is a schedule: periods, room numbers, a teacher's name scrawled in the margin, a bell time circled as if circling it once could make it manageable. I stare at the grid and feel my chest tighten— not with drama, but with recognition—because that's what high school was at first: a grid I tried to live inside while the rest of my life kept leaking outside the lines. The fan keeps pushing air. The refrigerator keeps humming. But the apartment's present-day quiet recedes, and behind it I can hear lockers slamming and shoes scuffing and the low roar of a building full of teenagers pretending they aren't afraid.

High school doesn't arrive like a clean doorway. It arrives like the same machine, turned up. Middle school already taught me the core mechanics—bells, hallways, shifting rooms, the way time becomes something that pushes you—but high school adds more gears, more noise, more spaces where you can vanish. The building is bigger than it needs to be. The hallways feel longer, the stairwells more crowded, the fluorescent lights more relentless. There are older kids everywhere, taller bodies with louder confidence, voices that carry like they own air. Teachers stop speaking to you like you're small and start speaking to you like you should already know what to do, as if knowledge of systems is something you're born with. I walk in with a backpack heavier than it needs to be, glasses on my face like a permanent attachment, and the sense that I'm stepping into a world where the rules are written in tiny print and enforced at full volume.

The strangest part is how easy it is to disappear. Not the dramatic kind of disappearance where someone is looking for you and can't find you, but the quiet kind, where your absence would barely register because there are too many bodies, too many names, too many faces passing under the same lights. In elementary school, a teacher could track a child's patterns because the class was a small ecosystem. In middle school, the day fragmented you across different rooms, but you still felt visible to adults in ways that mattered. In high school, there are too many corridors, too many entrances, too many side doors that lead to places nobody monitors unless they have a reason. You can become a shadow by choosing the right hallway at the right time. You can become a blank by staying quiet and keeping your eyes down. You can be physically present and still absent, and the machine will keep running as long as you don't interrupt it.

I learn that there's forced disappearance and chosen disappearance, and the difference matters. Forced disappearance is hiding because you're being hunted—by bullies, by attention, by trouble. Chosen disappearance is hiding because you want to, because being unseen feels like relief. High school gives me more of that second kind. Not because it's kinder, but because it's larger. A crowd is camouflage. A hallway is camouflage. A bathroom stall is camouflage. The library is camouflage. A corner of the cafeteria where the sound is still loud but you're not in the middle of it is camouflage. In this environment, invisibility feels like control. When you've spent years being tested, watched, measured, teased, and occasionally challenged into physical fights, the ability to move through a day without registering feels like a gift.

That gift comes with a cost: the better I get at disappearing, the harder it gets to show up on purpose. It starts as a practical skill—how to avoid certain clusters of kids, how to time my movement so I'm not caught in the most aggressive part of the hallway surge—but it becomes a habit. I learn to keep my face neutral, my body compact, my voice low. I learn to be efficient in a way that looks like maturity from a distance and feels like self-erasure from the inside. Teachers see a quiet student who doesn't cause trouble. They don't see the effort behind it: the constant scanning, the constant internal calculation of where to stand, how to move, what expression to wear so I don't invite someone else's boredom to land on me.

A kind of efficiency lives in my body by then—the same efficiency that helped me survive earlier years, the same efficiency that made me quick in a headlock, quick in a hallway, quick in a classroom. In high school, efficiency becomes camouflage. I can slide into a room without drawing eyes. I can sit in the back without becoming a target. I can keep my hands busy so my restlessness has somewhere to go. I can keep my attention split—half on the teacher, half on the room—because you never fully stop watching other people. Even when nobody is threatening you in that moment, some part of you expects a verdict to land anyway, and the expectation makes you live as if you're always on a low boil.

High school also gives me something else: a way to feel adult without actually becoming adult. It begins, like so many things in my life begin, with an older kid in my orbit —someone close enough to influence me, someone who moved through the world like rules were made for other people. That person had swagger that felt like gravity. He could be magnetic one moment and reckless the next, and he carried a kind of certainty I didn't have. When he introduced me to smoking, it didn't come with a sermon. It came like a casual handoff, a small ritual offered as proof of belonging. The cigarette felt ridiculous at first—thin paper, bitter smell, a thing people chose to inhale on purpose—but the moment the smoke hit my lungs and my body rebelled, coughing hard enough to make my eyes water, I understood what the ritual was really about. It wasn't about taste. It was about crossing a boundary. Coughing became evidence that I was stepping into an adult space, and the laughter around me—half amused, half approving—felt like a stamp.

Within the same year a friend reintroduced me to smoking as if it were a skill I should already own. The group gathered behind the building or near a fence line or in a place where adults didn't linger, and cigarettes appeared like a shared resource. The smoke hung in the air and made the light look different. There was a rhythm to it: flick of a lighter, inhale, exhale, the tiny moment of silence while your lungs held fire. Everyone pretended it was normal. Everyone pretended their throat didn't burn. Everyone pretended coughing was weakness. I learned quickly how to make the coughing smaller, how to tuck it into my chest, how to take a shallow inhale and still act like I belonged. It wasn't bravery. It was performance. The performance was rewarded with a seat inside the circle, and that seat felt better than being alone.

Smoking gave me a kind of control. A cigarette had a beginning and an end. It had steps that were predictable. It gave my hands something to do. It gave the minutes a structure when the rest of my life felt like drift. Smoke also gave me a subtle form of armor: it created a haze between me and the world. It softened edges. It gave me permission to stand apart and still be part of something. I could be quiet and still look like I was participating because the ritual itself counted as participation. In a school where attention could be dangerous, smoke made invisibility feel intentional rather than imposed. It said: I'm not hiding. I'm choosing not to engage. And in adolescence, the illusion of choice can be enough to keep you afloat.

At the same time, my mornings were being claimed by religion. Before the sun fully rose, before the rest of the neighborhood's lights came on, a caregiver insisted I attend an early-morning religious class. It was held in a separate building near the school, a room full of folding chairs and laminated posters and an adult voice teaching rules as if rules could stabilize a life. There were other teenagers there— some engaged, some half asleep, some clearly resentful— and we sat with our notebooks open while the world outside was still dark. The air smelled like stale coffee and carpet cleaner and winter coats. The lessons were about worthiness, obedience, purity, the idea that order can be maintained if you obey it. Some mornings it did feel like order. Some mornings it did feel like a path. Other mornings it felt like a pressure clamp, a requirement layered on top of a school day that already demanded everything.

High school didn't fit neatly into a system that promised peace through boundaries. It pulled me toward things that were messy and human and hard to moralize. So I learned to hold two worlds at once. In the early-morning class I could sit straight, nod at the right times, speak the right language. I could appear serious, appear committed, appear like I wanted the version of life being offered. Then the bell would ring later, the day would begin in full, and the hallways would remind me that rules don't protect you from other people. The cafeteria would remind me that hunger and noise don't care about doctrine. The group behind the building would remind me that belonging can be purchased with small acts of rebellion. I lived with that split without naming it as a split. I simply learned how to switch masks fast. Mask switching became a skill the way pacing became a skill: not because it solved the problem, but because it helped me keep moving.

In the house where I lived, adults told origin stories like they were medicine. Something went wrong in a kid's behavior, and an adult would reach back and try to find the one moment that "explained" it. The one influence. The one event. The one mistake. They did it because adults need causality to feel safe, and because blaming one thing is easier than admitting life is complicated. I absorbed that habit without realizing it, and it turned inward. If I drifted, I looked for the moment I "broke." If I made a mistake, I hunted for the point where the mistake began, as if every small failure was evidence of a deeper defect. That kind of thinking is seductive because it promises a solution—find the cause, remove it—but it also becomes a trap because it turns every misstep into a verdict. High school fed that trap. It offered endless data points: grades, attendance, discipline slips, social reactions. The machine recorded everything, and even when the records didn't matter, the existence of them made me feel watched.

A close relative of mine occupied the center of much of my adolescence like a bright object I couldn't look at directly. We were close in that intense, messy way teenagers can be close when the adults around them are inconsistent, when attention feels scarce, when affection is sometimes a reward and sometimes withheld. That closeness came with loyalty that didn't always make sense. It came with secrets. It came with the feeling that belonging wasn't something I built; it was something I borrowed. In the brightest moments, that relationship made me feel tethered, like I wasn't floating alone in my own head. In the darker moments, it trained me in silence. It trained me in the idea that secrecy can be proof of love. It trained me in the idea that doing something wrong together can feel safer than doing something right alone.

That relative also pulled me into risk in practical ways. We went into big-box stores and learned how to steal. Not the romantic version of stealing you see in movies, but the stupid, adrenaline-chasing version that teenagers do because they want to touch a boundary and return. We took small things—cosmetics, cheap accessories, whatever could fit in a pocket—and the thrill wasn't the item. The thrill was the shared silence. The thrill was the moment after, walking out with a straight face, pretending nothing happened while the heart hammered in the chest. The outside air would hit my lungs like relief. My hands would tremble slightly from the adrenaline, and I would smile in a way I tried to hide, because the smile felt incriminating. Later, at home, the stolen items were not even impressive. They were proof that we could. Proof that we were in control of something, even if it was the wrong thing.

The adults in the house responded to that relative in ways that fed the dynamic without ever acknowledging they were feeding it. Sometimes they punished harshly. Sometimes they shrugged things off. Sometimes they believed the version of the story that sounded most convenient. Sometimes they believed the version that matched their biases. Watching that taught me a quiet, corrosive lesson: truth isn't always what matters; the story people want to believe matters. Combine that with other shifting narratives in the household—different people saying different things depending on mood—and you get a kid who learns to hide by default. You learn to keep certain truths inside because you don't know which truth will be weaponized. You learn to show the version of yourself that is safest for the moment. High school gave me more opportunities to practice that kind of hiding, and the practice made it easier to do it everywhere.

Skipping school doesn't arrive like an explosion. It arrives like drift. At first, it's small: a missed class, a late morning, a deliberate "sick" day that isn't really sick. Then it becomes a pattern. There are days I slip out with other students and nobody stops us because nobody is positioned to stop us. We move through side doors and across parking lots like we belong there, and the simple fact of walking away feels like power. Time behaves differently when you skip. Hours become soft. Consequences feel unreal because they haven't landed yet. You can sit somewhere quiet—

behind a building, at a friend's place, in a room where the curtains are drawn—and the world seems paused. But the pause doesn't bring peace. It brings fog. The longer you live in the fog, the harder it is to step back into the machine and pretend you were never gone.

There's a particular kind of shame that follows skipping. It's not the shame of being caught. It's the shame of realizing you're choosing absence and you don't fully know why. Skipping becomes less about avoiding a specific class and more about avoiding the feeling of being pinned to a schedule. In high school, the day is a chain of obligations: be here, then here, then here, and if you fail to move when the bell says move, you're treated as wrong. When I skip, I get a brief taste of a day without those commands. I get a day where time belongs to me. Then the dread arrives: the moment you remember you have to return. The moment you realize the machine has been running without you and will require you to explain your absence. The fog turns into weight. It's easier, in that moment, to keep skipping than to face the return.

Around this time I try learning another language, believing it will be a clean kind of achievement, something that proves I'm still the "capable" version of myself adults used to point at. It makes sense on paper. The mind that sees patterns quickly should be good at grammar. The mind that learns music should be good at phonetics. But the language doesn't stick the way I want it to. Vocabulary slides away. Conjugations blur together. The embarrassment is quiet because nobody else cares as much as I do, but it irritates me because it cracks the story I've been handed: that being "smart" means being capable in every direction, that potential automatically becomes outcome. High school exposes how false that story is. You can be capable and still drift. You can be quick and still fail to sustain the larger pattern. The machine doesn't measure potential; it measures attendance, completion, compliance. And compliance is not a thing my nervous system offers easily when it's tired of being pushed.

At home, competence shows up in a place that feels safer than classrooms. Someone in the house upgrades a computer, and the old machine becomes mine to experiment with. I take it apart with a screwdriver, the case opening like a treasure chest full of parts that look both simple and mysterious. I learn what a hard drive feels like in the hand, heavier than it should be. I learn the satisfying click of a cable seating correctly. I learn how to swap components, how to troubleshoot, how to make something work again by understanding its logic. There is no crowd. There is no hallway. There is no bell. There is only cause and effect. When the machine powers on, when the screen glows, when the system boots successfully, the success feels honest. It doesn't require social performance. It doesn't require luck. It's proof that my mind can still build something, still solve something, still hold a sequence long enough to finish it.

That proof does not translate into school the way I want it to. In the classroom, the work is either too easy and boring or too scattered to hold my attention in a clean line. In the hallways, the social economy still runs on its own rules, and my competence doesn't buy me safety or belonging. In the early-morning religious class, the idea of order is offered like a cure, but order doesn't touch the daily texture of my life: the drift, the hiding, the smoke, the guilt that follows me like a smell I can't wash off. I begin to feel like I'm living inside contradictions that never resolve. I can be disciplined in one corner of my life and self-sabotaging in another. I can be praised for talent and punished for absence. I can want to be good and still reach for trouble when trouble is the only thing that makes me feel real.

In the background, the household carries its own strange fears. A group of teenagers brings a spirit board into the house one night and treats it like a toy, like a dare, like a way to manufacture meaning out of boredom. The room is dim. Laughter is louder than it should be. Fingers rest on the planchette lightly, and everyone pretends the movement isn't coming from anyone's muscles. In the moment it's spectacle, an adolescent performance of curiosity and rebellion. Later, the story changes. Later, adults speak about it with more seriousness, as if the night might have opened something. The meaning gets assigned afterward, and the assigned meaning sticks. That pattern becomes familiar: actions taken in confusion, then judged as if they were deliberate. The world loves to rewrite adolescent mistakes into moral lessons. The problem is that the lessons don't always teach what they claim to teach. Sometimes they only teach shame.

The shame around desire is its own atmosphere in high school. I carry earlier lessons about boundaries, about pressure, about becoming the kind of boy who does harm without meaning to. I distrust my own impulses because I've seen how quickly a moment can turn ugly when you try to force closeness. So when intimacy appears, it arrives braided with panic. I want to be wanted, but I also fear what wanting might make me do. Then I meet a girl—older by a year— and that difference matters in the way small differences matter when you're young. She carries herself with more confidence, more certainty, like she already belongs in her body. When she chooses me, it feels like a verdict in my favor. Not because she fixes me, not because she rescues me, but because her attention is deliberate. She makes me feel wanted on purpose, and that sensation is rare enough that I cling to it harder than I should.

At first the relationship is a mix of tenderness and intensity. There are moments of warmth that feel clean: sitting close, talking late, feeling the world narrow to two people instead of a whole building of judgment. There are also moments of volatility, the kind that teenagers confuse with passion because intensity feels like proof. We break up during the first summer, then orbit back toward each other because I don't have enough of that feeling in my life to walk away from it. The connection becomes a place I run to when school feels like fog and home feels like pressure and my own mind feels like a room I don't want to sit in alone. I learn to treat closeness like shelter, which means when the shelter shakes, I shake with it.

Homecoming night becomes a hinge. Not because it's glamorous—high school dances are mostly loud music and awkward bodies and cheap perfume—but because the night carries the weight of a line being crossed. I'm old enough to be convinced I'm making adult choices, young enough not to understand how irreversible certain choices can feel afterward. We end up alone. The moment is private and urgent and full of nervous laughter that tries to hide fear. When it happens, it is not a cinematic scene. It's two teenagers fumbling toward something they want and don't fully know how to hold. The aftermath is where the hinge lives. The boundary changes. The relationship becomes heavier. The world looks slightly different because now there's a secret that isn't just emotional; it's physical. I compartmentalize and keep moving because that's what I know how to do. But compartmentalizing doesn't erase weight. It only stores it.

We start skipping school together—not occasionally, but periodically, drifting out of the machine as if stepping out of a river. Some days the skipping feels like freedom: driving around, sitting somewhere quiet, talking in a way that feels more real than anything in a classroom. Some days it feels like dread disguised as freedom, because the longer you stay out, the harder the return becomes. An adult in her house uses marijuana openly, and that fact enters our relationship like another kind of permission. The air in certain rooms carries a sweet, skunky smell that clings to fabric. Smoke hangs in corners. The ritual looks casual, normal, like something you do while watching television. I'm not trying to rebel against God in those moments. I'm trying to feel real. I'm trying to quiet the restless, buzzing part of me that can't sit still inside my own head. The problem is that relief bought this way always has a bill later, and the bill shows up as guilt, as anxiety, as a tighter knot in the stomach when I sit in that early-morning religious class and hear lessons about purity and worthiness and consequence.

Religion starts to feel less like refuge and more like surveillance. Not because someone is following me with a clipboard, but because the rules hover over everything, turning ordinary teenage choices into cosmic judgment. I sit in that early-morning room and hear words like clean, unclean, worthy, unworthy, and my chest tightens with a quiet panic. It isn't that I don't believe. It's that belief doesn't protect me from myself. Belief doesn't erase desire. Belief doesn't erase the need for closeness. Belief doesn't erase the ways I've learned to hide. So I carry weight and keep my face neutral. I learn to wear guilt like a second skin, a constant background sensation, and the longer I wear it the more normal it feels. That normalization is dangerous, because once guilt becomes normal, you stop noticing it as something you could set down.

When she turns eighteen, her home life breaks into open conflict. The details shift depending on who tells the story, but the shape is clear: she can't stay where she is. She needs somewhere else. In the house where I live, an adult makes a decision that feels sudden and huge: she is allowed to move into a basement room. The basement becomes a strange imitation of adulthood. We live under the same roof as authority, but we pretend we're independent. We have a private space, but we don't truly own it. We have the illusion of being a couple building a life, but the life is still surrounded by rules we didn't write. The air down there is cooler. The light is dimmer. The sounds from above—footsteps, doors closing, voices—filter through the ceiling like reminders that we are not fully separate from the world that raised us.

In that basement, I learn how thin the line is between warmth and instability. There is comfort in waking up with someone beside you, in having a shared routine, in cooking small meals, in watching television together, in believing you're building something. There is also constant tension because the arrangement itself is fragile. Every noise from upstairs can feel like judgment approaching. Every disagreement carries the fear of collapse because if the relationship collapses, the living situation collapses with it. The basement becomes both refuge and pressure cooker, and the pressure makes small problems feel large. I don't have the skills to manage conflict cleanly. I don't have a model for stability that doesn't rely on silence. So I do what I've learned: I compartmentalize, I hide, I keep moving, even when "moving" now means emotionally moving—shifting feelings into a locked room so I can get through the day.

School administrators eventually notice the skipping. Not because they're especially attentive, but because the machine has rules, and persistent absence becomes an administrative problem. Meetings happen. Adults sit across from me with concerned faces and clipped tones, asking what's wrong in a way that assumes I have a neat answer. I don't. The truth isn't a single cause. It's drift layered on drift. It's smoke and shame and fatigue. It's the constant switching of masks. It's the feeling that the day is a chain of commands I can't always obey. But the machine doesn't know what to do with complexity, so it seeks a simple narrative. They talk about my intelligence like it's evidence—test scores, assessments, the language of potential—and the disappointment in their voices is sharp because they believe "capable" should automatically mean "compliant." They treat my drift like a choice to waste a gift. They don't see how drift can feel like gravity, how easy it is to fall when you're already tired.

At some point, an adult at the school introduces me to a recruiter. The introduction is framed as opportunity. A person in a uniform sits with me and speaks a language different from teachers and caregivers. Teachers talk about semesters and credits and grades and college applications like life is a ladder you climb in a straight line. Caregivers talk about morality and rules and the idea that being good will protect you. The recruiter talks about leaving. He talks about structure. He talks about a paycheck. He talks about travel. He talks about being part of something that already knows what it wants from you. He talks about a system that will hand you an identity and require you to wear it correctly. Leaving becomes a word that feels holy when you're trapped. It feels like a door in a room that has been shrinking for years.

The process unfolds with a strange mix of adult seriousness and teenage unreality. There are forms. There are appointments. There is the odd, clinical choreography of being measured—height, weight, hearing, vision—like the institution needs to verify you are an acceptable piece of equipment. There are conversations where the recruiter's confidence feels contagious. He speaks as if the future is already decided, as if all I have to do is step onto a track and let it carry me. Part of me resists because stepping onto a track means surrendering control. Another part of me craves it because control has not been kind to me. My attempts at controlling my life have often turned into hiding. Structure sounds like a cure. The recruiter doesn't promise happiness. He promises order. Order is enough to seduce a tired nervous system.

Only near the end—only when the exit has a name— does the word land with full weight: the Navy. It arrives not like a war story, not like a heroic narrative, but like a promise of clean lines. Uniforms. Rules. Clear hierarchies. A place where the day is scheduled for you and the expectations are explicit. The Navy is presented as an escape hatch from drift, from shame, from the feeling that I'm wasting potential. In the recruiter's office, it sounds like a way to become a person without having to invent myself from scratch. I don't know what it will take from me. I only know what I hope it will take away: the fog, the indecision, the constant mask-switching. I want a life where showing up is not optional. I want a life where belonging is guaranteed by membership, where I don't have to bargain for a seat in the circle with smoke and silence.

In the months leading up to that decision becoming irreversible, high school begins to feel like a room I'm already leaving, even while my body still walks its halls. The bells sound different when you know you're exiting. Teachers' voices feel farther away. Assignments feel less real. The social dramas that used to feel urgent start to look like tiny storms in a closed environment. That change isn't wisdom. It's detachment. When an exit is named, the mind starts packing early. It starts storing emotion in boxes. It starts treating the present as temporary, which can be both relief and danger. Relief because it reduces the pressure— why care about this quiz if your life is about to change completely. Danger because detachment can become a habit that follows you into the new life, and institutions don't like detached recruits. Institutions want devotion.

The actual act of dropping out happens without the cinematic weight people assign to it later. It isn't one dramatic argument, one door slam, one rebellious declaration. It's paperwork. It's meetings. It's the slow acknowledgment that the pattern of my life has become incompatible with the school's pattern, and the school doesn't have a softer solution than removal. I don't feel triumphant. I feel a hollow relief and a quiet dread. Relief because the daily machine stops demanding my body. Dread because now the drift has more space to spread. When you remove a structure from a life, you don't automatically become free. You become responsible for building your own structure, and I have not proven to myself that I can do that reliably. That fear pushes me harder toward the institution that promises structure in exchange for obedience.

The weeks after leaving school are full of strange, unclaimed hours. Days stretch long. The neighborhood looks different when you're not commuting to a building. The sun moves across the sky like a slow spotlight. I find myself awake at odd times. I sit in rooms that used to feel like home and now feel like waiting rooms. I spend time with the girl in the basement, and the relationship alternates between comfort and tension, because nothing about our situation is truly stable. There are moments we talk about the future with forced optimism, as if speaking it aloud will make it real. There are moments we fight over small things because small things are safer than the big fear we're both carrying: that this arrangement can end suddenly, that this closeness can turn to ash, that neither of us actually knows how to build a life.

I keep returning to the recruiter's language because his language is clean. It doesn't require me to explain my contradictions. It doesn't ask me to untangle guilt from desire. It doesn't ask me to justify why the school day felt like fog. It says: sign here, show up there, follow orders, become part of a system that has already survived bigger chaos than your teenage life. That promise is seductive. It's also a kind of surrender. I practice that surrender in small ways—taking instructions seriously, showing up on time to appointments, letting adults tell me what to do without arguing—because the Navy is already training me before I ever leave. The training is psychological: stop improvising, start complying. Stop drifting, start marching.

There is a night near the end—close enough to departure that the air itself feels charged—when the house is unusually quiet. The basement room is dim. A bag sits packed or half-packed, the zipper open like a mouth. Clothes folded in stacks that look too neat to be mine. Toiletries arranged like a checklist. Paperwork gathered, names printed, dates circled. The girl is asleep or pretending to be asleep, turned away, and the distance between us feels both normal and alarming. Upstairs, a floorboard creaks, a door closes, the house making its familiar sounds as if nothing is changing. Outside, the neighborhood is dark and ordinary, streetlights pooling light on empty pavement. Everything looks the same, and that sameness feels unreal because the future has been named and scheduled and is already moving toward me like a train.

In that night, the life I've been living starts to look like a series of rooms I've passed through without fully inhabiting. The school hallways. The early-morning religious class. The smoke circle behind the building. The basement that pretended to be adulthood. The recruiter's office with its posters and its confident promises. Each room offered something—belonging, structure, escape, warmth— and each room also demanded something I didn't always have. I sit on the edge of the bed and listen to the house settle, and the listening itself feels like a rehearsal for leaving: learning the last sounds of a place before you trade them for a new set. My chest tightens with the kind of feeling that doesn't have a clean name. It isn't just fear. It isn't just excitement. It's the awareness that a choice has been made and now the choice will start making me.

Morning arrives with the dull inevitability of light pushing through blinds. The house wakes in fragments— running water, footsteps, muffled voices—and I move through it like someone wearing borrowed skin. My bag is heavier than it should be, not because of the contents, but because of what it represents: a life being condensed into portable form. I step outside and the air hits my face with a clarity that feels almost rude. The sky looks too wide. The street looks too ordinary to be the threshold it is about to become. A vehicle is waiting, engine idling, and the sound of it vibrates through my bones. People speak to me in that careful tone adults use when they want to say something meaningful but don't know how. I nod. I keep my face neutral. I do what I've practiced: I hide the storm and perform steadiness.

The last moment before leaving is not a grand pause, not a slow-motion cinematic farewell. It is practical. It is stepping toward an open door with my bag in my hand. It is the sensation of crossing a small distance—sidewalk to curb, curb to vehicle—while the world keeps looking the same. The house behind me doesn't collapse. The neighborhood doesn't change color. The sky doesn't announce anything. The only thing that changes is the direction of my body. I am moving toward the institution that promised order, and I can feel the pull of it like gravity. The door is open. The seat is there. The engine's hum is steady. I lift my foot to climb in, and for a fraction of a second the entire life behind me feels like a room I've already exited, even though the door hasn't closed yet.

# CHAPTER 6

# *Borrowed Order*

The apartment had learned my patterns better than I had. It knew the difference between a quiet night and a false quiet night—the kind where everything in the room behaves, everything stays still, and my body is the only thing making noise. The first warning is never the pain. The first warning is the clock. It starts as a small tightening low in my abdomen —so subtle it could pass for nothing if I wanted it to—and then the clock in the kitchen becomes the only thing I can hear. The microwave glow is too bright for what it is. The minutes look clean and indifferent. I stand in the living room of my apartment, surrounded by the life I built to be quiet, and my body ignores the quiet completely. The tightening deepens, slow at first, then with a kind of certainty that feels like a decision being made without me. I tell myself it'll pass. I tell myself it's not that bad. I tell myself I can finish what I started. The lie lasts only as long as it takes for the sensation to sharpen into a countdown.

Denial is automatic, almost rehearsed. I can feel my mind trying to out-negotiate my nervous system, as if bargaining has ever worked. My mouth goes dry, the way it does before something urgent, and a thin film of sweat gathers along my back. I move toward the bathroom with that controlled, careful pace people use when they're pretending they're fine, and then—halfway there—the pace breaks. It turns into logistics. It turns into that humiliating math of distance and time: do I make it, how fast can I move without making it worse, what if this is the moment I lose control of my own body in my own home. The door closes behind me with a soft click that lands louder than it should, sealing me into a small room with tile and bright light and the knowledge that I am, once again, being managed by a timer I didn't choose.

What makes it worse is what my mind does while I wait for the wave to crest. It doesn't stay in the bathroom. It doesn't stay in the present. It starts scanning—searching for the origin point, the first domino, the moment where the rules changed. Sometimes my brain goes hunting through years like it's rifling a file cabinet, convinced that if it finds the right folder it can finally explain why my body treats time like a threat. And then, without permission, my attention locks onto the one place that trained me to worship the clock: the Navy. The way the day there was divided into commands. The way urgency wasn't a feeling—it was policy. The way you learned to measure your life in minutes because minutes were the difference between passing and being singled out, between blending in and being made an example.

I can't sit on a bathroom floor in a quiet apartment without hearing a different kind of countdown underneath it. Reveille. Lights snapping on. Boots hitting tile. A voice barking time like time was a weapon. The memory comes in with the same physical certainty as the cramps: not a story I choose to tell, but an atmosphere that floods in and fills my lungs. And suddenly I'm not here anymore, not really. I'm back in a world where every second belonged to someone else, where you learned fast that the system didn't care what your body needed, only what the schedule demanded. The bathroom light hums above me, and it becomes fluorescent barracks light. The clean quiet of the apartment collapses into the roar of hundreds of young men moving at once. The clock in the kitchen turns into a drill instructor's voice. And the past opens like a door that never stopped being close.

The Navy had not arrived in my life as war. It arrived as the promise of a schedule. It arrived as a system that said, *Stop improvising. Stop drifting. Stop making your life a loose pile of hours. Let us hold you.* That promise did not sound like romance. It sounded like relief. It sounded like a way out of a house full of tension and a school full of bells and a mind that kept slipping away from whatever it was supposed to be doing. The recruiting office language had been clean, almost gentle in its certainty—forms, signatures, tests, a path. The people around me at the time wanted the path to mean something noble, something respectable, something that could be talked about without embarrassment. I wanted the path to mean I didn't have to keep deciding how to live every day.

The leaving itself had felt less like a heroic departure and more like logistics with a hard edge. A bag packed with what I thought mattered. A ride. A last glance at a familiar street that didn't change color or shape just because I was leaving it. The car ride held a strange silence, broken by practical instructions and the kind of adult tone that tries to hide emotion by becoming efficient. There were signatures, then more signatures, then a day that started early and stayed clinical—lines, desks, papers slid across counters, questions asked in rooms that smelled like stale coffee and disinfectant. Each step removed another piece of my old identity and replaced it with a file. Each step made it harder to back out without becoming a story people would tell about weakness.

By the time I was on the bus headed toward Great Lakes, I already felt like I was being carried by momentum rather than choice. The windows showed dark, flat stretches of land and highway lights that passed like blinking eyes. The other young men around me were quiet in different ways: some talkative with forced bravado, filling the air because silence felt dangerous; some withdrawn, staring ahead like they were trying to hypnotize themselves into not feeling; some already performing toughness as if toughness could prepay whatever fear was coming. I kept my voice low, kept my body still, watched the way the bus interior light made everyone look pale and tired. The closer we got, the colder the world looked through the glass, and the cold felt personal, like the air was already trying to strip something from us.

Great Lakes greeted me with wind that didn't behave like weather so much as an intention. The cold cut through fabric and found skin as if it knew exactly where to aim. The first time I stepped off the bus, my eyes watered instantly— not from emotion, but from the shock of air that felt sharpened. The buildings were plain and official, the kind of architecture designed to be endured rather than admired. Even the pavement looked disciplined, lines painted crisp, corners squared. Voices found us quickly. Before I could fully orient myself, before my mind could build a map, there were commands—loud, clipped, unnegotiable—and bodies moved because the easiest way to survive the first minutes was to obey. Bags were grabbed. Lines formed. A crowd turned into something that resembled order by sheer force.

The processing days were the Navy's way of teaching a lesson without announcing it: individuality is malleable. Hair that had been part of my self-image became debris on a barbershop floor in seconds. The clippers buzzed close to my scalp, and the sensation was both humiliating and oddly cleansing, like the institution was erasing a version of me that had been allowed to drift. We shuffled through medical stations that smelled like antiseptic and rubber gloves, sleeves rolled up for shots, mouths opened for inspections, ears checked, eyes tested. We were weighed, measured, examined like equipment. We were issued uniforms that didn't fit right at first, stiff fabric that scratched, boots that made my feet feel like someone else's feet. We were handed numbers, paperwork, and a new way to be addressed that made my name feel distant.

Boot camp had a rhythm that was brutal in its simplicity. Wake up before the body was ready. Make the bed in a way that was less about comfort and more about proof—corners tight, blankets smooth, a surface that could be inspected like a table. Stand in formation. March. Eat quickly. Learn rules in classrooms where the air smelled like dry markers and tired breath. March again. Train the body until it shook. Clean until the knuckles burned. Be corrected for details that seemed ridiculous until I understood the point: the detail wasn't the goal. The goal was surrender. The goal was to build a person who could be commanded without discussion. Even the way we moved through doorways had rules. Even the way we held our hands had rules. The institution didn't care what I thought about any of it. It cared whether I complied.

There were moments in that rhythm where the world narrowed to senses. The smell of the barracks—bleach, sweat, damp wool, and the faint metallic scent of lockers. The sound of boots on tile in a hallway that echoed like a tunnel. The taste of cafeteria food shoveled in fast, swallowed more than chewed, because talking was dangerous and time was rationed. The feel of a uniform collar rubbing the neck raw. The way my shoulders ached from holding posture too long. The way fatigue turned everything slightly unreal, like the edges of the day softened and the only sharp things left were commands. Nights weren't restful. Nights were recovery at best—lights out, bodies collapsing into racks, the room full of breathing and occasional coughs, the constant knowledge that the morning would arrive no matter how little sleep I got.

Training filled in the gaps with standardized experiences, the common litany that turns recruits into something uniform. There was firefighting instruction, the heat and smoke simulated enough to make the body believe it, the mask pressing against the face, breath loud inside the seal. There was swimming qualification that made the pool smell like chemicals and fear, bodies tensing at the edge before stepping in, some men moving like fish, others moving like rocks and pretending they weren't panicking. There were drills that turned the day into marching geometry, lines and angles and synchronized motion, the strange satisfaction of doing something perfectly in time with others. There were classroom hours where attention fought exhaustion, where my mind sometimes floated above my body, watching myself sit and nod and copy notes like a puppet that had learned how to mimic compliance.

In that environment, accusation was a weapon sharper than any physical threat because accusation could attach to paperwork and become permanent. In civilian life, a false accusation can ruin a day. In basic training, it can ruin your future. A rumor became a hook. A misunderstanding became an investigation. Someone said something about me —something I knew wasn't true, something that should have been easy to dismiss in a normal world—and the institution treated it like a problem that needed sorting. I was pulled aside. I was questioned in a tone that pretended to be neutral but carried suspicion like a smell. The questions came in a pattern designed to trap: repeat the story, then repeat it again, then repeat it with tiny shifts and watch for inconsistency. They looked at my face, my posture, my pauses, as if my body language could be used as evidence.

The false accusation did something inside me that I didn't have language for at the time. It wasn't only fear of punishment. It was a sudden collapse of trust in the idea that the system would be fair if I was obedient. Boot camp had already taught me that fairness wasn't the point, but part of me still wanted to believe that truth mattered. Sitting there, answering questions I hadn't invited, feeling the air in the room tighten with suspicion, I realized truth was not a shield. The system didn't need to hate me to harm me. It only needed to suspect me. It only needed to decide I was a problem worth applying pressure to. My heart hammered. Sweat collected under my uniform. My mouth dried out, and every time I swallowed it felt like the swallow could be interpreted as guilt.

I tried to speak plainly. I tried to keep my answers consistent because consistency felt like proof. But consistency can look rehearsed, and rehearsed can look like lying. The trap of the situation wasn't the accusation itself; it was that any reaction could be used against me. Calm could be read as coldness. Anxiety could be read as guilt.

Anger could be read as defiance. I sat in the chair and felt my body vibrate with the need to escape, the kind of vibration that later in life would become familiar in other contexts for other reasons. In that moment, it was purely situational: a young man inside a machine that could punish him based on another person's words, with no meaningful control over the outcome.

Around the same stretch of time, another recruit tried to exit the machine in the most literal way possible. It happened fast enough that it felt like a glitch in reality. A shout. Footsteps. A sudden sharp change in the tone of the room. Someone lunged, bodies converged, and for a moment the barracks became a single frantic organism. The recruit had moved toward a second-story window with an intention that didn't need explanation. The air turned electric with panic. People grabbed at him, pulled him back, held him, and the scene carried the rawness of a thing nobody wanted to witness but couldn't unsee. The building that had felt like a controlled environment suddenly felt fragile, as if glass and gravity had been waiting all along to make a point.

The aftermath lingered in the body more than the mind wanted it to. The windows looked different after that. The height looked different. The idea that someone could decide, in a single desperate moment, to end everything rather than keep complying changed the atmosphere of the days that followed. The institution responded the way institutions respond: containment, procedures, a fast return to routine to prevent the disruption from spreading. We were told to get back in line, get back to training, get back to being shaped. But the image remained. It sat in my chest like a stone, not because I wanted to romanticize it, but because it proved something I had been avoiding: a person can break inside a system, and the system's first instinct is not tenderness. Its first instinct is control.

I didn't become the recruit at the window. I didn't want to die. What I wanted was out. What I wanted was release from a pressure I had underestimated, release from the constant surveillance of my own behavior, release from the feeling that my identity was being flattened and filed away. The system that had promised to hold me felt less like a container and more like a vise. I began looking for exits the way a trapped animal looks for light. I began telling myself stories about injury, about medical disqualification, about anything that could produce an official reason to leave without having to admit I couldn't endure it. Pride matters in environments like that. Pride becomes a second uniform. Admitting weakness felt more dangerous than admitting nothing.

Eventually, in a moment of desperation and calculation, I said something I'm not proud of. I told medical personnel—people whose job was to assess stability—that if they didn't send me home, I would harm myself. The statement was not a plan. It was not a method. It was a lever. It was me trying to force a door open using the only language I thought the system would take seriously. That doesn't make it harmless. It doesn't make it clever. It makes it what it was: a young man cornered by shame and fear, trying to turn his own body into evidence. The words landed heavy in the room. The adults' faces changed. The system heard the phrase it is designed to respond to, and suddenly my inner state became official business.

The irony was sharp. Up until that moment, my suffering had been mostly invisible—anxiety, pressure, fatigue, the slow stripping of autonomy. The second I put the right words on it, the machine paid attention. It didn't pay attention because it cared about me personally. It paid attention because liability has a language, and I had spoken it. I was monitored. I was questioned again, but this time the questions were about my mind rather than my alleged behavior. I could feel the institutional shift: from punishment to risk management. I had wanted out. Now I was inside another corridor of the system, one designed to sort out who is safe to keep and who is safer to release.

The separation process didn't feel like freedom. It felt like being dropped. One day I was inside the most structured life I had ever known, and the next day I was on my way back to civilian air with a head still buzzing from commands. The transition didn't come with decompression. It came with paperwork, signatures, and the strange emptiness of being told, effectively, *You're no longer our problem.* I left with a bag and a set of memories that didn't align into a heroic narrative. There was no war zone. There was no battlefield. There was a training pipeline that had pressed me until I reached for an exit that embarrassed me. That embarrassment rode with me like a passenger, quiet but present, shaping the way I talked about the experience— minimizing it, reframing it, trying to make it sound like something other than what it was.

Returning home after the Navy should have been a reset. That's what the imagination sells: come back, step into familiar rooms, feel comfort, rejoin the life that was paused. But life doesn't pause. The home I returned to—the house where I had left a version of myself behind—looked the same and felt altered at the same time. The rooms still held their furniture. The light still fell through the same windows. The sounds were still the sounds of domestic life: water running in pipes, doors closing, voices moving through hallways. Yet I walked through it with a strange detachment, like the part of me that had learned to stand at attention was still waiting for orders, and the part of me that had wanted a schedule didn't know what to do with a day that belonged to no one.

I expected the person I'd been with before I left to feel like an anchor. I expected closeness to act like proof that I was still connected to my old life, still accepted, still wanted in a way that mattered. That expectation was unfair, but it existed anyway. Instead, what I encountered was time: time that had moved while I was gone, time that had allowed patterns to change, attachments to shift, stories to get rewritten without my input. She looked familiar, and that familiarity made the distance feel sharper. Her expressions landed differently. Her timing in conversation felt slightly off. Small questions that should have been simple carried hesitation. It wasn't a single smoking gun. It was a collection of micro-signals that made my stomach tighten in a way that wasn't about food.

The suspicion arrived as an impression, not as proof. That made it worse because proof can be confronted cleanly. An impression spreads. It infects ordinary moments. A laugh becomes suspicious. A pause becomes suspicious. A glance at a phone becomes suspicious. I watched her talk and found myself scanning for what wasn't being said. It wasn't that I wanted to believe she had betrayed me. It was that my nervous system had returned from an environment where accusation could destroy you, and now my own mind was manufacturing accusations without a tribunal to settle them. The institution had trained me to live inside scrutiny, and now the scrutiny had turned inward and outward at the same time.

We lived under the same roof as other adults, in a basement space that had once felt like a rehearsal for independence. The basement had its own climate—cooler air, dimmer light, the steady reminder of footsteps above us. I had imagined coming back and stepping into that space like it was a private sanctuary. Instead, the space felt like a pressure chamber. Every unresolved thought echoed off the low ceiling. Every small disagreement felt amplified because there was no real escape from it. The household above continued its routines—dinner smells, voices through vents, the occasional vibration of a door closing—and down below, our world narrowed to two people trying to pretend we hadn't changed.

For a while, I tried to swallow the suspicion because swallowing felt like control. I tried to act normal. I tried to lean into routine—small chores, small talk, physical closeness—as if routine could overwrite uncertainty. But suspicion doesn't dissolve when ignored. It thickens. It becomes a film over everything. The more I pretended, the more I felt myself becoming false, and falseness made me angrier because it felt like losing. The Navy had already taken my autonomy and returned me with a sense of rawness I didn't know how to name. I didn't want to come home and discover that the one relationship I had been counting on had quietly moved on without me.

The confrontation happened on a walk around the block, because walking creates movement that makes difficult conversations easier to start. It was a familiar loop —sidewalk, curb, the smell of grass, a neighbor's dog barking behind a fence—ordinary scenery for a moment that didn't feel ordinary. At first I tried to keep my voice steady. I tried to phrase things like questions rather than accusations. But the words came out sharp anyway, because sharpness is what happens when fear pretends to be certainty. She responded in pieces—denial, defensiveness, fatigue, confusion—and the mixture didn't settle anything. The conversation didn't feel like two people trying to understand each other. It felt like two people trying to protect themselves from being the one who lost.

By the time we completed the loop and approached the house again, something had hardened in me. It wasn't mature. It wasn't wise. It was simple: the need to end uncertainty by making a decision. In the basement, under the ceiling that held the sound of the household above, the argument escalated quickly. Words moved faster than thought. Anger arrived with its familiar heat, the same heat that had pushed me into headlocks years earlier, the same impulse toward decisive action when a situation felt unstable. I told her the relationship was over. I told her she needed to leave. The sentences landed like doors slamming, and once they were spoken, they felt irreversible even if part of me wanted to take them back.

She left that night. The basement door opened and closed, and the sound of it was blunt and final in a way the rest of the house wasn't. Footsteps above us remained ordinary, which made the rupture below feel surreal. The world didn't acknowledge our collapse. It didn't pause. It didn't dim the lights. It simply continued. After she was gone, the basement felt too large and too empty at the same time, a room built for two now holding one person who didn't know how to occupy his own silence. I stood there with my heart still racing, listening for sounds that would confirm reality—car doors, voices, anything—and the absence of sound felt like punishment.

The next days were a blur of anger and damage control. Living under the same roof as other people meant the breakup wasn't private. Even if no one asked questions, the air in the house changed. There were new gaps in routine. There were spaces where someone used to be. There were small domestic reminders that felt like insults—a cup left behind, a stray hair tie, the faint scent of perfume lingering in fabric. I moved through the rooms with a stiffness that felt like leftover military posture, but inside I was churning. I replayed the conversation, searching for a moment where it could have turned differently, searching for a sentence that would have de-escalated instead of detonated. The replay always ended in the same place: the door closing, the finality of it, my own voice turning into something that didn't sound like me.

Within a week, she was with the person I believed she had been involved with. The speed of it hit like a slap. It didn't matter whether my belief was fully accurate or partly fueled by the paranoia of return; the outcome was the same. The world delivered a confirmation-shaped event, and the event felt like humiliation crystallized. It made me feel replaceable in the most basic sense—like I could leave to become something "better," something more structured, and still come back to find my spot filled. That feeling wasn't new in my life, but it was sharper now because it came after a system had already stripped me down and returned me raw. The breakup didn't create my future problems by itself. It didn't plant a seed that grew into everything. It was one more cut in a series of cuts, and later cuts would be deeper. But in that moment, it bled.

It also revealed something about the kind of stability I had been chasing. I had gone to the Navy believing structure could save me from myself. I had returned believing a relationship could save me from emptiness. Both beliefs were versions of the same mistake: outsourcing the job of holding me. The Navy held me by force, and I tried to escape it by speaking the only words that made the system take me seriously. The relationship held me by attachment, and when the attachment frayed, I tried to end uncertainty by severing it completely. In both places, my response to instability was decisive, physical in its finality, as if cutting a rope could stop the fear of falling.

The body responded the way bodies respond when the mind is overloaded: by choosing symptoms without asking permission. The abdominal timer that would later become familiar in other eras began showing itself more often—tightening, pressure, urgency that arrived like an alarm. Sleep became uneven. I could lie in bed exhausted and still feel my nerves vibrating, the same vibration I had felt in interrogation rooms and under fluorescent lights. I could snap awake at small noises—a footstep above, a door closing—because the nervous system stayed trained for surveillance even after the institution was gone. These reactions weren't proof of permanent damage. They were proof of context. They were what a young man's body did when it had been living under pressure and then lost the structure that had at least explained the pressure.

That context matters because later in life there would be experiences heavier than training, heavier than a breakup, heavier than the shame of escape. There would be events that carried more unmistakable weight, events that could plausibly be traced to the baseline state with less ambiguity.

What happened here—boot camp, accusation, the window, the desperate lever I pulled, the return, the rupture—was real, but it was not the singular origin of everything. It was one era where my nervous system learned specific lessons about systems and safety and shame. It was one era where I practiced disappearing in a new way: disappearing into compliance, then disappearing into escape, then disappearing into anger. The habits formed here mattered, but they did not explain the whole shape of the person who would exist later.

After the breakup, the house above continued as a house does. Meals were cooked. Conversations happened in other rooms. Televisions played. The world kept moving with its ordinary indifference, which is one of the cruelest things about private collapses: they don't register on the outside. Inside, I walked around with a kind of hollow energy, the sense of being both too full of emotion and strangely numb. I wanted to talk about it and also wanted to bury it. I wanted to be witnessed and also wanted to vanish. I kept replaying the Navy's promise—structure, purpose, belonging—and felt the bitterness of it. The promise had been partly true: the system had held me. It just hadn't held me gently.

In the quiet moments, when no one was demanding anything of me, I could feel a new problem emerging that I didn't yet know how to name: civilian time. In the Navy, time had been owned. Time had been divided into blocks with clear commands attached. In civilian life after a rupture, time spread out like an empty room. The emptiness wasn't peaceful. It was exposed. Every hour asked, *What are you now? What are you building? What are you doing with the fact that nobody is telling you what to do?* I wanted freedom until I had it. Then freedom felt like standing on a wide-open field with no cover, visible from every direction.

That era ended the way many eras end: not with a clean conclusion, but with a slow drift toward the next thing. The Navy was behind me, still present in muscle memory and in the way my posture tightened under stress. The relationship was behind me, still present in the way my mind scanned for betrayal even when there was nothing to betray. The house remained, full of routines that didn't pause for my internal state. I stood in the basement at night sometimes and listened to the footsteps above, trying to decide whether I had been held or whether I had been contained. The answer shifted depending on the day. The only consistent truth was that the system I had asked to hold me had let go, and now there was nothing between me and my own mind except whatever I could build next.

And the clock kept glowing in ordinary rooms, green numbers counting up, counting down, reminding me that the body has its own schedules, its own alarms, its own insistence. The system had trained me to live by a timer. The timer had followed me home.

# CHAPTER 7

# *After the Uniform*

A barcode scanner is one of the cleanest sounds in the world. A short, high chirp—so quick it barely qualifies as noise—followed by the soft thud of an item being set aside, the rustle of a bag opening, the polite murmur of a transaction finishing itself. I stand in a modern checkout line with my hands empty and my mind too full, watching the conveyor belt carry someone else's groceries forward, and the fluorescent lights above me behave like they're doing me a favor. Everything is bright. Everything is legible. The store has signs for every aisle and arrows for every flow, as if enough labeling could keep a life from spilling. The chirp happens again, and my chest responds faster than my thoughts, a small tightening like a door latching. Not pain. Not panic. Recognition—my nervous system noticing a place it used to live in.

I tell myself it's nothing. I tell myself it's only a sound. I try to focus on the ordinary details: the price display blinking, the card reader waiting, the tired impatience on the face of the person ahead of me. But the chirp doesn't stay in the present. It multiplies into a rhythm—the steady sequence of scans, the mechanical courtesy of a job that requires you to be pleasant no matter what you feel, the way hours can be murdered one item at a time. The store smells like plastic packaging and floor cleaner and the faint sweetness of candy near the register, and that combination cracks something open in me. I can feel the past moving closer, not like a memory I choose, but like a room I'm being guided back into. A uniform. A name tag. Break-room air with the stale taste of vending-machine coffee. A parking lot at night with heat still rising from asphalt. A version of me that had returned from a uniformed system believing civilian life would feel like relief—only to discover relief can be its own kind of emptiness.

The line inches forward. The scanner chirps again. The fluorescent ceiling becomes older, harsher, less forgiving. The place in my mind that handles logistics—what to say, where to stand, how to look normal—slides into gear without asking, and that is exactly what those years taught me: how to operate while something inside me stayed unsettled. The present-day store keeps moving. The world around me stays polite. But my attention drops backward into the fall when everything reset in a way that didn't feel like a beginning. It felt like returning to a house that had kept its shape while the inside of me had rearranged, and then trying to pass as if that rearrangement didn't matter.

I came back to the same household in the fall of 1998, and the first thing I noticed was the ceiling. That sounds absurd until you've lived in a basement room long enough for low light to become your normal. In the basement, sound had traveled through vents and floorboards like gossip, and footsteps above had always been part of the air. Down there, privacy had been conditional, borrowed, and full of reminders that I wasn't truly independent—only tucked away. After the breakup, after the door closed behind the girl who had lived down there with me, the basement stopped being "ours" and became what it had always been: an underlevel space with colder air and an atmosphere of being slightly separate from life happening upstairs. So I moved. Not in a dramatic way, not with declarations, but with a quiet shift that felt like being reassigned within my own house.

My new bedroom was the first one down the main hallway on the main floor, a room that caught more daylight than the basement ever did. It shouldn't have mattered as much as it did. Light is just light. A window is just a window. But that first week upstairs, waking up with sunlight cutting across the wall and hearing the house at my level—voices in the kitchen, cabinet doors opening, the ordinary traffic of morning—made me feel exposed in a way I didn't expect. The basement had been a hiding place. This room was not. From the hallway, anyone could see my door. Anyone could walk past and glance in. The change wasn't only physical. It was social. It said: you're back in the main flow of the house, back under the daily attention of the people who run it, back inside the routines you once tried to escape by joining a system that promised structure.

The breakup I had set off didn't stay contained to the basement. It rose up through the floorboards and spread through the household the way tension spreads—quiet at first, then obvious, then normalized. It would be easy to tell that story as if it were a turning point that explains everything about who I became, but it wasn't strong enough to deserve that kind of myth. What it did was smaller and more corrosive: it made ordinary interactions feel loaded. A question asked at dinner carried an extra edge. Silence in the hallway felt like judgment. The house didn't become a battlefield; it became a place where everyone adjusted their behavior in subtle ways, trying not to trigger the next conflict, trying to keep the story from becoming uglier than it already was. I was young enough to still feel like a kid in some rooms and old enough to be expected to act like an adult in others. That mismatch created a constant internal friction that nobody could see, and that nobody had a good name for.

I tried to become invisible again, the way I had learned in school hallways and in uniformed environments. I learned where to stand so I wouldn't be in anyone's path. I learned how to keep my face neutral when I didn't want questions. I learned to offer minimal information—enough to satisfy a caregiver's curiosity without inviting follow-up. The house functioned on stories: who was doing what, who was failing at what, who needed to be corrected, who needed to be watched. I didn't want to be a story. I wanted to be a person who could move through days without becoming an argument. The problem was that being invisible doesn't create a life. It only creates a gap where a life should be, and gaps get filled by whatever is loudest: anxiety, boredom, impulse, or the pressure of someone else's expectations.

Work became my first excuse to exist without explanation. I started working at Walmart after returning from Navy basic training, stepping into a world that was supposedly normal—customers, aisles, schedules—yet still felt like another institution. The store had its own rules and its own hierarchy and its own language that turned people into functions. There were time clocks, uniforms, policies posted in back rooms, supervisors who learned quickly how to speak with authority without raising their voice. The fluorescent lights never changed, which made every shift feel like the same hour repeating. On paper it was simple: show up, do the job, leave. In practice it became an environment that trained the same parts of me the Navy had touched—compliance, endurance, the ability to keep moving while my mind was somewhere else.

The store gave me something I could point to when the house felt too tight. *I have a shift.* A shift didn't fix anything, but it gave my day a spine. It gave me a reason to leave the hallway bedroom, a reason to put on clean clothes, a reason to speak to people in a predictable way. Retail conversations are scripted without being written down: greetings, small talk, problem-solving, apologies delivered with a practiced tone. In that script, I could perform competence even if I felt hollow. I could be polite. I could be efficient. I could keep the machine running. The paycheck didn't feel like independence yet—more like proof I was not entirely stuck—but it mattered, because money in that house carried moral weight. Earning it meant I was less vulnerable to accusation. It meant I was at least doing something.

What I wasn't prepared for was how quickly the store could turn my body into public property. Customers felt entitled to comment on anything they could see: my face, my posture, my tone, the way I moved. Coworkers made jokes that landed too close, testing boundaries under the cover of humor. A workplace that should have been neutral became another place where being watched mattered. Someone could say something about my appearance with a laugh, and suddenly my skin would feel too tight, as if attention had weight. It wasn't always cruel. Sometimes it was casual. Sometimes it was meant to be friendly. The problem was that even friendly attention can feel threatening when you're already living in a state of internal vigilance. I would walk out into the parking lot after a shift and realize my jaw was clenched hard enough to ache, and I hadn't noticed the clenching while it was happening.

At home, secrecy became a routine rather than an exception. The household ran on the assumption that certain things should not be discussed outside the walls, and that assumption wasn't a single rule spoken out loud. It was a posture everyone adopted without admitting they were doing it. There were topics that made the room quiet immediately. There were names that, when mentioned, changed the temperature of the conversation. There were events that had happened recently—fresh enough to still sting—that were treated as if revisiting them would be dangerous. So the past became a set of locked doors inside the house, and everyone learned to walk past those doors without touching the handles. The result was an atmosphere where silence didn't feel peaceful. It felt strategic. It felt like everyone was working together to keep certain truths from detonating again.

In that atmosphere, even small assignments could become controlling. A caregiver in the house—meaning well, or at least believing they were—decided I needed containment through structure and gave me an assignment that wasn't about learning a skill so much as keeping me occupied. The instructions were clear. The expectations were strict. The tone suggested that doing the task correctly would earn approval and failing it would prove I wasn't trying. The strangest part was how quickly I accepted the bargain. I didn't love the work. I didn't always see the point. But the assignment created a narrow corridor where I could succeed, and narrow corridors were easier than open rooms. If I stayed inside the corridor—do the required thing, follow the steps, produce the result—I could avoid larger conversations about what I wanted or what I was becoming. Containment disguised itself as guidance, and I let it.

A caregiver's attentiveness became intense in those months, the kind of attention that can feel like love and suffocation at the same time. Questions arrived disguised as concern: where I was going, who I was with, how I was feeling, whether I had plans. The attention wasn't always hostile, but it kept me from relaxing. When someone is watching you for signs of collapse, you start monitoring yourself more harshly than you would otherwise. Another adult in the house grew quieter, patience thinning into a tight-lipped endurance that didn't express itself in long lectures—more in the way a door closed, the way a sigh landed, the way silence stretched after I answered a question wrong. I learned to store truth like dangerous cargo. I learned that the safest version of myself in that house was the version who needed nothing.

Independence, during that period, didn't look like rebellion. It looked like movement. Any movement. Driving to work. Driving to class. Driving to nowhere in particular just to feel my own thoughts shift with the scenery. The moment I was in a car, the house's attention loosened. I could breathe in a way I hadn't noticed I was holding back. The car became a private room that traveled, and travel created the illusion of control: my hands on the wheel, my foot on the pedals, the road responding. That illusion mattered because I didn't feel in control anywhere else. In the store, rules shaped my body. In the house, expectations shaped my speech. In my own head, the future felt like a fog. In the car, at least, I could choose a direction.

Around that same time, an adult in the household offered me a different kind of independence: a computer. The offer came with conditions, but the conditions were clean. If I could build it and make it work, it would be mine.

No moral lectures. No emotional negotiations. Just a mechanical challenge and a reward. I took the leftover components like they were pieces of a secret language. I liked the honesty of it—the way hardware either fit or didn't, the way a cable either seated or refused, the way a system either booted or failed with no concern for my feelings. I assembled the machine slowly, carefully, learning what each part did by touching it, by making mistakes, by correcting them. When it powered on, when the screen glowed, the satisfaction landed deep because it didn't depend on anybody's approval. The computer worked because I made it work.

Windows 98 was new. That mattered because it pinned the era in place—the late 1990s feeling of technology arriving with fanfare, the promise that new software would make everything smoother, faster, cleaner. I bought it with money that felt heavy in my pocket because earning it had required hours under fluorescent light. The operating system wasn't just a program; it was a symbol. It suggested modernity, progress, a future that was supposed to be brighter than the basement and the breakup and the household tension. I spent nights at that machine in the hallway bedroom, the glow of the monitor painting my hands, the rest of the house quiet beyond the door. In those hours, I wasn't being watched. I wasn't being measured by a supervisor or a caregiver. I was simply solving problems, moving through menus, learning systems. It would be tempting to romanticize that as salvation. It wasn't. It was a refuge. Refuge is different. Refuge doesn't fix the war; it gives you a place to sit down for a minute.

Evenings brought another attempt at structure: community college classes. I went after work, sliding from the retail machine into the classroom machine without a real gap between. The campus at night had its own atmosphere —parking lot lights buzzing, buildings quiet except for a few lit rooms, the faint smell of old carpet and whiteboard marker. Many of the students were older than me, already working, already carrying adult lives that made my own mess feel smaller and more embarrassing. I tried to focus. Sometimes I could. Sometimes my mind drifted the way it always drifted when something didn't feel urgent. The difference was that community college didn't have the same social cruelty of earlier school years. The room didn't care who I was outside the work. That anonymity should have been liberating. It mostly felt lonely. I was surrounded by people and still floating.

A person from my household attended evening classes too, and that coincidence created an odd companionship. We shared the commute. We shared the fatigue. We shared the silent understanding that the day had been long before the class even started. On nights when the air inside the car felt too tight with household tension, the drive to campus felt like a corridor of shared neutrality. We didn't have to talk about the hard things. We could talk about assignments, about traffic, about nothing. That "nothing" mattered because it was safer than "everything." But safety has a shadow. When you practice avoiding "everything" long enough, "everything" starts to feel unspeakable. It starts to feel like a threat rather than a reality you can face.

Drinking entered those months as a shortcut to quiet. Not the kind of drinking that looks like celebration, but the kind that looks like subtraction: take a mind that won't settle, remove the edges, soften the vigilance. We skipped classes sometimes—not often enough to call it a lifestyle, but often enough to recognize the pattern. The logic was simple and adolescent: we were tired, we were restless, we wanted the night to be ours, and alcohol offered ownership in a bottle. One particular night became the model for how quickly that ownership could turn into danger. We mixed orange juice and Everclear, poured it into cups that made the mixture look harmless, and drank as if we were proving something. Each of us drank about half, the sweetness disguising the strength until it was too late to pretend we hadn't taken in something volatile.

Afterward, the night kept moving because we didn't know how to stop it. We drove to a local bar, still underage, still pretending the rules didn't apply if we carried ourselves confidently enough. The bartender saw through it immediately and forced us to leave after the driver finished a first beer. That should have been the end. It wasn't. We drove to a local lake instead, the kind of place that feels peaceful in daylight and slightly unreal at night. There were people fishing. A small fire glowed by the water, orange light flickering on faces and tree trunks. The scene looked like a postcard, but inside my body things were deteriorating. I passed out briefly sitting on the ground, my consciousness dropping out like a light switching off, then returning with a disorienting snap.

Police lights appeared reflecting off the trees, blue and red moving through branches like something alive. The driver told me to get up, voice sharp with fear, and I stumbled in the wrong direction, falling into a ditch as the car moved. For a second, the tires came close enough that I understood how easily the night could end under rubber. We got back into the car. We tried to look normal. We were pulled over anyway. Questions were asked. The driver answered with the brittle confidence of someone trying not to be exposed. I sat there dizzy and sweating, feeling my body betray me with every small movement. The police called an adult from the household to pick us up, and while we waited, I vomited several times beside the car, each time more humiliating because it was proof of how little control I had.

That night didn't stop the drinking. It changed the way it felt. Before that, alcohol had been fantasy—freedom, rebellion, relief. After that, alcohol carried the shadow of flashing lights and the cold dread of a phone call made to the house. It taught me that risk isn't always dramatic. Sometimes it looks like sitting on the ground by a lake while a fire glows nearby and your consciousness slips away for a moment you can't account for. Sometimes it looks like a ditch you don't see until you're already in it. The adult who arrived to retrieve us didn't need to say much. The disappointment was physical, thick in the air, and I absorbed it the way I had absorbed other household atmospheres: silently, as if silence could make the event smaller. It didn't. It just stored it.

Between work and classes and the occasional disaster, life filled itself with ordinary gaps. Late-1990s afternoons where the light outside looked too cheerful for the heaviness inside the house. Weekends where the day stretched long and empty, making boredom feel like pressure. Nights in the hallway bedroom where I sat at the computer and felt relief simply because nobody was speaking to me. Music played through cheap speakers— songs that now feel welded to that era—while I scrolled through menus, installed programs, learned my own small power: the power to make a machine obey. Sometimes I went out with coworkers after a shift, the kind of hanging out that had no plot. Parking lots. Fast-food booths. Cigarettes smoked outside because the air inside the restaurant was too bright and too full of eyes. These weren't deep friendships. They were temporary shelters against solitude.

Being young and empty is dangerous because any attention can feel like rescue. At Walmart, proximity did what proximity does. You spend hours beside someone, laughing at the same stupid customer story, complaining about the same supervisor, sharing the same boredom, and the closeness starts to imitate intimacy. Sometimes the imitation turned physical. I learned quickly that sex can be used as a shortcut to feeling chosen, and that the shortcut doesn't build anything stable. The moments were private, fast, threaded with secrecy because the store's social world was full of gossip and moral judgments. I didn't frame it as romance. I framed it as proof: proof that I was wanted, proof that I could still matter to someone, proof that the person I was becoming wasn't only a problem carried around by the household. The proof never lasted. Afterward, the emptiness returned with sharper edges.

The household's moral atmosphere made those choices feel heavier than they might have otherwise. I could feel judgment even when it wasn't spoken, as if the walls themselves had absorbed doctrine and would reflect it back at me. That didn't make me stop. It made me compartmentalize harder. In one compartment, I was the person who went to work, took classes, built a computer, tried to be competent. In another compartment, I was the person who drank too much, chased attention, hid details, acted out. Compartmentalization can look like adaptability, and in the short term it is. In the long term it becomes a habit of splitting life into sealed rooms, and sealed rooms develop pressure. During those years, the pressure hadn't found its most destructive outlet yet. There were later experiences that would strike deeper and leave more obvious marks. This era was more like a steady wear on the edges, a grinding rather than an explosion.

In the summer of 2000, a few days before July 4th, the pressure found a public stage. A person from my household and I went to a park near our house, the trunk of the car loaded with fireworks and beer purchased by him. The night had the hot, restless energy of early summer—people gathering, voices carrying, the air smelling like cut grass and barbecue smoke. We fired aerial fireworks over a shelter where friends were drinking, and the scene looked like a celebration until the wrong angle made it look like a threat. Patrons at a nearby baseball game called the police. The mood shifted instantly. The park's normal noise became a hush with fear underneath it, and the people who had been laughing a moment earlier started moving like prey.

When police arrived, lights flashing, the group scattered. The person from my household ran into the woods with others. I stayed with the car, partly because I didn't know what else to do and partly because my instinct, even then, was to remain near an object that could anchor me. The police asked me to call out the friends who had fled. I called, voice carrying into the dark, and only the person from my household emerged. He made a gesture toward a nearby neighborhood—something meant to indicate where people had gone, nothing more—and the officer interpreted the gesture as threatening. The situation detonated. The officer knocked him down and sprayed him with mace. It happened fast, brutal and messy, the kind of violence that doesn't need a weapon to feel like a weapon.

Afterward, charges followed. The story hardened into paperwork. The person from my household was later charged with assault on a police officer. In that world, consequences don't care about nuance. They care about narratives that fit legal language. The household absorbed the event like it absorbed other crises: with anger, shame, and strategic silence. The air in the house thickened again, familiar and suffocating. The incident didn't create my future, but it added another layer to the lesson I had been learning since school: systems simplify. They punish what they can document. They ignore what they can't. In the months that followed, the household treated the situation like a wound that had to be covered, and I learned again how to speak in partial truths.

Somewhere inside that chaos, I bought a new car. The purchase should have felt like progress, like a clean marker of adulthood—ownership, freedom, the ability to leave whenever I wanted. In reality, it felt like making a promise to myself I wasn't sure I could keep. A new car is a contract with the future: you are claiming you will continue to exist in a stable enough way to make payments, maintain it, treat it like something worth protecting. I signed anyway. The keys in my hand felt heavy. The smell inside the car was sharp and synthetic, that new-vehicle scent that tries to convince you the world is fresh. I sat behind the wheel and felt a brief rush of control—the kind that always arrived when I was moving, when scenery could shift, when I didn't have to be watched by the house.

Not long after, I took a road trip that felt like a deliberate escape attempt. We drove through Utah, through

Las Vegas, and back, chasing distance the way some people chase answers. The road had its own hypnosis: lines rolling beneath the car, mountains rising, desert stretching out like a dare. We took pictures on film because that was still how you proved you had been somewhere. Film felt physical, precious. You couldn't check the shot immediately; you had to trust the moment and wait for the evidence to be developed later. That waiting gave the trip a strange sacredness, as if the proof of it existed in a future we had to survive long enough to reach. On the road, conversation could be shallow or deep without consequence. Silence could be shared without suspicion. Movement made me feel less like a problem and more like a person.

When we returned, reality was waiting in the most ordinary, efficient form. My car was parked on the street in front of the house. It was broken into. The damage wasn't dramatic; it was precise. The kind of break-in that says the person knew exactly what to take and didn't care about anything else. The film was stolen. The custom sound system was stolen. It felt like being robbed twice—once of the objects and once of the meaning attached to them. The film mattered more than the equipment. The film held the road trip's proof, the pictures that would have become memory anchors. Without it, the trip turned into something I could describe but not show, and the loss landed in my chest as a quiet grief. It also carried a message I had been collecting for years: even when you try to build something good, the world can reach in and remove it without explanation.

That break-in didn't ruin me. It didn't create a permanent fracture. But it contributed to a slow internal shift: the sense that investing in the future was risky because the future could be stolen. This is where it becomes tempting to draw a straight line from those feelings to my present-day condition, to treat late-1990s disappointments as the seed of everything that came later. That would be dishonest. Later experiences would strike with more force and clearer cause. This period was not the storm. It was weather—unpredictable, sometimes harsh, sometimes bright, teaching me small habits of distrust and self-containment that would resurface in other contexts. The distrust didn't become destiny here. It became a posture I could slip into when life felt unstable, a posture that would be reinforced and complicated by heavier years ahead.

As the summer after that road trip faded, the shape of my days settled into a routine that looked adult from the outside and felt unresolved from the inside. Work shifts under fluorescent light. Evening classes that I attended with varying success, sometimes focused, sometimes drifting. Nights in the hallway bedroom with the computer humming, the monitor glow painting my hands while the house quieted. Occasional drinks that promised relief and sometimes delivered danger instead. Attempts at intimacy that provided brief proof of being wanted and then left me emptier when the proof evaporated. Household tension that never fully resolved, only changed form depending on what crisis was most recent. I moved through it all with a kind of functional numbness, learning to do what was required without trusting the larger story.

Toward the end of that window—just before the next relationship entered my life in a way that would reshape everything—I began to feel the pull of being seen again. Not in the shallow sense of attention at work, not in the dangerous sense of being watched by the household, but in the deeper sense: someone noticing me and choosing me without a transaction attached. The hunger for that kind of recognition had been present for a long time. It had driven bad decisions, small rebellions, secret shortcuts. Now it sat quieter, more patient, as if it had learned to wait. I didn't yet understand that being seen can be both salvation and risk, depending on who is doing the seeing and what they want from you. I only knew that the routine I had built—work, school, hiding, occasional escape—could not be the full shape of a life.

In the hallway bedroom, at night, I would sometimes lie awake listening to the house settle. Pipes ticking as they cooled. Footsteps somewhere down the hall. A door closing softly. The ordinary soundtrack of a domestic world that kept existing regardless of my internal state. I would stare at the ceiling and feel time passing like a slow current, carrying me toward something I couldn't yet name. I wanted a future that felt solid. I wanted a version of myself that didn't rely on hiding. I wanted to stop living in compartments. Those wants were still mostly wishes, not plans. But wishes can act like gravity. They pull you forward even when you don't know what you're walking toward.

And in that last stretch before the next hinge, I kept showing up—at the store, at class, at home—carrying the quiet knowledge that this era was transitional even if I didn't have the language for it. The uniformed system had failed to hold me the way I hoped. The household had failed to feel fully safe. Work had given me structure without meaning. School had offered possibility without direction. None of it was the ultimate source of what I would become. It was simply the terrain I crossed between one collapse and the next beginning, a long corridor of late-1990s days where I learned how to keep moving even when I didn't feel whole.

# CHAPTER 8

# *The Ring Dish*

The ring is still here. Not on my finger—never on my finger anymore—but in a small dish on the dresser, mixed in with other objects that have lost their original purpose: a bent key that doesn't fit anything, a coin with the face rubbed smooth, a screw I've kept for no sane reason, a dog tag chain that isn't attached to anything now. The ring itself looks harmless, almost cheap, a dull band that catches light only when I tilt it just right. I pick it up and it's colder than the room, a little weight that shouldn't be able to steer a whole life, yet my body responds as if it can. My throat tightens. My jaw sets. My breath goes shallow without me choosing it. That's how the present works now—systems that were built for other moments still firing their alarms, even in a quiet apartment with no one watching.

It would be easy to tell myself the ring is just metal, that it's only an artifact from an early era, long before the heavier years, long before the things that left more obvious damage. But the mind doesn't obey fairness. The mind obeys triggers, and the ring is a trigger because it carries a particular kind of failure—one that looks simple from the outside and feels bottomless from the inside. The failures that came later were louder and more undeniable. This one is quieter. It's the kind that doesn't explode; it drains. It teaches the nervous system to brace for abandonment as a normal state. It teaches the heart to treat warmth as temporary, to treat attachment as something that can be pulled out by the root without warning. In my present life, that brace shows up in a hundred small ways—hypervigilance, dissociation, the constant sense of being slightly detached from the room I'm in, and even the humiliating physical symptoms that arrived much later, after other uniforms, after other traumas, after my body learned too many lessons the hard way.

I turn the ring between my fingers and watch the dull surface flash once under the lamp, a small, sterile glint. The apartment stays silent. The refrigerator cycles. The fan pushes air like a slow breath. Nothing in the room demands a memory, yet the memory rises anyway, not as a story I choose, but as a scene that grabs me by the collar. The ring isn't only a symbol of marriage. It's a symbol of acceleration—the way my life, at twenty, went from drifting to sprinting, from a job and a bedroom in a crowded house to promises spoken like life rafts. That shift didn't happen gradually. It happened like a door opening under my hand, and once it opened, I ran through it without checking what was on the other side.

She entered my life as if someone had reached into my orbit and pulled her into place, as if the world had decided I was done wandering and it was time to lock something down. We weren't introduced at my job, not in the fluorescent sameness of aisles and break rooms. It happened through a friend—someone I trusted enough to take the suggestion seriously, someone who spoke her name like it meant possibility. The first time I saw her, she didn't look like fate. She looked like a person in motion: a quick smile, a laugh that came easily, eyes that stayed on me a beat longer than they had to. The room around us could have been ordinary—chairs, cheap lighting, a background hum of other people talking—but my attention narrowed the way it does when hunger thinks it's found food. She made space for me without requiring performance, and that alone felt like a miracle.

We started fast because I didn't know any other speed. Slow felt like danger. Slow felt like losing the moment. In my life, whenever something good appeared, it had always felt as if it might be taken—by someone else's boredom, by a system's judgment, by a random turn of luck. So when she leaned in, when she chose me, when she offered closeness without making me audition for it, I didn't treat it as something to build carefully. I treated it as something to grab before it vanished. Our early days were saturated with that bright, irrational confidence that comes from finally being wanted: long drives with the windows down, music too loud, hands on each other in the car like we were proving the connection was real. When we were apart, my mind stayed on her like a held note, vibrating with need.

There was a sweetness to those first weeks that felt almost clean, as if the world had finally softened. We sat in diners late at night under harsh lights that made everyone look tired and honest, splitting cheap food, laughing at nothing. We walked through big stores with carts we didn't need, just to have a place to wander side by side. We talked about the future with the casual certainty young people use when they don't understand how expensive the future can be. She told stories from her life and I listened the way thirsty people listen, absorbing details as if knowing her better would guarantee she stayed. When she touched my hand across a table, my nervous system exhaled. In those moments, the rest of my world—my crowded house, my uneasy routines, my unresolved sense of who I was supposed to be—fell back behind a curtain.

The relationship turned physical while I was still living in the house where I'd been staying, in a room that didn't feel fully mine no matter how many of my objects were in it. Privacy in that house was always conditional. Doors could be opened without warning. Footsteps in the hallway carried meaning. The air itself felt monitored, as if the walls had absorbed decades of rules. But desire doesn't negotiate with household atmospheres. We found moments anyway—stolen time, quiet time, bodies pressed together like we were trying to fuse into one certainty. The sex wasn't pornographic or poetic. It was urgent, messy, and full of the belief that closeness could become a plan. Every touch carried a second message underneath it: *Stay. Choose me again. Don't disappear.*

The discovery came the way discoveries always come in a house like that—sudden, humiliating, and wrapped in moral authority. A door opened. A voice cut through the air, sharp with disbelief and anger. The room's temperature seemed to drop in a single breath. We separated like startled animals, pulling fabric into place, trying to look like nothing had happened even while the evidence was still warm in the sheets. The adult who confronted us didn't need to say much. The meaning was embedded in posture, in tone, in the way the house itself seemed to lean in and listen. The message was simple: not here. Not under this roof. Not where rules and judgment could be disrupted by two bodies acting like they belonged to themselves.

That confrontation should have slowed us down. It did the opposite. It forced a decision, and the decision felt like proof of commitment. If we couldn't be together there, we would be together somewhere else. We talked about moving out as if moving out would solve everything, as if a new address could erase the fear and the scrutiny and the shame. The idea took on momentum fast. It became a project, and projects are seductive because they give anxious minds something concrete to do. I began turning my life into boxes. I began measuring my days in tasks: find a place, gather money, coordinate schedules, convince the world that two young people with shaky foundations could build something stable. In my chest, the urgency felt like love. In hindsight—only in the present—does it look like survival wearing romance as a mask.

We moved into an apartment with another person, someone connected to her work life, someone who made the rent seem possible by splitting it into manageable pieces. The apartment smelled like new paint and old carpet, that particular combination of hope and mildew that cheap places wear like a badge. The rooms were small, but they were ours in the way the house had never been. No one could open the door without knocking. No one could enforce rules without being invited in. The first night there, we sat on the floor because we didn't have enough furniture yet, eating something out of plastic containers, laughing at how adult it felt. Outside, traffic hissed on wet pavement. Inside, the walls held our voices and reflected them back like proof of independence.

Not long after we moved, she told me she was pregnant. The sentence landed in my body like a sudden weight. It changed the air. It changed her face in my perception. It changed the meaning of everything we had done. "Pregnant" wasn't only biology in the world I came from; it was consequence, identity, the beginning of a story you couldn't walk away from without being judged. My mind did what it always did with high-stakes information: it accelerated into planning. I imagined cribs and bills and responsibility. I imagined being a father because a sentence had been spoken. I imagined my life becoming respectable overnight, as if obligation could transform drifting into purpose. At the same time, fear rose like bile. I was young. I was unstable. I was barely holding my own hours together. The idea of caring for another life felt both holy and impossible.

We didn't have the luxury of processing slowly. Rent didn't pause for emotions. Work schedules didn't pause. The household we had left behind didn't suddenly become supportive simply because we had crossed a boundary. We moved through days as if speed could keep us from collapsing. I worked and came home tired, shoulders tight from hours under fluorescent light, hands smelling faintly of cardboard and plastic. She moved through her own routines, sometimes bright, sometimes distant. We bought cheap groceries and tried to make meals feel like domestic stability. We lay in bed at night listening to the building settle—pipes clicking, neighbors arguing through thin walls—and I stared at the ceiling, imagining the future as a narrowing corridor: pregnancy, birth, bills, responsibility, adulthood arriving whether I was ready or not.

When a friend introduced what he called an opportunity, it felt like salvation disguised as business. It wasn't a job in the normal sense. It was one of those glossy schemes that sells the image of success more than the work itself: motivational language, hotel ballrooms, smiling speakers promising a life that didn't require grinding under fluorescent lights. I clung to it because I needed a miracle. I needed a way to pay rent and prepare for a baby without admitting how fragile our foundation was. The workshop was out of town, a trip that felt important because it was framed as the beginning of a new life. I sat in a ballroom under warm lighting that made everything feel slightly unreal, listening to applause and rhetoric, watching people nod like believers. The speaker's voice rose and fell like a preacher's. The crowd responded on cue. For a few hours, I could pretend there was a ladder out of my financial panic.

Before I left, I handed her my car keys because she needed transportation and I wanted to be generous. The gesture felt intimate and adult—trust made physical. She watched me pack with an expression that held something I couldn't read. I kissed her goodbye with urgency, telling myself the distance was temporary and the reward would be worth it. The travel itself felt like movement toward purpose: highway lights at night, the hum of tires, the brief anonymity of being in a hotel room alone, surrounded by generic furniture and the smell of industrial detergent. I called her between sessions, hearing her voice through the thin distortion of a phone line, imagining her at home touching her stomach, carrying our future. The idea made my chest ache with a strange tenderness and dread.

The call that ended the illusion came fast, like a blade. Her voice on the phone was broken in a way I hadn't heard before—ragged, breathy, full of shock. She said there had been an accident. A hit-and-run. She said she had lost the baby. The words didn't feel real. They bounced off the inside of my skull like hail. I sat on the edge of a hotel bed with the phone pressed to my ear, staring at a patterned carpet that suddenly looked obscene in its normality. My body went cold. My heart hammered. I felt a roar fill my ears, not tinnitus, not the present-day ringing that would arrive later, but a situational flood of adrenaline and disbelief. I asked questions that didn't form properly. She answered in fragments. The room around me stayed unchanged, and that made the news feel even more violent.

I left immediately. The workshop, the applause, the speeches about success—all of it evaporated. I drove home fast enough that the road blurred. My hands clenched the steering wheel until my fingers hurt. The world outside the windshield looked wrong, as if the landscape hadn't been informed that my life had just collapsed. When I arrived, I found her shaken, pale, moving as if she were trying not to fall apart. I held her the way people hold each other in tragedies: tightly, desperately, as if pressure could keep pieces from breaking off. Grief moved through our apartment like smoke. It settled into the corners. It sat on the furniture. It made the air heavy enough to taste.

The pain of believing you have lost a child you never met is a specific kind of horror. It doesn't have memories attached to it, only imagined futures. There are no photographs, no birthdays, no stories—only the sudden vacuum where a life was supposed to unfold. I walked through days after that as if underwater, every movement slowed by weight. I went to work and performed normalcy because work requires performance. I smiled when customers spoke to me. I nodded when coworkers joked. I went through motions like a man obeying a script he didn't understand. At home, I held her when she cried and felt helpless because there was no fix, no repair kit, no instruction manual for how to survive a grief that had no physical proof.

We tried to make it official. That impulse came from both grief and practicality—if there had been an accident, there should be records; if there were records, there should be a path to justice; if there were a path, perhaps it would make the chaos feel less random. We sat in offices that smelled like paper and stale coffee, speaking to professionals who used measured language the way people do when they don't want to be responsible for your pain. Questions were asked. Dates were discussed in careful tones. Names of institutions were mentioned. We were told what documentation would be needed. The process had the cold, bureaucratic texture of modern life: without paperwork, the world treats your tragedy as rumor.

The problem was that the paper trail didn't behave the way my mind needed it to. Records were hard to locate. Phone calls led to transfers. Transfers led to dead ends. We were told things that didn't match the story we had in our hands. The mismatch didn't resolve quickly, and that uncertainty is its own kind of torture. Grief needs an object. Grief needs something solid to press against. Uncertainty dissolves the object, leaving grief to float free, unanchored and endless. I watched her face for signs—guilt, fear, truth, anything—and found only more emotion, more volatility, more exhaustion. I didn't know what was real and what wasn't, and not knowing made my body tense as if waiting for a second tragedy to land.

Around the same time, the practical world tightened its grip. Rent was due. Bills arrived. The apartment's smallness began to feel less like freedom and more like confinement. The third person sharing the space became not just a roommate but a constant reminder that we were improvising adulthood with too many bodies in too few rooms. Privacy frayed. Tension gathered. Small irritations became sharp because everything else was already too sharp. We tried to comfort each other, but comfort kept colliding with resentment: resentment at money, resentment at stress, resentment at the feeling that life was punishing us for trying to build something. At night, I would lie awake and listen to breathing in the dark, the building's distant noises, and feel an old familiar sensation creeping back in—hypervigilance without a clear target, the sense that safety was conditional and could be revoked without warning.

Within the first half year, financial strain became a constant background roar. I started asking for help from people who, in my mind, represented stability—adults in my orbit who had money, authority, and the power to soften consequences. The requests were humiliating because asking for help required admitting I wasn't in control. I sat in living rooms under warm lamps, hearing my own voice explain our situation, hearing the shame in my own tone. I watched faces tighten with judgment. I heard refusals delivered politely, as if politeness could erase the cruelty. Some refusals came wrapped in morality—talk about sin, talk about doing things "the right way," talk about how suffering was the natural result of stepping outside rules. The message wasn't only no. The message was: you deserve this for moving too fast, for wanting too much, for trying to build a life without permission.

I went to a religious community for help as well, because religion had been offered to me as a system that caught people when they fell. I sat in offices that smelled like carpet and old books, listened to voices speak about worthiness as if worthiness could be measured like a receipt total. I asked for assistance the way a drowning person asks for a hand, and I was met with judgment disguised as counsel. The lesson landed hard: you can be desperate and still be evaluated. You can be hungry and still be told you don't qualify. I walked out into sunlight afterward and felt my stomach hollow, not from hunger alone but from the knowledge that even "good" systems prioritize rules over relief. That knowledge didn't destroy me in the dramatic sense. It simply added another layer to the internal file my nervous system was building: *don't rely on anyone. Don't trust warmth. Don't assume care is unconditional.*

With money tight and grief unresolved, the relationship began to change shape. The warmth that had felt effortless early on became something we had to manufacture. We tried to go out and pretend we were normal—movies, restaurants, evenings where laughter was forced into existence like a performance—but the effort made the cracks more visible. In the apartment, arguments ignited over small things: dishes, schedules, a tone of voice, who forgot what. The fights weren't cinematic. They were domestic and exhausting, the kind that leave no dramatic aftermath, only a residue of bitterness in the air. In between fights, we clung to each other in a way that felt less like romance and more like two people holding onto the same plank in rough water, each terrified of being the one who lets go first.

The idea of marriage entered as both hope and pressure. Hope, because marriage promised legitimacy—a status that might quiet the moral judgment we kept encountering, a certificate that might convince adults and institutions to take us seriously. Pressure, because marriage was also an escalation, another step taken at speed, another lock clicked into place on a door we had already rushed through. We spoke about it in late-night conversations where the room was dim and the world felt distant. We imagined a ceremony, imagined rings, imagined the relief of being "official." The imagery was seductive. It suggested a clean beginning. It suggested that paperwork could become safety. It suggested that if we did the right thing, the world might stop punishing us for earlier choices.

When we did it, it wasn't the fairytale version. It was legal and practical, carried out in a bright room that smelled like ink and cleaning products, with witnesses who were there because someone had to be there. The vows were spoken with sincerity, but the sincerity had weight under it —fear, urgency, the desire to make something permanent so it couldn't be taken away. I slid the ring onto her finger and watched the metal disappear past her knuckle, a small act that carried an absurd amount of meaning. My hands trembled slightly. My throat tightened as if I were swallowing a stone. The room around us stayed ordinary, and that ordinariness felt surreal because inside me it was thunder. I wanted marriage to be a wall against chaos. I wanted it to turn our unstable life into something solid. I wanted it to prove that my speed had been love, not desperation.

Marriage didn't erase strain. It changed the kinds of strain that were allowed. We were now bound together in a way that made leaving harder, which meant every argument carried a heavier shadow. We moved again when our lease ended, packing boxes in a small apartment while daylight faded through blinds. The act of packing is always emotional even when people pretend it isn't—each object lifted is proof of time passing. We relocated into someone else's space for a while, living under another roof with another set of invisible rules, the way young couples do when money is thin and pride has already been spent. I felt parts of my identity detach with each move: the fantasy of independence, the fantasy of control, the fantasy that a new address could fix the inside of my life.

Work became a scramble. I moved through jobs like stepping stones across a river, trying to land on something stable and finding each stone slick. I did temporary work that treated bodies as disposable. I took what I could get, woke up early, drove through cold mornings, watched my breath fog the windshield, and told myself endurance would eventually pay off. Every paycheck arrived with relief and left too quickly. Every bill felt like a verdict. The anxiety wasn't constant in a dramatic way; it was constant in a mundane way, a background vibration that never fully shut off. In the evenings, when the two of us sat together, the air between us was crowded with unspoken calculations: how long until rent, how long until the car needs work, how long until another crisis, how long until one of us breaks under the weight.

The grief from the claimed pregnancy loss didn't resolve cleanly. It sat in the relationship like a third presence. Sometimes it was spoken about directly, raw and heavy. More often it was implied through mood swings, through sudden tears, through anger that didn't fit the current moment. I found myself walking on invisible eggshells, trying not to trigger something I didn't fully understand. When you love someone volatile, you start tracking their emotional weather like a sailor tracks clouds. You study tone. You study silence. You learn which subjects make the room colder. That tracking felt like care at first. Over time it became exhaustion. And exhaustion made me less gentle. It made my responses sharper. It made me resentful of how much effort it took to keep the day from collapsing.

There were still good moments, and those good moments were dangerous because they renewed hope. We would have a quiet evening where she laughed easily again, where the room felt light, where our bodies fit together in a way that made everything else recede. We would drive somewhere at night—no destination, just movement—and the city lights would blur into streaks on wet pavement, and for a while it would feel like we were simply two young people in love. In those moments, I could believe the story again: marriage as rescue, love as anchor, the past dissolving behind us. Then morning would come, bills would still exist, tension would still exist, the world's judgment would still exist, and the hope would look naive in the harsh light of practical life.

The relationship also existed in a social ecosystem that didn't belong to us. Friends, acquaintances, people who loved drama because drama made their own lives feel interesting—those people hovered around the edges, offering opinions, offering gossip, offering interpretations. In our world, perception was power. If someone believed a story about you, that belief could become reality regardless of truth. I had seen that dynamic in school, in workplaces, in institutions. Now I watched it enter my marriage like a slow leak. Someone could mention a glance in a store, a comment overheard, a moment at a gathering, and suddenly that moment would be retold with sharper edges, transformed into evidence of betrayal. I wasn't prepared for how quickly a relationship could be shaped by other people's sentences.

The trigger that ended everything came from that ecosystem, not from a dramatic confession or a clear, private rupture. It started with a conversation I wasn't in. Someone connected to my old household spoke to her friends and described me as if I were hunting other women with my eyes, as if I were unfaithful in spirit even if I hadn't done anything in action. The story traveled the way stories travel—fast, embellished, carrying emotional certainty because emotional certainty is more contagious than truth. It reached her in a form that felt like proof, and once the story had landed, it didn't matter what I said. Denial sounded like lying. Anger sounded like guilt. Calm sounded like manipulation. I watched her face harden as if she were sealing a door from the inside.

The confrontation didn't happen in a clean, cinematic setting. It happened in ordinary space—kitchen light, living room clutter, a hallway that smelled faintly of laundry detergent—because that's where most lives break. She told me what she'd heard, the words coming out sharp and rehearsed, as if she had repeated them to herself until they became solid. My chest tightened. My mind raced through memory, trying to locate the supposed offense: a glance, a smile, a moment of being human in public. I tried to explain. I tried to argue. I tried to plead. Each attempt landed wrong. The more I talked, the more trapped I became in the role the rumor had assigned me. I could feel the old panic rising— the same panic that comes when a system has decided you are guilty and your innocence is irrelevant. Only this time it wasn't a system. It was the person I had married.

When she left, it wasn't slow. There was no long negotiation. There was no shared counseling, no careful unpacking of misunderstandings. There was movement— fast, decisive movement that made my body go cold. A bag appeared. Keys were grabbed. A door opened and shut. The sound of that door closing didn't have drama attached to it. It was a simple domestic sound, which made it worse. Domestic sounds aren't supposed to mark endings. They're supposed to mark routines. After the door shut, the space she'd been standing in looked the same, and that sameness felt like a trick. I stood in the room with my hands half-raised, as if my body had been preparing to stop her and hadn't been given instructions for what to do when stopping her failed.

I didn't chase in a heroic way. I moved in confused fragments, stepping toward the window, stepping toward the door, stepping back, as if the right direction might suddenly reveal itself. Outside, the world continued—cars passing, distant voices, a neighbor's dog barking—ordinary life refusing to acknowledge my collapse. I felt something inside me detach, not as poetry but as sensation: a hollowing behind the ribs, a sudden absence where certainty had been. I sat down on the floor because standing required too much coordination. The room smelled like her shampoo and my sweat and whatever meal we'd eaten earlier, and that mixture made nausea rise. The marriage had been a wall I believed in. Now it felt like paper, torn quickly, leaving me exposed to air that didn't feel breathable.

The days immediately after were not dramatic in the way movies depict heartbreak. They were administrative. People asked questions. Paperwork existed. Obligations remained. I still had to work. I still had to pay bills. I still had to move through public spaces with a face that didn't announce that my life had just been gutted. That forced functioning is a particular kind of cruelty: grief doesn't pause the world, and the world doesn't slow down to match grief's pace. I moved through those days as if in a trance, doing tasks by muscle memory, nodding when spoken to, smiling when required. Inside, my mind replayed the last conversation over and over, searching for the moment where a different sentence might have changed the outcome. The replay never solved anything. It only wore grooves deeper into my attention.

Eventually, I returned to the house I had once moved out of, because there was nowhere else with a door open. Returning felt like swallowing pride and swallowing failure at the same time. The hallway looked the same. The air smelled the same—cooked food, cleaning products, old furniture holding years of human presence. But my body walked through it differently. The house didn't greet me like home; it greeted me like a tribunal I couldn't avoid. I moved back into a room and tried to make it mine again, tried to place my objects in ways that suggested continuity. The attempt felt hollow. A room can hold your things without holding your dignity. At night, I lay on a bed and stared at a ceiling and listened to voices in other parts of the house, feeling both surrounded and isolated.

There was a night when the pressure finally broke through the surface. I didn't cry in a clean, cinematic way. I fell apart in fragments—breath catching, chest tight, hands shaking, an ugly sound escaping my throat that didn't feel like my voice. The breakdown wasn't only about her leaving. It was about the speed of everything: meeting, intimacy, pregnancy claim, grief, financial collapse, judgment, marriage, and then abandonment delivered on the back of rumor. It felt like I had built a life out of wet paper and then acted surprised when rain destroyed it. I sat on the floor in that room, shoulders hunched, trying to pull air into lungs that refused to cooperate. I wanted someone to tell me what the next step was. I wanted a schedule. I wanted orders. Civilian life offered neither.

An adult from the household eventually came and sat nearby—not in my arms, not holding me like a child, but present enough that I wasn't alone with the worst of it. The presence was quiet, heavy, uncertain. No perfect words arrived. No rescue speech. Just another person sharing air with me while I shook. That moment didn't heal anything. It didn't rewrite the story. It simply kept me from disappearing entirely into the dark. In the years that came later, darker moments would arrive with sharper edges and more obvious causes—experiences that would carve deeper grooves into my mind and body. But in this moment, in the aftermath of her leaving, the world narrowed to a small room in a familiar house, a man on the floor trying to breathe, and the knowledge that love, when used as a wall against chaos, can collapse fast enough to take your sense of self with it.

# CHAPTER 9

# *Years of Vanishing*

The apartment has the kind of quiet that doesn't soothe—it audits. The refrigerator clicks, the vents sigh, and somewhere beyond the wall a stranger's life makes the smallest proofs of itself: a faucet turned, a latch set, a footfall that disappears as soon as it's made. When the room stays like this long enough, a thin line of sound in my ears becomes impossible to ignore, as if the silence is brightening it. I stand at the kitchen counter with a stack of unopened mail in front of me and feel my hands hesitate over paper like it's a living thing. Envelopes are harmless until they aren't. Envelopes are how consequences learn to travel.

One of them is heavier than the rest, stiff in a way that usually means an institution. The return address is printed in that cold, standardized font that never admits it belongs to a human being. I pick it up, turn it once, and my throat tightens as if my body recognizes the ritual before my mind does: the moment right before a decision is made for you. The apartment's air is warm. My palms are damp anyway. I set the envelope back down, not because I'm afraid of paper, but because I know what paper can do when it lands at the right moment in a person's life.

On the counter beside the stack is a small object I keep within reach without admitting it counts as a habit—something that gives my hands a task when my thoughts get too loud. I touch it, then stop, as if contact alone could trigger a memory. The taste of certain rituals doesn't matter as much as what they promise: a lever you can pull, a small sense of control, a way to cut the edge off an hour that won't sit still. My fingers hover, then pull away. I don't need the ritual to do its job. Its presence is enough. It reminds me of earlier years when I tried to manage emptiness with tiny, repeatable actions—ways to feel like I was steering, even when I was only circling.

The present doesn't fade politely. It slips. The envelope on the counter becomes a different kind of letter in my mind—deadlines, eligibility, warnings dressed up as neutral language. The apartment's quiet reshapes into campus quiet: late-night hallways, distant laughter, the thump of music leaking through walls, the sense that everyone else has somewhere to go while I'm still searching for a place to stand. That shift carries me back to the spring after my marriage ended, when I returned to familiar rooms and discovered familiarity doesn't equal safety. I kept trying to outrun absence by moving faster, and the faster I moved, the more my life started to feel like a blur I could live inside without having to look at it directly.

After she left in the spring of 2002, there wasn't a clean collapse that people could recognize as a turning point. There was no grand, public implosion that forced the world to treat my pain as real. The ending was quieter than that, and the quiet made it worse. The absence didn't come with a final conversation I could replay and annotate. It came as a missing presence, a space where a person used to be, a life rearranged by decisions made elsewhere. I woke up for weeks with the muscle memory of attachment still in my body—reaching for warmth that wasn't there, hearing silence and expecting footsteps, feeling the slight dizziness of realizing the day had started and I was already alone in a way I hadn't planned for. That kind of loss isn't dramatic; it's humiliating. It makes you feel like you didn't even fail correctly. It makes you feel like you were removed from your own story and left holding a prop with no stage.

I drifted back into the house I had grown up in because drift is what happens when you don't have a stable place to land. The first bedroom down the main hallway on the main floor became mine again, not as a triumph of return but as a quiet surrender to practicality. The room caught more light than the basement ever had, and that light felt invasive at first, as if it could expose what I was trying to keep hidden. I brought in boxes, folded clothes, a few objects that still smelled faintly like the life I'd been living—laundry detergent from a different apartment, the stale trace of shared spaces, a hint of perfume that clung to fabric in a way that made my stomach tighten. The adults in the house moved around me carefully, sometimes offering help in the form of silence, sometimes offering questions in the form of concern, and I learned again how to answer without revealing anything that might become a lecture. The hallway outside my door became a runway for judgment I couldn't see but could always feel.

Smoking was the one ritual I didn't have to explain. It was a reason to step outside when the air inside the house felt too thick. It was a way to slice time into pieces small enough to survive. I would stand under whatever weak light reached the porch, the night air cooling the heat that had been building in my chest, and I'd inhale until the smoke filled my lungs with something sharp and tangible. The smoke leaving my mouth felt like proof I could still release something on purpose. The world outside was quiet in that late-hour way—no traffic, no voices, just the occasional insect sound and the far-off rumble of a car passing on a road I couldn't see. The cigarette ember glowed, then dimmed, then glowed again, and for those minutes I didn't have to be a husband who'd been abandoned or a failure who'd returned home. I could be a body doing a simple thing, a body with a small, manageable plan: finish the cigarette, stub it out, go back inside.

In the fall of 2002 I stepped into a university like it was a costume I could wear. I registered, moved into dorm life, and tried to let the architecture convince me I had a future. The dorm smelled like carpet that had been cleaned too many times and never cleaned enough, a mix of detergent and old sweat and the faint mold of a building that held too many bodies every year. My room had the early-semester neatness of a place not yet lived in—a bedspread pulled tight, a desk cleared, my few possessions arranged with the kind of precision that implies control. A roommate occupied the other half of the space, his belongings forming a parallel life just inches away from mine. During the day there were voices everywhere—doors opening and closing, laughter in hallways, music thumping through drywall—but at night the noise thinned, and the dorm's fluorescent hum became more noticeable, and the room started to feel like a box designed to contain silence rather than comfort it.

The first weeks were a blur of introductions and schedules and the illusion of a clean start. Students moved in clusters, hungry for friendship, walking as if they already belonged. I watched them with a kind of quiet disbelief, the way you watch people speak a language you don't know and still understand each other perfectly. I went to classes and sat in lecture halls where the air felt dry and the seats creaked when someone shifted. I wrote notes sometimes, not because I felt engaged but because writing made me look like I belonged. I ate in dining halls where trays clattered and food tasted like it had been designed for efficiency rather than joy. At night I smoked outside with other smokers, strangers gathered into temporary tribes by nicotine, and the conversations were short, repetitive, easy to escape without consequence. The cigarette offered me a role: quiet guy, casual smoker, someone who can nod and laugh at the right moments without having to reveal what he's thinking.

Weekends were the first real test because weekends remove structure and ask you to define yourself without the excuse of a schedule. When Friday night arrived, the dorm changed temperature. The hallways grew louder, doors stayed open, and groups formed with the urgency of people chasing a party before it vanished. I joined those movements not because I felt invited but because being alone in a dorm room with my thoughts felt worse. There's a particular kind of walking you do when you're searching for a party you weren't exactly invited to, carrying yourself like you belong while your eyes scan porches and driveways for the evidence of music and bodies. You read sound the way sailors read weather—bass thumps, sudden cheers, the roar of conversation spilling into the street. Sometimes you'd find a house overflowing with noise and step into heat and sweat and cheap beer, and sometimes you'd be turned away by a look that said your face didn't match the guest list, and either way you'd keep walking because the goal wasn't the party itself. The goal was to avoid returning to your room feeling like a person no one had noticed.

Inside those crowded rooms, I learned how to be present without connecting. I would stand in a kitchen with strangers, holding a plastic cup, laughing when they laughed and nodding when they nodded, and the whole time my mind would be running a translation process: what are the rules here, what's the correct amount of eye contact, how close is too close, when is it my turn to speak. I didn't have the inner ease other people seemed to carry, the kind that lets them flirt without looking like they're calculating each word. I moved carefully, almost clinically, aware that one wrong move could make me the story people told later. The fear wasn't only rejection; it was perception. It was the dread that I would come off as predatory simply because I didn't know how to be relaxed. I watched women laugh with other men and felt a tight, mean awareness rise in my chest: if I approached, would I look desperate, would I look strange, would I look like someone waiting to pounce. The nights would end, and I would walk back to the dorm under cold streetlights, replaying conversations as if I could correct them retroactively, and the replay never produced improvement. It only produced exhaustion.

By spring of 2003, I had learned something about the university system that mattered more to me than the education itself. The institution rewarded you for staying technically enrolled. It wanted you full-time on paper, compliant with credit requirements, and it would keep money flowing as long as you stayed inside that definition. I took the minimum number of credits needed to be considered full-time and chose classes that were light, easy, designed to be survived rather than mastered. The academic side of my life became a mechanism, not a mission. I would show up just enough, sign attendance sheets, turn in the simplest versions of assignments, and then use the rest of my time as if it were my actual life: nights out, weekends out, bars and clubs where the lighting was dim enough to make everyone look better, loud enough to drown out self-consciousness. I didn't frame it as scam. I framed it as survival. I told myself that people do what they have to do, that my life had been disrupted, that I deserved some relief. The relief I chased wasn't peace. It was anesthesia.

The bars were different than the parties. At a party you could still pretend the chaos was communal, that everyone was messy together, that belonging could be measured in volume and proximity. Bars were transactional. Bars had sticky floors and bouncers and the sense that everyone was evaluating everyone else even if no one made eye contact. The light was designed to flatter and conceal at the same time, and the music made conversation optional, which meant you could stand near people without being required to actually know them. Outside the bars, smokers gathered in clusters under weak lights, and those clusters became the closest thing to social comfort I could reliably access. A cigarette gave me something to do with my hands and something to look at besides faces. It gave me a reason to step away from the pressure of being watched. The smoke curled upward and disappeared, and I would watch it like it was a lesson in how to leave without anyone noticing.

Spring break that year carried me away from campus in a caravan of vehicles, a group trip organized by someone close to me and their classmates, people with plans and energy and a belief that chaos could be fun. We drove for hours through highways and gas stations and fast-food wrappers, passing time with playlists that looped and jokes repeated until they were no longer funny. When we arrived, the air tasted like salt and heat and sunscreen. The place was built for staged freedom—beach, pool, clubs, bodies everywhere, the constant soundtrack of someone else's good time. About ten of us shared one suite, which meant there was never a moment fully alone. There were always feet on carpet, someone in the bathroom, someone laughing, someone sleeping with sand stuck to their skin. Daytime held activities that would sound normal if described cleanly—horseback riding one morning, shopping, restaurants—but the true gravity was at night, when the pool became a bar and the bar became a blur and the blur became the point.

One night we moved through clubs as if we were collecting scenes rather than experiences. Bass vibrated through ribs. Lights cut the room into fragments like a shattered mirror. People shouted into each other's ears and called it conversation. In one hotel club we met a pair—a confident older woman and a younger woman beside her—who announced themselves like they were conducting an experiment. The older one spoke about teaching the younger one what men think in clubs, framing the whole interaction as a lesson rather than a risk. There was laughter, a kind of staged permissiveness, and then a brief performance that was kept in bounds by clothing and distance and the older woman's sanction. It lasted only minutes, but the feeling of it stayed longer than it should have, not because it was erotic in any clean way, but because it was strange: a situation where consent and power and spectacle were all tangled, and I went along with it because the entire trip had been built on not stopping to ask questions. Later, the older woman claimed she could read fortunes, and in the roar of the club I barely caught anything she said, except a detail repeated to me afterward like it was prophecy. I carried it home like a joke and like a warning at the same time.

When the trip ended, I returned to campus exhausted and hungover in a way that felt almost spiritual—like the body punishing me for trying to pretend that drowning in noise counted as living. The dorm smelled the same as before, but I smelled different, my clothes holding beach salt and smoke and alcohol, my skin dry from sun and dehydration. Classes resumed as if I had never left. The calendar didn't care about my fatigue. The university kept demanding minimal compliance, and I provided it with the same half-hearted precision as before. The trip didn't change me in any dramatic way. It didn't create my later collapse. It simply added another layer to a pattern: chasing intensity, waking up empty, repeating the chase. The intensity became a habit, and habits are quiet architects. They don't build skyscrapers overnight. They build corridors, one day at a time, until you look up and realize you've been walking in the same direction for years.

That summer I moved into campus apartments with the same roommate from spring, a supposed step toward adulthood that mostly became a wider container for the same loop. The apartment had a kitchen I rarely used properly, a living room that became a staging area for pregame drinking, and a television that glowed late into the night when I couldn't tolerate silence. Some weekends I went out and returned with my ears ringing from bass and my mouth tasting like stale beer. Other weekends, when money thinned or energy collapsed, I stayed in and played video games for hours, the clean rules of the game offering a kind of relief that real life refused to provide. There's a special numbness that comes from gaming after a night at bars: the room quiet except for the fan hum of electronics, the television light making walls look pale, the body heavy as if gravity has been turned up. Progress becomes measurable in levels and achievements while real life stays stubbornly unmeasurable. Smoking fit into that rhythm perfectly. It became punctuation—the comma between matches, the period at the end of a night, the brief pause where I could stare out a window and pretend I had chosen this life on purpose.

Sometime in that season, I went for a fertility test, a clinical errand that felt like stepping into a sterile version of my own fear. The waiting room had chairs designed to be cleaned, not to be comfortable, and the lighting was bright in a way that felt unkind. Paperwork asked questions in neutral fonts that still managed to feel personal. I was directed into a small room with a plastic cup and a request that turned my body into a machine expected to perform on command. The moment wasn't dramatic; it was awkward, quiet, and full of a cold awareness that the future can be altered by numbers you don't get to negotiate with. When the results came back, I was told my count was extremely low, so low it sounded like a mistake, like a measurement taken from the wrong person. The numbers lodged in my mind like a weight. I didn't cry. I didn't explode. I went blank in a way that frightened me more than panic would have, because blankness felt like something shutting down.

In my head, I reached for a cause the way a drowning person reaches for anything solid. I connected it to an early-life medical correction, to the idea that something that should have been handled cleanly had been handled late, and now the consequences were arriving years later like a bill. I didn't research it. I didn't consult experts. I simply needed a story that made the low number feel less random, because randomness is intolerable when it touches your future. The deeper meaning didn't settle fully then. It arrived later in small waves, not as wisdom but as a quiet bitterness: how many times sex had happened without protection, how many confusing claims and false alarms had swirled around me, how little confirmed proof existed that I had ever created a child. The test made my body feel less like mine and more like an unreliable instrument, a thing that might not do what it was supposed to do even when asked politely. It didn't define my life, but it became a private fact I carried like a defect no one could see.

As summer bled into fall, stories about my former wife began reaching me through the shallow pipes of gossip, arriving as fragments rather than truth. Someone mentioned pregnancy claims connected to her past. Someone implied another claim involving someone else. Nothing came with documentation, nothing came with a neat conclusion, but the mere suggestion of pattern made something inside me go cold. I had lived through the administrative confusion of the hit-and-run and miscarriage claim while I was still married, the way reality refused to provide receipts for the tragedy I had been told to grieve. That absence of records didn't become a clean conclusion immediately. It sat in me like an unsolved problem, a question mark that made me feel cruel for wanting certainty and foolish for accepting ambiguity. The new rumors didn't prove anything by themselves. They simply pressed on the same bruise: the fear that I had been living inside a story someone else was writing, where my feelings were material rather than sacred. I didn't have the courage then to declare that out loud. I did what I was already good at doing. I kept moving. I kept drinking. I kept smoking. I kept trying to outrun the parts of my life that didn't make sense.

Fall of 2003 brought a new roommate into the apartment, an international student with a guitar, and the guitar changed the soundtrack of the place. Some nights he would sit and strum, the notes threading through the air in a way that made the apartment feel briefly alive, briefly intentional. Music can fill a room even when the people in it don't know how to fill themselves. The sound should have soothed me, but sometimes it only sharpened my awareness that other people seemed to possess an inner ease I couldn't access. He could sit in a chair and let his hands move and produce beauty. I could sit in a chair and feel like my own body was an awkward object, a thing that didn't know where to place itself. My schedule became a mess of half-attended classes and fully attended nights. I skipped lectures to play games. I skipped lectures because the idea of sitting under fluorescent lights pretending to care felt unbearable. I skipped lectures because no one stopped me. College gives you freedom in a way that can feel like kindness until you realize it also gives you permission to dissolve quietly, and the institution will still cash the checks.

The parties continued, and with them the same spike of self-consciousness. I would stand in a crowded room and suddenly feel myself from the outside—my posture, the angle of my shoulders, the way my face probably looked when I tried to smile. My eyes would scan too quickly, searching for a person to talk to and simultaneously searching for danger. In those moments the paranoia would surge: do I look strange, do I look desperate, do I look like someone who doesn't understand the rules. The fear wasn't about being rejected; rejection was familiar. The fear was about being labeled, about becoming the story people told later with a word attached to it that meant I wasn't safe. I tried to approach women and felt like I was interrupting their lives. I tried to be confident and felt like I was faking it. I didn't know how to fake it well enough to make it real. So I stayed on the edges, hovering, drinking, letting the noise do the work of covering my silence. I would stumble back to the apartment afterward, smoke on the balcony or by the doorway, and watch the ember glow as if it could tell me what to do next.

Spring of 2004 replaced that roommate with another international student, someone who liked to cook, and the smells changed—garlic, butter, something rich and unfamiliar. The kitchen would fill with heat and aroma, and for a moment the apartment would feel like a home, a place where human beings lived with intention. Then the meal would end, the dishes would sit, the glow would fade, and the loop would resume. My days became a repetition so steady it started to feel like a kind of self-hypnosis: bars at night, games during the day, minimal classes attended just enough to keep the paperwork alive. The repetition wasn't comforting. It was numbing. It was the same coin flipped over and over while the rest of life waited in a stack of unopened mail. Smoking remained constant, a thread stitched through every scene. Between classes, outside bars, late at night when the screen finally went black, the cigarette made me feel like I was doing something even when I wasn't. The smoke became a companion, a small ritual that asked nothing of me except breath.

By summer of 2004, the administrative consequences I'd been avoiding arrived as a letter, as if the universe finally decided to put my denial into an envelope and slide it under my door. The mailbox held it like any other piece of paper—plain, unglowing, indifferent. When I opened it, the message was blunt: financial aid was ending after one more semester because my GPA had fallen below threshold. I read the letter, then read it again, then set it down carefully as if gentle placement could soften what it meant. But the reality was already inside my body. Student loans had been piling up behind me like a trail I refused to look at. I had been living as if the money was endless because the consequences were delayed. Now the delay was ending. My stomach tightened. My shoulders rose toward my ears. My mind ran numbers it didn't want to run, calculating debt, calculating time, calculating the shape of a future where I wasn't a student on paper but still owed the world for pretending to be one.

That was when the Army began forming in my mind as something like an exit. Not a dream. Not a calling. Not a patriotic awakening. An exit. The idea didn't arrive with heroic imagery. It arrived with practicality: a way to get benefits, a way to address loans, a way to return to a structured life because my own structure had collapsed into addictions that looked harmless from the outside. I had already proven that when I was given freedom, I used it to avoid myself. The Army promised the opposite: a machine that would make decisions for me, a schedule that would own my hours, a system that would drag me forward whether I felt ready or not. The thought felt both relieving and humiliating. Relieving because it offered a door out of the mess. Humiliating because it meant admitting I couldn't steer. I didn't feel brave. I felt cornered. I felt like I was choosing a uniform because my life had become too soft and shapeless to hold itself together.

I entered the delayed entry program, which meant the rest of the year acquired a countdown quality even when I tried to ignore it. Everything became "lasts" without ceremony: last semester of pretending, last months of late-night bars, last afternoons wasted on screens, last cigarettes smoked with no thought for consequences. The countdown didn't make me more disciplined. It made me more frantic. Part of me kept trying to squeeze as much numbness as possible out of the remaining time, as if I could store it up and carry it into the future. Another part of me watched myself doing that and felt disgust, the quiet kind that doesn't motivate change so much as deepen shame. The Army demanded clarity in ways my life had not been demanding it. Paperwork. Legal status. Clean definitions. On paper I was still married, separated but not divorced, tethered by law to a person who had vanished from my daily life. The system didn't care about the emotional reality of abandonment. It cared about documents. It told me bluntly that if I didn't make the divorce official, I could be obligated to provide support. The idea that I could be haunted financially by someone I couldn't even speak to made my chest tighten like a fist.

So I went back to the household and asked one of the older adults there for help. Asking was its own humiliation, because asking meant admitting I had created a problem I couldn't solve cleanly alone. The request wasn't framed as pain. It was framed as logistics. I needed filing fees, I needed a process, I needed someone with the authority and resources to make the paperwork move. The conversation happened under ordinary light, in ordinary rooms, the way life-changing moments often do when there's no audience. The adult listened with a face that carried its own judgments, its own fatigue, and then agreed in a way that didn't feel warm but did feel functional. The help came with strings made of silence: no long comfort, no reassurance, just the cold, practical assistance that kept the situation from becoming worse. We dealt with forms and offices and the measured language of bureaucracy, and I learned again that institutions don't care what something felt like. They care what it can be proven to be.

The divorce process itself was not dramatic. It was waiting rooms and signatures and the strange sensation of closing out a marriage without seeing the person you were married to. I would sit in a chair with the air too cold, holding paperwork like it was evidence of a life I barely recognized. There were moments where the absurdity hit: how quickly I had moved from meeting someone to making vows, how quickly the vows had become silence, how the legal system treated the whole thing as a file to be processed. I didn't spend those moments in poetic reflection. I spent them in a kind of numb compliance, because feeling too much in a courthouse waiting area is a good way to fall apart in public. When the paperwork moved forward, it didn't feel like relief. It felt like a door being shut quietly, without ceremony, and the quiet made it hard to believe it was real. The loose end wasn't resolved in my heart. It was resolved on paper, which meant the world could stop caring about it even if I still did.

Fall of 2004 arrived like the last stretch of a bad habit you can't quite quit. I went through the motions of being a student, attended some classes, skipped others, and spent more time in bars and clubs than I did in lecture halls. The campus felt familiar by then in a way that wasn't comforting. It was familiar like a loop is familiar. I knew which streets led to which parties. I knew which bars had the dimmest light and the easiest entrances. I knew where to stand outside to smoke without being in anyone's way. Nights blurred into each other—beer foam, bass, laughter that sounded real until it didn't. Days were spent recovering, staring at screens, letting games provide a sense of progress that my real life refused to provide. Somewhere beneath it all was the knowledge that the countdown was nearing its end. The Army date sat on the calendar like a stone. I could feel it without looking at it, the way you can feel a storm coming from pressure change alone.

The last days of 2004 arrived carrying the dull weight of logistics. Packing. Paperwork. Approved items arranged to satisfy an institution that did not care what kind of life I was leaving behind. Clothes folded into a bag. Documents stacked. A toothbrush and a razor, the small maintenance tools that remind you how much of living is simply keeping a body presentable enough for other people to tolerate. I moved through my apartment like someone already gone. The place smelled like months of stale smoke sunk into fabric, like old beer dried into carpet fibers, like the residue of a life spent in loops. Boxes sat in corners, sealed stories —video games, cheap furniture, the remnants of a college life that had been more about anesthesia than education. I looked at those boxes and felt no nostalgia, no pride, no sense of completion. I felt only the pressure of the next morning, the threshold waiting like a door that wouldn't negotiate.

That evening I stepped outside for a cigarette because habit doesn't vanish just because a new uniform is coming. The cold air bit at my lungs in a way that felt clean and cruel at the same time. Campus night sounds drifted around me— distant laughter, a car door shutting, footsteps on concrete— ordinary life continuing as if my life wasn't about to be claimed by a machine. I stood under a weak light, watched the ember glow, watched the smoke rise and vanish into darkness, and tried to picture the Army as a series of manageable steps: wake up, go here, obey, survive. I tried to imagine discipline reshaping me the way heat reshapes metal, turning my soft drift into a harder form. But another part of me—the part that had been collecting evidence for years—didn't believe in easy transformation. That part understood, even then, that you can change your surroundings and still carry the same interior weather.

When I went back inside, the apartment felt smaller, as if the walls were already beginning to close behind me. I lay down—if it can be called sleep—and floated in and out of shallow rest with the knowledge that the night was only time moving forward, one minute at a time, toward morning. Toward the moment when I would step out of the life I had been wasting and into the life that would claim me. There was no comfort in that knowledge. There was only the fact of it, heavy and plain. And somewhere in that heaviness was the quiet truth that these years hadn't destroyed me in a single, spectacular way. They had worn grooves into me— habits of avoidance, hunger for numbness, fear of perception —that would later be eclipsed by heavier events. The eclipse was still ahead. For now there was only the threshold, the packed bag, the last cigarette taste lingering, and the corridor opening.

# CHAPTER 10

# *The Machine Moves*

The airport security line moves in tiny shuffles, the kind that feel like progress only because everyone agrees to pretend they're progress. Plastic bins slide along stainless rails with a dry scraping sound, shoes thump into place, belts coil like discarded snakes, and strangers lift their arms on cue as if surrender is just another travel step. A uniformed voice repeats instructions in the same calm cadence, over and over, until the words stop sounding like language and start sounding like a metronome. I watch my own hands follow the routine—pockets emptied, pockets checked again, palms turned up for a moment as if proving there's nothing hidden—and the strange part is how quickly my body relaxes inside the process. Not because it's pleasant, but because it's clear. The rules are posted. The expectations are blunt. You move when you're told to move. You stop when you're told to stop. No one asks what you're feeling.

When the scanner beeps for someone ahead of me, I feel the sound behind my ribs before I interpret it with my mind. It isn't fear exactly. It's recognition, like my nervous system has been waiting for a reason to return to an older posture. The line has the same choreography as other lines I've stood in—lines where your name becomes a number, where your body becomes a checklist, where you learn to keep your face neutral because expressions can invite attention. A bin bumps the metal stop at the end of the rail, a small, sharp clack, and the clack pulls something loose: the memory of being processed into a new identity, not once but twice, the sensation of giving up the right to improvise. The present stays bright and orderly, but the inside of my head begins to darken with a different kind of order.

I step forward when the line tells me to step forward. I place my hands in the right place, I angle my feet the right way, and my compliance feels too practiced to be explained by modern travel alone. The posture doesn't belong to this airport; it belongs to a different system, one that didn't ask whether I wanted to participate after I signed my name. That's the part that matters. I chose that system on purpose. I walked into it because I had been living in years where freedom looked like drifting and drifting looked like disappearing, and I was tired of being the kind of man who could dissolve quietly. When the scanner hums and the uniformed voice says, "Go ahead," the words become another voice, another command, and the floor under me turns from polished tile into the dull, scuffed hardness of a place built to reshape people.

The shift into the past isn't gentle. It isn't a soft nostalgia. It's a snap of context, like a camera switching lenses. The plastic bins become duffel bags and paperwork. The travelers become recruits, heads shaved, eyes wide, pretending they aren't afraid. The calm security instructions become louder, sharper, less patient. The smell changes too, from perfume and fast food to disinfectant and sweat and the faint chemical tang of institutional cleaning. A line is still a line, but now it's a line with consequences, a line that marks the moment when my life stops being shaped by my own hesitation and starts being shaped by a schedule with teeth.

I entered the Army at the beginning of that year the way some people step onto a train: with a bag, a decision, and the private hope that motion itself would become a cure. I did not frame it as destiny. I framed it as structure. College had become a loop I used to numb myself. Debt had accumulated behind me like a shadow I refused to turn around and face. My days had been full of easy exits—skipping, drifting, swapping obligations for distractions—and the longer I lived that way, the more I felt my life thinning into something that didn't count as living. The Army offered a different bargain than civilian life had offered: surrender your autonomy, receive a spine. Show up, obey, become part of a system that will not allow you to vanish quietly.

The first days were pure processing. I learned quickly that the Army doesn't begin with training; it begins with paperwork and reshaping. There were forms for everything—medical, legal, financial—each one reducing me to boxes and signatures. We moved through stations like parts on a conveyor belt, shuffled forward by voices that didn't need to be angry to be absolute. Someone checked my eyes, someone checked my hearing, someone checked my teeth, someone checked my joints as if evaluating whether I was worth the institution's investment. Hair fell again, shorter than I would have chosen, and the loss of it was a minor humiliation that carried a larger message: personal preference is not relevant here. Uniforms were issued that smelled like fabric stored too long in a warehouse. Boots were stiff and unforgiving, turning my feet into raw, aching instruments within hours. Even standing still became work.

The bus ride to Fort Sill had its own bleak quiet, broken by the occasional forced joke and the constant sound of bodies shifting in seats. Outside the windows, the landscape flattened into winter-bare shapes—fields, fences, gray sky—and it felt as if the world was stripping down to essentials to match what was happening to us. The men around me were young enough to still carry a teenager's face in some angles, but old enough to be held accountable like adults. Some spoke about the Army with bravado, saying "I can handle it" as if speaking the sentence could create the reality. Others said almost nothing, staring forward like they were trying to avoid becoming a person on record. I stayed quiet and watched, taking in the social atmosphere the way I always did: scanning, measuring, deciding what kind of presence would keep me safe.

Reception at Fort Sill was a controlled storm. We stepped off the bus into cold air that cut through thin layers, and within seconds we were being sorted—told where to stand, how to hold our bags, when to move, when not to move. The voices weren't cruel for sport; they were loud because loudness is an efficient tool for establishing hierarchy quickly. The first lesson was immediate: the Army has no interest in your inner life. It wants your body in the right place, at the right time, doing the right thing without debate. We were directed into large rooms where dozens of recruits stood shoulder to shoulder, waiting for instructions that arrived in bursts. There were moments of boredom so thick it felt like glue, followed by sudden frantic movement when someone decided we were behind schedule. The day alternated between hurry and waiting, and both were forms of control.

When basic training truly began, it began with the stripping away of comfortable habits. Sleep became a ration, not a right. Mornings arrived as an event, not a gentle transition: lights on, voices cutting through darkness, bodies moving before the mind fully caught up. The barracks smelled like bleach and damp fabric and the sharp metallic odor of stress sweat. Beds had to be made not for comfort but for inspection, corners tight enough to pass a hand test, surfaces smooth enough to look like nobody had slept there. The floor had to shine. The toilets had to shine. Dust was treated like a moral failure. We learned to fold clothing into uniform rectangles, to align boots precisely, to make our small spaces look like someone else's idea of perfect. In the beginning, I hated the detail. Later, the detail became a kind of relief because detail gave me something to do besides think.

The drill sergeants were not characters; they were forces. They moved through our days like weather systems, appearing suddenly, changing the temperature of a room with their presence, leaving behind a wake of tension and compliance. They spoke in commands because command language creates simple outcomes. They corrected posture, tone, speed, and even facial expression if expression suggested disrespect. They didn't need to hit anyone to make the body behave. Their authority was enough, their unpredictability enough. In those early weeks, I learned to treat every moment as potentially supervised, every moment as a test. Even when they weren't there, the possibility of them shaped behavior. That's how institutions make themselves permanent: they build an internal observer that continues policing you after the external observer leaves.

Basic training filled in the days with a predictable blend of physical exhaustion and ritual. Physical training happened in the cold morning air, breath fogging, muscles stiff, bodies moving together because the alternative was being singled out. We ran in formation, boots thudding, arms pumping, cadence calling and response echoing across open space. We did pushups and sit-ups until arms trembled and abdomens burned. We learned that pain is not necessarily an emergency in this environment; it is often just information. Chow was fast and loud, trays sliding, metal utensils clattering, brief windows of nutrition treated like privileges to be earned. We learned to eat with speed and silence, to finish before the next command, to accept that hunger would sometimes remain because time mattered more than appetite. The days were long, but the hours were owned.

Weapons training introduced a different kind of seriousness. The first time I held the rifle, it felt both familiar and alien—familiar because the object has an undeniable physical logic, alien because I was being asked to merge with it as if it were an extension of my identity. We learned to clean it with obsessive care, to treat carbon buildup like it was a moral stain. We learned the mechanics—sight alignment, breathing, trigger squeeze—and then we moved to the range where the air carried the sharp smell of gunpowder and the sound of shots cracked like brittle wood. The range was one of the few places where anxiety had a clear target: the paper downrange, the scoring rings, the simple fact that performance would be measured without ambiguity. When I hit well, it felt like competence. When I missed, it felt like humiliation. Either way, the rifle forced focus, and focus became another form of relief.

There were rites every soldier seemed to share, designed less for tactical necessity and more for psychological binding. The gas chamber was one of them. We lined up in protective masks, learned to trust the seal, learned the odd claustrophobia of breathing through a filter, and then stepped into a space filled with chemical bite. Even knowing it was controlled, even knowing it was meant to be endured, the body responded with primal alarm when the mask came off. Eyes burned. The throat tightened. Mucus surged. Coughing shook the ribs. The message was physical and blunt: your body will betray you under certain conditions, and you will still be expected to function. Later, we would laugh about it in the tired way people laugh after surviving a shared misery. In the moment, it felt like swallowing fire.

Field training widened the environment, turning the world into mud, dust, cold wind, and the uncomfortable reality of sleeping outside with limited control over anything. We marched with heavy packs that turned shoulders into bruises and made hips ache. We learned to keep moving even when the feet were already raw. We learned to dig positions, to set security, to rotate through watches that turned the night into a sequence of short sleeps and long vigilance. The sky above Fort Sill looked enormous in the dark, cold stars sharp as pins, and there were moments when the quiet of the field felt almost peaceful until a command snapped through it and reminded us we were never fully off duty. My mind, which in civilian life could dissolve into drift, found fewer places to disappear. The environment demanded presence.

The Army's structure did not heal me in those weeks, and it did not need to. It contained me. It replaced the freedom to wander with the requirement to show up. It took the question "what should I do today?" and replaced it with "do what you're told." In a life that had become too fluid, that containment felt like a temporary kind of stability. Yet even while basic training built discipline, it also built a specific kind of tension: the habit of monitoring myself constantly. I learned to anticipate correction before it arrived, to adjust posture before someone commented, to keep my mouth shut unless spoken to, to move with urgency even when my body was exhausted. That hypervigilant efficiency did not originate here—later years would carve it deeper in harsher ways—but basic training gave it a new uniform and a new justification.

By the time graduation approached, my body had adapted to a rhythm I hadn't believed I could sustain. I was stronger in obvious ways—endurance, coordination, the ability to function on little sleep—and also altered in less obvious ways: the quiet flattening of emotion, the way joking became sharper and more fatalistic, the way compliance started to feel automatic. We stood in formations that looked impressive from a distance and felt like endurance from the inside. We marched past families and flags and speeches, and the moment carried ceremony that suggested transformation. Part of me wanted to accept the narrative—new soldier, new life, new direction—but another part of me stayed cautious. Institutions are good at producing appearances. The deeper question—whether the person inside the uniform had found meaning or only found containment—remained unanswered.

From Fort Sill, I moved to Fort Huachuca for the Human Intelligence Collector training course, and the contrast was immediate. The air was different—drier, brighter, warmer—and the landscape felt less like winter discipline and more like an open, sunlit test. Where basic training had been about physical compliance, this course was about attention, language, ethics, and the uneasy work of extracting information. The classrooms were clinical in their own way: rows of desks, whiteboards, instructors who carried authority without needing to shout. The pace demanded a different kind of endurance, the mental kind. We studied procedures, reporting formats, collection principles, the boundaries that separate legitimate questioning from abuse. We learned that words can be tools and weapons depending on how they are used. We learned that a conversation can be a battlefield without anyone firing a shot.

Role-play became a major part of the course. Scenarios were staged, and trainees practiced interviewing and debriefing with instructors watching, grading tone as much as content. The rooms used for these exercises were designed to be controlled—plain walls, minimal distractions —because the focus was supposed to be on the interaction. In those exercises, I discovered something about myself that was both useful and unsettling: I could become very calm when a situation had rules. I could ask questions with a steady voice. I could maintain a neutral expression. I could take notes and track details while the person across from me tried to manipulate or evade. That calm looked like professionalism. It was also a kind of dissociation, a compartment I could step into where emotion was muted. Later experiences would deepen that skill and make it more costly, but here it was rewarded. The course praised composure. It praised control.

The training also introduced the complicated truth that information is rarely pure. People lie for survival. People lie for advantage. People lie because they don't trust you. People tell partial truths to see what you already know. Instructors taught us to listen not only to words but to patterns: inconsistencies, timing, hesitation, overconfidence.

We practiced writing reports that had to be accurate, measured, and stripped of drama, because the institution doesn't want your feelings; it wants usable facts. That discipline appealed to the part of me that liked systems, liked clear formats, liked problems with solutions. Yet there was always an undercurrent of discomfort. This job required stepping into other people's stories and asking them to open doors they might want to keep closed. Even in training scenarios, that reality could be felt. A conversation can be invasive without being violent. That truth sat quietly in my chest.

Life at Fort Huachuca had its own atmosphere outside the classroom. The days were structured, but not as brutally as basic training. There was more personal time, more opportunity to drift, and with that opportunity came old habits trying to reassert themselves. Some evenings were spent studying in a dull, determined way, the mind holding on to details because failure had consequences. Other evenings were spent letting off steam in the limited ways available—small social gatherings, jokes that ran darker than they needed to, the constant sense that everyone was both young and trying to be taken seriously. The heat pressed down in the afternoons. Dust collected in corners. The sky at night looked different than it had at Fort Sill—wider, warmer, less harsh—and sometimes I would stand outside and feel the odd mix of pride and uncertainty that comes when you're becoming something official without fully believing in your own stability.

During the course, I made a mistake that followed me into paperwork, and paperwork is how the Army turns a mistake into a lesson you can't forget. A relationship formed with another trainee, the kind that grows in pressured environments where people are far from home, where loneliness is common, where attention feels like relief. The relationship was not graphic, not romantic in a clean, healthy way—more a collision of need and proximity, a brief sense of being wanted inside a world that is otherwise indifferent. The complication was her status. She was married, and she spoke as if that marriage was already ending, as if the paperwork was just a delay. I let myself believe the story because believing it kept the moment simple. Believing it allowed me to pretend I wasn't stepping into a moral trap.

The truth arrived the way truth often arrives in institutions: through discovery, not confession. The cadre found out. The tone shifted immediately from instruction to discipline. I was called in, questioned, and placed under a kind of scrutiny that made my skin feel tight. The Army does not care about the emotional complexity of a situation like that. It cares about rules. It cares about what can be documented. I received an Article 15 and the consequences were blunt: loss of rank, loss of pay, extra duty. The punishment wasn't only financial or administrative; it was social. It marked me. It changed how certain leaders looked at me. It changed the way I looked at myself. The strangest part was the imbalance in consequence. The story didn't land evenly. The system's weight fell harder on me than on her, and that asymmetry lodged in my mind like grit—an early lesson that rules don't always apply with equal force.

Extra duty was its own kind of humiliation because it turned time into penance. While others rested, I cleaned. While others had personal hours, I performed tasks designed to remind me that I had stepped out of line. The labor itself wasn't the worst part. The worst part was the way the punishment reinforced an older fear: that being seen can be dangerous, that intimacy can become evidence, that a private moment can be converted into a public verdict. I carried shame through those days in a controlled way, keeping my face neutral, doing the work, avoiding any display that could be interpreted as attitude. The Army didn't need to break me. It only needed to correct me. The correction worked. It made me more cautious. It also made me harder in small ways, less trusting, less willing to take people's stories at face value.

Despite the disciplinary hit, I finished the course and moved into the next phase of Army life: assignment to a unit and the slow pivot toward deployment. Unit life had a different texture than training. Training environments are built to reshape individuals. Units are built to perform missions, which means they tolerate imperfection as long as performance is maintained. Days became a cycle of maintenance, briefings, equipment layouts, physical training, and endless small tasks that exist because large organizations must keep moving to justify themselves. The social environment shifted too. In a unit, reputations matter. The story of what happened at training can follow you even when nobody speaks it out loud. I could feel people measuring me, not with hostility but with that quiet evaluative glance soldiers use when deciding whether someone is reliable. I responded the way I always responded: by becoming efficient, by keeping my mouth shut, by doing the work.

As the unit prepared to deploy, training intensified and became more mission-shaped. Gear was issued and reissued. Equipment was inspected, loaded, unloaded, inspected again. Vehicles became objects of obsession, maintained with the seriousness of lifelines. Briefings multiplied. Threat awareness entered the language—how to look at roads, how to look at crowds, how to look at a horizon. Even before we left the country, the mind began adapting to the idea that danger would become ordinary. That adaptation did not create the deeper injuries that would come later; it was preparation, a tightening of focus. Yet preparation has a cost. It teaches you to scan constantly. It teaches you to treat uncertainty as a baseline. It trains the body to stay slightly tense, slightly ready, because readiness is praised and relaxation is treated like negligence.

Pre-deployment training at the National Training Center at Fort Irwin pushed that readiness into a full-body experience. Fort Irwin's environment was unforgiving: vast stretches of desert, heat that pressed down in the day, cold that surprised at night, dust that found its way into everything. The training there was designed to simulate deployment stress without the actual stakes. We wore MILES gear that turned movement into a game of sensors and lasers, yet the exhaustion was real. We moved in convoys that stretched along dirt roads, engines rumbling, radios crackling with constant traffic. We set up positions, tore them down, set them up again, slept in fragments, ate when we could, learned to function with grit in our teeth and a film of dust on our skin that never fully washed off. The desert didn't care about morale. It demanded endurance.

The National Training Center rotation introduced the unit to controlled chaos. Opposing forces harassed, ambushed, probed, forcing constant adaptation. Small mistakes were amplified because the training environment was designed to punish complacency. A vehicle that drifted from its lane could become a tactical failure. A moment of inattention at a checkpoint could become a simulated casualty. We were evaluated not only on our ability to execute tasks but on our ability to recover when the scenario shifted. After action reviews were relentless, dissecting decisions in detail, turning every move into a lesson. The tone was clinical but the effect was intimate; being analyzed that closely makes you feel exposed. Yet exposure was part of the purpose. The Army wanted us accustomed to scrutiny, accustomed to correction, accustomed to the idea that performance could be measured and judged constantly. In the desert, there was no hiding.

At Fort Irwin, nights were their own world. The sky was enormous, stars sharp, and the darkness carried a different kind of silence than any city ever could. That silence was not peaceful. It was the silence of waiting—waiting for radio calls, waiting for movement, waiting for the next scenario to begin. Sleeping was never deep. You learned to doze with one ear open, to wake quickly, to pull boots on fast. The body became a machine in smaller and smaller increments: two hours here, thirty minutes there, a brief collapse against a vehicle tire, a quick meal eaten standing. In those moments, the mind sometimes drifted toward civilian life—toward what I had been trying to escape by joining the Army—and the drift felt like a temptation to soften. I resisted it instinctively, because softness in that environment felt dangerous. The desert didn't just train tactics; it trained posture. It trained hardness.

When the rotation ended, there was no celebratory relief, only a brief exhale before the next stage. We returned to garrison life with dust still embedded in gear, and the routines continued: checklists, inspections, packing lists, medical readiness, final briefs that grew more serious with each repetition. The language around deployment hardened. Conversations among soldiers shifted from hypothetical to practical: what to bring, what to leave, how to handle money, how to handle fear without calling it fear. I watched people around me adopt different masks. Some became louder, as if volume could drown anxiety. Some became quieter, storing emotion in a locked place. I became more controlled, more efficient, more determined to avoid attention for the wrong reasons. The Article 15 had taught me what institutional attention could cost. I didn't want any more lessons like that.

Late in the year, the unit staged in Kuwait, and the world changed temperature and texture in a way my body registered immediately. The air felt heavier, as if heat had substance. Dust carried a particular smell—dry earth, exhaust, sweat baked into fabric—and that smell clung to everything. Kuwait was not the battlefield, not the mission zone, but it was the threshold, a waiting room built on sand. We lived in camps with their own routines: meal lines, briefings, equipment checks, training refreshers, endless waiting punctuated by sudden urgency. The waiting was its own psychological pressure. You could feel the future pressing toward you without being able to touch it. You could feel the anxiety building in the spaces between tasks. The mind had too much time to imagine what was coming, and imagination is rarely kind.

Life in Kuwait created a strange double reality. On one hand, there were mundane rhythms—standing in line for food, cleaning gear, talking with other soldiers about ordinary things as if ordinary things could keep the world normal. On the other hand, every mundane action was shadowed by preparation. Every vehicle check felt like a rehearsal for harm. Every brief seemed to carry an unspoken message: this is the last time you will hear these instructions in a place where the stakes are controlled. The camp's lights at night created islands of visibility surrounded by darkness, and those islands felt both safe and exposed. I would stand outside sometimes, looking at the horizon where nothing moved, and feel my body buzzing with a readiness I couldn't turn off. It wasn't panic. It was tension with a purpose, the kind an institution cultivates because it believes purpose makes tension useful.

In those weeks, I learned a quieter truth about myself: even when I chose the machine on purpose, the machine still reshaped me in ways I didn't fully authorize. The structure I had wanted did arrive—schedules, routines, clear expectations—but structure also came with a cost in softness. It narrowed what emotions were acceptable. It rewarded suppression. It praised endurance even when endurance meant ignoring internal warning signs. Those lessons mattered, yet they still weren't the deepest drivers of my present-day condition. Heavier experiences lay ahead, experiences that would offer clearer, harsher cause and effect. What happened here, in training and staging, was not the storm. It was the tightening of the sky. It was the moment the body learns to brace before the impact.

Kuwait also taught me about anticipation as a physical state. Anticipation isn't an idea; it's a sensation. It lives in the jaw, in the shoulders, in the way sleep becomes shallow because the mind refuses to fully surrender. It lives in the way laughter sounds slightly forced because everyone is trying to prove they're fine. It lives in the way small irritations flare—someone's tone, someone's mistake— because the nervous system is already carrying too much voltage. I watched men snap at each other, then apologize, then snap again, trapped in the loop of stress seeking an outlet. I watched others become oddly serene, as if they had accepted the future by making themselves numb to it. I didn't become serene. I became more controlled. I kept my hands busy. I checked my gear again and again. I treated preparation as prayer, because action felt safer than waiting.

The chapter of my life that began with enlistment and led through Fort Sill, Fort Huachuca, and Fort Irwin was full of reshaping, but the reshaping was still largely mechanical. It created habits—attention, compliance, vigilance—that would later interact with far more intense experiences. It created a posture of readiness that the body would carry forward. Yet at this stage, I was still on the edge of the deeper story. Kuwait was the threshold where the air tasted like dust and the future sounded like engines idling. It was the place where the machine's promise—structure, purpose, belonging—felt both real and insufficient, because beneath it all was the quiet knowledge that structure can prepare you for danger but cannot guarantee what danger will do to you once it arrives.

By the end of that year, the waiting had hardened into inevitability. The camp routines continued, briefings repeated, equipment checked until the motions became automatic. The sky stayed bright and indifferent. The sand stayed everywhere. And inside me, a version of discipline had formed—less idealistic than the recruiters' promises, less naive than my own hopes. It was a discipline built not from inspiration but from repetition, from the daily practice of doing what had to be done even when the mind wanted to run. I stood in that threshold space with my unit and felt myself becoming something narrower and stronger at the same time, like metal heated and shaped. The true heat—the kind that leaves lasting marks—was still ahead. But the shape was already being set.

# CHAPTER 11

# *Dust and Silence*

A red light holds me in place on a four-lane road that looks harmless enough to forget the way my body behaves in it. The day is warm, and the air inside the car carries that trapped, sun-baked smell of upholstery and faint plastic. Ahead, a garbage truck eases out of a side street and lumbers into the lane, hydraulics whining, diesel breath hanging low. When it accelerates, the wind from its wake pushes a sour, rotting stench into my open window—hot refuse, wet cardboard, something sweet gone wrong—and my stomach rolls before my brain can tell me I'm safe. The smell isn't merely unpleasant. It has a shape. It climbs the back of my throat, presses behind my eyes, and starts rearranging the room inside my head as if it has permission.

The light stays red. My fingers tighten on the steering wheel without my approval. The garbage truck's exhaust hangs in the air like a veil, and a small curl of smoke rises somewhere farther up the road where a man is burning yard debris in a metal drum behind a chain-link fence. It's just smoke. It's just a neighborhood doing what neighborhoods do. But my body doesn't live in the logic of "just." My body lives in association. The smell of heat and rot and burning takes the present and folds it until it fits inside another place, another air, another year. My jaw sets the way it used to set when I was trying to look calm in a situation that had no reason to be calm. The sound of the truck's hydraulics becomes the grind of armored doors. The wind becomes dust moving across flat land. And the simple fact of being stopped—being unable to move forward even though I want to—becomes something older and sharper than traffic.

I don't close the window right away. Part of me tries to out-stare the reaction, like I can win by refusing to flinch. The smell keeps coming, and the inside of my chest tightens around it, a clamp I recognize as preparation. My mind starts doing the thing it does when it can't tolerate uncertainty: scanning for threat even when the threat is imaginary. The light is still red. The garbage truck is still there. My car is still a car. But my nervous system doesn't care about labels. It cares about the old equation: heat + rot + smoke = danger, heat + rot + smoke = the place where you learned that the world can kill you quietly, without announcement, while you're doing something ordinary.

When the light turns green and the cars begin to move, the present doesn't fully return. It only loosens its grip. The road remains in front of me, but the other road— the one etched into muscle memory—has already opened. The smell becomes a corridor, and I step into it without moving. The garbage truck fades into a line of armored vehicles. The fence line becomes a wall line. The small burn barrel becomes a horizon filled with smoke that never seemed to end. And the year begins again, not as a calendar fact, but as a lived environment: the year we crossed over, the year the air itself felt contaminated, the year I learned that time can be measured in routes cleared and routes not cleared, in days survived and nights spent writing down what happened so it would count as real.

We crossed into Iraq at the start of that year, and the first thing that registered wasn't ideology or mission language. It was sensory. The light looked harsher, as if the sun had fewer filters here. The air felt thicker and drier at the same time, a contradiction that made breathing feel like work even before anything happened. Dust wasn't a nuisance; it was a constant presence, fine enough to get into pores, into seams, into every piece of gear no matter how carefully you sealed it. The smell of burning—trash, fuel, something organic—sat in the background like a permanent low note. Even when you couldn't see smoke, you could taste the idea of smoke. It coated the back of the throat. It lived in the tongue. It turned water into something you drank for function rather than relief.

We lived on a base that was both real and unreal: real because it had walls and barriers and routines, unreal because it was not designed for comfort, only for staging. The base had its own noises—generators, radios, vehicles starting and stopping, distant booms you learned not to react to too dramatically. The ground was hard, the buildings functional, the spaces crowded with men trying to pretend their minds were ordinary. It didn't take long to understand that the war wasn't a continuous firefight the way movies sell it. It was waiting punctuated by spikes. It was long stretches of routine—maintenance, briefs, meals eaten too fast—followed by moments so sharp they felt like the world had broken open. The spikes trained your body to stay partially braced all the time, because the alternative was being surprised, and surprise is expensive.

My job was Human Intelligence, and that meant the war touched me in two directions at once. On one side, I was part of convoys, missions, movement through hostile space—armored vehicles, radios, weapons, the physical language of survival. On the other side, I was supposed to gather information: talk to people, build sources, conduct questioning, interpret motives, file reports that could steer operations. The work lived in a strange tension. You needed trust in an environment where everyone assumed everyone was lying. You needed patience in an environment designed to punish hesitation. You needed empathy without softness, composure without detachment, and you had to do it while your body was scanning rooftops and doorways for a flash that meant you were about to die.

A typical day began with the kind of routine that looks almost civilized from the outside. Gear laid out. Weapons checked. Radios tested. A brief delivered in a room full of men trying to absorb details while their minds drifted toward fear. Maps with lines drawn, routes discussed, last-minute changes based on whatever intelligence had arrived overnight. "Actionable" became a word with weight. Actionable meant the difference between moving with a plan and moving into an ambush. We would step out into the heat and light, climb into vehicles, settle into positions that were both familiar and never fully comfortable. The seat belts cut into gear. The armor made movement clumsy. Every strap and buckle had a purpose, and every purpose was a reminder of what could happen.

When I rode in the gunner position, the world narrowed into an elevated tunnel of scanning. Up-armored vehicles turned you into a moving target wrapped in steel and glass. In the gunner seat, your job was to be the eyes and the warning system: watch the road for disturbances, watch the shoulders for buried shapes, watch the crowds for the wrong kind of stillness. You learned to look for tiny anomalies—fresh dirt where there shouldn't be fresh dirt, a piece of trash placed too neatly, a wire that didn't belong, a gap in a line of people where a gap didn't make sense. The brain became an engine for pattern recognition, and the cost of missing a pattern was so high that your body treated every pattern as potentially lethal. You could feel your own adrenaline like a second heartbeat.

Convoy life is not heroic in the cinematic sense. It's cramped, dirty, loud, and repetitive. Engines vibrate through bones. The air inside the vehicle carries sweat trapped under armor, metal warmed by sun, the faint chemical smell of equipment. The radio never truly shuts up—call signs, updates, clipped voices trying to stay calm. Outside, the world moves past in frames: walls with faded paint, market areas full of motion, children watching with expressions you can't safely interpret, men standing too still in doorways. You learn to distrust stillness and distrust motion. You learn that anything can be a decoy. You learn that being watched is not always a threat, but you also learn that it can be, and you won't know which until it's too late.

Sometimes the route would stop not because we chose to stop but because the ground decided for us. A suspicious object, a disturbance, a report from another element. The convoy would slow, then halt, vehicles stacked in a line that suddenly felt like a spine exposed to knives. You would hear the radio shift tone—less casual, more precise. EOD would be called. And then you would wait, in place, with the world still moving around you, with civilians watching from behind walls and corners, with your own mind producing images you didn't request. Waiting for EOD is a particular kind of fear because it combines helplessness with awareness. You know that if there's an explosive device, you are already inside its territory. You know that the device might be command-detonated, which means someone could be watching you wait. You know that a secondary device is possible, placed to hit whoever responds. You know all of this, and you still sit there because sitting there is what the situation demands.

The waiting stretches time. Minutes become long enough to have texture. You feel sweat under armor and can't wipe it without exposing skin. You feel the sun pressing down and can't move because movement might mean drifting into the wrong space. You keep scanning, scanning, scanning, because scanning is the only action available. EOD arrives and becomes the center of gravity: men in gear moving with deliberate slowness, robots rolling forward like insects, a controlled approach to an object that could turn everything into smoke. You watch the process and try not to think about how fragile it all is. One mistake, one misread, one hidden secondary, and the story ends. When the device is cleared—when the radio announces the route is good—relief doesn't arrive as peace. It arrives as a temporary loosening in the chest, a permission to breathe that never fully becomes a normal breath.

Then you move again. Movement itself becomes addictive, because motion feels like agency even when it's forced. The convoy surges forward, engines growling, dust rising behind tires, and you re-enter the same scanning posture as if nothing happened. That's one of the strangest aspects of that year: how quickly the body learns to reset. You can be in a state of near-panic, then receive a simple confirmation—cleared—and your nervous system snaps into the next task. There isn't room for processing. Processing is for later. Later often doesn't come. So the unprocessed stacks up, and you carry it in your shoulders, in your jaw, in the way you wake up too quickly at night even when the base is quiet.

The base itself was not clean. None of it was clean. Burn pits were a constant presence—trash, waste, materials you didn't want to think too hard about—set on fire because disposal is a logistical problem and fire is a crude solution. The smoke didn't behave like normal smoke. It had density. It had a greasy, chemical weight that clung to clothes and hair and the inside of the mouth. You would be eating a meal and smell it. You would be trying to sleep and smell it. You would be standing in formation for a brief and smell it. The smoke made the air feel inhabited by something hostile that wasn't an enemy fighter with a weapon, something more indifferent and persistent. You didn't need to be told it wasn't good for you. Your body already knew by the way your throat felt at the end of a day, by the way your lungs burned after a run, by the way the taste never fully washed out.

Outside the wire, the environment was worse in ways that were hard to communicate without sounding exaggerated. Streets filled with raw sewage were not a metaphor. They were real, knee-deep in places, moving slowly as if the city itself was leaking. The smell hit first—ammonia and rot and human waste warmed by sun. Then you saw it: brown water holding debris, sometimes still, sometimes moving, sometimes churning where a vehicle had passed through and stirred it. You would step around it when possible, step through it when not, because missions don't pause for hygiene. The boots that carried you back to vehicles carried that contamination with them. The smell followed. The idea of "clean" became a memory rather than a reality. Your skin itched. Your mind tried not to imagine what was in the water. Your body moved anyway, because disgust is not an excuse the mission accepts.

The movement from vehicle to foot was its own transition, and it always carried a spike of vulnerability. In the convoy, you had armor and distance. On foot, you had your own body and the thin promise that someone else was watching your angles. Source operations were often like that: arrive in a vehicle with a show of force, then become suddenly quiet and human. You'd dismount, weapons at the ready, scanning doorways and windows, and then the tone would shift because the goal was not simply to intimidate. The goal was to talk. To persuade. To gather. The buildings were often cramped, dim inside compared to the brutal sunlight outside, with stairwells that smelled like damp concrete and cooking oil and too many bodies living too close together. You would walk into a room and feel eyes on you—curiosity, resentment, fear—and you would have to keep your posture controlled, because posture communicates more than words in a place like that.

Sometimes the absurdity of the job became clear in the most immediate way: protecting someone you knew was the enemy because your source was in the same building. That's not a moral puzzle you solve with philosophy in the moment. It's a tactical reality you manage while your heart is beating too fast. You can't set off a firefight inside a building where you're trying to extract information. You can't spook a source who might disappear forever if they believe you can't control your own side. You can't ignore the presence of hostile individuals either, because ignoring them invites ambush. So you become a strange kind of guardian: holding the perimeter of a conversation while standing a few feet away from men you would fight under other circumstances, men whose expressions you read too carefully because the wrong twitch might mean a weapon is coming out.

There were missions where it was just me and an interpreter on foot, moving through streets that felt too narrow, too exposed, too alive with possible threats. The supporting unit would say they had us covered from afar, meaning eyes on rooftops, overwatch somewhere distant, a radio promise that help would arrive if needed. That promise was both comfort and insult. Comfort because any support is better than none. Insult because the distance between "we got you" and "we can physically stop a man with a weapon from stepping around a corner" is enormous. Walking with only an interpreter means every sound is amplified—the scrape of your boots, the echo in an alley, the sudden shout in a language you don't understand until it's interpreted. It means your awareness is split: one part scanning for physical danger, one part trying to read the interpreter's face for cues, one part trying to maintain a calm that doesn't invite panic in the people watching you.

The interpreter was a bridge and a vulnerability at the same time. You had to trust them, because without them your words were blunt instruments. At the same time, you knew trust in that environment was complicated. Everyone had pressures. Everyone had loyalties. Everyone had survival strategies. So you learned to watch subtle things: timing, hesitation, the way a phrase was delivered. You learned to speak in short, controlled sentences because long sentences create opportunities for distortion. You learned to keep your tone neutral even when you wanted to sound warm, because warmth can be read as weakness. You learned, in other words, to make yourself smaller emotionally while still performing engagement, and that practice—emotional contraction while staying outwardly functional—is one of the habits that followed me out of that year more clearly than I wanted to admit.

Combat missions during the day were often a blend of routine and chaos. You'd roll out with a plan, and the plan would meet reality. Sometimes it was quiet enough that the silence felt suspicious. Sometimes you'd take small arms fire —pops that sounded almost like fireworks until you recognized the crack and the way it made your body flinch. In a firefight, time behaves differently. The mind narrows. The world reduces to angles, cover, return fire, communication. You hear your own breathing louder than you should. You hear the radio and have to force your attention to it because the radio is how the unit stays coherent. You see dust kick up on walls, see flashes in windows, see movement you can't fully interpret. You make decisions that feel automatic in the moment and later you realize how thin the margin was between automatic and fatal.

Some firefights ended fast. A burst, a response, the enemy breaking contact. Those were almost worse in a way because they didn't give closure. They left you vibrating, adrenaline with nowhere to go, scanning the same alley after the sound stopped because silence can hide the next move. Other engagements were longer, more complex, with multiple elements moving, calls going out, coordination with other units shifting based on what you were seeing in real time. "Immediately actionable intelligence" sounds clean in a report. In reality, it can mean standing in the middle of a street while rounds snap nearby and someone is shouting into a radio about a vehicle, a building, a person who needs to be stopped now. It can mean making a quick judgment about credibility while knowing a wrong judgment could send men into an ambush or let a threat slip away.

There were times when the aftermath of violence was the mission itself. Local police trucks with dead bodies piled in the back for transport weren't rare in the way a civilian mind wants to believe. You'd see the truck, metal sides stained, the air around it heavy with a smell you never fully forget. The bodies were treated with a rough practicality because the system around them was overwhelmed, because dignity requires resources and time, and those were always short. My role, at times, included documenting: photographing the dead for identification so someone could match names to faces, so the event could become official in whatever bureaucratic way existed there. Taking those photographs did something quiet and permanent. You are looking at a human face emptied of expression, and you are being told to frame it, focus it, capture it clearly. You're not allowed to look away. You're not allowed to treat it as unseeable. You're forced to make it into data. That conversion—human to evidence—reshaped the way my mind stored images.

Interrogations sometimes happened on location because time mattered more than comfort. Capture a person, exploit the shock, get information before it hardens into rehearsed denial. That is a reality of the job, and some of the details around how we operated cannot be fully described because parts of the work were classified. The classification wasn't always about drama; sometimes it was simply about methods, sources, and the delicate facts that could put other people at risk if written too plainly. But the feeling of it can be described: sitting in a room that is not secure in any comforting sense, knowing danger is still nearby, hearing noises outside that could be innocuous or could be the beginning of an attack, and still pressing questions because the mission demands it. The suspect's eyes would be wide, breathing fast, sweat on their face, and the air in the room would carry the smell of fear mixed with dust and old concrete. Your own fear has to be folded and put away. You can't be seen as frightened. Fear reads as weakness. Weakness invites manipulation.

After those operations, the day didn't end. It shifted. Evening would arrive and the base lights would flicker on and the generator hum would fill the background, and I'd move into the second half of my job: writing. Reports had to be filed. Details had to be captured while fresh—names, descriptions, locations, statements, the subtle impressions that might matter later. Writing was not creative. It was precise and stripped. You learn to write in a way that makes emotion invisible. The report format becomes a kind of armor. You can describe violence without sounding shaken. You can describe a dead body without letting grief leak into the sentence. You can describe fear without using the word fear. Sometimes I would write through the evening and into the night, fingers moving, eyes gritty, head aching from dehydration and tension, because the paper trail is how the institution decides something happened. If it isn't written, it didn't exist in the system's memory, and I learned early that invisible events can eat you from the inside.

That rhythm—mission by day, reports by night— created a life with almost no genuine downtime. Sleep came in fragments. Sometimes you'd lie down and the body would refuse to shut off, still scanning, still replaying images, still braced for impact. Sometimes exhaustion would win and you'd fall into a heavy, dreamless block that felt like drowning. Waking up was rarely gentle. You'd snap awake to a loud sound, a distant boom, a shouted voice, and for a moment you wouldn't know if you were in a safe place or a kill zone. The nervous system doesn't differentiate well when it has been trained for threat. It simply reacts. That reaction, over months, becomes a baseline, and a baseline reaction is hard to unwind later no matter how safe the room becomes.

We ran hundreds of combat missions away from the base that year, and the number matters less than what it implies: repetition under threat until the body treats threat as routine. On mission one, your mind tries to narrate everything. On mission fifty, your mind starts compressing because narrating would be too costly. On mission two hundred, you might not even realize you're holding your breath until someone says your name. Repetition builds competence, but it also builds grooves. Those grooves include practical skills—scanning, moving, communicating —but they also include psychological habits: expecting betrayal, expecting sudden noise, expecting death to be nearby even when you can't see it. Those habits didn't originate in that year entirely. They were shaped by earlier experiences and later ones would deepen them. But this was the year they became constant, the year the habit had enough repetition to become muscle memory.

The IED came in the part of the year when my body already felt worn down in small ways—sleep debt, dehydration, the chronic tension of living in armor. We were in an up-armored vehicle, and I was in the gunner position, eyes forward, scanning as usual. There are moments like that where your mind is both focused and drifting, not because you're careless but because sustained vigilance has limits.

You can't stay at peak intensity for hours without something in you dulling to survive the strain. The road looked like a road. The shoulders looked like shoulders. The world looked almost normal in the way war sometimes tricks you into believing it has rules.

Then the ground broke.

The blast was not a sound first. It was force. A sudden, violent shove from below that turned the vehicle into a kicked object rather than a controlled machine. The pressure wave hit my lower back right below where the body armor stopped, a cruelly precise line where protection ended and vulnerability began. The seat and the frame transmitted the shock through my spine. My body launched forward, not in a dramatic arc but in an involuntary slam, and my head smashed into the buttstock of the mounted weapon hard enough that the world went white at the edges. For a fraction of time that felt both instant and endless, I wasn't in my body. I blacked out momentarily—not a long unconsciousness, but a flicker where continuity snapped.

When my awareness returned, it came back in fragments. Black smoke. The smell of explosive residue mixing with dust. The sound of men shouting inside the vehicle, voices sharp with panic and urgency. Someone was screaming my name, asking if I was okay, asking if I could hear them. The radio was alive with overlapping calls. The vehicle's engine noise had changed, strained, as if the machine itself was trying to decide whether it still worked. My vision was tunneled for a moment, and my hands were gripping something without me remembering when they grabbed it. That's the part civilians don't fully understand about a blast: you can't rely on your own narrative. Your body acts. Your mind tries to catch up. The order of events is not clean.

In the seconds after, training takes over because training is what you have. You scan for secondary threats because secondary threats exist. You look for fire. You look for movement. You try to re-establish communication. You try to keep the unit coherent because coherence is survival. Somewhere in that scramble, the pain still wasn't the center. That is part of the cruelty of the body in shock. The adrenaline floods so hard that it covers sensation like a blanket. You can be injured and not know it yet. You can be damaged and still functioning. In that moment, I felt more confusion than pain, more urgency than awareness. I was aware of my heart punching against my ribs, aware of the taste of dust, aware of the way my mouth had gone dry. I was aware of other people's fear in their voices. Pain, the real pain, waited.

We moved, because movement is what you do after an attack if you can move. You don't sit and admire the crater. You don't stay still and become the target for the next trigger. The convoy adjusted, secured, pushed through, because stopping is how you become a stationary problem. Later, the details of what exactly happened around the vehicle became part of briefings and reports, part of the institutional memory. But in my body, the memory was simpler: the punch from below, the slam forward, the blackout, the smoke, the voices asking if I was alive. That sequence became a loop my brain could replay without permission, especially in quiet moments much later, when nothing around me resembled a road in Iraq and my nervous system still acted as if it did.

The pain arrived later, delayed like a bill that doesn't show up until you've already spent what you had. At first it was stiffness, a deep ache in the lower back that I tried to treat as normal wear. Everyone hurt. Everyone had aches. You didn't want to be the man who complained. You didn't want to be the component that slowed the machine. So I kept moving, kept lifting gear, kept climbing into vehicles, kept doing the job. But the ache grew teeth. It sharpened when I sat too long, when I stood too long, when I tried to sleep. It began to shape how I moved before I admitted it was shaping me. That's one of the ways injury becomes permanent: not in a single dramatic moment, but in the way the body starts making accommodations that become habits.

There were other violent moments that year that were not "my" injury but still became part of what I carried. Seeing fellow soldiers bleeding after an RPG strike is not the kind of scene the mind files neatly. The body's response to blood is primal—shock, nausea, urgency—and the professional response is immediate action: tourniquets, pressure, calls for medevac, security maintained even while someone is dying. The worst part is the helplessness that lives inside the task. You can do everything right and still watch a man fade. You can press your hands to a wound and feel warmth and life and then feel the warmth change as the body loses the fight. You can hear someone's voice go thin. You can watch eyes look past you. Those moments create a particular kind of silence inside a person, a silence that isn't peaceful. It's the silence of knowing the world can take someone away in seconds and the only witness is you and whoever else was close enough to see it.

In between the spikes, the work kept demanding that I be human in the middle of inhuman context. Meeting people who smiled at you because they needed you. Meeting people who hated you and still needed something from you. Sitting in rooms with men whose hands were clean and whose eyes were not. Conducting source operations where you had to maintain the appearance of control while knowing the building you were in could be surrounded by hostile forces you couldn't see. Protecting someone you knew was aligned against you because the source you needed was under the same roof. That moral complexity didn't feel like a philosophy seminar. It felt like grit in the teeth. It felt like holding two truths at once and being punished by both.

Classified work added another layer of isolation because you couldn't always explain what you were doing even to people in your own unit. You could say "we went out." You could say "we talked to someone." You could say "we got information." But the details—how, why, who— were often things you held in your own head and then transferred into controlled reporting channels. That secrecy is functional, but it also creates a private compartment where stress accumulates. When you can't fully speak about what you're carrying, you carry it alone. Even when you are surrounded by men going through similar danger, you can still feel alone because your particular slice of the danger is sealed behind classification.

By the end of that year, the cumulative effect was not a single dramatic breakdown. It was more like erosion. The constant scanning. The constant readiness. The smoke in the air. The filth in the streets. The bodies turned into evidence. The fear folded and stored and never fully released. The back pain that grew from a dull ache into a persistent presence. The sleep that came in fragments and never felt restorative.

The shift in how I related to ordinary life—how quickly my body tightened at a sound, how easily my mind returned to routes and corners and rooftops. This is the period that most directly shaped my present state, not because it created every symptom alone, but because it trained my nervous system in a language it still speaks fluently: the language of threat as normal.

We finished the deployment because finishing was the only available outcome besides not finishing. The calendar moved whether we felt it moving or not. The missions kept coming until they didn't. The reports kept stacking until someone else's shift took over. The dust kept coating everything until the idea of being clean became almost imaginary. And inside me, something had changed that I didn't have a name for then. I didn't call it anything. I didn't frame it as injury. I simply lived inside it and performed competence because competence was required. The person I would become later—the person living in a world where a garbage truck smell can pull a year out of storage and drop it on the kitchen counter—that person was being built here, mission by mission, route by route, image by image.

The year ended with me still in my body and not entirely inside it. The back pain was no longer hypothetical. It was real enough to shape posture, real enough to influence sleep, real enough to remind me that the blast had left a mark even if the mark wasn't visible from the outside. The mental pressure was harder to name, but it was there in the way quiet felt suspicious, in the way laughter sometimes sounded far away, in the way I could be surrounded by other soldiers and still feel as if I was operating behind glass. The machine had taken what it needed from me and kept moving. I kept moving with it, because that's what you do when movement is the only way to survive the day.

And even as the year closed, even as the routines began shifting toward the idea of leaving, the environment didn't soften to offer closure. The air stayed hot. The smoke stayed present. The streets stayed contaminated. The danger stayed possible. Closure is a luxury war doesn't provide on schedule. All it gives you is the next task, the next route, the next room, the next report written under harsh light while your body tries to pretend it isn't trembling from exhaustion. That was the year. That was the language my nervous system learned. And the lesson it kept, long after everything else changed, was simple and brutal: ordinary can become lethal without warning, and the body never fully forgets the difference between a green light and a cleared route.

# CHAPTER 12

# *The Long Debrief*

The eye chart is supposed to be simple. Black letters on a white wall. A clean test with clean outcomes. But when the technician slides the occluder into my hand and tells me to cover my left eye, the letters don't stay put. They split. Not dramatically—no surreal kaleidoscope—but enough to make the world feel untrustworthy in a way I can't explain to someone who has never had to negotiate with their own vision. The big letter at the top has a faint twin, offset like a bad print, and the smaller lines below it shimmer into soft duplicates, as if the wall itself is vibrating. The room is quiet except for the soft whir of an air vent and the flip of paper in a folder. I blink, hard, the way people do when they want their body to behave out of respect for the situation. The letters remain doubled. I try to focus harder, as if focus is a lever I can pull. The harder I try, the more my right eye seems to argue back.

The technician asks, gentle, "Better… or worse?" and my mouth opens with no clean answer. *Better* and *worse* are words that assume a stable baseline, a world where the only variable is the lens. What I'm looking at isn't only a test; it's a reminder. A reminder that some damage doesn't announce itself with blood or a cast. Some damage is invisible and constant, a private distortion layered over everything else. The doubled letters pull a chain of associations so fast my chest tightens before I can name why.

My brain goes to the desert. Then it goes to fluorescent hallways. Then it goes to a small accidental impact—something absurdly minor in isolation—that changed the way light behaves in my right eye permanently. The technician keeps waiting for my answer. I swallow and force myself to pick a letter, to perform the test like a normal person, even while the act of choosing feels like lying.

I hear myself say a letter anyway, and the sound of my own voice—controlled, polite, trying not to betray frustration—feels like a skill I learned somewhere else. I keep my tone even. I keep my breathing quiet. I do not let my face show what my mind is doing, which is stepping backward through time like a hand sliding along a scar. The letters on the wall stop being letters. They become the beginning of a different sequence: coming home from Iraq and being expected to reset, pushing through training with a back that didn't feel right, volunteering for a procedure that promised clarity, and then being moved into a unit designed for soldiers whose bodies had stopped meeting the machine's needs. The eye chart stays on the wall. The room stays clean. But the past opens anyway, and it opens at the moment when "home" was supposed to mean relief and instead became another theater where I had to pretend I was fine.

When we returned to Fort Hood, the first thing that hit wasn't joy. It was the shock of normal shapes. Parking lots. Curbs. Trees that didn't look scorched. Buildings with clean lines and predictable entrances. People walking without scanning rooftops. The world looked like the same country I had left, but it didn't feel like the same reality. I had expected the homecoming to be an emotional event— tears, gratitude, some kind of internal release—and what I got instead was numbness wrapped in routine. The Army did not bring us back and then ask how we were. It brought us back and processed us, the way a system processes anything returning from stress: checklists, stations, medical screens, briefings, signatures, gear turn-in, and the quiet message underneath it all—*thank you, now get back in line.*

Post-deployment processing has its own atmosphere, and the atmosphere is strangely sterile for what it is. There are rooms where you sit in rows and listen to instructions delivered in that neutral tone institutions use when they don't want to be responsible for emotion. There are forms you initial to prove you were present for information you can barely absorb. There are medical questionnaires with yes/no boxes that cannot hold the truth of what a year did to a nervous system. There are moments where someone asks if you have any concerns, and the room is full of men who have been trained to treat concern as weakness, so the answers come out minimal. Everyone is tired. Everyone is hungry. Everyone wants to go home. The system gives you an orderly corridor to walk through, and if you make it to the end of the corridor, you are "home," as if the word is a stamp.

I moved through that corridor with the same controlled efficiency I had used overseas. I stood where I was told. I answered what was asked. I signed where the line indicated. I turned in equipment that still smelled like dust and oil and sweat baked into fabric. I watched people around me joke too loudly, laugh too hard, like volume could prove they were okay. I watched others stay silent and stare forward, eyes flat, the way you stare when you're holding too much inside and you don't trust the room to deserve it. My own body behaved as if we were still on mission. Shoulders tight. Jaw set. Eyes scanning. Even when I was standing under safe lights with safe walls around me, I couldn't fully stop monitoring the environment. It felt less like anxiety and more like readiness that had nowhere to go.

In those first weeks back, I told myself the stiffness in my lower back was ordinary. Everyone had aches. Everyone had carried weight and sat in armor and bounced through rough terrain and slept wrong. Pain was part of soldiering. Pain was not special. Pain was not, in my mind, something that justified attention. The blast I'd been in during deployment had been violent, but the body has its own delayed accounting. At first I could move. I could work. I could bend and lift with discomfort that felt like a price, not a problem. Then the discomfort sharpened. It started showing up at night when I tried to sleep. It started showing up in the morning before I had done anything. It started showing up when I sat too long, when I stood too long, when I tried to twist my torso the way you twist without thinking when you're healthy. The pain wasn't a dramatic spike; it was a steady, growing insistence that something inside me had changed.

There is a particular frustration in having an injury that does not perform the way injuries are supposed to perform. You want a clean story: an event, immediate pain, diagnosis, treatment, recovery. What I had instead was a delayed invoice. Weeks after we were home, my lower back began to feel as if a knot had been tied deep inside it, a knot that could not be massaged out. Over time the knot grew teeth. There were days it would ease enough that I'd convince myself I was overreacting, and then there were days it would catch hard and make me freeze mid-motion, breath held, as if any movement might tear something further. I did what soldiers do in that environment. I tried to tough it out. I tried to move carefully. I tried to let pride outweigh pain. Pride is a powerful anesthetic in a culture that rewards endurance.

Post-deployment leave—what people picture as rest—didn't arrive as rest for me. It arrived as dissonance. I would stand in civilian spaces and feel the difference in sensory load as if it were a pressure change. Crowds were too close. Noise felt too loud, not because I had sensitive ears in a delicate way, but because my mind kept trying to map the noise for threat and the threat wasn't there. People would ask how it was "over there," and I would answer in the same clipped, controlled manner I had used in briefs: simple, safe, unprovocative. The truth didn't fit the question. The truth was too big and too specific and too stained. I learned quickly that many people didn't actually want the truth. They wanted a version that made them feel grateful and supportive and then allowed them to return to their own lives without disruption. So I gave them a version that didn't inconvenience anyone.

When leave ended, we returned to the base routines as if the deployment had been a long field exercise and now it was time to train for the next one. Cycling soldiers in and out is one of the strangest rhythms of the Army. People who had become part of the unit's fabric were suddenly gone—transferred, separated, moved to other roles—and new faces arrived carrying fresh energy and fresh ignorance, eyes that hadn't yet learned the cost of the job. The unit became a place where two timelines overlapped: the timeline of men who had been there and carried the memory, and the timeline of men who were about to be shaped by it. I watched new soldiers try on the unit's culture like a uniform that didn't fit yet. I watched old soldiers become instructors without meaning to, teaching small habits—how to pack, how to move, what to watch for—because those habits had been learned the hard way and nobody wanted to watch someone else learn them from scratch.

North Fort Hood training exercises filled the calendar the way they always do in garrison—field time that is meant to keep the unit sharp, to justify readiness, to simulate stress without the real stakes. There were days in dusty training areas where vehicles lined up in rows, radios crackled, and leaders walked up and down making sure everyone looked busy. There were convoy rehearsals that felt like ghosts of the real thing, with routes and contact drills practiced on familiar ground. There were ranges where you fired weapons under controlled conditions and tried not to think about the way controlled noise still made the body flinch. There were mornings where physical training resumed as if nothing had happened, as if the body was a tool that could simply be recalibrated by routine. My lower back pain threaded through all of it like a quiet sabotage. I could still perform, but performance began to come with an internal cost that I kept paying without admitting I was paying it.

Sick call culture is its own ecosystem, and it's not built for subtle injuries. You learn quickly that if you don't look broken, you will be treated as if you are fine. Back pain is especially suspect because it is invisible and common, and common things are easy to dismiss. I would sit in waiting areas under bright lights, surrounded by other soldiers with obvious injuries—wrapped ankles, bruised limbs, coughs that came from whatever virus was making its way through the barracks—and I would feel like a fraud for seeking help for something that couldn't be shown. The language offered was always the same at first: rest, medication, stretches, maybe physical therapy. I did the stretches. I took the medication. I tried to be patient. But the pain kept returning, not as soreness but as something deeper, as if the structure of my spine had been altered in a way that simple solutions couldn't reverse.

Somewhere in that long post-deployment stretch, the Army approved PRK surgery for me. It was supposed to be a practical upgrade, a way to remove the need for glasses and make me more effective, more deployable, more streamlined for the work I was expected to do. Glasses in a combat environment are not just an inconvenience; they are a vulnerability. They fog, they get knocked, they break, they complicate protective gear. PRK was presented as a solution with a clean promise—clear vision without the extra object on your face—and I accepted the promise because I needed to believe some part of the system could still improve me. There was also something psychologically seductive about it. A procedure approved by the Army felt like the machine investing in me again, choosing to repair rather than shelve.

The day of the procedure had a clinical calm that didn't match the intimacy of what was happening. Eyes are personal in a way most body parts are not. Your eyes are how you confirm reality. Handing them over to a process, lying back while bright lights and measured voices took control, required a kind of surrender that felt both ordinary and terrifying. The surgery itself was fast in the way modern medicine can be fast, but recovery was not. Recovery felt like living inside rawness. Light became aggressive. Wind felt like an attack. The world was still the world, but my ability to access it smoothly was compromised, and that compromise made me feel exposed. I sat through days where my eyes burned and watered and my vision shifted in small, unpredictable ways, and I told myself it was temporary because temporary pain is tolerable when you believe in the payoff.

During that recovery period, a relationship entered my life—one I did not anticipate and did not introduce to the unit the way people introduce relationships when they feel stable. She worked in an adult entertainment environment, and that fact is easy for outsiders to reduce to a stereotype. The reality was more human and more complicated. She had children. Her life was busy in a way that wasn't romantic, busy with obligations and fatigue and the constant pressure of keeping things moving. The relationship carried a mix of intensity and practicality, the way relationships sometimes do when two people meet while both are in unstable terrain. I will not dress it up as healthier than it was, and I will not strip it down into moral caricature. It was what it was: closeness offered during a period when I was not functioning in a fully integrated way, closeness that felt like relief simply because it made me feel less alone.

Children have their own physics, and one of her kids —still very young—collided with me in a moment that should have been nothing. A head bumped into my right eye while I was still healing, an accident with no malice, no intention, just movement in a small space and a body that didn't have the coordination adults assume. The pain was immediate and sharp in a way that made my stomach drop. I remember pulling back, hand to my face, not wanting to panic in front of a child, not wanting to make the household feel unsafe. In the days that followed, I realized something had changed. My right eye developed a persistent distortion —double vision, ghosting, a faint duplicate image that refused to go away. The world's edges became slightly unreliable, and that unreliability added a strange layer to everything else I was already carrying: pain in my back, tension in my mind, and the constant demand to keep performing like a soldier who could be relied on.

It is hard to explain how psychologically wearing it is to have your perception compromised while you are trying to convince an institution you are still fit. Vision isn't just about seeing; it's about trust. When the image doubles, even slightly, the brain works harder to correct it, to filter it, to choose which line is real. That extra effort becomes fatigue. Fatigue becomes irritability. Irritability becomes more isolation because you don't want to explain why you're suddenly short-tempered about things that seem minor. I began to notice that certain lights at night caused the ghosting to flare, that certain angles made it worse, that reading for long periods gave me a headache that felt like pressure behind the eye. I didn't have the luxury to treat it as an existential crisis. I had tasks. I had training. I had the constant churn of a unit resetting itself for the next deployment cycle.

The Army, in its own indifferent way, kept moving toward the next major readiness event, and that meant we went back to the National Training Center again. NTC the second time carried a different emotional tone than the first. The first rotation, before deployment, felt like the machine tightening the sky. The second one felt like reenactment under a different kind of weight. We returned to the desert, returned to the dust, returned to the long convoys, the simulated chaos, the exhaustion that comes from sleep broken into fragments. The training was designed to be punishing by intention. It forces mistakes out into the open.

It forces friction between units and personalities. It forces you to practice functioning when the environment is hostile to comfort. The desert at Fort Irwin doesn't need to invent misery; it simply offers conditions where misery arrives naturally: heat, cold, wind, grit, and the constant sensation of being coated in a layer you cannot scrub off.

This time, I carried a lower back that had stopped being merely sore. Armor and gear pressed into the wrong places. Sitting in vehicles for long periods made the pain build until it felt like a hot rod laid along my spine. Standing too long made muscles tighten as if they were trying to guard the injured area by turning the whole lower body into a rigid frame. Sleeping on the ground or on thin pads did not restore anything; it only reset the pain into a different shape. I would wake up stiff and angry at my own body, then force myself to move because the training schedule didn't care about my internal argument. When people around me laughed about the discomfort, I laughed too, because that's what you do in a culture where admitting you're failing at endurance is treated as weakness. But inside, the laughter didn't land. It felt like performance layered over panic.

NTC also magnified the effect of the vision problem because everything there demands quick, accurate perception. You're scanning horizons. You're reading hand signals. You're interpreting silhouettes at distance. You're trying to maintain situational awareness in a landscape that offers few landmarks and many mirages. A faint ghost image in the right eye might not seem like much in a clinic. In a training environment that simulates combat, it becomes another small uncertainty, and small uncertainties are heavy when stacked together. I found myself compensating without admitting it—closing one eye briefly to check an image, blinking hard to reset focus, shifting my head angle to find the clearest line. The compensations were subtle, but the fact that I needed them added to a growing internal conclusion I tried not to say out loud: the machine was still demanding readiness, but my body was beginning to refuse the demand.

When we returned to Fort Hood after that rotation, garrison life resumed with its predictable cruelty: paperwork, schedules, formations, the constant pressure to look ready even when you're not. My lower back pain did not fade. It escalated. There were days it felt like a deep internal bruise, and days it felt like a sharp pinch that traveled into my hips and made me move like an old man. I began to live with a low-level calculation running constantly: how far can I walk before it catches, how long can I sit before it flares, how can I climb into a vehicle without triggering that hot spike. The pain started dictating my posture without permission. I would stand with my weight shifted in unnatural ways to protect the injured side. I would avoid certain movements instinctively. Those adaptations kept me functional, but they also fed into a long-term problem: the more you adapt around an injury, the more your body learns a new normal, and the new normal becomes a cage.

Eventually, the injury was taken seriously enough to be diagnosed with clarity. The moment of diagnosis was not a victory; it was a strange relief threaded with anger. Relief because the pain finally had a name attached to it, proof that I wasn't imagining it. Anger because the name arrived late, after months of pushing through, after the injury had already reshaped my movement. The disk was damaged—herniated and torn in a way that explained the sensation of instability, the sudden catches, the deep ache that wouldn't leave. Knowing the structure of the damage did not fix it. It simply made the future clearer, and the future was not comforting. Treatment options were discussed in clinical language that tried to sound optimistic. Profiles were written. Restrictions were put on paper. Paper, in the Army, is how your body becomes official.

This is also the period where I felt the absence of institutional acknowledgment in a way that went beyond ego. The injuries from the blast during deployment had not earned me a Purple Heart. People can argue about medals all day, and I know the arguments: what counts, what doesn't, what the criteria are. For me, the absence mattered less as a symbol of honor and more as a symbol of legitimacy. The blast had happened. The pain had grown out of it. The damage was real. Yet without that particular recognition, the injury felt less anchored in the institution's story. It felt like something that existed in my body but not fully in the Army's memory. When you're dealing with a system, memory matters. Memory affects speed of care, tone of leadership, how quickly people believe you, and whether your suffering is treated as "combat-related" or merely inconvenient.

As the unit continued moving toward the next deployment cycle, I became a problem the machine didn't know how to solve easily. The Army can handle a soldier who is fully functional. It can handle a soldier who is obviously broken. It struggles with the soldier in between—the one who can still show up but is accumulating limitations, the one whose pain is real but not spectacular, the one who is still technically in uniform but increasingly incompatible with the demands of the job. The decision arrived not as a dramatic confrontation but as a slow narrowing of options. I was deemed undeployable. The word carries a blunt weight. It does not mean "take a break." It means "you do not fit the forward-moving mission." In a culture built on readiness, being labeled undeployable is a kind of exile. You are still there, still in formation, still wearing the same uniform, but you are no longer part of what the unit is preparing itself to do.

That is how I ended up transferred to the Warrior Transition Unit at Fort Hood, and the WTU had an atmosphere unlike any other Army environment I had been in. It was quiet in a way that didn't feel peaceful. The halls were full of appointments. The days were measured in medical visits and paperwork rather than training events. The people there were still soldiers, but many of them moved with the careful stiffness of injury, the slow caution of bodies that had been damaged. Some wore braces. Some carried scars. Some had a vacant look in their eyes that wasn't stupidity or laziness—it was the look of someone who had been running on stress for too long and had finally been forced to stop. The WTU felt like a shelf. You were still part of the Army, but you were stored. You were kept in place while the system decided what to do with you.

Being placed on that shelf did something to me that was hard to admit at the time. In the unit, pain could be disguised as toughness. In the WTU, pain became the central fact, and that centrality made it harder to pretend I was normal. I was surrounded by other injured bodies and injured minds, and the environment made me more aware of my own symptoms: the way I woke too quickly, the way my shoulders stayed tense, the way loud sounds still made my heart jump, the way my lower back felt like an anchor even when I was just walking down a hallway. The WTU was supposed to be a place of recovery, but it was also a place of identity loss. Soldiers define themselves by what they can do. WTU life asks you to define yourself by what you cannot do, and that shift is brutal for someone who has been trained to equate value with performance.

WTU routines were a slow grind of bureaucracy and waiting. There were medical evaluations that felt like interrogations because you were constantly asked to prove your pain in words, asked to quantify sensations that don't fit numbers. There were physical therapy sessions where you learned stretches that helped slightly, then stopped helping, then helped again depending on the day, as if the injury had moods. There were profiles that restricted certain activities, but restriction didn't erase the Army's expectations. People still wanted you to be "a good soldier." People still wanted you to show up on time, maintain uniform standards, keep a clean space, complete tasks that could be completed. The machine doesn't fully let you rest even when it has decided you are damaged. It simply changes the kind of work it demands—less mission, more compliance.

In the middle of that strange limbo, the relationship I'd begun continued in a way that felt both grounding and destabilizing. She had her own life pressures, and I had mine, and we met each other in the overlap. Her children, especially the youngest who lived with her, brought a kind of chaotic normality into my days. Children do not care about medals, profiles, or medical boards. They care about snacks and attention and play. There was something both healing and painful about that. Healing because it forced me to exist in a world that wasn't only military. Painful because it highlighted how far my own internal state was from simple. I could smile with them, laugh at small things, and then feel the laughter fade quickly when my back caught or my vision ghosted or my mind snapped into scanning mode for no reason. I was trying to live in two worlds at once: the bureaucratic limbo of the WTU and the human mess of civilian life, and neither world fully fit.

At the same time, the Army was still cycling forward without me. Units trained. Units deployed. New soldiers arrived. Old soldiers left. The forward motion of the institution continued as if my shelf did not exist. That indifference is part of what makes WTU life psychologically corrosive. You can feel yourself becoming irrelevant. You can feel your identity thinning. You can watch the machine you once belonged to move on without looking back, and the only proof you still exist is the next appointment slip, the next form, the next evaluation that determines whether you are repairable or whether you will be released. Release sounds like freedom until you remember that you joined because freedom had once turned into drift. Now, release arrived not as a triumphant separation but as a decision made after months of being measured by limitations.

The medical discharge process is its own long corridor, and corridors are a theme in my life for a reason. In a corridor, you move forward because you can't go sideways. You do what the next step requires because the next step has a signature line and a deadline. There were moments during that corridor where the absurdity hit me: I had gone to war, I had done work that often involved classified elements and responsibilities that weren't easily described, I had watched bodies become evidence and violence become routine, and now my future depended on paperwork moving correctly through offices. This is how the modern world works. It reduces everything to forms. It converts pain into codes. It takes a person and turns them into a case. I moved through the case process with a kind of cold obedience, because cold obedience was easier than rage, and rage would have nowhere to go anyway.

By the time the separation became real, I was exhausted in a way that wasn't just physical. The exhaustion felt structural, as if the years had rearranged my internal wiring and the wiring was now frayed. My back injury wasn't a temporary flare anymore; it was a permanent factor. The ghosting in my right eye wasn't a recovery phase; it was now part of how I saw the world. And the mental shifts from deployment—hypervigilance, difficulty relaxing, the way quiet could feel suspicious—had become habits that no one had named yet. Later, those mental elements would be recognized and categorized in ways that came with official language and disability ratings, but in this period, the reality was simpler and more isolating: I was carrying things that didn't fit into casual conversation, and I was being asked to return to civilian life as if returning was as easy as changing clothes.

The move to Arizona happened quickly after separation, not because I felt ready for a fresh start, but because a job opportunity existed near Fort Huachuca and I needed a frame for my days. A frame is what I have always reached for when my internal world threatens to become too loud. The Army had provided a frame. Losing the Army meant losing the frame, and I didn't trust myself in an unframed life. So I drove west—out of Texas, across long stretches of highway where the landscape slowly changed texture, the sky widening, the air drying. The desert in Arizona is not Iraq, but it carries an echo: open space, bright sun, hard ground. As I crossed into that new environment, I felt both relief and dread. Relief because distance can feel like escape. Dread because I knew, even then, that escape doesn't remove what you carry. It only changes the scenery around it.

Arizona greeted me with heat and light that felt too familiar for comfort. The horizon looked clean, the kind of clean that makes you believe you can start over. I told myself the move was a reset. I told myself the job would stabilize me. I told myself I would heal with time. But my body was already writing its own terms: lower back pain that dictated how I slept and moved, an eye that refused to produce a single clean image, and a nervous system trained for threat that didn't stop simply because the uniform was gone. The machine had released me, and the release did not feel like freedom. It felt like being handed back to myself with damage I hadn't fully inventoried yet, and being expected to build a life anyway.

# CHAPTER 13

## *Wide Sky*

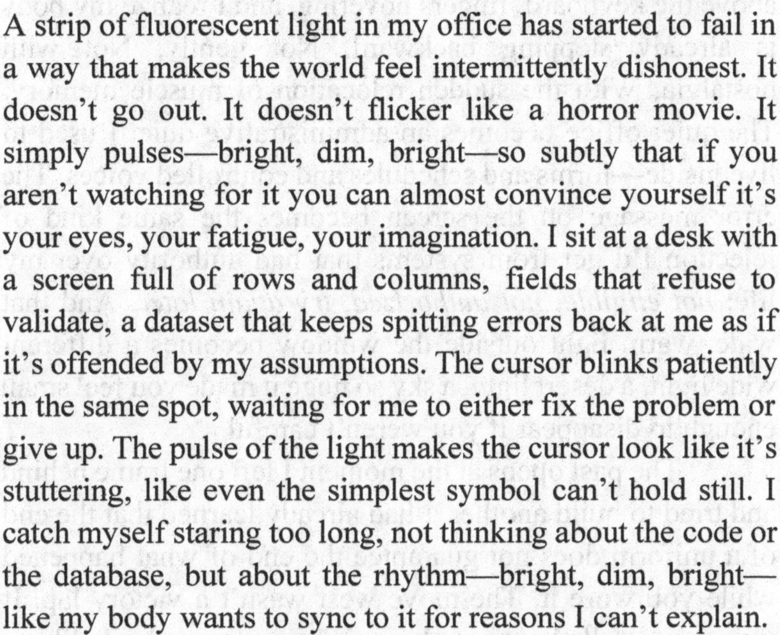

A strip of fluorescent light in my office has started to fail in a way that makes the world feel intermittently dishonest. It doesn't go out. It doesn't flicker like a horror movie. It simply pulses—bright, dim, bright—so subtly that if you aren't watching for it you can almost convince yourself it's your eyes, your fatigue, your imagination. I sit at a desk with a screen full of rows and columns, fields that refuse to validate, a dataset that keeps spitting errors back at me as if it's offended by my assumptions. The cursor blinks patiently in the same spot, waiting for me to either fix the problem or give up. The pulse of the light makes the cursor look like it's stuttering, like even the simplest symbol can't hold still. I catch myself staring too long, not thinking about the code or the database, but about the rhythm—bright, dim, bright— like my body wants to sync to it for reasons I can't explain.

The room is quiet except for the soft fan noise from the computer tower and the occasional click of keys. Outside the window, the late-day light drapes the yard in a color that looks almost theatrical, too warm to be trusted. Nothing is happening. No one is shouting. No radios. No engine rumble. No sense of urgency. And yet my shoulders are up near my ears, my jaw set, my breath shallow. The problem on the screen is solvable. I know it is. I've solved problems like it before. But the feeling inside my chest is not about the problem. It's about being trapped in place with something that refuses to behave, about the way my mind starts scanning for exits when the only thing in front of me is a stubborn line of text.

The fluorescent pulse and the blinking cursor begin to match a different rhythm: structured days, scripted roles, repeating questions that never change. My hands pause above the keyboard, fingers hovering, and I realize my body is already stepping backward. Not gently. Not with nostalgia. With the sudden relocation of muscle memory. The quiet office becomes an administrative quiet I used to live inside—forms and schedules and controlled voices. The error message on the screen becomes the same kind of rejection I'd get from systems that had authority over my life: *not eligible*, *not authorized*, *try again later*. And that wide, warm light outside the window becomes a different wide light, a desert light, a sky so huge it made you feel small enough to disappear if you weren't careful.

The past opens at the moment I left one frame behind and tried to build another. I had already learned that the end of a uniform does not guarantee the end of what happened while you wore it. The move west wasn't a victory lap. It was a controlled retreat. I carried my lower back like a private injury that refused to be private, and I carried the rest of my internal wiring like contraband. I told myself the new landscape would do something the old landscape couldn't. I told myself the space would make room for me. I told myself the distance would break the scent trail of what I didn't want following. Then I crossed state lines, watched the scenery change, and discovered the most dangerous passenger was always sitting in my own seat.

The move to Arizona happened fast enough that it didn't give me time to second-guess it. Packing was efficient

—clothes, papers, the few objects that felt essential—and everything else was treated like clutter, like proof of a life I wanted to shed. The desert intelligence schoolhouse in southern Arizona was a known quantity to me, a place I had passed through earlier in my Army life, a location with a mission and a schedule and an institutional vocabulary that could swallow my days. That mattered more than the geography. I didn't move because I loved the state. I moved because I needed a new routine to replace the one that had been stripped away. The transition out of the Army had left me with too much unstructured time, and unstructured time has never been neutral for me. It becomes a pressure chamber.

The first place I rented was a house on a plot of land so large it felt like an accusation. Five acres is not luxury when you don't know what to do with your own mind. Five acres is distance. Five acres is silence you can't escape. The house sat back from the road, and the road itself felt thin and far away, a line of asphalt that carried other people's lives past mine without invitation. The yard wasn't manicured in the way suburban yards are manicured. It had the rough honesty of desert property—scrub, hard ground, scattered vegetation that looked like it survived out of spite. When the wind moved across it, the sound was dry. When the sun set, the shadows fell long and clean, and the sky opened like a door into a larger darkness.

At first, the space felt like relief. The nearest neighbors were far enough away that I couldn't hear their televisions or their arguments or their footsteps. There were no apartment walls to transmit other people's lives into mine. No shared hallways. No constant incidental contact. I could stand outside at night and hear almost nothing—no traffic hum, no sirens, no city buzz—only insects, wind, and the faint sound of my own breath. The quiet did something to my nervous system that I wanted to interpret as healing. The quiet felt like a promise: *Here, you can stop scanning. Here, the world won't sneak up on you.*

I brought a girlfriend with me from Texas, and that decision was less romantic than it sounds when spoken cleanly. She came from an adult entertainment environment, a world of late nights and money that arrives in strange ways, a world where attention is both currency and threat. She also had children, and children change the temperature of a house in ways adults rarely understand until they live it. The older ones were tied to other households, other schedules, other adults. The youngest lived with her, which meant the house —this big, quiet desert space—was suddenly filled with small-footed motion, random laughter, sudden crying, questions that arrived like thrown objects. The kid would run from room to room, dragging toys, leaving small evidence of life in corners: plastic pieces on the floor, a blanket wadded up on a couch, a cup left half-full somewhere it didn't belong. The chaos was messy, but it was also human. It disrupted the kind of silence that can turn poisonous.

We tried to make a life out of borrowed parts: a rented house, an oversized yard, a new job, the idea that a fresh start could be purchased with relocation. In the first weeks, I could almost believe it. We woke to bright mornings and long horizons. We drove into town for groceries and supplies and came back to a house that felt temporarily ours. I did chores not because I loved them, but because chores gave me something physical to do, something that wasn't thinking. Fixing small things around the property gave me a sense of competence that didn't require anyone to praise me. I could tighten a hinge, replace a part, build a simple structure, and the result would hold. It wouldn't shift like emotions. It wouldn't betray me like people could. It would simply function.

Work pulled me into a different kind of structure. Being an instructor at the Human Intelligence Collector training course wasn't the same as being a student. As a student, I had been anxious and hungry, trying to prove I belonged. As an instructor, I was supposed to be calm and authoritative, a person who could shape other soldiers into something the Army needed. The training course has a public-facing simplicity when it's described on paper: learn interviewing and debriefing; learn the principles of collection; learn reporting; learn ethics; learn to operate inside a system that depends on information. The lived reality is more intimate. It's a schoolhouse where stress lives in the walls because everyone knows that a mistake in this field doesn't just mean a bad grade. It can mean bad intelligence. Bad intelligence can move units into danger. Bad intelligence can get people killed.

The days started early in the way military-adjacent work always does, even when you're technically a civilian or contractor. Briefings. Schedules. The classroom environment with its dry markers and fluorescent lights. PowerPoint slides that reduce complexity into bullet points. Students sitting in rows trying to look engaged while their minds run ahead into what this training might mean downrange. Many of them were young. Some carried the stiffness of men who had already been somewhere dangerous. Some carried an overconfident swagger that looked like armor and was armor. They asked questions that betrayed fear without using the word fear. They laughed at things they didn't find funny because laughter is how people signal they're okay.

As an instructor, I learned to read faces the way I had learned to read streets: quickly, habitually, without mercy. Who was listening. Who was drifting. Who was trying to impress. Who was quietly panicking. I could see the students who wanted to be good at this work for the right reasons—because they believed in protecting others—and I could see the ones who wanted the job because it gave them power over people. I could see who thought interrogation was a fantasy of domination and who understood it as a disciplined, ethically constrained tool that still carries moral weight. Those differences mattered. They mattered because the course didn't just teach skills. It filtered personalities. It rewarded composure. It rewarded control. And control is not always the same thing as character.

Some of the training required realism that bordered on theater. Role-play is common in this field because you can't teach human interaction without practicing human interaction. You can't teach someone to ask questions under pressure without putting them into a pressure simulation. You can't teach someone to hold their posture steady while a person lies to their face without giving them a liar to practice on. That meant we used role-players—people who acted as detainees, sources, hostile witnesses, cooperative informants—and those role-players became a mirror. They reflected the student's temperament back at them. A student who came in thinking this job was about intimidation would reveal themselves quickly when facing a role-player who wouldn't bend. A student who came in thinking this job was about kindness would reveal themselves when the role-player turned manipulative.

I ended up in the role-player seat more often than I expected. It wasn't glamorous. It wasn't a fun break from instruction. It was the part of the job that got under the skin. I would put on a new identity—different name, different background, different posture—and sit in a small room while students came in one after another to practice. Twice a day, sometimes more, I would be "captured" again. Questioned again. Pressed again. Watched again. It was controlled and scripted on paper, but the body doesn't always respect paper. The body responds to tone, to proximity, to the feeling of being cornered. The body remembers rooms.

Some students were clumsy, nervous, apologetic. They asked questions too softly, backed off too soon, tried to be polite to the point of uselessness. With them, the role-play felt like teaching. You could nudge them, guide them, show them the difference between pressure and cruelty. Other students were too eager. Their eyes would sharpen when they walked into the room, like the scenario had given them permission to become someone they wanted to be. They'd lean forward too hard, speak too loudly, try to "break" the detainee like it was a contest. In those moments, I would have to keep my face neutral and play my part, because the exercise had to continue. But inside, something would tighten. Not anger exactly—something colder. A recognition that the line between training and reality is thinner than we like to admit.

The mental toll wasn't only in the interrogations themselves. It was in the repetition. Being placed in that chair again and again made my own nervous system start to buzz in a way I didn't want to name. The controlled environment could still trigger uncontrolled reactions: a pulse in the throat, a sudden heat in the face, a tightening in the chest when a student raised their voice. I had to absorb other people's aggression as if it were harmless because "it's just training." I had to watch their body language and simulate fear, simulate defiance, simulate cooperation, all while keeping my own real reactions hidden. After the sessions, I would walk out into sunlight and feel slightly unreal, like my identity was lagging behind my body. I wasn't back in war. I knew I wasn't. But the role-play was rubbing against old grooves, and old grooves have a way of waking up.

At the same time, my lower back was doing what it had been doing since deployment: refusing to let me forget. The pain didn't always announce itself with a sharp spike. More often it was a constant, heavy ache that made standing in classrooms feel like endurance. Long periods of sitting weren't relief either; sitting compressed the injury in a different way and sent heat down into my hips. Some mornings I would wake up stiff enough that rolling out of bed felt like negotiating with an angry machine. I learned to move carefully. I learned to avoid twisting. I learned to pick things up with a controlled squat instead of bending at the waist. Those accommodations helped me function, but they also made me feel older than I wanted to admit. In a schoolhouse full of young soldiers, being the instructor who moved slightly too stiff became another quiet humiliation.

The relationship at home mirrored that instability. Living with someone isn't only sharing space; it's sharing rhythms, and our rhythms didn't naturally match. She worked odd hours. I worked structured hours. She carried the emotional residue of her own world. I carried mine. The house was big enough that distance could be created without anyone leaving, and we started using that distance as a coping mechanism. We could be in different rooms for hours and call it normal. We could avoid conversations by filling time with noise—television, music, errands—anything that prevented silence from becoming an invitation to talk. When we did talk, the conversations were often about logistics: the kid's needs, the next grocery run, the bills, the maintenance tasks on the property. We were building a life out of function. Function can last a long time. Function can also feel like slow starvation.

The desert property became a character in our lives. In the mornings, light would pour through windows with no softness, illuminating dust in the air like the house was filled with tiny floating ash. In the afternoons, the heat would make the world shimmer beyond the glass. At night, the darkness outside the yard lights was absolute, a blackness so complete it felt like a physical wall. Sometimes the kid would be asleep and she would be out or exhausted, and I would stand outside and look up at the stars and feel a strange kind of vertigo. The sky in that part of the country is not polite. It doesn't hide its size. It doesn't let you pretend the universe is small enough for your problems to matter. That bigness can feel like freedom. It can also feel like erasure.

After the lease ended, we moved into a new house that had been built for me. New construction carries its own emotional trick. Everything is crisp. Everything is clean. Everything smells faintly of paint and new carpet and materials that haven't yet absorbed human history. The walls haven't heard arguments. The floors haven't held footsteps. The rooms feel like blank pages, and blank pages can make a person believe in reinvention. I walked through the new rooms and felt the brief, bright lie of possibility: *This is where you become normal. This is where you settle. This is where the past loses its grip.*

But the past doesn't lose its grip just because the drywall is new. It simply finds new corners.

We arranged furniture. We unpacked. We established routines. The kid found favorite spots on the floor and favorite hiding places in closets. We hosted small gatherings sometimes, the kind that are meant to prove you're living a stable life—meals, laughter, casual talk about weather and work. I could perform stability for a few hours at a time. I could smile and make jokes. I could appear like a man whose life was moving forward. Then the guests would leave, the house would quiet, and the largeness of the rooms would return. A big house is comforting only when it's filled with the right energy. Without that, the big house becomes an amplifier. It takes small loneliness and makes it echo.

Work became the anchor I used to keep myself from floating off. The training course demanded output, demanded schedules, demanded measurable improvement. I leaned into that demand because leaning into demand has always been easier for me than leaning into emotion. I became the instructor who could be relied on. The one who showed up on time. The one who delivered content cleanly. The one who could step into a role-play room and take student aggression without flinching. The machine rewarded that reliability. The machine doesn't care if it's costing you something internally, as long as you keep producing.

Then the world shifted in a way that reminded me how fragile employment is when it's tied to budgets rather than human need. The training course was impacted by large-scale cutbacks—contract positions reduced, numbers trimmed, priorities rearranged by people who would never meet the instructors whose lives were being altered. It didn't feel personal. That's what made it colder. If it had been personal, at least it would have acknowledged my existence as a person. Instead, it was a spreadsheet decision, and spreadsheets can dismantle a life with no emotion.

The shift landed like a delayed punch. Contractors were cut. Only a limited number of civilian positions remained. I was not initially selected for one of those positions. I was placed on a waiting list, a bureaucratic limbo where your future hangs on whether other people accept or decline an offer. Waiting for a decision you cannot influence is its own kind of torture when your nervous system is already trained for threat. The mind starts producing scenarios. The stomach stays tight. Sleep becomes shallow. The house feels less like a home and more like a cost you might not be able to justify. When the phone rings, you flinch. When the phone doesn't ring, you feel the hours dragging past like a slow insult.

I was called back only after others turned down offers. That fact matters, not because I needed to be flattered by the machine, but because it taught me something about my position in the world: I was near the edge. I wasn't chosen because I was indispensable. I was chosen because I was available. Being the last person called is a specific kind of humiliation. It means you were almost excluded from stability. It means your life was nearly restructured by someone else's refusal. I accepted the position immediately, not with gratitude, but with the grim relief of a man who knows what it feels like to have the floor disappear.

The new role came with different responsibilities. The course was always evolving—new lessons learned from downrange, new threats, new doctrinal emphasis—and that evolution created problems that couldn't be solved only with lectures. The course needed systems. It needed a way to track student performance, role-play scenarios, feedback, improvements, adjustments. It needed a way to capture what worked and what didn't so the same mistakes wouldn't be repeated across classes. Over time, my work began shifting toward building the tools that helped that improvement happen. Databases. Software. Structured ways to store and retrieve information about training cycles. If the course was a living organism, I was building part of its nervous system.

There was a satisfaction in that work that had nothing to do with pride and everything to do with control. A database either works or it doesn't. Code either compiles or it doesn't. You can troubleshoot. You can isolate variables. You can test. The logic is harsh but honest. Human beings are not harsh but honest in the same way. Human beings lie, stumble, contradict themselves, change their minds, punish you for being too quiet or too intense, and sometimes leave without providing a reason you can accept. Software didn't do that. Software could be annoying, stubborn, and time-consuming, but it was fair. It didn't abandon you out of boredom. It didn't accuse you of being wrong as a person. It simply returned errors until you corrected them.

The more I leaned into the structured work, the more I noticed what the training environment was doing to my internal state. Days filled with interrogations—real or simulated—create a kind of residue. Even when you're teaching ethics and procedure, you are steeped in confrontation. You are steeped in the language of suspicion. You are steeped in the idea that people hide truth and that your job is to extract it. That mindset can be useful in a warzone. In a domestic life, it becomes corrosive. It makes you read tone too sharply. It makes you search for motives behind ordinary words. It makes relaxation feel like negligence. I found myself bringing that posture home without meaning to. Listening too hard. Watching too closely. Interpreting silence as tension. Interpreting normal mood shifts as warning signs. The house became another place where I was always working, even when I wasn't.

The relationship began to crack not because of one single betrayal, but because of accumulated mismatches and the slow erosion of trust. There was an incident that became the official trigger—she caught me looking at pornography —and the situation was ugly in the way private shame becomes ugly when it's dragged into daylight. I won't pretend it was noble. I won't pretend it was harmless. What matters is the way it played out emotionally: she treated it not as a mistake or a symptom, but as a verdict about my character. There was hypocrisy tangled in it too—her own history, her own choices, the way we both lived with contradictions—and hypocrisy doesn't soften the sting. If anything, it sharpens it because it makes the judgment feel less like morality and more like power.

She left. The departure didn't come with closure that felt satisfying. It came with boxes, with arguments that looped, with the sense of a door closing without ceremony. Watching her leave carried a specific kind of emptiness that I recognized too well: the emptiness of being rejected by someone who had been woven into daily life, someone whose presence had been part of the house's temperature. When she was gone, the rooms didn't simply become quieter. They became hollow. The kid's noise disappeared. The random chaos vanished. The house reverted to a kind of too-clean stillness that made me feel like I was living inside a showroom rather than a home. And in that stillness, the parts of my mind I had been outrunning began to catch up.

I stayed in the job. I stayed in the routine. I kept building systems. I kept teaching. I kept role-playing. I kept adjusting databases and course modules as if improving the training course could also improve me. Workdays were filled with other people's needs and other people's futures. Nights were filled with my own silence. I began to understand something I had not wanted to admit: my ability to function was not the same as my ability to be okay. Functioning can look like health from the outside. Functioning can be a disguise. The more competent I appeared at work, the less anyone would suspect how thin the inside of my life had become.

During that period, I tried to find companionship in ways that weren't always wise. Some attempts were brief and almost forgettable—dates that fizzled, conversations that didn't land, relationships that never fully formed. Others were more intense, driven by the hunger to not be alone in the big house. There is a particular kind of vulnerability that comes after someone leaves. You become susceptible to attention. You become susceptible to anyone who can fill a room with warmth for even a few hours. You can mistake intensity for compatibility. You can mistake closeness for healing. I did some of that. I was not looking for love in the clean, patient sense. I was looking for relief.

Work provided another kind of intensity. I returned to the National Training Center as cadre, but this time I wasn't a trainee bracing for deployment. I was part of the training machine, a person tasked with helping teams practice HUMINT operations under simulated combat conditions. Fort Irwin's desert has a way of scraping away pretense. Dust gets into everything. The heat makes tempers short. The nights drop cold enough to remind you the environment doesn't care about your comfort. The training scenarios are designed to force friction and expose weakness. HUMINT teams were evaluated under pressure— rapidly changing intelligence, role-players acting as locals, controlled chaos meant to resemble what these soldiers might face downrange.

That rotation mattered to me for reasons I didn't advertise. One of my siblings was tied to a unit preparing to deploy, and some of the teams I was helping train would be operating in the same ecosystem as that unit. I understood the chain of cause and effect in a way that felt brutally simple: if these HUMINT teams did their jobs well, they would generate better information; better information could reduce blind movement; reduced blind movement could lower the risk to everyone else, including someone I cared about. I couldn't control the deployment. I couldn't control the enemy. I couldn't control fate. But I could contribute to training that might make the next cycle of war slightly less lethal for the people caught in it.

I worked hard during that rotation. Harder than my back wanted to allow. The pain followed me through the desert the way it always did—heavy and persistent—but the purpose gave me a kind of stubborn energy. I watched teams struggle with source operations, watched them wrestle with language barriers and distrust, watched them make mistakes and then learn, watched them practice protecting sources while navigating a hostile environment full of ambiguous threats. I pushed the lessons I had learned the hard way without making them sound dramatic. I focused on discipline: verify, document, don't overreach, don't become addicted to assumptions, don't treat people like props. I emphasized that the job is never only about extracting information. It's about doing it in a way that doesn't create more enemies than it neutralizes.

At night in the desert, when the training slowed and the camp quieted, I would lie on a thin pad and feel my lower back pulse with heat. The pain had a rhythm. It would build when I moved, ease slightly when I stayed still, then build again because staying still too long also hurts. There's no perfect posture for an injury like that. There's only management. I would stare into the darkness and listen to distant vehicles, distant voices, the wind moving grit across ground, and I would feel the strange collision of purpose and despair. Purpose because I was doing something that felt meaningful. Despair because the meaningful thing did not fix my internal state. Despair because my house back in Arizona was still waiting with its hollow rooms. Despair because even the desert, which once felt like escape, had become familiar in a way that didn't soothe.

When I returned home from that rotation, the big house still felt too large. The quiet still felt too sharp. The job still demanded performance. I had moments of pride when the systems I built worked—when a database improvement reduced errors, when the course ran smoother, when student feedback reflected genuine learning. Those moments were real. They just didn't last. They were sparks in a room full of dry wood. The larger mood kept settling back into me like dust. It coated everything. It dulled things that should have felt bright.

During that time, an older family member became increasingly invested in "fixing" me in a way that had less to do with my happiness and more to do with their own discomfort. Some people cannot tolerate an unmarried man living alone in a big house. They treat solitude like a moral failure. They treat grief like a weakness. They treat depression as stubbornness. Their solution is often simple and insulting: find a woman, join a community, become normal, stop making everyone else nervous. I didn't argue with that family member directly because arguing would have required me to admit what was really happening inside me, and I didn't yet have the language to describe it without sounding like a man begging for understanding.

Instead, I allowed myself to be set up.

She entered my life through an introduction that came preloaded with certainty I didn't share. A well-meaning intermediary framed it as something more than chance, something guided, something meant to be received rather than evaluated. We spoke by phone first, the conversations spaced out like appointments, and I let the momentum build because momentum can feel like proof when your own instincts are dulled. When she flew down to visit, the arrival carried that strange energy of a story already half-written—luggage at the door, polite smiles, the sense that everyone expected me to step into a role. The relationship turned physical quickly, and that speed worked like a blindfold. Physical closeness can mute the part of the mind that asks hard questions. I mistook intensity for compatibility and treated the warmth of being wanted as evidence that the fit was real.

After she returned home, we stayed on the phone, and the plan shifted from "visit" to "move." It happened the way decisions sometimes happen when you're trying to escape your own quiet: the future gets announced before you've actually agreed to it internally. She had a teenage daughter with roots of her own—friends, a school world, a sense of identity tied to a place—and the idea of relocating sparked resistance immediately. That resistance didn't soften the plan; it sharpened it. The move itself was assisted by someone who wanted this to work badly enough to do the heavy lifting, and their effort became part of the pressure. When the moving truck arrived, it didn't feel like the start of a relationship. It felt like a decision landing in my driveway with no easy way to reverse it.

The shift in her behavior was visible before the dust from the move had even settled. Control entered the house like an uninvited roommate—small corrections, rules delivered as if they were obvious, expectations announced rather than discussed. Her drinking wasn't a side detail; it became part of the weather. Some nights she drank until the volume of the house changed, until words sharpened and moods flipped without warning. Her daughter responded to the new environment with a kind of escalating rebellion that wasn't theatrical so much as desperate—arguments that turned loud, doors slammed, accusations thrown like objects. The mother-daughter relationship felt less like a family bond and more like a constant contest for power, and I was pulled into the center whether I wanted to be there or not. I learned quickly that a household can be unstable without any single moment being "the" crisis.

What I didn't understand at first was how much of that instability was being manufactured before I even walked in the door after work. There were patterns that only revealed themselves over time: the daughter would already be inflamed when I arrived, the mother would already be primed to present herself as the victim, and I would be handed a scene mid-argument like I was expected to rule on it. The daughter began interpreting my presence through a lens that made me uneasy—reading intentions that didn't exist, treating me like a threat simply because I was there. That misunderstanding raised the stakes for me in a way I couldn't ignore, because my livelihood depended on being beyond suspicion. When police became involved more than once, I didn't feel relief; I felt cold practicality. At least there was documentation. At least there was a record that showed I wasn't hiding anything. In a life where perception can become accusation, paper can function like armor.

There were evenings when I came home and found her passed out on the couch, the television talking to an empty room, the house smelling of stale alcohol and resentment. On one of those nights I used the quiet the way I always do when the inside of me is too loud: I made order. I cleaned the kitchen with a compulsive thoroughness— counters stripped, dishes washed, floors scrubbed—because cleaning is one of the few ways to produce an immediate, visible result. When she woke up, the quiet didn't stay quiet. She came into the kitchen and began to press into my space, taunting and provoking, pushing for a reaction that would make her the center of a new story. She wanted me to become the villain in her narrative. I did not touch her. I did not give her what she was baiting for. But I did something I hate admitting: I lost control of my volume. I screamed— full force, face-to-face—because it was the only way I could create distance without using my hands. The moment left my throat raw and my nerves buzzing, and it clarified something I'd been refusing to name: the household wasn't merely difficult. It was dangerous to my stability.

Once that clarity landed, the ending didn't take long. I stopped negotiating with hope. I stopped telling myself it would settle. Within a week, I did what I had avoided doing because I felt guilty about the daughter and what displacement would do to her: I ended it decisively. I packed her belongings, arranged transportation, and sent her back to where she had come from. It wasn't a noble goodbye. It was logistics under emotional pressure, the kind of cleanup you do after you realize you've been living inside someone else's storm. When the truck pulled away, the house didn't feel healed. It felt emptied out, scrubbed of noise but not scrubbed of residue. The quiet returned, and this time it didn't feel like peace. It felt like the after-sound of a slammed door, the kind your body keeps hearing long after the room stops shaking.

After she left, I did something I often do after emotional upheaval: I made a concrete purchase, a physical decision meant to prove I still had agency. I bought a pickup truck. The decision was practical on paper—utility, reliability, capability—but psychologically it was something else. It was a way of saying, *I can still move. I can still choose. I am not trapped.* The truck smelled like new materials and had that heavy, mechanical promise of power. I drove it on open roads and listened to the engine and tried to feel something like strength settle into me. For brief moments, it worked. Motion has always been a seduction for me. Motion feels like escape. Motion feels like control.

But motion doesn't erase what you carry. It only changes the scenery around it.

The months after the breakup carried an emotional weather that became harder to ignore. The job still demanded output, and I still produced. The training course still moved students through its pipeline, and I still taught, still corrected, still evaluated. The role-play sessions continued, and the repetition continued doing its quiet damage: being "captured" again and again, sitting in that chair again and again, absorbing other people's aggression while calling it instruction. My back continued to ache in a way that made every long day feel like a test of endurance. The house continued to echo. And the attempts at companionship continued to fail—not always in dramatic breakups, but in slow fizzles that left me more aware of my own isolation.

There were evenings when I would sit in the living room with the lights off and feel the size of the house pressing down like a weight. There were mornings when I would wake up with a heaviness already in my chest, a heaviness that didn't feel like sadness in the traditional sense. Sadness implies tears, implies story, implies catharsis. What I was feeling was flatter, more constant, more physical. It was like gravity had been turned up. Getting out of bed required negotiation. Showering felt like a task, not a refresh. Eating felt like maintenance. Even the desert sky—the wide, bright thing that had once felt like salvation—began to feel indifferent in a way that stung. The sky did not care if I was healing. The sky did not care if I was failing. The sky did not answer.

That indifference became an echo of something I had encountered overseas, but here it was dressed as domestic life. In war, indifference feels honest because danger is honest. In civilian life, indifference feels like abandonment because everyone expects you to be grateful you're "safe." Safety is not always relief when your nervous system refuses to believe in it. Safety can become another kind of prison if the mind inside it is still wired for threat and still hungry for meaning.

I began to feel the edge of something approaching, not as a clear thought, not as an announced intention, but as a change in internal pressure. Like a storm forming far away, visible only in subtle shifts: irritability that arrived too fast, moments of blankness where hours passed without memory, a sense of detachment when people spoke to me as if I were behind glass. I would be at work, mid-brief, and suddenly feel as if I were watching myself from the outside. I would be driving and realize I had taken an exit without remembering deciding to take it. I would be standing in the grocery store aisle and feel overwhelmed by choices that should have been simple. These weren't cinematic breakdowns. They were small fractures, hairline cracks spreading quietly.

The training course environment did not help with that. Teaching human intelligence work means living in a world where motives are always questioned. You train students to look for deception. You train them to assume that what they are being told is incomplete. You train them to treat trust as something that must be earned and verified. That mindset is necessary for the mission. It also seeps. It made it harder for me to relax around people. It made it harder for me to accept kindness without searching for what was behind it. It made it harder for me to believe in simple affection. And as my attempts at companionship continued to collapse, the mindset grew more entrenched: *Of course it didn't work. Of course people leave. Of course you are not built for this.*

At the same time, I could feel myself becoming more invested in systems—data, software, process—because systems didn't judge. Systems didn't demand intimacy. Systems rewarded effort. I poured myself into course improvement, into building tools that made training more efficient, more trackable, more adaptable. I became the man who could solve problems in the database while failing to solve the problem of his own interior life. The irony wasn't lost on me. It simply didn't change what I did, because changing would have required me to admit how bad it was getting, and admitting would have required me to risk someone else's reaction.

The arranged relationship failure left a particular residue. It wasn't only the awkwardness of sending someone back. It was the message embedded in it: that the people closest to me—people who believed they were helping—did not see me as a person navigating damage. They saw me as a broken appliance that needed replacement parts. Their solution was to attach me to a woman, to a community, to a moral structure that would "fix" me. When I rejected that, I felt the silent accusation: *If you won't take the cure offered, then you must enjoy being sick.* That accusation is poison. It makes a man isolate further. It makes him stop asking for help before he even asks.

That is where the chapter ends—not with a dramatic collapse, not with a clear decision, but with the quiet stacking of conditions. A big house that had become too quiet. A job that demanded constant performance while keeping me steeped in confrontation and suspicion. A body that carried persistent pain and visual distortion as background noise. A failed relationship that left emptiness. A failed arrangement that left shame. A growing sense of internal pressure that I couldn't yet name without feeling like I was confessing weakness. I stood in my driveway sometimes and looked at the truck and the open road beyond it, and the road looked like the only honest thing left: a line you can follow without having to explain yourself.

The idea of leaving—of taking the road, of going somewhere vast enough to hold my silence—began to form quietly, not as a vacation plan, but as a survival instinct. The breakup had cleared space in the house, and the space had started to feel dangerous. The desert sky stayed wide and indifferent. The training course kept moving students toward deployment. My own internal pressure kept rising, like a tide that doesn't care whether you're ready to swim. And in that environment, the thought of driving away toward empty landscapes began to feel less like escape and more like the only remaining method of breathing.

The national parks were still just an idea at the edge of the mind, not yet a story. But the need that would send me there—away from rooms that echoed, away from people who wanted to fix me with arrangements, away from my own house becoming a witness—was already present. It was in the way I lingered too long in parking lots before going inside. It was in the way I stared at maps without committing. It was in the way the wide sky over Arizona began to feel less like freedom and more like a silent, unanswered question that I was tired of asking.

# CHAPTER 14

# *Winter Roads*

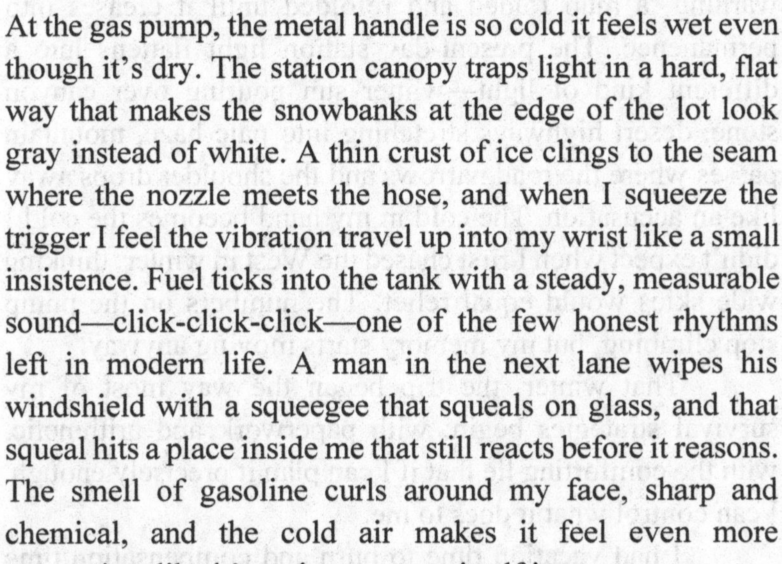

At the gas pump, the metal handle is so cold it feels wet even though it's dry. The station canopy traps light in a hard, flat way that makes the snowbanks at the edge of the lot look gray instead of white. A thin crust of ice clings to the seam where the nozzle meets the hose, and when I squeeze the trigger I feel the vibration travel up into my wrist like a small insistence. Fuel ticks into the tank with a steady, measurable sound—click-click-click—one of the few honest rhythms left in modern life. A man in the next lane wipes his windshield with a squeegee that squeals on glass, and that squeal hits a place inside me that still reacts before it reasons. The smell of gasoline curls around my face, sharp and chemical, and the cold air makes it feel even more aggressive, like it's trying to carve itself into memory.

I watch the numbers climb on the digital display and realize my breathing has gone shallow. The station is safe. The road beyond it is ordinary. A winter afternoon in a place that has nothing to do with war, nothing to do with deserts, nothing to do with training rotations. Yet my body is bracing, and I don't even have a clean explanation for what it thinks is coming. The pump clicks and the sound is too similar to another sound—gravel under tires, a chain snapping tight, a door latch closing behind me as I step away from everything that is supposed to be "normal." I stand there holding the cold handle and feel the old urge rise, the one that has never been about travel for its own sake. The urge is simpler than that. The urge is to keep moving so the inside of my head doesn't have to settle into a room and start echoing.

The nozzle shuts off with a blunt clunk, and for a moment my mind is somewhere else entirely: a truck loaded with the idea of escape, a weather report that reads like a warning, a map folded and refolded until it creases into permanence. The present-day station light flattens into a different kind of light—winter sun pouring over canyon stone, desert highways stretching into pale haze, mountain passes where the road narrows and the shoulder drops away like an accusation. The cold in my hand becomes the cold I didn't expect when I first chased the West in winter, thinking wide skies would equal relief. The numbers on the pump stop climbing, but my memory starts moving anyway.

That winter, the trip began the way most of my survival strategies begin: with paperwork and arithmetic, with the comforting lie that if I can plan it precisely enough, I can control what it does to me.

I had vacation time to burn and compensation time I'd earned earlier doing long, grinding days in a training environment that treated exhaustion as normal. Those hours sat on a ledger like a permission slip. I stared at the leave balance and felt a strange kind of hunger—hours that could be converted into distance, into silence, into landscapes where no one expected anything from me. I didn't frame it as a vacation. I framed it as a project. Projects are safer than feelings. I sat at a table with maps spread out, drew lines with a pen, looked at the order of places the way you look at a sequence of tasks: start here, drive there, sleep, repeat. The plan wasn't designed for comfort. It was designed for motion.

I loaded the truck with the kind of supplies people bring when they're pretending they're only being practical: extra water, blankets, food that wouldn't spoil, a small shovel, a flashlight. Winter adds a layer of seriousness to travel that summer never requires. You can be reckless in summer and still survive because the world isn't actively trying to freeze you. In winter, the environment has teeth. I checked tires. I checked fluid levels. I checked weather reports and told myself I was being responsible. Beneath that responsibility was a quieter truth: I liked the danger. Not because I wanted to die—my mind hadn't admitted that out loud yet—but because danger is a clean sensation. Danger cuts through numbness. Danger makes the body feel present, even if the presence is painful.

The first miles out of Arizona felt like stepping away from a house that had turned into an amplifier. The new-built rooms had started to echo in a way that made me feel watched by my own emptiness. Driving was the opposite. Driving gave my eyes a horizon to hold. It gave my hands a task. It gave my mind a sequence of decisions small enough to handle: speed, lane, exit, fuel, the next place to sleep. I rolled north toward the Grand Canyon's South Rim with the desert thinning into higher elevation, the air cooling, the sky widening and sharpening. The farther I drove, the more the land seemed to strip away distractions until there was only the road and the big, indifferent backdrop. That indifference felt honest. Human beings carry judgment like perfume; it leaks into everything. The land did not judge. The land only existed.

By the time I reached the South Rim, winter had already changed the park's personality. The crowds that fill it in warm months weren't there. The parking lots weren't jammed. There were fewer voices, fewer camera clicks, fewer groups shuffling in choreographed awe. Snow lay in patches along the rim, gathered in shadowed corners like it had been saved there. The air tasted clean in the way cold air tastes clean—sharp, almost metallic. I walked toward the edge and felt my body tighten with a primal caution even though there were railings and signs and safety built into the experience. The canyon doesn't care about railings. The canyon doesn't care about signage. It simply drops away into scale so vast it makes human concerns look like dust.

Standing at the rim in winter is different than standing there in a crowd. In a crowd, you share the moment. In winter, the canyon feels like it has singled you out. The silence is larger. The wind moves along the rock and seems to speak in a language that predates you. Snow clings to ledges and highlights contours, making depth more visible, making distance more dramatic. I leaned on a railing and stared down until my eyes started to lose their ability to measure. The canyon makes you small in a way that can either be humiliating or relieving. That day it was relieving. Being small meant my problems were not the center of the universe. Being small meant I didn't have to perform. I could simply stand there and be a body under a huge sky, held in place by awe rather than obligation.

From the canyon, I drove toward Zion, and the shift in landscape felt like the world changing chapters. The road dropped and rose through desert and scrub, through long stretches where the horizon looked empty enough to be a dare. Winter light flattened color, turned reds darker, made shadows crisp. In Zion, the canyon walls rise close and vertical, red rock towering like architecture built by a god with patience. Even in colder months, the place carries a kind of quiet intensity. The river moves through the valley like a vein, and the cliffs hold the day's light for only so long before the shadows slide in and the temperature falls fast.

I parked, stepped out, and felt the cold settle into my joints. Zion in winter was calmer, less trafficked, more open to solitude. The paths weren't crowded. Some facilities were closed or minimally staffed. I walked under sheer walls streaked with mineral stains, and the scale made me feel both protected and trapped. The canyon holds you. It funnels your movement. It decides where you can go. There is a comfort in that kind of constraint when your internal world feels too wide and chaotic. The land gave me boundaries I couldn't create for myself.

From Zion, the plan bent toward the Hoover Dam. The drive carried me through stark terrain where wind had nothing to slow it down. Approaching the dam, the architecture of control appeared—concrete carved into curves, water held in place by a structure built to argue with gravity. The dam is a monument to the human belief that we can contain massive forces if we engineer hard enough. Standing near it, feeling the cold air coming off the water, I felt a strange envy toward that clarity: force identified, force contained, force turned into power. My own life had been full of force without containment, pressure without output. The dam's clean purpose felt almost insulting.

Las Vegas came next, and it hit like an artificial punch. After rock and river and winter air, the city's lights felt loud even before I stepped out of the truck. Las Vegas is built to be a distraction that never sleeps. It offers constant stimulation so you don't have to hear yourself. Part of me wanted that. Part of me despised it. I drove into the city and watched neon smear across my windshield, watched the glow bounce off low clouds. The Strip looked like a machine designed to convert attention into money, and I was a man trained by other machines—military machines, training machines—so I recognized the logic immediately.

Inside the casino air, everything smelled like carpet and cleaning chemicals and something sweet meant to mask smoke and sweat. Sound was constant—slot machines chiming, voices overlapping, music engineered to keep you moving. Winter outside was irrelevant here. Time was irrelevant. I wandered for a while, letting the noise wash over me, and felt the familiar problem appear: stimulation can numb you for a few hours, but it doesn't cure anything. When the noise fades, you're still you. I didn't stay long. I didn't come here for entertainment. I came here because the itinerary demanded it, because I wanted the contrast, because I wanted to test whether a city built on distraction could drown out what was rising in my chest. It couldn't. It only proved the thing I already knew: the inside of my head travels with me.

From Vegas, the route tilted toward the coast—Santa Monica, the pier, the Pacific. The drive was long enough to become its own kind of meditation. Desert gave way to more traffic, more signs, more visible human density. By the time I reached Santa Monica, the air smelled different—salt, exhaust, dampness. The ocean was a moving flatness under a winter sky, gray-blue and restless. The pier stretched out into it like a gesture of confidence, lights strung along it like someone trying to make the edge of the continent feel festive.

Walking out onto the pier in winter, with fewer tourists and more locals bundled in jackets, I felt a strange emptiness and a strange relief at the same time. The ocean doesn't have the canyon's vertical drama. It has horizontal infinity, a different kind of scale. Waves rolled in and broke, repeating with a patience that made my own internal urgency seem ridiculous. I stood near the railing, watched the water, and felt my shoulders drop a fraction. Not peace—my body wasn't capable of that yet—but a small loosening, like the nervous system had found a rhythm bigger than its own.

After the coast, I drove inland again toward a relative's home—someone older than me, someone settled into a family life that looked stable from the outside. The visit was both comforting and difficult. The house was warm in the ordinary way homes are warm: cooking smells, children's toys, voices that rise and fall without fear. There were photos on walls, a visual record of years that had been lived in a straight line rather than in loops. Being there made me feel like a visitor from a different universe. I could sit at a table and laugh at a joke and still feel detached, as if the laughter was happening in another room and my body had only been invited to perform it.

The children moved through the house with the careless confidence of people who assume the world will hold. Their energy filled spaces in a way my own life no longer did. I watched them and felt something twist—envy, grief, maybe both. The adults talked about ordinary things, about work schedules and school events and plans for next week, and the ordinariness felt like a foreign language. I contributed where I could. I kept my tone calm. I didn't drop any of my heavier truths onto their floor like a mess they didn't deserve. The visit wasn't a confession. It was a pause. It reminded me what "normal" looks like in a way that didn't inspire me so much as underline how far away I felt from it.

From there, the route swung toward Yosemite, and this leg of the trip included a companion—another relative who joined me for that stretch. The drive into Yosemite in winter carries a particular kind of awe because the park's famous granite faces and waterfalls and valleys look different under cold air. The crowds thin. The silence grows. Snow gathers in shaded areas and along higher elevations. The road winds through forest where trunks stand like dark pillars, and then the valley opens and the stone rises—El Capitan, Half Dome in the distance—monuments that look less like geology and more like something carved by time with deliberate patience.

Yosemite in winter felt like a cathedral with fewer worshippers. The valley floor held cold, and the sky above the walls looked impossibly high. We drove slow, not only because of ice patches and cautious conditions, but because the sight demanded slowness. There's a kind of reverence that arrives when the land is that large and your own mind is that tired. My companion talked, pointed out features, shared small facts, and the conversation was normal enough to be soothing. Traveling with someone else changed the emotional texture. Solitude can be relief, but it can also turn sharp. Having another person in the vehicle created a buffer between me and my own spiraling thoughts. It gave me a place to put my attention besides the internal pressure I'd been carrying.

We left Yosemite and returned to that relative's house again, and the return felt like stepping from a dream into a warm room. The house held the same domestic noises as before, the same sense that life was ongoing and continuous. I slept in a guest space and woke up to ordinary morning sounds—pans, footsteps, conversation—without the abruptness of a base or the loneliness of my own empty home. Those mornings were almost gentle. Almost. The "almost" mattered. Even in a safe house, even around people who cared, my body remained tense, and the tension made me feel ungrateful. I didn't know how to explain that to anyone without sounding broken.

When I finally returned to the truck alone again, the itinerary moved north toward Crater Lake, and winter began showing its teeth more clearly. The farther north I drove, the more snow appeared along shoulders, the more the temperature dropped, the more the sky took on that heavy winter tone that suggests weather can change its mind quickly. Crater Lake sits high, and high places in winter do not negotiate. The roads began to narrow between snowbanks. Visibility shifted. The truck's tires sounded different on the surface—less a roll, more a hush. I watched the snow deepen and felt the old sensation of danger tightening around the edges of the day.

Crater Lake in winter is beauty with a warning label. The lake itself is a dark, impossibly blue bowl, held inside the remnants of a volcano, surrounded by snow-covered rim. When I reached the viewpoint, the wind was sharp enough to sting exposed skin. The air tasted clean and cold, and the lake looked unreal—too blue, too calm, framed by white snow that made the color even more intense. The quiet there was profound. Not the quiet of absence, but the quiet of containment. The world felt held in place by cold.

I stayed longer than was wise, letting the sight soak into me, letting the cold force my body into a kind of alert presence. Then the weather shifted the way it can shift in mountains: wind rose, snow began to move sideways, the sky thickened. The road back began to look less like a route and more like a question. There was a moment—standing by the truck, looking at the way snow was starting to erase edges—when I realized I could get trapped up there. Not metaphorically. Literally. Snowed in. Unable to drive out. A person alone in winter mountains with a truck and supplies and no one expecting them in a specific hour is not a romantic figure. It's a headline waiting to happen.

That realization snapped me into motion. I drove carefully, hands tight on the wheel, eyes scanning the road for ice sheen, for drift buildup, for places where the edge disappeared into white. The truck handled it, but my heart stayed elevated until lower elevation returned and the snow thinned. Surviving a near trap doesn't bring relief the way it should. It brings a strange disappointment, like the body had prepared for something final and then had to accept continuation instead. I didn't name that thought at the time. I only felt the residue of it like an aftertaste.

From there, Seattle came as another sharp contrast—urban density after remote cold. The Space Needle rose above the city like a stylized promise, a landmark designed to be photographed and consumed. Winter rain and dampness clung to everything. The air felt heavy with water. I stood under gray sky and looked up at the structure and felt small in a different way than the parks made me small. In the parks, smallness was relief. In the city, smallness felt like being one more body moving through a system that didn't care whether I existed.

I moved through Seattle quickly, not because I disliked it, but because I wasn't there for the city itself. The itinerary was still chasing something older and quieter: the places where nature could overwhelm my internal narrative. Olympic National Park pulled me west, toward coastline, rainforest, and mountains held in one region like a condensed version of the world. Winter amplified Olympic's mood. The beaches were emptier, the wind harsher, the surf louder. Trees in the rainforest held moisture like they were built to drink the sky. Moss clung to everything, thick and green even in cold season, a reminder that life can thrive in damp darkness.

The Hoh rainforest was where the trip's atmosphere shifted again into something almost dreamlike. Walking under towering trees draped in moss, the light filtered into a dim green glow that made time feel altered. The ground was soft with dampness. The air smelled of earth and decay and living growth, not the rot of human waste or burn pits, but the honest rot of forest cycles. Each step sank slightly into leaf litter, and the sound of movement was muted. Winter rain fell in fine mist, clinging to hair and jacket. The world felt quiet enough that my own thoughts became louder at first—then, gradually, quieter, as if the forest was absorbing the noise.

That quiet was the drug I had been chasing. Not excitement. Not distraction. Quiet. But quiet of the right kind: a quiet that didn't feel like judgment, didn't feel like abandonment, didn't feel like an empty house watching me. The forest quiet felt impersonal. It allowed me to exist without being evaluated. I walked longer than necessary, watched moisture drip from branches, watched fog hang between trunks, and felt a strange tenderness rise—toward the trees, toward the ground, toward the simple fact that something in the world could be this old and still standing.

Then I left the Hoh and returned to the truck, and the quiet left with me, proving again that I couldn't keep it.

Hells Canyon came later in the route, and winter turned that drive into one of the more dangerous moments of the trip. The road along parts of that region can narrow, twist, and offer views that are breathtaking in the literal sense—breath stolen by height and exposure. Snow in those conditions is not decoration; it's a hazard. The truck climbed into higher terrain, and the road's shoulder began to fade under white. Snow capped the edge. The sky was bright in that winter way that makes ice harder to see. There were stretches where the drop on one side was severe enough to make my hands sweat despite the cold. The cliffside didn't need to be dramatic to be deadly. It only needed to exist.

There was a moment when the truck's tires slid a fraction—just a fraction—on a patch that looked safe until it wasn't. The slip wasn't long. It was enough. My stomach dropped, my heart surged, and for a second my entire body went cold as if it had already accepted impact. I corrected, slowed, found traction again. The truck stayed on the road. The world continued. But the realization landed hard: one bad decision, one misread patch of ice, and the trip would end there, not with meaning, not with insight, but with the indifferent finality the land always offers. I pulled over later where the road widened, sat with my hands still on the wheel, and breathed until my pulse returned to something like normal.

That near-miss didn't scare me into turning around. It did the opposite. It made me feel alive in a way that was unsettling. The danger sharpened my senses. It forced my mind into the present. And the fact that I responded to that sharpness with something close to relief was a quiet warning I didn't want to hear.

Glacier National Park came after, and winter there is not a season so much as a takeover. Glacier in warm months is famous for alpine beauty and dramatic roads, but winter changes access, closes routes, compresses the human experience into what's still possible. Snow piles heavy. Mountains become quieter, more guarded. The cold is more serious, the kind that can kill if you pretend it's only uncomfortable. I drove toward the park with the sky bright and the land white, and the sense of isolation grew as services thinned. Snowbanks rose along roads. The world became a corridor.

Near East Glacier—near a lake that in summer would be a clean, reflective mirror—winter turned the landscape into a white field broken by dark trees and distant mountain shapes. I found myself on a stretch where snow drifted across the road in a way that didn't look threatening until the truck slowed into it and the tires began to dig. The engine strained. The wheels spun. The truck settled lower. The sound changed from movement to effort. Snow drifted against the undercarriage and packed. For a moment, the situation was absurd: a man alone in a beautiful, empty winter landscape, stuck because he had insisted on chasing solitude into conditions that didn't welcome it.

I tried the usual methods—rocking the truck, clearing snow with the shovel, placing material under tires for traction—but winter drifts have a stubbornness that feels personal even though it isn't. I could feel my frustration rising, sharp enough to make me want to slam the door, shout into the cold, do something dramatic just to prove I had a voice. Instead I worked. I dug. I cursed under my breath. And then, in the distance, movement appeared: a couple of figures on skis, hikers moving over snow with the slow confidence of people who belonged there.

When they reached me, they didn't treat the situation like a rescue from a movie. They treated it like winter reality. They looked at the drift, looked at the truck, gave calm instructions, helped push and guide and clear. Their faces were red from cold, their breath visible. They spoke with the casual tone of people who know the land doesn't care and you either adapt or you don't. With their help, the truck moved, tires found bite, and the vehicle rolled free. Relief hit me in a wave that made my knees feel briefly weak. I thanked them more than once, words coming too fast, because their arrival had cut through something darker than inconvenience. Being stuck alone in winter silence had started to feel like a metaphor that my mind didn't want to finish.

After Glacier, Yellowstone was next, and winter there demanded a different kind of compromise. Parts of the park become inaccessible to normal vehicles when snow takes over. The roads close, the distances become more serious, and the park shifts from a drive-through wonderland into something that requires planning. I wanted to see it anyway. I needed to see it. I hired a track-wheeled tour vehicle—an ungainly, specialized machine designed to move over snow where tires would fail—and the decision felt both ridiculous and necessary. Ridiculous because it was expensive and elaborate for a man traveling alone. Necessary because I had come this far chasing the emptiness of winter parks, and I wasn't willing to let a closed gate be the thing that turned me around.

The track vehicle moved with a heavy, deliberate vibration, its treads biting into snow and rolling forward like a slow animal. Inside, the air was warm, fogging windows with breath. The guide talked—facts about geysers, wildlife patterns, winter survival—and the facts floated around me like background noise. Yellowstone in winter looks like another planet: steam rising from hot springs into freezing air, bison moving like dark shapes through white fields, trees rimed with frost. The contrast between boiling water and frozen ground felt like the park's own internal contradiction made visible. I watched steam billow, watched it drift and vanish, and felt the old thought return: the earth has heat and violence under it at all times, whether we see it or not. We stand on a thin crust and call it stable.

The tour gave access, but it also made me aware of my own limitations. I wasn't a man thriving in wilderness. I was a man visiting wilderness with paid assistance, with heated transport, with a schedule. The land was still indifferent, but I was insulated. Part of me wanted to strip that insulation away and test myself more directly. Another part of me—the part that still wanted to live, even if it didn't know why—was grateful for the boundary. In winter, boundaries keep you alive.

Mount Rushmore came later, a human monument after so many natural ones. The faces carved into granite looked stern and permanent under winter sky, an attempt to make history literal. Snow gathered around the base, and the cold air made the place feel quieter than it probably does in summer. I stood there and felt the odd emptiness of symbols. The monument was impressive, yes. It was also static. It didn't move me the way canyons and forests had moved me, because it didn't contain the same kind of indifferent truth. It was a human assertion. Nature had been offering me something else: a reminder that my life is not the center and never has been.

From Rushmore, I drove back toward the region where I had grown up, returning to a familiar house for the holiday season. The drive felt like reverse motion through time. The roads looked more familiar. The towns carried the particular architecture of my earlier life—strip malls, familiar brands, the sense that the world is smaller here. Winter holidays bring their own atmosphere: lights strung on houses, stores crowded, people moving with a manufactured cheer. I stayed through the turn of the year, existing inside the familiar routines and familiar expectations that come with being in that environment. Conversations happened around tables. Television played in living rooms. Meals came and went. People asked questions and expected answers that fit the holiday mood.

Being there wasn't purely bad. Familiarity can soothe. But familiarity can also press on old wounds. In that house, under those holiday lights, I could feel how much of my life had become a series of departures. I could feel how hard it was for people to understand a man who keeps leaving and returns without bringing a clear story of improvement. I kept my face calm. I laughed in the right places. I performed the role required. At night, in a guest room, I stared at the ceiling and felt the internal pressure still there, still building, still not addressed by food or conversation or the symbolic warmth of holidays.

After the holidays, the trip turned south again, but not alone. A close relative traveled with me for the next stretch, and the presence changed the trip's emotional temperature. With someone else in the passenger seat, I couldn't dissolve into silence as easily. I had to talk. I had to answer questions. I had to be polite when my mind wanted to retreat. We drove toward the South Padre region, toward the national seashore and then the island, trading winter's biting cold for a different kind of winter: coastal wind, damp air, sunlight that still lacked true warmth. The Gulf looked calmer than the Pacific, but it carried its own seriousness, its own endlessness.

At the national seashore, the sand stretched long and open, and the sky felt bigger than the buildings. Winter kept the crowds away. The beach was less a party place and more a wide, empty line where the world met water. Wind pushed at jackets. Waves came in steady. The air smelled of salt and wet sand and seaweed. We walked along the shoreline, letting the cold wind carve thoughts out of us. The relative spoke about ordinary things—plans, worries, family matters —and I listened and responded in measured ways. Being there with someone else kept me tethered to human reality. It also made me aware of how much I had been using solitude as a drug.

South Padre Island itself was a different mood— more built-up, more evidence of tourism even in off-season. There were restaurants, lights, the sense that in warm months the place becomes crowded and loud. In winter, it felt like a stage after the show: empty patios, fewer cars, the ocean still there doing its indifferent work. We ate meals. We drove along the island. We watched the water in late-day light. The days were simple in a way that should have been restful. Rest didn't come easily. Even on a beach, even with someone else beside me, my nervous system stayed half-braced, like it was waiting for something to happen.

The return journey back to Arizona with that relative carried its own mixture of relief and pressure. Relief because the trip was still movement, still distance, still a line of road that gave me something to do. Pressure because returning meant going back to my house, back to the quiet rooms, back to the life that had been waiting for me like an unopened letter. We drove long stretches. We stopped at motels. We ate in roadside places that all smelled the same—fried food, coffee, disinfectant—ordinary America in transit. At some point near the end, I took the relative to an airport and watched them disappear into the logic of travel: ticket counters, security lines, gates. I stood outside afterward in cold air and felt the loneliness return fast, like it had been crouched nearby waiting for its turn.

Then it was just me again, the truck and the road and the last miles back to my own driveway.

The national park tour began and ended as a loop of winter landscapes, and the loop did not cure me. It did something else, something more complicated and more dangerous. It proved that emptiness can feel like relief. It proved that the land's indifference can feel cleaner than human judgment. It proved that I could stand in places so vast they made my problems look small, and for a few minutes that smallness felt like peace.

It also proved that winter can kill you without drama, that a drift can trap you, that a cliffside road can end everything with one bad slide, that the body can respond to near-death with a kind of calm that should be questioned. The trip offered beauty and silence and danger in a blended dose, and my nervous system accepted the blend too readily. I didn't articulate that to myself then. I only knew that when I returned to my own house, the walls felt closer than they had before. The rooms felt emptier. The quiet felt louder. The landscapes I'd visited had been honest in their indifference, and now I was back in human-made space where indifference feels like abandonment.

I parked the truck, turned off the engine, and sat for a moment with my hands still on the wheel, listening to the cooling metal tick as it contracted. Outside, the winter air held stillness that wasn't the stillness of a canyon or a forest. It was the stillness of a neighborhood night. I looked at the front door, at the windows, at the clean lines of a house that was supposed to represent stability. The trip had begun as a plan built from leave balances and routes on paper. It ended with me staring at my own home as if it were a place I didn't fully belong.

The parks had been empty. The roads had been long. The sky had been wide enough to swallow thought. I had chased that wideness like a medicine. And now, at the end of the tour, the medicine's effect was fading, leaving behind the same internal pressure—sharper, more defined, no longer disguised by motion. The winter road had carried me through wonder after wonder. It had also carried me back to myself, and that was the part I had been trying to avoid.

# CHAPTER 15

# *Frozen Time*

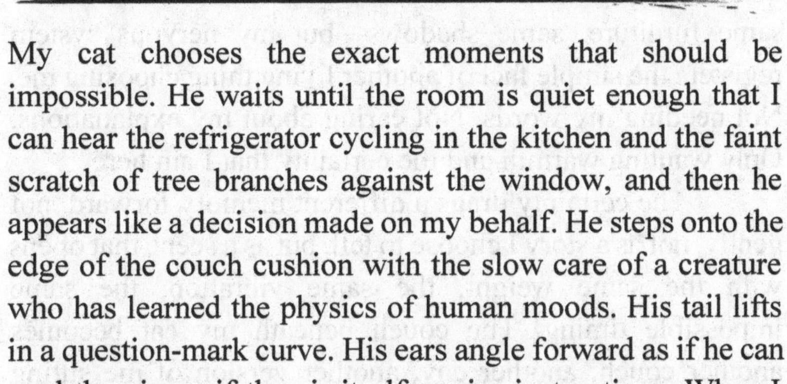

My cat chooses the exact moments that should be impossible. He waits until the room is quiet enough that I can hear the refrigerator cycling in the kitchen and the faint scratch of tree branches against the window, and then he appears like a decision made on my behalf. He steps onto the edge of the couch cushion with the slow care of a creature who has learned the physics of human moods. His tail lifts in a question-mark curve. His ears angle forward as if he can read the air, as if the air itself carries instructions. When I don't move, when I keep my hands still, he closes the distance anyway, placing one paw on my thigh and shifting his weight like he owns the next five minutes of my life.

He turns in a tight circle—once, twice—kneading fabric with deliberate pressure, not affectionate in a sentimental way but methodical, as if he is testing whether I'm solid enough to hold him. His fur is warm from wherever he has been sleeping. His body is small but dense, a compact engine of heat and insistence. When he settles, his weight lands fully, and it is impossible not to feel it. It pins me to the present in a way nothing else does. The purr starts low and steady, vibrating through bone, a sound too simple to argue with. He doesn't ask permission. He doesn't negotiate. He simply arrives and makes contact like contact is a law.

I look down at him and notice the way his eyes half-close in trust, and something in my chest shifts—not relief, not happiness, but a loosening that feels like a knot giving up a fraction of its grip. My hand lifts without thinking and rests on his back, fingers moving through fur in slow passes. The purr deepens. His breathing stays calm. His body behaves as if the world is safe, and for a moment I borrow that belief. The room remains the same room—same walls, same furniture, same shadows—but my nervous system registers the simple fact of another living thing choosing me. Not needing my words. Not caring about my explanations. Only wanting warmth and the certainty that I am here.

The certainty drags a different memory forward, not gently, not as a story I choose to tell, but as a scene that opens with the same weight, the same vibration, the same impossible timing. The couch beneath my cat becomes another couch, another day, another version of me sitting inside a house that had started to feel like a trap built out of quiet. The purr in the room becomes the one sound that cut through a frozen second and restarted time. My hand on his back becomes my hand trying to unclench, trying to let go, trying to stop being a fist around my own throat. The present doesn't disappear so much as it tilts, and the tilt drops me into the winter after the national park tour—when the roads had ended, the motion had stopped, and the inside of my head began to fill the empty rooms again.

The trip had been winter's version of freedom: long miles, empty overlooks, snow-edged roads, landscapes so vast they reduced me to a speck. It had also been an experiment I didn't admit I was running—testing whether beauty and danger could substitute for meaning, whether cold air and open space could quiet the part of me that kept searching for exits. For a while, movement had worked like a drug. It kept me occupied. It kept me outside myself. It offered new horizons faster than my mind could poison them. Then the loop closed, and the truck rolled back into my driveway, and the engine shut off, and the house waited with the same blank stillness it had been holding in reserve.

Winter in the desert doesn't behave like winter in the places people imagine when they hear the word. There wasn't a constant white blanket, no soft hush of snow covering everything. Instead there were cold nights that cut sharp, mornings with frost clinging to shaded corners, and afternoons that could still feel sun-warm until the light slipped away and the temperature dropped like a punishment. My house—newer, clean, built to represent stability—held that temperature swing inside its walls. Heat clicked on, shut off, clicked on again. The air dried. The rooms remained wide and quiet. The quiet had a quality that wasn't peaceful. It felt like the house was listening.

The days after the trip did not restart the way I had told myself they would. I didn't unpack with purpose and feel refreshed. I didn't return to work with a full tank of energy. Instead, the moment the motion ended, exhaustion that had been waiting behind my ribs rushed forward like floodwater. I woke up late and still felt tired. I stood at the sink and stared at dishes as if they belonged to someone else's life. I opened the refrigerator and closed it again without choosing anything, not hungry, not satisfied, only stalled. The routines that were supposed to keep me functional—showers, meals, driving to work—began to feel like tasks assigned by an indifferent supervisor. My body moved because bodies keep moving, but it moved with less conviction, as if the muscles had started to question the point.

Work had been my anchor for years. Even when everything else wobbled—relationships collapsing, pain flaring, sleep breaking into fragments—work had offered structure. It offered deadlines and expectations and a role I could perform. But the post-trip weeks brought a subtle unraveling that didn't look dramatic from the outside. I called in sick more often. Not because I was contagious, not because I had a visible injury that demanded rest, but because getting dressed felt like lifting a weight off my own chest with bare hands. The thought of sitting under fluorescent lights, talking through training objectives, watching students perform interrogations, hearing the same aggressive tones in the role-play rooms—those thoughts made my stomach tighten before I even moved. I would lie in bed and stare at the ceiling and feel time sliding past like oil, slick and unstoppable.

When I did go in, I performed, but the performance had begun to thin. My voice still sounded calm. My face still showed the controlled neutrality that had served me in other harsh environments. I still delivered instruction, still corrected mistakes, still looked competent. Underneath that competence there was a growing vacancy, a sense that my thoughts were moving through mud. My attention drifted at the wrong moments. I would catch myself staring at a screen full of data fields and realizing I hadn't processed anything for several minutes. Students would ask questions and I would answer automatically, hearing my own words as if they were coming from a speaker in the corner of the room. The job still mattered. The work still had purpose. It just stopped reaching the part of me that needed saving.

At home, the emptiness became physical. The house was not small enough to hold me tightly. It was large enough to let me vanish inside it. A person can live in a big house and never truly occupy it, moving from room to room like a visitor, leaving lights off to avoid admitting the space exists. I would walk down the hallway and feel the sound of my footsteps echo. I would stand in the living room and look at furniture that felt like props—couch, chair, table—objects placed where objects are supposed to go, not because they belonged to a life I wanted. The silence inside those rooms didn't feel like privacy. It felt like abandonment. It felt like the house had been built to prove I could be stable, and the proof was failing.

Spiritual language started creeping into my thoughts during that period because ordinary language couldn't contain what was happening. I didn't stand up one morning and declare a transformation. It was quieter than that, more like a desperate reaching for a framework that could explain why I felt hollow. When the mind begins to collapse, it looks for interpretation. It searches for a story that makes the suffering meaningful. I had already tried practical stories: pain as a medical problem, loneliness as a temporary phase, work as an anchor, time as a healer. Those stories were fraying. In the vacuum, the older stories—the ones people hand you as children, the ones communities repeat with confidence—began to shine with the appeal of certainty.

I started listening to sermons again, not in a social way, not inside a building full of people, but alone, with the volume low, as if I didn't want the walls to hear me reaching. I would sit with a laptop open, letting a steady voice talk about purpose and sin and redemption. The words would roll through the room like smoke, and sometimes they comforted me. More often they sharpened something painful. Redemption implies you need saving. Sin implies you are wrong at the core. Purpose implies there is a reason you should still be here. I wanted the comfort. I feared the implications. My mind turned spiritual ideas into weapons against itself, because my mind was already practiced at turning anything into a reason for self-contempt.

Prayer became less like conversation and more like bargaining. It wasn't poetic. It wasn't reverent. It was blunt. It was me sitting on the edge of my bed in the dark, hands clasped because that's what people do in the movies, whispering promises I didn't fully believe I could keep. *If you fix this, I will change. If you make the weight lift, I will be better. If you give me one clear sign, I will follow it.* The problem was not that the sky refused to answer. The problem was that silence became an answer in my head. Silence became rejection. Silence became proof that I had already been weighed and found unworthy.

That interpretation didn't arrive out of nowhere. It built itself out of old material. It pulled from years of feeling like a misfit in ordinary social spaces, years of surviving by performance rather than belonging. It pulled from the way my body had been damaged and then treated as a bureaucratic inconvenience. It pulled from relationship failures that left me feeling like I was always one mistake away from being discarded. It pulled from the shame of wanting relief so badly I was willing to chase it into winter roads and empty parks, as if solitude could cure what was wrong. Spiritual language gave those experiences a harsh coherence. Instead of being unlucky, I became cursed. Instead of being wounded, I became broken. Instead of being exhausted, I became weak. Instead of needing help, I became the kind of person help doesn't stick to.

The loneliness got sharper because the religious frame made it feel earned. It wasn't just that I was alone. It was that I deserved to be alone. That thought is poison because it doesn't simply describe pain; it recruits pain as an ally. It turns suffering into a judge. It makes you stop reaching out because you believe reaching out is an imposition. I would pick up the phone and set it down again. I would start composing a message and delete it. The idea of telling anyone the truth—how empty the days felt, how heavy the nights were, how often the thought of stopping had begun to feel practical—felt like confessing a crime. I had spent years learning to look steady in unstable environments. Admitting instability felt like stripping naked in public.

Even my physical pain became part of the spiritual problem. The lower back injury was always there, a constant pressure that colored everything. Some days it flared into a sharper ache, and I would move carefully, avoiding sudden twists, avoiding lifting anything heavy. Other days it stayed at a low simmer, a reminder that I wasn't the version of myself I had once imagined. Pain has a way of making the future feel smaller. It narrows possibility. It turns ordinary tasks into negotiations. That narrowing fed the depression, and the depression fed the spiritual despair, and the spiritual despair fed the sense that my life was becoming a corridor with no doors.

The house reflected that narrowing. I began closing off rooms, not physically locking them, but treating them as unused territory. I kept curtains drawn. I let mail pile on the counter without opening it. I avoided mirrors because my face looked dull, eyes slightly vacant, skin tired. I ate enough to keep the body running but not enough to feel pleasure. I slept too much and woke up exhausted anyway. The days began to lose edges. One afternoon bled into the next. Weekends arrived without meaning because workdays had already become numb. The national park tour began to feel like something that had happened to someone else—another version of me with more motion, more nerve, more ability to chase the horizon.

In that atmosphere, suicide didn't arrive as a dramatic impulse. It arrived as a practical idea, like a door you notice in a room you've been trapped in for too long. The thought wasn't, *I want to die.* The thought was, *I want this to stop.* There is a difference, and that difference matters, because the mind can talk itself into stopping without believing it is doing something monstrous. Stopping becomes framed as mercy. Stopping becomes framed as necessary. Stopping becomes framed as the only remaining agency when everything else feels out of control. I didn't have the language to describe it cleanly to anyone. I only had the sensation of the idea becoming less frightening the more it repeated, like exposure therapy performed by my own despair.

The first attempt was not cinematic. It wasn't poetic. It was domestic and ugly, which is part of why it still carries its own kind of shame. It happened inside the ordinary architecture of my life—driveway, garage, bedroom— spaces designed for safety and routine. Winter had cooled the nights enough that the garage held a faint, trapped cold, and when I opened the door between the house and that space, the air smelled like rubber, oil, and stored dust. The garage was a mechanical room, a place for tools and tires, not a place for endings. That day it became a passageway anyway.

The truck sat there like it always did, solid and familiar. The metal of the door handle was cold in my palm. When I climbed inside, the interior smelled faintly of upholstery and the residue of long drives. I started the engine, and the vibration filled the small space with a living hum. The sound was ordinary—an engine doing what engines do—yet in that moment it felt like a heartbeat that didn't belong to me. I let the truck run. I didn't sit there and watch it. I didn't make speeches. I stepped back out and closed the door behind me with the same casual motion I used every other day, because treating it casually made it feel inevitable.

Then I walked back into the house and went to bed.

That sentence should not be possible. It should not be something a person can do without hysterics or tears. But the mind in that state doesn't behave like the mind people imagine. It narrows. It becomes procedural. It becomes focused on completion rather than experience. I lay on the bed fully dressed at first, then shifted under the blanket because the room was cold. The sheets were familiar against my skin. The ceiling above me held the same cracks and shadows it always held. I listened to the faint sound of the engine through the walls, a distant rumble like an animal breathing in another room. My body didn't panic. My body felt heavy, as if gravity had increased. My thoughts came in dull waves: not memories, not visions, just a steady certainty that this was the nearest door.

Time moved strangely. It didn't race the way it does when you're frightened. It didn't slow into a dramatic crawl. It thinned. It became soft around the edges, like the day had been wrapped in cotton. I waited without feeling like I was waiting. My breathing stayed shallow. My heart beat steadily. The engine sound remained. Winter air held the house in a quiet that felt sealed. In the middle of it, there was a part of me that still looked for something—a voice, a sign, a sudden surge of fear that would force me to stop. Nothing like that arrived. The absence of interruption felt like confirmation, and the confirmation was oddly calming. It was the calm of surrender.

Then the world did not do what I had arranged for it to do.

At some point, the engine sound changed, not loud enough to startle me but different enough to register. Or maybe it didn't change at all and my mind simply noticed my own breathing continuing. The exact detail matters less than the moment of awareness: I was still alive. I was still in the bed. Air was still moving in and out of my lungs. The room still held the same shadows. The ceiling still watched. I lay there and felt a slow confusion spread through me, followed by a hard, bitter clarity. Whatever I had attempted had not completed. Something about the setup—ventilation, leakage, the ordinary imperfect boundaries of a garage connected to a house—had prevented the outcome. The boundary between mechanical space and living space had refused to be airtight. The world had kept feeding me oxygen while I waited for it to stop.

I got up and moved through the house in a numb, stunned way, not running, not frantic, only mechanical. I opened the door to the garage and the smell hit—exhaust layered over rubber and oil, a harsh chemical bitterness that made the air feel contaminated. The truck was still there, still running, still vibrating like a dumb animal that didn't understand what it had been recruited for. I shut it off. The silence after the engine stopped was immediate and thick. I stood in that silence and felt the failure settle into my bones. Not relief. Not gratitude. Failure. The mind that had framed death as mercy framed survival as incompetence. The attempt had failed, and the failure became another piece of evidence in the case against myself.

That evidence did not push me toward health. It pushed me deeper into distortion.

In the days that followed, the spiritual desperation sharpened rather than softened. If I had believed, even secretly, that some force might intervene to stop me, the failed attempt complicated that belief. Survival could be interpreted as grace—another chance, an undeserved mercy. My mind refused that interpretation. It chose the crueler one. Survival became proof that I couldn't even escape correctly. Survival became proof that my pain wasn't serious enough to earn an ending. Survival became proof that I was trapped inside my own body with no competence even in leaving it. Those thoughts were not rational. They were relentless. They behaved like a prosecutor who never sleeps.

I went through motions anyway. I showered because the body smells if you don't. I ate because the body gets weak if you don't. I drove to work some days and called in sick other days, the decision made hour by hour rather than planned. The training course continued without caring about my internal collapse. Students still needed evaluation. Systems still needed maintenance. Data fields still needed validation. I could still solve technical problems, still write code, still troubleshoot database errors, and the ability to do those things made my despair feel even more shameful. It is hard to justify wanting to die when you can still be useful. Usefulness becomes a chain. It makes you look healthy to outsiders. It makes you look functional enough that asking for help feels like exaggeration. I kept my face controlled and my voice even and felt my insides rotting.

The religious pull tightened because it offered an explanation for rot. It offered a cosmic reason: spiritual failure. Moral failure. Inadequacy framed as sin. I began to read my own life as a long pattern of falling short. Not in a normal human way, but in a fundamental way. I would sit alone in the house at night and replay scenes like a punishment reel: earlier relationships collapsing, moments when I had been harsh or distant, moments when I had wanted closeness and couldn't allow it, moments when I had been injured and couldn't fix myself back to usefulness fast enough, moments when I had chased distraction and called it healing. Each memory became a bead on a string pulled tighter around my throat.

The house became a sanctuary in the worst sense— sanctuary as isolation, sanctuary as hiding. I stopped inviting anyone over. I stopped answering calls quickly. I let the days fill with quiet because quiet felt safer than the risk of being seen. In that safety, thoughts grew bolder. They began to articulate themselves more clearly. The mind that had once treated suicide as an abstract exit began testing specifics. It began turning the idea over like an object, examining angles, considering certainty. The first attempt had failed because the world is messy and boundaries leak. The mind began seeking a cleaner method, a more decisive door, something that would not depend on air movement and imperfect seals.

That search is not something I describe with pride. It is something I describe because it is true. The mind in that state does not behave like a moral philosopher. It behaves like a wounded animal looking for a den where the pain stops. It begins to treat death as logistics. It begins to think in terms of certainty, speed, and control. The spiritual frame didn't prevent that. It intensified it. If I was already condemned, then stopping became not only an escape from pain but a conclusion to a story that felt already written. My prayers turned darker. They stopped being bargains and started being accusations. *Where are you? Why is this still happening? Why am I still here?* The silence that followed each question felt like a door closing.

The second attempt happened on a day that did not look special from the outside. Winter light came through the windows in pale stripes. The air inside the house felt dry from heating cycles. The rooms were still. The world outside continued without me—cars passing occasionally, distant human noise softened by distance—yet inside the house the atmosphere had thickened into something almost tangible. It felt like oxygen had been replaced with a heavier substance, something you had to push through with each breath. Movement felt slow. Decision felt inevitable. The mind had been narrowing toward this point for days, and that narrowing had the sensation of a corridor: walls close, forward motion forced, no side exits left.

The pistol was not a dramatic symbol in that moment. It was simply an object that existed within the house, metal and weight, a tool that carried certainty. My hand found it the way a hand finds something it has already decided to use. There was no ceremonial pause. No trembling over a drawer. No dramatic sobbing. The mind in that state is frighteningly calm, not because it is peaceful, but because it has stopped imagining alternatives. I held the weight of the object and felt how real it was compared to my thoughts. My thoughts were vapor. The metal was solid. The metal did not argue.

The metal did not require faith. It simply existed with a single purpose built into it.

I moved to the couch because it was there, because it was the most ordinary place in the house, because ending in an ordinary place felt like confirmation that nothing about my life deserved ceremony. The couch cushion sank beneath me. The room's light stayed the same. The air vent hummed softly. The house did not change expression. My body felt distant, as if I had stepped half an inch outside myself. I raised the pistol and pressed it to the side of my head, and the contact was not just physical. It was psychological. It was the moment the mind believes it has reached the final door, the moment the imagination of escape becomes a tactile fact.

From that contact forward, time nearly stopped.

The house did not freeze in a magical way. The clock did not visibly slow. It was my perception that altered. The world narrowed down to a few sensations: the cold hardness against my skin, the weight in my hand, the pressure of my own finger settling toward the trigger, the sound of my breathing too loud in my ears. Everything else—the room, the furniture, the winter light—fell into a distant background as if it were a painted set. In that slowed space, thoughts did not arrive one at a time like normal thinking. They arrived in a whirlwind, overlapping and serrated, a storm of internal voices competing to deliver the most crushing verdict before the last second ended.

*This is what you are.*

The thought did not come with explanation. It came like a stamp. My mind immediately began supplying evidence, ruthless and efficient. It pulled the winter trip back into view—the empty overlooks, the dangerous roads, the way danger had felt clean. It framed that craving as proof of corruption. *You went looking for places where you could disappear.* It pulled the return home into view—the quiet house, the echoing rooms—and framed that as proof of failure. *You built a life and you can't live in it.* It pulled the work environment into view—the training course, the role-play rooms, the interrogations—and framed that as proof of hypocrisy. *You teach control and you have none.*

Another thought rose, sharper, nastier: *You have always been this. The ending is simply catching up to the truth.*

The whirlwind did not allow mercy. It did not allow context. It did not allow the human understanding that wounds accumulate. It chose the harshest interpretation of every chapter. Childhood scenes became early evidence of wrongness—being an outsider inside normal rooms, learning to perform instead of belong. Adolescence became proof of drift—wanting things without knowing how to get them, making choices driven by impulse, then paying for them in shame. Early adulthood became proof of instability—relationships formed under pressure and broken under pressure, intimacy turning into conflict, the sense of being unable to hold a shared life steady. Military life became proof of damage—being shaped by environments built for violence, then coming home and discovering the shaping didn't reverse. Injury became proof of uselessness—back pain, visual distortion, the slow realization that the body would not return to its old reliability.

My mind recapped each of those as if it were reading charges in court, and each recap carried a justification for the thought that sat inside the trigger finger: *It makes sense to stop.* It made sense because the pain had lasted too long. It made sense because the house had become a box. It made sense because the spiritual silence had become unbearable. It made sense because I could not imagine a future that wasn't simply more of the same—more hollow mornings, more forced performances, more nights spent bargaining with an absent sky. The mind framed suicide not as destruction but as a correction, a way of aligning reality with what it claimed had always been true: that I did not belong in the world the way other people seemed to.

In that slowed time, religious thoughts cut through like blades. They did not comfort. They condemned. The mind held up every private shame and turned it into a spiritual verdict: *Unclean.* It held up every failure of self-control and turned it into proof that I was beyond redemption: *If grace existed, it would have reached you by now.* It held up the silence after prayer and turned it into a divine rejection: *You asked. You received nothing. That is your answer.* It held up the survival of the first attempt and turned it into mockery: *Even when you try to leave, the world keeps you here to suffer.* The spiritual frame became a trap with no exit, because leaving could be interpreted as damnation and staying felt like punishment anyway.

The internal voice grew crueler. It began listing people who had passed through my life and left—without naming them, without allowing them to become human again, only using them as proof. *They didn't stay. They saw what you are. They left because you are not safe to love.* It turned the job cutbacks into humiliation. *You were not chosen first. You were not wanted. You were tolerated.* It turned the house into an accusation. *A man with a house and a job should be grateful, and you can't even hold gratitude inside your ribs.* It turned my own competence into evidence against me. *You can build systems. You can improve training. You can solve problems. And you still can't fix yourself. That means the problem is you. Not circumstances. Not bad luck. You.*

The finger on the trigger tightened slightly, not because I consciously decided to pull, but because the body responds to the mind's momentum. The mind had been pushing toward completion for days. In that frozen second, it pushed harder. *Do it.* The command felt like an instruction from a voice that had been living in my head longer than I wanted to admit. It wasn't frantic. It wasn't panicked. It was calm and final, the way a person speaks when they have stopped negotiating. The calm was terrifying because it felt true.

Then another thought flashed—thin, desperate, still relentless but different: *You are not brave. You are tired.*

The mind tried to crush that thought immediately, tried to smother it with shame. *Tired is an excuse. Everyone gets tired. You don't get special rules.* But the thought had already left a crack. It reminded me, brutally, that I had been surviving by exhaustion for years—sleep debt, pain, constant vigilance, constant performance. It reminded me that the war had trained my body to live at high stress, and the home world had expected the body to downshift without instruction. It reminded me that the training environment had kept me steeped in suspicion and confrontation even after I had left combat. It reminded me that the solitude I had chased had turned into isolation. It reminded me that the spiritual frame I had grabbed had become a weapon because my mind was already skilled at weaponizing anything.

The crack didn't widen into hope. It widened into grief, and grief hit like a wave inside the frozen second. Not dramatic sobbing. A heavy internal ache that made my chest feel full. The grief carried images: empty national park overlooks under winter sky, the wide blue bowl of a crater lake, a cliffside road with snow on the edge, a drift that had stopped my truck, strangers on skis pushing me free. Those images were not heroic. They were proof that the world had still offered me moments of contact, moments where life had touched me even when I didn't deserve it. The mind tried to reject those as irrelevant. *Moments don't justify living.* The grief didn't argue. It simply existed, pressing against the internal command to end.

In that pressure, I felt my trigger finger tremble—not visibly, not in a way a spectator could photograph, but a small quiver of muscle fatigue. The finger had been holding tension for tooo long, as if it had been waiting for permission to relax or permission to complete. My breath caught in my throat. The metal against my head remained cold. Time remained nearly stopped. The world stayed narrow.

And then my cat entered the scene like a law.

He didn't sprint. He didn't leap heroically from across the room with cinematic timing. He simply moved with the quiet confidence he always carried, padding across the floor, jumping onto the couch with a soft thump that should have been insignificant. In the frozen second, that thump was thunder. The cushion shifted under his weight. The shift traveled up into my body, a physical interruption. He stepped onto my lap without hesitation, turned once, and settled as if he had been invited. His warmth spread through the fabric of my pants. His purr started immediately, a low vibration that cut through the whirlwind like a tuning fork.

The vibration did something time could not resist.

Time restarted.

Not all at once, not with a snap, but with a loosening. The room came back into focus: winter light on the wall, the quiet hum of the vent, the distant sound of something outside. My breathing became audible to me again as breathing rather than as a countdown. The pressure of the pistol against my head remained, but now it was one sensation among many instead of the only sensation. The cat's weight on my lap was undeniable, anchoring. His purr climbed through my ribs and shook something loose. My trigger finger, which had been clamped by the mind's momentum, relaxed a fraction—not because I forgave myself, not because hope arrived, but because another living thing had made contact and demanded attention in the simplest possible way.

The finger loosened again. The muscle fatigue turned into release. The internal command—*Do it*—lost volume, not silenced, but interrupted. In the resumed flow of time, I felt a strange, involuntary relief wash through me, the kind that makes the body tremble. Relief not that I had chosen life with conviction, but that the decision had been delayed. Relief that the frozen second had cracked. Relief that I had not yet crossed the final line. The cat's purr continued, steady and indifferent to my crisis. He behaved as if this was a normal lap, a normal afternoon, a normal human body beneath him.

That normality was devastating.

It made my shame flare hard, because it highlighted how close I had been to ending everything in the same room where an animal could still trust me. It made my grief deepen, because it showed me a version of innocence that still existed in my house. It made the religious condemnation wobble, because I couldn't easily fit the cat's timing into the narrative of total rejection. The mind still tried to be relentless. It tried to twist even this into cruelty. *You were stopped by a cat. That is how weak you are.* The thought landed. It stung. It did not regain control, because the physical reality on my lap kept insisting on the present: warmth, weight, vibration, breath.

I lowered the pistol away from my head, not in a dramatic flourish, not in a triumphant decision, but in the same mechanical way I had done other things while numb. My hand moved because the tension had released enough to allow movement. The metal's weight shifted. The cold against my skin disappeared. The cat adjusted slightly and settled deeper, purring as if satisfied with his own work. The attempt failed for a reason so ordinary it felt unreal: a small animal chose contact at the exact moment time had nearly stopped, and that contact restarted time long enough for my finger to relax.

I remained on the couch with the cat on my lap, the winter light still painting pale stripes on the wall, the house still quiet, the air still dry, my body still alive. The decision had not been resolved into a clean lesson. It had only been interrupted. The first attempt had failed because the world's imperfect boundaries leaked air. The second attempt failed because my own muscle released under the weight of a purring animal. No sirens. No dramatic rescuer. No cinematic redemption. Only failure—and the unbearable fact that failure meant continued breathing.

The chapter ends there, in the moment the trigger finger relaxed and time resumed, because everything that came after belonged to a different scene: the aftermath of survival, the collapse that follows an interrupted ending, the new kind of corridor that opens when you are still alive and you no longer have the illusion that stopping is easy.

# CHAPTER 16

# *Learning Help*

A small orange prescription bottle sits in the cup holder of my car like it belongs there, like it has always belonged there. The label is rubbed soft from fingers and time, the printed letters worn at the corners where I've peeled it and pressed it back down again, as if I could change what it says by worrying it like a scab. When I shake the bottle, the tablets rattle with a dry plastic clatter that sounds almost cheerful—tiny objects bouncing inside a container, proof of something contained, manageable, official. The sound is too light for what it represents. It's a sound you'd expect from candy, not from a system's attempt to name and medicate a mind that has learned to run hot without permission.

The bottle knocks gently against the cup holder when I take a turn, tapping out a quiet rhythm—tap, tap, tap—like it's trying to get my attention. My hands stay on the steering wheel. My eyes stay forward. Outside the windshield the road moves in its normal way, the world behaving as if everything inside me is ordinary. The bottle's tapping becomes louder in my awareness than the traffic, louder than my own breath. It brings with it a particular kind of memory: a waiting room smell, the sterile friendliness of laminated posters, the way institutions speak in calm voices while people inside those walls are falling apart.

The rattle and tap are present-day facts, but they pull backward, through time, into the first months after the attempts—when survival wasn't relief and getting help wasn't a decision I made from hope. It was a decision I made because the alternatives had proven themselves too close. The road outside stays stable, the bottle stays in its holder, but the scene in my mind shifts to a different kind of drive: not a commute, not an errand, but the slow, reluctant movement toward a place where I would have to admit, out loud, that I had nearly ended my life and didn't trust myself not to try again.

After the cat interrupted the gun and the frozen second released its grip, the house did not transform into a sanctuary. It stayed the same—wide rooms, dry air, winter light cutting pale stripes across the wall. The difference wasn't in the architecture. The difference was in me. A door had been opened in my mind and it didn't close. The first attempt had failed because the world leaked air where I had assumed it wouldn't. The second attempt had failed because a small animal made contact and restarted time at the exact moment my finger was turning intention into action. Those failures didn't erase the desire to stop. They didn't heal the despair. They simply proved something I hadn't known before: the line between living and ending wasn't theoretical. It was reachable. It was tactile. It was one movement away.

In the days that followed, shame became the weather of my house. Shame sat in the corners like dust. It drifted into every routine. If I brushed my teeth, shame watched. If I stood at the sink, shame leaned over my shoulder. The shame wasn't only about trying to die. It was about surviving. It was about how ordinary it had all been—how domestic, how procedural, how quiet. People imagine suicide as an explosion of emotion, an operatic collapse.

What had happened in my house was more disturbing than that because it had been calm. It had been a man moving through a series of steps as if he were following instructions, and the calmness made me feel monstrous. The calmness made me wonder what else I was capable of.

Winter didn't help. The nights were long enough that darkness felt like a second ceiling lowering. The mornings arrived too slowly, and when they arrived, they didn't bring renewal; they brought the same weight in the chest, the same dry throat, the same heavy limbs. Some hours were filled with an eerie, brittle clarity—moments when the mind seemed sharp, capable, almost normal—followed by stretches of blankness where time softened and slid away. I would sit on the couch and realize the light had changed outside without being able to account for the minutes in between. It wasn't sleep. It wasn't rest. It was dissociation in the plainest sense: a mind stepping sideways from itself because being fully present hurt too much.

The turning point wasn't a sudden decision to choose life. It was a practical fear. The fear wasn't death itself. The fear was that I had proven I could get close, and closeness changes the math. Before the attempts, suicide had been an idea that appeared and disappeared like a shadow. After the attempts, it became a known path through the woods. Once you know a path exists, the mind can find it faster. Once you have put your hand on the door, the door becomes easier to open again. That frightened me in a way I didn't want to admit, because fear implied I still cared about staying alive. Caring implied responsibility. Responsibility implied more work. I was exhausted to the bone by work that didn't look like work—just surviving hour after hour without relief.

Reaching out for help began in a state that felt like humiliation. It wasn't the kind of humility people praise, the noble kind that signals growth. It was humiliating because it required me to reveal weakness to a system. I had spent years performing competence. I had spent years being the person who could teach, evaluate, build, troubleshoot, adapt. Admitting collapse felt like stepping onto a stage and confessing I didn't know my lines. I dialed numbers and hung up before anyone answered. I started to speak to a person on the other end of a line and felt my throat close around the words. It was easier to confess to empty rooms than to another human voice, because a human voice might react. A human voice might judge. A human voice might sound tired of me before I even finished.

Eventually, the call went through anyway. The person on the line didn't sound shocked. That fact was both comforting and horrifying. Comforting because it meant I wasn't the only one. Horrifying because it meant the world contained enough people like me that my confession was routine. The questions came in a calm sequence—safety questions, direct questions—spoken in a tone designed to keep me from spiraling. I answered with short phrases at first, then with longer ones as the dam cracked. Saying the words out loud changed them. They became heavier once they existed in the air between me and another person. They became more real. They became less romantic, less abstract. The attempts had already been real; the telling made them official.

The first appointment felt like stepping into a building where everyone was trying not to look at each other too closely. Waiting rooms have a specific atmosphere: chairs arranged for compliance, muted televisions playing noise that isn't meant to be watched, posters on walls offering hope in clean fonts. I sat with my knees slightly apart, hands clasped, eyes scanning without meaning to. My body still ran on an old operating system—always aware, always braced. People around me held their own shapes of pain. Some looked exhausted. Some looked angry. Some looked blank. No one made prolonged eye contact because prolonged eye contact invites conversation, and conversation invites disclosure, and disclosure is dangerous when you're barely holding together.

When someone finally called my name, the sound of it—my name spoken in that neutral clinical tone—felt like a jolt. In an office with a closed door, the questions returned, more detailed now. I answered with the same controlled voice I had used in other high-stakes environments. I described what I could. I omitted what felt too raw. I watched myself doing it, watched the way my mind tried to keep the story tidy, and I hated myself for that too. Even in collapse, I was still trying to perform. Even in a room designed for help, I was still guarding my own vulnerability like it was contraband.

Therapy began as a strange kind of labor. People think therapy is talking. Talking is the surface. The deeper work is tolerance—the ability to sit with memories and sensations without fleeing. My body was not built for that yet. Sitting in a quiet room and being asked to describe internal states felt harder than sitting in loud places with external threats. External threats can be met with action. Internal threats require stillness. Stillness is where my mind had become most dangerous. The therapist spoke in measured ways, guiding, not forcing. The guidance sometimes felt gentle enough to be insulting. I didn't want gentleness. I wanted a switch to flip. I wanted the weight to lift. I wanted the night thoughts to stop offering exits. I wanted spiritual silence to either turn into comfort or admit it was absent. Instead I got slow questions and slow progress and the painful realization that healing is rarely dramatic. Healing is mostly repetition, mostly showing up when you don't want to, mostly tolerating discomfort without solving it.

At the same time, life demanded that I keep functioning. My job didn't pause because I was in therapy. The training course kept moving students through its pipeline. The systems I had built kept needing maintenance. I kept driving into work, kept walking through familiar hallways, kept sitting at a desk with screens full of data fields. But something changed in how I moved through that environment. After the attempts, student contact began to feel intolerable. It wasn't the students themselves as individuals. It was the role: standing in front of rows of faces, pretending I was stable enough to teach mental discipline while my own mind was negotiating whether to exist. Watching students role-play interrogations and hearing voices rise and press and push, even inside controlled training, started scraping me raw. The repeated posture of confrontation—the constant drilling of suspicion and pressure—was amplifying the worst parts of my internal state.

So I did what I've always done when an environment becomes unlivable: I adapted by narrowing my exposure. I began shifting my work priorities in a way that looked logical on paper. I leaned harder into software development and course systems—the parts of the job that involved building tools, improving databases, tightening processes.

Those tasks were socially safer. A database doesn't watch your face. A database doesn't ask how you're doing. A database will accept your effort without demanding eye contact. I worked with leadership to frame it as efficiency: better tracking, better evaluation tools, improved course quality. All of that was true. Beneath that truth was my private truth: distance from students meant fewer triggers, fewer human moments where I might crack, fewer times I'd have to stand in a room and pretend I was strong.

In that shift, I became more valuable in a specific way. I became the person who could build and maintain the invisible machinery that made the course run smoother. I wrote code that reduced errors. I designed fields that captured performance data more cleanly. I built reporting tools that helped instructors see patterns across classes. The work had a cold satisfaction to it. It was measurable. It had endpoints. It rewarded persistence. The problem was that my mind began treating those endpoints as proof of worth: if I could make the system better, maybe the system would let me stay. If I could keep producing, maybe I could keep outrunning the part of me that wanted to stop. Production became a spiritual practice of its own, a form of worship offered to a god that never speaks: the god of usefulness.

The VA involvement continued in parallel. Therapy sessions came and went. Some were productive in the way people imagine—moments where a thought changed shape, where a pattern became visible. Many were productive in a less romantic way: I showed up, I spoke, I endured. There were days when leaving a session felt like walking out of a room where I'd been scraped open. I would sit in my car afterward and stare at the steering wheel, hands resting on it without turning the key, because I didn't trust myself to drive while emotionally unsteady. Other days, the sessions felt almost pointless—talking into the same air, naming the same despair, leaving with no immediate relief. The point, I learned slowly, wasn't immediate relief. The point was keeping me alive long enough for different choices to become possible.

Spiritual transformation didn't resolve neatly during this period. It shifted the way a wound shifts: sometimes closing, sometimes reopening. For a while, I chased religious certainty hard. I tried to read, to listen, to pray with discipline. I tried to interpret survival as mercy. I tried to interpret the cat's interruption as a sign. The problem was that signs are hard to believe in when your nervous system is still braced for threat and your mind is still trained to find exits. I could accept the idea of grace intellectually and still feel condemned emotionally. Those two states can coexist, and they make a person feel divided. In that division, I kept reaching. Reaching was easier than surrender. Reaching let me pretend I was still moving toward something, even when I couldn't name what.

Work, for a while, held. The house remained mine. The desert sky remained wide. The pain in my lower back remained a constant undertone. The distortion in my right eye remained part of how light behaved at night. Those were known facts. The unknown was whether I could keep my life assembled while the larger world shifted around me. Budgets change. Contracts change. Priorities change. Institutions cut and rehire as if human lives are items in a storage room. I had seen it happen once before and lived through it with a bitter kind of luck. I assumed—without admitting it—that my usefulness would protect me the next time too.

It didn't.

Another round of cutbacks arrived like a cold hand on the back of the neck. The announcement didn't come with drama. It came with meetings and vague language and that institutional tone that tries to sound compassionate while delivering harm. The number of positions shrank again. The frame that had held my days—the routine, the role, the reason to get up—began to feel unstable. I watched coworkers' faces tighten. I watched people calculate silently. Who would be cut. Who would be kept. Who could move. Who had savings. Who could risk being unemployed. The environment filled with a quiet desperation that didn't show in polite conversation but leaked through every hallway.

When the decision point arrived for me, it didn't feel like a choice between two good options. It felt like choosing the shape of a loss. I could fight to stay, cling to the position, gamble on being selected. Or I could accept a severance package, take the money, and remove myself from the slow humiliation of waiting for a system to decide whether I deserved to keep living the life I had built around it. Pride and exhaustion met in the same place. Pride didn't want to be cut. Exhaustion didn't want to beg. So I chose the severance. I told myself it was strategic—better to leave with a check than to be pushed out empty-handed. The truth was harsher: I didn't trust myself to survive another prolonged uncertainty. I had already learned what it feels like to sit alone in a house and watch the mind turn on itself. I wasn't willing to invite that again while also watching my income disappear.

Losing the job in late spring of 2017 felt like the floor dropping out, not because the job was my identity in a proud way, but because it was my structure. Without it, my days became wide and dangerous again. The house I had built, the one that had promised stability, began to feel like a dare. The mortgage didn't care about my mental state. The bills didn't care about my therapy schedule. The desert didn't care about my prayers. I walked through rooms and felt the space closing in, not physically, but psychologically. The house had been survivable when it was a place I returned to after work. When it became the place I stayed all day, it became an amplifier again.

I tried to sell it. The decision was practical, humiliating, and necessary. I hired a realtor, signed a contract, and watched my house become a product. Photos were taken. Listings were made. The price was set, then lowered, then lowered again. I dropped it by an amount that should have made it irresistible, an amount that made my stomach twist because it meant losing money on a thing that had been sold to me as an investment in a future. The house did not sell. Weeks turned into months. Showings were rare. Feedback, when it came, was vague. The longer it sat, the more it felt like a public judgment: even the market didn't want what I had built.

I began to direct my anger at the realtor because anger is easier than despair. It gave me a target. I could tell myself the failure was incompetence rather than fate. I could tell myself property values were supposed to rise, that the universe owed me appreciation, that losing money meant I had been cheated. Those beliefs were partly economic myth and partly emotional defense. The deeper truth was simpler: I was watching the last major proof of my attempted stability fail to convert into an exit. I was trapped in a house I couldn't afford and couldn't sell, in a state of life where "moving on" had become more complicated than packing a truck.

In the middle of that, the severance money began to thin. Savings don't disappear in one dramatic moment. They disappear through ordinary expenses—utilities, insurance, groceries—each one small enough to seem manageable until you add them together and see the slope. I watched the numbers in my accounts and felt a cold dread settle. Dread isn't always panic. Sometimes it's a slow, constant weight that makes the future feel like a narrowing hallway. I had lived inside narrowing hallways before. I knew where they could lead. The memory of 2013 wasn't a distant chapter. It was a warning light that never fully turned off.

So I did what I had done before when life cornered me: I moved. Not as an adventure. Not as a fresh start. As a retreat.

In mid-summer of 2017, I left the desert house behind and returned to the region I had grown up in—back to flat land and familiar roads, back to a house that existed inside my mind as a specific kind of time capsule. The move wasn't only geographic. It was a psychological reversal. It meant stepping backward into an earlier version of myself, into an old bedroom that carried the residue of the man I had been decades before. When I carried boxes in and set them down, the room felt both too familiar and unreal, like a set rebuilt from memory. The walls were the same. The light through the window was the same kind of light. The air had a different humidity, a different smell. But the person placing items on the floor was not the boy who had once lived there. The person was a middle-aged man with injuries and ghosted vision and a mind that had walked up to the edge and been interrupted.

Living in that house came with conditions that were never spoken as cruelty but felt like control. There were expectations about routine, about behavior, about where I went and what I did, about attending religious services as proof of stability. I complied because compliance bought shelter. I sat in pews and listened to familiar cadences, the language of sin and redemption and salvation poured over me like water that didn't quite penetrate. Part of me wanted to believe again with simple faith. Part of me felt resentful —resentful that church attendance was treated as medicine, resentful that my internal collapse was being handled through external rituals. Yet another part of me was grateful for the structure. The house imposed a schedule. The schedule kept me from drifting too far into isolation. Structure, even borrowed, can keep a man alive.

During that period, an older adult in the house began showing signs that something was shifting cognitively, though no one named it yet. It appeared in small ways at first —repeated stories told with absolute confidence, details slightly off, the same questions asked more than once in the same conversation. Sometimes the older adult would speak about past work years as if they were recent, as if time had folded. Sometimes there would be irritation at small confusions, the kind of irritation that comes when a person feels themselves slipping but doesn't know what to call it. In those moments, the household atmosphere tightened. No one wanted to say the word that would make it real. So the word stayed unspoken, and the small signs became part of daily life like an additional piece of weather.

Watching that slow cognitive shift did something complicated to me. It made me angry in a protective way, then guilty for the anger, then terrified because it felt like another example of the body betraying itself. My own body had betrayed me with pain and vision distortion. Now I was watching a mind begin to betray someone else in a way that would eventually become undeniable. The house held that tension quietly. Some days were normal. Some days carried a faint edge of confusion that made every conversation feel slightly fragile. I found myself becoming more patient than I expected, not because I was naturally gentle, but because I recognized the terror underneath: the terror of losing control of your own system.

Work, in the traditional sense, wasn't available to me then. The job had gone. The house sale had failed. The desert life was now at a distance, still technically mine but not physically present. In that vacuum, I needed something to pour myself into, something that could provide structure without requiring permission from a budget committee. That's how game development entered my life—not as a childhood dream fulfilled, not as a whimsical hobby, but as another attempt to build a frame strong enough to hold me.

I downloaded Unreal Engine 4 and began teaching myself the tools the way I had taught myself other systems: obsessively, methodically, with the belief that competence could produce meaning. Game development is a strange mix of logic and imagination. It has the satisfying harshness of code—things either compile or they don't—and the soft unpredictability of design—things either feel right or they don't. I built small test environments: a room, a hallway, a landscape. I learned how lighting changes mood. I learned how collision works, how physics behaves inside a simulated world. I learned how to make an object respond to an input, how to trigger an event, how to animate simple actions. The work pulled my attention into a space where I could control outcomes. The world inside the engine responded to me in ways the real world rarely did.

I joined a startup effort that promised future profit but offered no pay, a gamble framed as opportunity. The arrangement was thin—people scattered, remote, talking in bursts of enthusiasm and then vanishing into their own lives. We discussed concepts and roles. We imagined a finished product. We assigned tasks and deadlines and pretended momentum existed. Nearly two years passed inside that effort, and nothing tangible emerged. No finished product. No release. No paycheck. Only the slow realization that passion doesn't always become output when the adults involved are exhausted and under-resourced. The failure was predictable in hindsight. At the time, it still stung, because it was another structure I had tried to build that didn't hold.

While I was learning UE4 and trying to make a game development path real, the desert house remained unresolved. The realtor contract ran its course. The listing remained stale. The market did not rescue me. Eventually, the strategy shifted from selling to renting, not because renting felt like victory, but because it was a way to stop hemorrhaging. That shift required me to return to the house in the desert state again for a period—go back alone, open doors that had been closed, ready it for someone else's life. Returning to the house after living elsewhere felt like visiting a previous self. The rooms were familiar and wrong. The air smelled different, dustier, like an unoccupied space that has been holding its breath. I walked through and heard my footsteps echo again, and the echo brought back the danger of too much quiet.

Preparing a house for rental is intimate in an odd way. You're cleaning not to enjoy your own space but to make it acceptable to strangers. You patch small holes. You repaint scuffed walls. You check appliances. You replace bulbs. You walk through each room and try to see it the way someone else will see it, someone who doesn't carry the memories you carry. I scrubbed and repaired and organized with a grim focus, because focus kept my mind from slipping. I told myself this was practical—asset management, financial survival. Underneath, it was emotional: I was turning a chapter of my life into a commodity, letting other people live inside the shell of the stability I had failed to inhabit.

At night, when the work stopped and the house went still, the silence turned predatory. I slept on an air mattress in the master bedroom because the rest of the house felt too empty to choose from, and because the bare floor and the thin cushion matched the way my life had been reduced. Several nights, while I was trying to fall asleep, I heard what sounded like a group of people talking too loudly outside— voices layered over each other, the indistinct swell of conversation, like a crowd that didn't care who it disturbed. I got up and checked more than once. I walked the rooms. I looked out windows. I stepped outside into the cold air and listened. There was no one. No cars. No laughter. No footsteps. The voices kept going anyway.

They weren't clear enough to quote. More like mumbling, like a cluster of human sound without words, but my brain received it as real. That was the part that scared me most: how easily it slipped past logic, how the house could be empty and my body could still react as if people were out there. Later, I could tell myself it had the texture of old patrols—moving through crowds where you couldn't separate threat from noise, where too many mouths and too many languages turned into one continuous pressure. Back then, after Iraq, I learned to keep silence filled—music, television, white noise—anything to keep my mind from inventing its own atmosphere. In that house, alone, with nothing running but the heater and my own breath, the silence had room. And in that room, the voices crept in while I was trying to make the place clean enough for strangers.

The VA remained part of my life through all of this, sometimes steady, sometimes frustrating, always bureaucratic. Appointments, forms, assessments. The system's language attempted to reduce my experience to categories. Sometimes that reduction felt like validation—proof that what I carried had a recognized shape. Sometimes it felt insulting—like the complexity of my internal world was being turned into a number on a form. I attended group sessions at one point, sitting in a room with others whose eyes carried a similar mix of exhaustion and vigilance. In that setting, people spoke about symptoms without always naming them as symptoms. They described sleep that wasn't rest. They described irritability that arrived like a switch. They described bodies that flinched at ordinary sounds. Listening to them was like hearing my own life echoed through different voices. It was comforting and unsettling at the same time.

That group exposure taught me language. Not the language of excuse, the language that says, *This is why I can't*. The language of recognition: *This is what is happening*. That recognition mattered when it came time to file for service connection. Paperwork asks you to translate pain into narrative, to make suffering legible to a system that measures it. I had spent years being reluctant to do that, partly out of pride, partly out of exhaustion, partly out of the old belief that needing help is weakness. Eventually, necessity and accumulated knowledge forced action. The claim process was slow, impersonal, and heavy. When a rating finally arrived—substantial but not complete—it felt like a strange kind of truce. On paper, the system acknowledged that something real had happened and continued to happen. In my day-to-day life, the acknowledgement didn't fix anything. It simply gave me a small foundation of stability to build on, and stability, even when imperfect, changes what choices become possible.

During the years between returning to the old house in the plains and enrolling in school again, I lived inside a paradox. On one side: dependence and regression—moving back into a bedroom that belonged to an earlier era, living under household expectations, watching an older adult's cognitive changes deepen slowly without being named. On the other side: self-directed ambition—learning complex tools, building projects in UE4, trying to pivot into a new identity built from creativity and code. The paradox didn't resolve; it simply became daily reality. Some days I felt like I was rebuilding. Some days I felt like I was hiding. Most days I felt like I was doing both at once.

The decision to return to university for a second time didn't arrive as inspiration. It arrived as a calculation: I needed a path that had institutional legitimacy. Game development alone was too unstable without credentials, without a finished product, without a network that could translate skill into income. The job I had lost was not coming back. The training-course world had moved on. My body still carried pain. My mind still carried a door that had opened in 2013 and never fully closed. The question became less about what I wanted and more about what I could build that might keep me alive in a sustainable way.

Enrollment required its own kind of courage, not the loud kind. Paperwork courage. Schedule courage. The willingness to be a student again, to sit in classrooms or online portals and accept instruction, to risk feeling old among younger people, to risk feeling slow because trauma and depression can blunt attention. I filled out forms. I requested transcripts. I chose a program that felt practical enough to matter. When acceptance and start dates arrived, the calendar suddenly held a future again—weeks with assignments, semesters with structure, goals measured in credits. That structure had saved me before. It might save me again.

By fall of 2019, the second university attempt began, and the start carried a quiet significance. Not triumph. Not redemption. It was simply movement in a direction that wasn't an exit. After years of survival that often felt like stalling, I was stepping into a system designed for progress. Whether progress would happen was still uncertain. The older adult in the house still repeated stories with increasing frequency. The desert house still sat in my life like unfinished business, now prepared for renters rather than sold. The game development dream still hovered in the background, both alluring and unreliable. The VA still held my file, still scheduled appointments, still measured my life in forms. My mind still contained the memory of frozen time and a trigger finger that had relaxed under a small animal's weight.

But the semester started anyway.

And that—more than any dramatic revelation—was the shape of my survival in those years: not choosing life with joy, not finding a cure, not discovering a clean spiritual answer, but continuing to take the next structured step because structure, once again, was the only thing strong enough to keep the inside of my head from becoming the only place I lived.

# CHAPTER 17

## *Altered Semesters*

A stack of accommodation letters sits in a folder I keep like a private passport. The pages are ordinary—clean fonts, checkboxes, polite language—but they carry the quiet power of permission. Extra time. Reduced-distraction testing. A separate room. The right to ask for what my brain can't manufacture on demand. I don't read them for comfort, not exactly. I read them the way someone rereads a diagnosis, half hoping the ink has changed. The words never change. What changes is my relationship to them: some days they feel like a lifeline, proof that I'm not imagining the friction; other days they feel like a receipt for damage, a formal acknowledgment that I don't move through the world like other people do.

The folder has softened at the corners from being opened too often. The pages inside have faint creases where I folded them in a rush before walking into an office, before meeting a coordinator, before asking a professor for patience without sounding like I was bargaining for pity. When I touch the paper, I can feel the timeline braided into it—how a single decision to return to school turned into a long sequence of tests, laboratories, deadlines, illnesses, and increasingly strange attempts to lift the weight off my mind by pushing it through doors I didn't fully understand. The present is a thin film over that memory. Peel it back, and I'm there again, stepping into a campus apartment building in the fall of 2019, carrying more history than any syllabus could hold.

I returned to university that season through a veterans' program designed to rebuild broken careers. The paperwork that got me there was its own course load—forms, meetings, evaluations—each one asking me to translate my life into categories that administrators could approve. I told myself I was doing it for stability, for a legitimate path out of drifting, but the deeper motive was simpler and more desperate: I needed structure that couldn't be negotiated with my moods. Work had once done that for me. Work had collapsed. I needed a new frame, a new set of rails. University offered rails: assignments due at midnight, lectures at set hours, labs that demanded attendance, exams that didn't care if I slept poorly or woke up with my thoughts already armed.

The apartment assigned to me was in a university housing building that felt like a self-contained ecosystem—hallways that smelled faintly of detergent and microwaved meals, common areas designed for the kind of casual social life I never quite learned, a steady churn of people moving through doors with backpacks, earbuds, and the unearned confidence of the young. I was older than most of them. Not ancient, but old enough to feel the difference in how time sat in my body. They moved fast and loose, as if injuries were hypothetical and sleep was optional. I moved like someone who had learned that the body keeps receipts. I walked carefully when my back flared. I watched my right-side peripheral distort under certain lights. I built routines the way you build scaffolding around a fragile structure—meal times, study blocks, notes, checklists—because if I didn't, the days would dissolve.

Accommodations were introduced early, not as a favor but as a formal arrangement. I had recently been diagnosed with dyslexia and attention issues layered on top of other invisible damage, and those diagnoses changed the way I understood my past more than they changed my daily skills. I could read. I could write. I could solve problems. What I struggled with was the invisible tax: the extra time it took to decode, the way letters would swap places under stress, the way my attention would slip at the worst moments, the way fatigue turned simple instructions into puzzles. The accommodations didn't make me smarter. They made me less likely to lose points for the brain's misfires. I started taking exams in a testing center room that was too quiet, like a chapel for anxious minds. I would sit alone under sterile lighting, the clock on the wall louder than any crowd, and try to do math as if math was the only reality.

Computer engineering was the most honest kind of challenge I had found in years, because it didn't care about my story. It cared about whether my answers were correct. It was equal parts abstract and physical—equations that described invisible forces, circuits you could touch, code that either compiled or didn't. The curriculum demanded a kind of disciplined thinking that felt almost soothing. Calculus and physics were brutal but fair. Digital logic was a world of gates and truth tables where a single flipped bit could make the whole system lie. Programming required patience and precision, which I could supply in obsessive quantities when my brain latched onto a problem. Labs smelled like solder and plastic and metal, the air faintly warm from equipment. I liked the certainty of it: wires in, signals out, predictable laws governing what should happen. After years of living in a mind that could change the rules without warning, predictable laws felt like mercy.

I held a 4.0 in core classes, not because I was gifted in some effortless way, but because I treated school like a mission. I studied the way I once prepared for things that had real consequences. I took notes like my future depended on it because it did. I sat through lectures with my attention chained to the front of the room, forcing myself to refocus every time my mind drifted. I solved practice problems until my hand cramped. I went to office hours when I didn't want to be seen. I learned to ask questions without apologizing for existing. The grades were evidence that structure worked. They were proof that a part of me could still perform at a high level if the environment had clear rules and if I had enough scaffolding to keep my symptoms from turning into failure.

But success didn't erase the weight. It only made the weight harder to explain. When people see a strong GPA, they assume you're fine. They assume you've solved yourself. They don't see the hours of forced concentration, the way a single misread symbol can spiral into panic, the way your body can sit in a chair while your mind fights a private war to stay present. I would finish an exam and walk back to my apartment feeling both proud and hollow, like I had won a battle but not moved the front line. At night, the building would quiet down, and I would hear doors close, voices fade, laughter drift away. Then I would be alone with the part of my mind that didn't care about grades. The part that asked the same question in different disguises: *Is this enough to keep you here?*

That winter break, I traveled to see an older relative who lived near the coast. The trip was supposed to be normal

—holidays, family time, a change of scenery—but it became the first pivot of this chapter. When I was picked up from the airport, a small device was placed in my hand like a gift, offered as a way to relax. I didn't think much of it at first. I had used mild marijuana in the past and never treated it as anything more than a soft edge, a small chemical permission to loosen. At the house, after days of ordinary conversation and meals and the quiet tension that always exists when people who share history try not to talk about what history did, the relative told me he could fix my depression. Not cure it in a clinical way, but fix it in the way a person says when they believe they have discovered a lever.

He invited a childhood friend over—someone who knew him well, someone who moved through the house as if he belonged there—and that night they laid out small squares of paper like they were tools. No ceremony, no warning tone, no reverence. Just paper on fingertips, a casual little distribution like it was gum or aspirin. They talked about it the way people talk about something they've already survived: confident, slightly amused, almost bored by the magnitude of it. One tab for me, they said. Two for the friend. Three for the relative.

I watched them handle the squares and felt the first thread of unease start to pull at the back of my throat. I knew what the word *LSD* meant in culture—colored posters, old cautionary tales, a punchline—yet I didn't know what it meant in the body. I didn't know how it would feel to have my own mind rearranged from the inside. Still, I agreed. I agreed because I was tired of being heavy. I agreed because the promise of relief can make a person reckless even when he thinks he's being cautious. I agreed because the two of them acted like this was normal, and normal is contagious.

I held the paper for a moment before placing it on my tongue, as if delaying could preserve control. The tab softened with saliva, a small, bitter hint of something chemical, then nothing at all—just wet paper dissolving into the ordinary. I swallowed, and for a brief stretch of time the world remained perfectly unchanged. The same room. The same furniture. The same air. The same hum of household electricity. I told myself that was proof I was fine. Then I told myself it was proof it wasn't going to work. Then I told myself I should have taken more. Then I told myself I'd made a mistake taking any.

For the first thirty minutes, nothing happened, and that nothingness became its own anxiety. I kept checking myself like a man checking a wound that hasn't bled yet. *How do I feel? Do I feel different? Is that different or am I imagining it?* Every small sensation became suspect. A shift in stomach. A swallow. The warmth of a lamp on skin. I waited for a switch to flip, for the experience to announce itself with a clear border between before and after.

Somewhere between forty minutes and an hour, the border arrived—quietly, without fanfare—and I noticed it only because my balance changed. Not like nausea, not like spinning, but like the hidden calibration inside my head had loosened. I stood up and felt the room slide a fraction beneath me, as if my inner ear had been filled with something that moved too slowly. I wasn't loose and social drunk. I was disoriented drunk—careful with my steps, aware that my body was suddenly a machine I didn't fully trust.

The friend suggested marijuana to smooth the come-up. He said it like it was a known trick, like adding a second chemical was simply adjusting a thermostat. I hesitated, then inhaled anyway, because I was already committed and commitment has its own momentum. The inhale felt too large, too deliberate, like stepping on the gas while I was still learning where the brakes were. The smoke hit the back of my throat and settled in my chest with an oily weight. I exhaled and watched the vapor curl, and I felt the air in the room begin to change—not visually at first, but atmospherically. The way the air changes before a storm. The way a room can feel crowded even when no one new has entered.

Sound sharpened. Not louder, just more *present*. Their voices seemed to have texture. The refrigerator's cycling felt like an event. The tiny creaks of a house settling took on significance, like the structure itself had opinions. I tried to keep my face neutral and my tone steady, but I could already feel myself shifting into a more careful kind of listening, the way you listen when you're trying to detect something you can't name.

Around ninety minutes in, a pizza arrived. That detail is ridiculous and sacred at the same time because it anchored the experience to something normal. Someone opened the box, and the smell rose—hot dough, grease, sauce, a blunt, comforting smell that belongs to ordinary life. I took a bite expecting simple relief, expecting food to ground me.

Chewing became a loop.

It wasn't just that it took longer. It was that the act of chewing refused to reach its end. I could feel each movement of my jaw in exaggerated detail—the teeth pressing, the tongue shifting, the swallow beginning and then restarting. I became aware of my own mouth in a way I had never been aware of it before. I could not stop tracking the process. The pizza didn't dissolve into "eating." It became a series of mechanical steps that insisted on being monitored.

Time stopped behaving like a line. It stretched and folded. The space between chews felt vast, like I could spend an entire minute inside the sensation of my tongue touching my teeth. I tried to force myself to swallow just to finish the loop, and the forcing made it worse, because the body doesn't like being commanded when it's already confused. My breathing turned heavy—not because I was exerting myself, but because attention became a life-support system. It felt like if I stopped monitoring my own breath, something could go wrong. I could feel my chest rise and fall with the exaggerated clarity of a machine, and that clarity wasn't calming. It was a warning. *This is happening inside you. Pay attention. Don't let go.*

I remember thinking, with a sudden blunt fear, that I had broken the autopilot. Most people don't realize how much of living is automatic until automatic stops feeling automatic.

They tried to reassure me. They spoke to me as if I were simply overthinking, as if the mind could be talked out of its own altered physics. I nodded and tried to act like I could ride it, like I could be competent in this too. Inside, I felt the first true panic flicker: the recognition that I couldn't "logic" my way back to baseline.

Someone put a psychedelic tapestry on the floor and told me to open my eyes and look. I did, and the room changed—not into a different world, but into a deeper version of the same one. The tapestry's colors weren't just colors anymore; they were *active*. Too saturated. Too meaningful. The pattern seemed to hold motion inside it, as if the design was a river and I was finally seeing the current.

Orange and yellow began to move through the image in a slow flow, like glowing paint sliding along hidden channels. The motion wasn't fast. That was part of what made it unsettling. It felt patient, inevitable, as if the pattern had always been alive and I had simply lacked the sensory equipment to see it.

The moment I recognized the motion, another thought landed immediately behind it: *If this is real now, what else has been hidden?* The thought didn't feel philosophical. It felt threatening. It made the room feel less stable, like reality had layers and the normal layer could peel away at any time.

I tried to narrate what I was seeing, to keep the experience in language, to shape it into something coherent. Coherence kept slipping. Words would form and dissolve before they reached my mouth. I could feel a sentence arrive intact in my mind and then fracture into fragments mid-flight. The slipping created its own panic because language is one of the last structures I trust. When language fails, it feels like the floor giving way.

I could hear myself speaking, but the timing felt wrong, like my voice was arriving a half-second after I intended it. I'd start to say something and then lose the thread, and the loss made me feel embarrassed in a childlike way, like I was failing a simple test in front of two men who seemed perfectly fine. Their casual confidence—earlier—now felt like a kind of authority I didn't have. They weren't just "experienced." They were *stable* inside the instability, and I couldn't understand how.

Late in the night, the conversation shifted into something heavier. My relative talked about faith with a sudden certainty I didn't share, and he framed that certainty as proof that belief was no longer possible for him. He spoke as if something had clicked into place, as if the path ahead was obvious. I disagreed, and the disagreement wasn't intellectual—it was survival. Belief, for me, had been a beam in a collapsing house. I had leaned on it when I couldn't lean on anything else. The idea of losing it—of watching someone else tear it out and call it clarity—felt like watching the roof come down.

The disagreement didn't become a fight, not outwardly. It became a pressure in the room. My emotions grew sharper, too sharp, like the volume on my inner reactions had been turned up. Everything he said landed harder than it should have. Every casual phrase carried double meaning. I couldn't tell if I was hearing the actual words or hearing my own fear inside them. I remember sitting there thinking: *This is what it means to be vulnerable. This is what it means to have no armor.* The armor I used in daily life—rational distance, controlled tone, strategic silence—wasn't working. The drug had slid under it.

The peak didn't arrive as a single overwhelming explosion. It built like a tide until the room felt too full of sensation to hold. The tapestry kept moving, not wildly, but insistently, as if it had become a living thing that wouldn't stop breathing. Colors intensified until they felt almost loud. Shadows in corners seemed deeper than they should be. Faces held too much detail—creases, pores, micro-expressions—and that detail made people feel slightly unfamiliar, like I was seeing the raw material of them rather than the social mask.

Time continued to behave badly. Minutes would stretch and then snap forward without warning. I would think I'd been sitting for an hour and then look at the clock and see only ten minutes had passed. Or I would feel like only a brief moment had gone by and realize the conversation had moved far ahead without my awareness. That temporal instability made me doubt my own continuity. It made me fear I could lose track completely, lose myself in a gap and not return the same way.

At some point I lay down—not because I wanted to sleep, but because upright living had become too complex. Lying down reduced the world to a smaller set of tasks: breathe, keep eyes open or closed, tolerate sensation. Even then, my mind kept working, trying to interpret, trying to solve. I would close my eyes and see faint shifting patterns —residual impressions, a gentle flicker behind the eyelids— but nothing like a separate universe. The dominant experience was still the room, still the sense that ordinary reality had been turned up too high, still the feeling that my own mind had become too loud to escape.

Fear moved in waves. It would crest—*I've gone too far*—and then recede—*no, you're still here, you can still speak, you can still recognize the room*—and then crest again. Each time it crested, I would grab for an anchor: the feel of the couch fabric, the sound of someone's voice, the weight of my own hand on my chest. I kept testing myself with small proofs of sanity: *I know where I am. I know who they are. I remember my name. I can choose to stand or sit.* Those proofs mattered because the alternative was terrifying: the idea that the mind could be altered in a way that doesn't reverse.

Eventually, the intensity began to soften, not like a switch flipping back, but like pressure slowly releasing from a sealed container. My relative seemed to sense when I was starting to break and shifted the environment with practiced ease—lowering stimulation, changing rooms, offering calmer tones. He didn't treat me like a spectacle. He treated me like someone riding out weather. That helped, even though part of me resented needing help.

The tapestry returned as an anchor. Its motion became less aggressive, more like a lingering afterimage. The room began to regain its ordinary proportions. My mouth stopped feeling like a complicated machine. Breathing became less of a monitored task and more of a background function again. The fear didn't vanish; it thinned, stretched out, turned into a tremor rather than a flood.

When the night finally ended, I felt wrung out—like my mind had been clenched for hours and was now releasing soreness. I also felt strangely calm, not enlightened, not cured, but quiet in a depleted way. The calm had the flavor of survival: *You went there. You came back.* I didn't know what lesson to take from it. I only knew that a door existed, and I had put my hand on the handle.

The next day I woke up with the world intact, and that intactness felt like a miracle and like disappointment. Miracle, because I had feared permanence in the worst way —feared that I'd altered something fundamental and wouldn't get it back. Disappointment, because part of me had wanted the door to close forever, wanted to never feel that kind of vulnerability again. And another part of me— the part that had been hungry for relief—wanted it to stay open because open meant possibility, even if possibility came with teeth.

A few days later, still under the residue of that first experience, we took mushrooms—five grams dried, a heroic amount by any casual definition, though labels didn't matter once the wave came. The mushrooms were different. Less cinematic, more internal. The experience was euphoric and unsettling in a quieter way, like the depression had been lifted without the world turning into a spectacle. I remember complaining about the lack of brilliant color, and I hate that part of myself—how I wanted healing to be dramatic enough that I could trust it. Afterward, I slept and woke feeling refreshed in a way that felt almost unfamiliar. In the weeks that followed, I felt a small shift, not a cure, but a loosening, as if something in me had been pried open enough to let air in.

Before I left the coast to return to university, the relative pressed tabs into my hand as if he were handing me a tool kit. He sent me away with them like a person sending someone into the wilderness with matches. I took them back to my campus apartment, back to quiet hallways and fluorescent lights and lab assignments, and I didn't become a new person. I became the same person with a new door in the wall. In the spring of 2020, roughly every few weeks, I took LSD alone and called it exploration because exploration sounds healthier than escape. The first solo experience is the one I remember most clearly: I put on fast music and stared at a tapestry image until it began to shift. The pattern moved like it was breathing. I believed I fell in love with a woman in the art, which sounds ridiculous until you remember what loneliness does to a human mind. It didn't feel like fantasy. It felt like presence. My heart latched onto that presence like it had been waiting for any shape to hold.

I tried to control the shifting chaos in the art. I tried to manage the storm. The harder I tried, the more the image refused to be pinned down, and the refusal taught me something uncomfortable: control was not the lesson.

Surrender was. The idea would have sounded spiritual in another context. In my context it felt dangerous, because surrender had always been what happened right before things went wrong. Yet the experiences kept offering the same pressure point: relax your grip or suffer. After each trip, I returned to my textbooks and assignments with a slightly altered lens, as if the abstract worlds of calculus and circuit theory had gained an extra dimension. The next morning, I would still have deadlines, still have labs, still have lectures. The trips didn't remove responsibility. They simply added a strange, private layer of meaning to everything, a layer I didn't know how to share without sounding insane.

Between spring and summer of 2020, I went back to the coastal house again, carrying the memory of my earlier trips like a private weather system. Nothing about the place had changed in a way that mattered—same rooms, same light that seemed to linger longer near the windows, the same mild ocean-damp smell clinging to fabric. What had changed was my expectation. I wasn't walking toward the unknown anymore. I was walking toward a door I had already opened, and that knowledge made me both calmer and more reckless.

This time we each took three tabs. It wasn't a dare exactly, but it had the shape of one. We didn't count down like astronauts. We just did it, and then we waited, trying to act normal, trying to let the minutes pass without staring at the clock as if the clock could protect us.

The come-up didn't hit like a slap. It rolled in like warm water, rising around my ankles, my knees, my chest. My body loosened first, as if someone had unlatched tension I'd been wearing for years. Then the room began to soften at the edges. Colors warmed and thickened, like the house had been painted with light instead of paint. Shadows stopped behaving like empty spaces and started behaving like substances—velvet, smoke, something you could almost reach into.

Objects lost their crispness. The corners of the coffee table didn't look sharp anymore; they looked agreed-upon. The line where the wall met the ceiling wavered like it was deciding whether it wanted to stay a line. Light became viscous, like honey poured across the room. When I turned my head, the air seemed to drag, leaving a faint smear of color behind motion. Sound changed too. It wasn't louder. It was closer. It had texture. A voice in the room didn't just enter my ears; it felt like it pressed lightly against my skin, like sound had become touch.

At some point we tried to play video games—one of those ordinary choices people make when they want to keep their hands busy and pretend they're still in control. The controller sat in my palms with an unfamiliar weight, as if it wasn't plastic but some artifact with rules I didn't know. The buttons looked too shiny, too meaningful. The screen's colors were impossible—saturated beyond what a screen should be able to produce, as if the game had been upgraded to a version only altered perception can run.

I tried to focus on the objectives, to keep my mind tethered to something simple: move, aim, jump, collect. But the visuals on the screen began to trail. The characters left ribbons behind them. The menu text pulsed like it was breathing. The background music turned into a living thing that crawled into my chest and rearranged my heartbeat. I would press a button and watch my thumb move, and there would be a tiny delay between the motion and my certainty that I had caused it, as if my brain had to submit a request to reality and wait for approval.

For a while, it was funny in that uneasy way—two adults staring too hard at a game like it was a sacred test. Then it stopped being funny because the game began to feel like a mirror. Every effect on the screen felt like it was happening to my perception rather than to a character. I could feel myself slipping from "playing" into "being played," and the loss of that boundary made me set the controller down like it had grown hot.

When I closed my eyes, the real show started.

Behind my eyelids, darkness wasn't dark. It was a stage. Patterns bloomed in the black like living geometry. At first it was faint—soft grids, the suggestion of a mandala— then it intensified into bright, rotating designs that felt older than language. The shapes weren't static. They moved with purpose. They assembled and disassembled like machines made of stained glass. Colors I didn't normally see—greens too electric, purples too deep, gold that looked molten—spun in layers, folding inward, unfolding outward.

The closed-eye visuals had a strange authority. Open-eyed reality was melting, yes, but it was still recognizably the house. Closed-eyed reality felt like it belonged to a different rulebook entirely. I would open my eyes and see the room swaying gently, the furniture soft-edged and glowing. Then I'd close them again and get pulled into a tunnel of geometry that felt like traveling without moving. Time didn't behave in that tunnel. A single second could feel like a long hallway. A long minute could collapse into a single image.

Somewhere in the middle of that, the relative stood over me.

I remember looking up and seeing him shirtless, flexing, his face intense with confidence that didn't seem entirely his. He proclaimed, "I am God."

The words were so absurd they should have collapsed under their own weight. A human body making that claim is obviously human. Muscles, skin, breath, the whole fragile biology of it. And yet the moment the words landed, my nervous system reacted as if the claim carried force. Not because I believed him in any rational sense, but because altered states treat declarations like spells. Authority can be spoken into existence inside a mind that has loosened its grip on skepticism. My heart kicked. My stomach tightened. My body tried to decide whether it was in danger or in the presence of something holy, and it couldn't resolve the conflict.

Absurdity and terror lived in the same second. I wanted to laugh. I wanted to flinch. I felt the old reflex—the one that responds to dominance before it responds to meaning—rise up like a guard dog. Then, just as quickly, the sensation shifted again. The room snapped into a hyper-clarity that was almost painful. It wasn't sobriety. It was clarity turned past normal, like the universe had turned up resolution and contrast and said, *Look*.

Every object looked perfect and impossibly real. The grain of the wood. The fibers in fabric. The tiny imperfections in paint. Reality had the sharpness of revelation. In that clarity, the proclamation "I am God" didn't feel like a joke anymore; it felt like part of a larger theme—ego swelling, identity dissolving, the mind searching for a crown to place somewhere. I could see the mechanism of it and still feel its pull. That double-awareness was its own kind of torment: understanding doesn't always protect you from sensation.

We went outside because inside felt too enclosed for what was happening.

The night air hit my face like a reset—cooler, cleaner, salted with the invisible presence of ocean somewhere beyond the dark. The backyard or porch space (whatever shape it had) expanded into a wide bowl of sky. And the crickets—those ordinary summer-night insects— became an orchestra.

Their sound wasn't background anymore. It had structure. It came in waves and patterns, call-and-response, like the night itself was speaking. I could hear individual chirps as distinct events, tiny clicks of existence, and at the same time I could hear the mass of them as one continuous field of sound. The chorus pressed into my ears and then into my chest, vibrating against bone, syncing with my breath. Every time the crickets surged, it felt like the universe was inhaling. Every time they eased, it felt like exhaling.

Above us, the stars did something that still doesn't sit right in memory. They didn't just sparkle. They arranged.

Constellations became more than human-imposed shapes; they became geometry that seemed intentionally placed. Lines appeared between points without me drawing them, not as hallucinated neon but as a sense of connection —triangles, lattices, repeating patterns that seemed too clean to be random. The sky felt engineered, like the cosmos had been built by a mind that loves symmetry and was now briefly showing its blueprints.

I stood there and felt awe rise the way panic rises— fast, bodily, undeniable. My mind tried to grab a tool it trusted: math. If I could do calculus under that sky, I thought, if I could take something infinite and translate it into symbols, maybe I could stand inside it without falling over.

So I tried.

I tried to hold derivatives in my head, tried to picture slopes and curves, tried to reach for the comforting idea that logic can bridge anything. But the formulas slid away. Not because I'd forgotten them, but because the environment had turned too large. The crickets were too loud in their meaning. The stars were too structured. The night air felt too alive. Every attempt at calculation felt like trying to measure the ocean with a teaspoon.

And then the failure became humbling instead of humiliating. It made sense. My brain was not meant to solve derivatives while reality was singing. The failure didn't feel like stupidity. It felt like a boundary being revealed: there are experiences that don't want to be reduced. There are moments when the right response is not mastery but witness.

In that space—crickets pulsing like a heartbeat, stars arranged like proof—faith and logic stopped feeling like enemies. They felt like two languages describing the same vastness from different angles. Logic wanted a model. Faith wanted a relationship. Under that sky, both felt inadequate and both felt honest. I didn't resolve anything. No grand conclusion arrived. What arrived was a quiet, aching recognition: my ordinary life—exams, housing, budgets, schedules—was a thin slice of a much larger thing, and the larger thing was not necessarily kind or cruel. It was simply immense.

That immensity was comforting and destabilizing at the same time. Comforting because it made my suffering feel less central, less like the entire story. Destabilizing because it suggested there might be truths too big for my defenses.

When we went back inside, the house felt smaller, like it had been gently folded while we were outside. The video game screen was dark now, the controller abandoned where we'd left it, an artifact of our attempt to stay ordinary. I closed my eyes again and watched the geometry return—spinning, blooming, assembling like a living machine. I listened to the crickets through the walls, still singing their steady chorus, and I felt myself caught between two realities: the one made of furniture and syllabi and human roles, and the one made of patterns and sound-fields and stars that seemed arranged on purpose.

I didn't come away healed. I came away with a scar-shaped memory: warm current, melted edges, a proclamation that lit up my fear reflex, and a night sky that made my mind reach for math and then, for once, accept the limits of what math can hold.

The first time I took four tabs alone, it wasn't framed as a dare. It was framed as a controlled test—my apartment, my rules, no unpredictable conversation, no one else's energy bleeding into mine. The on-campus place was quiet in that pandemic-era way: hallways muted, fewer footsteps, fewer door slams, the building feeling half-occupied, like a hotel after the season ends. Inside my unit, the same desk and the same chair faced the same screen. The blinds were half-drawn. A thin stripe of outside light cut across the carpet and made the dust in the air visible when I moved. I told myself I was prepared because I had prepared the room—water nearby, lights dim, a playlist queued, nothing sharp or cluttered left out to snag my attention.

I swallowed the tabs and waited.

The waiting was its own kind of pressure. I paced and checked the clock and then tried to stop checking the clock because checking the clock made me feel like I was trying to bargain with the chemistry. The first stretch felt too normal, and that normality made me restless. I could feel my mind scouting for symptoms—*Is it starting? Is this it?*—like a guard dog sniffing at the air. I sat on the edge of the bed, then stood again. I adjusted the volume on my music and then turned it down. I kept trying to find the right setting, as if there was a configuration where this would be easy.

At around forty minutes in, a sudden burst of energy hit me so cleanly it felt artificial, like a switch had been thrown in my spine. It wasn't euphoria at first. It was momentum. My body felt charged, warm, awake. My hands tingled slightly. My thoughts sped up, not in a scattered way, but in a focused, almost athletic way. I stood in the middle of the room and didn't know what to do with the electricity. So I dropped to the floor and did pushups—fast, hard, with that old reflex that says physical exertion will burn off whatever is building inside.

The pushups didn't discharge the energy the way I expected. They amplified it.

When I stood back up, my breath came heavier, my heartbeat loud in my ears, and the room felt subtly different, as if the air had gained density. I told myself to slow down. I told myself to sit. I lowered myself into my desk chair— my normal chair, the one I used for homework, the one that belonged to ordinary life—and the instant my weight settled, the world ripped open.

There isn't a polite metaphor for it. It didn't feel like visuals "starting." It didn't feel like colors getting brighter. It felt like reality itself had been peeled back, like someone had grabbed the edge of the scene and pulled it away from the frame. The walls were still there, the desk was still there, but the *meaning* of them dissolved. The room stopped being "my apartment" and became an exposed stage of sensation —light, texture, sound—too raw, too immediate. My vision fractured into impossible clarity and impossible motion at the same time. The edges of objects shimmered, not like heat waves, but like the outline of the world couldn't decide where to land.

Time broke at the joints. Seconds stretched thin. My thoughts arrived in stacks. I could feel my own mind as a physical thing, loud and bright and overflowing, and the overflow wasn't beautiful—it was terrifying. It felt like I had stepped behind the curtain of perception and seen the machinery, and the machinery was moving too fast to be safe. I remember gripping the arms of the chair, knuckles tightening, because the chair was the only thing that still felt solid. My breathing became something I had to manage consciously. Inhale. Exhale. Inhale. Exhale. The simple act of breathing felt like a job I could fail.

The peak came with a kind of cosmic violence. Not violence in imagery—no monsters, no blood—but violence in intensity. My mind insisted, with total certainty, that I had done it this time: I had peeled the world back too far and I wouldn't be able to put it together again. The thought wasn't, *This is scary*. The thought was, *This is permanent*. It felt like I had snapped a mental bone. Like I had triggered a break that sober life wouldn't be able to repair. My body responded to that certainty the way it responds to a real emergency. My pulse surged. My stomach dropped. The room seemed to tilt without moving. I could feel adrenaline flooding through me, and the adrenaline made everything sharper, faster, worse.

And then—without my permission—the peak began to release.

Not instantly, not kindly, but like a wave pulling back from shore. The ripping sensation faded in degrees. The furniture reasserted itself. The room's edges stabilized. The world started behaving again, but my nervous system didn't trust it. Coming back didn't feel like relief. It felt like the moment after an accident when you're still shaking and trying to figure out what you damaged. My hands trembled. My thoughts came in panicked fragments: *What if that was a psychotic episode? What if I'm insane? What if I don't fully return? What if I changed something and it's going to show up later?*

I remember sitting there in my chair, staring at the wall, trying to test myself the way you test a limb after it goes numb. Can I think clearly? Can I remember my name? Can I hold a sentence without losing it? The fear wasn't abstract. It was humiliatingly practical. I was alone. There was no one to reassure me that what I'd experienced was "normal" for the drug. There was no witness to confirm I hadn't done something irreversible. In that moment, the apartment didn't feel like a safe container. It felt like a sealed box holding a man who might be breaking.

I needed something to anchor me that wasn't my own thoughts.

That's when I turned to the screen—not as entertainment, but as structure. I needed a narrative with a beginning and an end, something that would keep time moving in a predictable line. I needed visuals strong enough to occupy the part of my brain that was scanning for catastrophe. I put on a movie I knew could overpower my panic with sheer spectacle.

*Avengers: Endgame.*

The first moments hit like a controlled burn. The soundtrack carried momentum. The dialogue gave me pacing. Then the special effects arrived and the experience shifted. The visuals weren't just impressive—they were *overwhelmingly satisfying*, like they had been designed for the LSD state without knowing it. Light and motion and impossible physics filled the screen in a way that didn't threaten my mind the way the peeled-back room had threatened it. The movie gave the intensity a track to run on. Instead of my brain generating chaos, the chaos was curated. It was framed. It was scored. It had stakes that weren't mine.

I watched the battle scenes and felt my fear loosen its grip in small increments. Not because the fear was gone, but because the movie kept catching my attention before my mind could spiral fully back into the question of insanity. The colors were too rich. The motion too clean. The scale too grand. For the first time in that night, intensity felt like pleasure instead of danger. I realized—almost with surprise—that the same chemistry that could rip the world open could also make art feel like a direct pipeline into awe. The discovery didn't justify what I'd done. It didn't erase the panic. But it gave me a new tool: if the trip tried to become a courtroom where my mind prosecuted itself, I could redirect the jury with spectacle.

When the movie ended, the apartment was still my apartment. The chair was still a chair. The walls were still walls. But I wasn't unchanged. I could feel the residue of the peak like a bruise—tender, alarming, impossible to ignore. I lay down later with exhaustion that felt earned through fear, and I kept circling the same thought as I drifted: *If my mind can be peeled back that easily, what else is behind it?*

That question didn't feel curious. It felt compelled. And that compulsion—half hunger, half dread—was the state I carried with me into the next doorway, the one people spoke about with reverence and warning.

Near the end of that summer, I went back to the coastal house again. This time I was introduced to DMT in that same house, and the mood changed immediately—less like curiosity, more like ceremony. It started in the garage, but not the kind of garage that smells like oil and cold concrete. This one had been converted into a recreation room: cleaned out, repurposed, softened around the edges with furniture that didn't quite belong in a space built for cars. The overhead door was still there like a sealed mouth, the walls still carried that faint, hollow acoustic of unfinished architecture, but someone had tried to make it comfortable —chairs pulled into a loose circle, a small table, a few objects positioned with intention as if the room itself needed to be arranged into permission.

The air held a mixed scent—old concrete, stale summer heat trapped in the walls, and the cleaner, sharper smell of the substance that was about to change everything. It didn't feel casual. Nobody was laughing the way people laugh when they're trying to convince themselves this is harmless. People spoke with an odd quietness, like the volume had been turned down before the experience even began. There was preparation—small movements with careful hands, checking, adjusting, making sure the tool was ready. The setup felt like a lab disguised as a living room, except we weren't measuring anything external. We were measuring how far the mind could go before it stopped recognizing its own rules.

I sat on the floor, legs folded, the way a person sits when they want to appear grounded. The posture didn't help. The floor was firm under me, the kind of firm that reminds you you're a body. That was the last time "body" felt like a stable concept.

I remember being told what to expect in broad strokes—breakthrough, doorway, leaving the room—words that sounded like metaphors until they weren't. I expected something like the other experiences: a wave, a climb, an altered angle on reality. I expected intensity, yes, but I still expected continuity. I still expected a thread that would connect the moment before to the moment after.

The first breath brought a hum into the room. Not a sound anyone else made—an internal hum, like the air itself had grown a motor. It was low and smooth and then instantly louder, climbing in pitch the way a power line sounds when you stand too close. The second breath made the hum wrap around everything. The third breath made the hum become the only thing. It flooded my skull, pressed against my teeth, filled my chest, and the world began to collapse inward as if someone was folding space like paper.

My vision didn't "change." It detonated.

The room didn't melt or warp gradually. It snapped away. Darkness arrived with force, not because my eyes closed but because the interface—whatever normally translates light into "living room," "garage," "walls," "people"—simply shut off. In that shutdown, color erupted. Not pretty color. Not decorative color. Color with mass. Color with authority. It was as if the universe had been hiding a second, brighter engine behind the one I knew, and someone had opened the casing.

Kaleidoscope geometry slammed into place with the crispness of machinery. Shapes locked together like gears. Patterns rotated too fast to track, then faster, then faster again, until speed became a solid wall. The movement wasn't fluid. It was mechanical—precise, relentless, indifferent. The patterns didn't feel like hallucination. They felt like an infrastructure I had never been allowed to see before. I had the absurd, terrifying sense that I was watching the operating system beneath reality, and it didn't care whether I understood it.

Sound changed next. The hum didn't fade; it transformed. It rose into a pitch that should have been unbearable, and then—like a switch—everything muted. Not silence as in quiet, but muting as in someone had cut the audio feed from the entire universe. The absence was so complete it felt violent. The muting made the visuals louder, heavier, more dominant, as if the brain had rerouted all bandwidth into sight because it had nothing else to process.

Then time stopped behaving.

There are moments in life when time feels slow. This wasn't slow. This was time ceasing to be a concept that mattered. The rotating machinery of geometry snapped into a stillness so sudden it felt like impact. Everything froze— pattern, motion, meaning—held in place by a force that felt absolute. The stillness wasn't calm. It was total. It was the kind of stillness you imagine exists outside the universe, where nothing changes because change requires time and time had been removed.

In that frozen eternity, a thought arrived with perfect clarity, clean and final:

I've broken something permanently. I will see the world like this forever.

It wasn't worry or speculation. It was certainty in the way a body knows pain is real. The thought didn't sit politely in my mind; it took over my physiology. Fear flooded through me like an electric current. I felt it in my stomach, in my throat, in my hands—even though "hands" didn't make sense anymore. It was a fear beyond panic, beyond adrenaline, a fear that felt cosmic because it wasn't about dying. It was about being trapped. Trapped outside the interface that makes "normal life" possible. Trapped in a place where geometry is law and the self is a broken translation.

The fear tried to reach for anything familiar—my name, my history, the idea of a room, the idea of a body— but familiarity had no traction there. The frozen machinery didn't respond to pleading. It didn't respond to logic. It didn't even acknowledge that I was frightened. It simply existed, perfect and indifferent, and that indifference made me feel erased. Not killed—erased. Like my ordinary self was a small, temporary story that had just ended.

I remember trying to hold on to one anchor: breath. But even breath became abstract. It wasn't "in and out." It was the concept of breathing floating somewhere far away, and I couldn't tell if my body was doing it. The terror sharpened into a single demand—*get back, get back, get back*—but there was no "back" visible. There was only the frozen, authoritative display and the certainty that I had stepped through a door I could not unstep.

And then, as abruptly as it began, the machinery released me.

The return was not gentle. It wasn't a gradual descent where reality reassembled piece by piece. It was like being dropped from height into a body that suddenly weighed a thousand pounds. Sound snapped back in with a rush—air moving, someone shifting in the room, the faint buzz of electricity in the walls. Light returned as "light," not as cosmic architecture. The garage recreation room reappeared around me, and for a second it looked foreign, like a movie set built to imitate normal life. My heart was hammering. My skin felt too tight. My mouth was dry. I had the immediate, animal need to confirm that my senses were still working the way they used to.

I blinked hard. I looked at the floor. I looked at the walls. I looked at the objects in the room, naming them silently like a spell: chair, table, door, window. Each label was a test. Each label was a plea: *stay stable.*

But the experience wasn't done. The door had closed enough to let me breathe, not enough to let me forget what I'd seen. The residue clung to perception like an afterimage burned into the retina. My mind felt scraped clean and then hastily put back together. I could feel the edges of myself— where "me" ended and "world" began—still vibrating, as if the boundary had been loosened and might tear again.

Someone close to me noticed that I wasn't okay. Not in a dramatic way—no sobbing, no collapse—but in the particular stillness that follows a private catastrophe. They came over and helped me up. Their hand on my arm was grounding, not comforting. It told my nervous system: *You are in a room. You are upright. You are not lost.*

They escorted me from the converted garage space into the living room—into a familiar arrangement of furniture and light that my brain recognized as safe territory. The transition mattered. The living room had history. It had ordinary angles. It had the kind of warmth that comes from a space being used the same way over and over. I sat down there, and the familiarity acted like a brace. The trip's intensity continued to ebb, but the fear stayed lodged: the fear that I had permanently altered my vision, my mind, my access to reality.

I breathed in shallow pulls at first, then deeper. My hands stopped shaking. The room stayed still in the normal way a room stays still. Yet inside me, something had shifted. Not enlightenment. Not healing. Not a clean lesson I could write down and keep.

What remained was knowledge—hard, undeniable knowledge—that there are doors inside the mind that open into places where time does not behave, where perception becomes machinery, where the self can be reduced to a frightened witness with no authority. And once you know those places are real, you can't unknow them. You can return to your life, to your classes, to your deadlines, to your routines, and still carry the awareness like a hidden weight: there is an underside to reality, and you have seen it, and your mind is capable of falling through.

Back at university, the pandemic era blurred days together. I studied. I passed exams. I maintained the appearance of forward motion. The on-campus apartment became a quiet bunker: the same walls, the same desk, the same screen glow. My world shrank to classes, assignments, and the private chemical experiments I treated like medicine. I didn't talk much about the psychedelics because I didn't want to turn them into a personality. I wanted them to remain a tool. Yet each experience carried a narrative arc that tugged at my identity: fear of permanent change, moments of intense joy, flashes of spiritual meaning, and the steady return to ordinary life where depression still waited like a heavy coat hanging by the door.

That fall, around a major holiday, I spent time in the plains with a relative—someone whose household had its own gravity, its own tension, its own routine. The air there always felt slightly charged, like conversations were built on invisible agreements: what you can say, what you should avoid, what gets laughed off, what gets taken personally. I arrived carrying my own quiet agenda. I didn't announce it as an agenda. I framed it as curiosity, as a willingness to try something that might loosen the clamp inside my chest. With his knowledge, I took a far larger dose of LSD than I had before, and I told myself—because I needed to believe it— that bigger would mean clearer, that intensity would equal truth.

The come-up didn't feel like a gentle slope. It felt like a floor shifting under the furniture. At first it was only a subtle wrongness, as if the world's edges had softened. Then it sharpened into a strange clarity that didn't match sobriety —more like sobriety turned past normal, the way cold weather can make distant objects look unnaturally crisp. Time began to lose its steady rhythm. Minutes stretched thin and then snapped. My thoughts stopped lining up in a single file and started arriving in clusters, overlapping, competing for the center. I could still speak, but speech felt like dragging meaning through thick water.

The movie started—*Across the Universe*—and at first it was just a screen, just light and sound in a room. Then it wasn't. The visuals stopped being images and became architecture. Scenes didn't "play"; they built themselves around me. Color had weight. Motion had intent. Dialogue wasn't simply heard; it landed in my body like a physical touch, like the film was pressing on nerves I didn't know I had. Some moments felt harmless, even playful, and then a scene would shift and the emotional temperature would spike so quickly my nervous system would recoil like it had been burned.

A love song arrived—familiar enough that, in ordinary life, it would have been background—and it hit me like a direct transmission. Not sentiment. Not nostalgia. Something wider. The feeling wasn't about the characters on screen. It was about the existence of love as a force, as if love was not an emotion inside human bodies but a field the universe runs on, a fundamental layer beneath matter. For a few minutes I felt that field fully, without the filters that usually protect me from intensity. It wasn't doctrinal. It wasn't tied neatly to any religious symbol I could name. It was simply infinite—too large to be safe, too bright to look at directly—and it made me weep without planning to. The tears weren't sad. They were overwhelmed. I felt grateful and suspicious at the same time, because joy that arrives too fast can feel like a trap when you've lived too long expecting the floor to drop.

That was the peak: that impossible certainty that love is real in the largest sense, and that I was touching it for a moment the way a fingertip touches the surface of a hot stove—briefly, intensely, and with the knowledge that it could burn me if I stayed too long.

After the peak, the experience didn't end. It layered.

The room changed as the night thinned out. The person I was staying with eventually went to bed, and the house took on a different kind of quiet—less social, more exposed. The silence was not peaceful. It was the kind of silence that leaves you alone with every sensation your body can generate. I was still profoundly altered. Coordination was a struggle, like my limbs were slightly delayed versions of my intentions. Standing up required planning. Walking across the room felt like navigating a ship through a narrow channel. Small tasks—picking something up, turning a knob, even changing my posture—became deliberate acts with consequences.

Then the dog's kennel became its own problem. The smell came first, thick and immediate, the kind of smell that doesn't politely stay in one corner. The dog had soiled the kennel, and the odor filled the room with a hot, sour presence that refused to be ignored. In ordinary circumstances I would have dealt with it quickly—clean it, fix it, restore order. In that state, order was a distant concept. The thought of opening the kennel and managing the mess felt like trying to solve a complex machine with gloves on. My coordination was already fragile, and the idea of making it worse— spreading it, stepping in it, failing to clean it properly—felt unbearable. I made a decision that I hated even as I made it: I left it as it was. I tried to tune out the smell like it was another intrusive thought. I tried to pretend the air wasn't contaminated, but my body kept registering it, a persistent insult that made the room feel hostile.

That smell became a strange counterpoint to the earlier revelation. The peak had been cosmic. The aftermath was bodily. The universe had just shown me infinity through a love song, and now I was sitting in a room trying to breathe around the stench of something ordinary and unavoidable. It felt like a lesson delivered with cruelty: transcendence doesn't remove the animal realities. You still have a body. You still have a nose. You still have responsibility waiting in the corner while your mind tries to float above it.

I needed something to anchor the experience without crushing it, something bigger than the smell and steadier than my scattered thoughts. I put on Beethoven's Ninth Symphony.

The first notes didn't simply play. They assembled.

With my eyes closed, the music became a full spatial environment—an interior landscape that formed itself out of sound. Each instrument in the orchestra was given a permanent object in my vision, as if my mind had built a private set of symbols and assigned them roles. Those objects didn't drift randomly; they had rules. They *jumped* when their instrument played a note. The jump wasn't uniform. The intensity of the jump depended on the volume and frequency of the note, like the object had a physics engine tied directly to pitch and amplitude. Low notes created heavy, slow movements. High notes snapped and flickered. Crescendos didn't just get louder—they grew taller, larger, more forceful, as if the entire structure of my inner world was being pushed outward by pressure.

The strangest part wasn't the visuals. It was what happened to my attention.

I could deconstruct the orchestra in real time. Not the way a trained musician might isolate a line by familiarity, but in a way that felt impossible: I could listen to the strings *alone* while the brass still played, then shift and hear the brass as a separate entity, then isolate a woodwind line as if it were being piped directly into my ear, then widen again and hear everything together, and somehow the "together" didn't blur the "separate." It felt like my mind had become a mixing board with infinite sliders. I could pull one instrument forward and push another back without losing the whole. I could hear the pattern of percussion like a heartbeat under everything. I could hear how themes returned, transformed, argued, resolved. The symphony became less like music and more like a living machine—complex, precise, emotional, and exact.

And in the middle of that precision, the smell still existed.

It didn't vanish. It hovered at the edge of my awareness, a foul reminder that I was still in a room, still in a body, still bound to ordinary consequences. But the music built a second room inside my head—a room where the odor couldn't reach as easily. For stretches of time, the symphony was large enough to eclipse the stench. Then a gap between movements would open, or my attention would falter, and the smell would rush back in like a punishment. The experience became a tug-of-war between the sublime and the grotesque, between Beethoven's architecture and the crude fact of a kennel in need of cleaning.

By the time the symphony moved toward its final sections, the closed-eye world had its own momentum. Objects leapt and settled. Patterns formed and dissolved. My breathing slowed, then sped up, then slowed again, syncing itself to dynamics as if my body was trying to conduct from the inside. The earlier peak—love as an infinite field—was still present, but now it had context. The universe wasn't only love. It was also mess. It was also smell. It was also the humiliating limits of coordination. It was also the astonishing capacity of the mind to turn sound into structure and find meaning in vibration.

When the music ended, the silence that followed felt enormous. Not empty—charged. I opened my eyes and the room returned, unchanged, with its ordinary objects and its ordinary problems. The film was over. The house was quiet. The kennel still smelled. My body still felt like it belonged to someone else by half an inch. The cosmic certainty of the peak didn't disappear, but it receded, like a tide pulling back from the shore, leaving behind wet sand and debris and the uneasy question that always follows: what do you do with what you felt when you're back in the room with the same air, the same mess, the same life waiting?

By the end of 2020, I repeated the pattern again—another large LSD experience, more movies, more attempts to chase the same relief. Some trips were beautiful. Some were confusing. The beautiful ones made me believe the door could be used responsibly, like a tool for insight. The confusing ones made me fear I was playing with my own wiring. In the spring of 2021, when supply ran dry, I filled the gap by researching other people's stories, reading about mystical experiences and terror trips and the way people talk about ego death like it's a baptism. In the same period, THC and CBD became more common in the house I would later live in, used casually, used daily, used as background. I absorbed that culture the way a person absorbs weather. I told myself it was benign. I told myself it was lighter than the heavier doors.

University continued, and for a while the rhythm held. I remained in on-campus housing through fall of 2021. Then illness came in like a derailment. I caught a respiratory virus that lasted for weeks, and I quarantined as if the world's larger crisis was still pressing its thumb on every door handle. The days of sickness blurred into a feverish, exhausted loop: sleep, cough, sweat, drink water, stare at the ceiling, check the clock, realize time has passed without meaning. When your body is sick, your mind loses its last excuses. You can't pretend you're lazy. You can't pretend you're dramatic. You are simply broken down. Classes don't pause for that. Labs don't pause. Deadlines pile like snow. I missed too much. I dropped the fall semester intending to restart in spring, telling myself it was a strategic retreat, not another collapse.

Dropping classes triggered consequences that weren't emotional—they were logistical, and logistics can be cruel because they don't care how close you are to the edge. Student housing has rules. Fall out of enrollment status, and the apartment is no longer yours. I was forced out, and that forced movement shoved me into another household, another ecosystem: the plains house of the relative I had tripped with. Moving into his home felt like stepping into someone else's gravity field. The air had different rules there. People moved with a different kind of confidence. The household carried its own friction—spouse, younger family member, routines, expectations—and I entered it already frayed from illness, already raw from school collapsing again, already carrying the strange residue of psychedelics in my perception.

In that house, THC and CBD were common, almost ambient. It wasn't presented as a moral issue. It was presented as normal—a way to relax, a way to soften, a way to get through. I was already hungry for relief, and relief was readily available. Then LSD supply returned, and with it came routine. Every few weeks the dose increased, framed as exploration, framed as building tolerance, framed as proof that fear could be mastered. One tab. Then three. Then five. Each step made the next step easier to justify. The logic was seductive: if you can survive a bigger dose, you're not fragile. If you can handle it, you're stronger. The problem with that logic is that it measures strength in units of dissociation.

In December of 2021, we went to seven tabs. It was the first and only time at that level, and it did not feel like a larger version of a smaller trip. It felt like a different species of event. The first thirty minutes felt like a lower dose, which is part of what made it strange—my brain expected a curve and got a flat line, as if reality was delaying the punch. Then the architecture of the trip cracked. The first hour felt broken. Not scary in a clean way, but wrong, jagged, untrustworthy. I remember telling him it felt broken, and I remember him disappearing for hours, leaving me alone inside a state where time had already started to lose its shape.

Solitude in that condition is not simply being alone. It is being trapped inside a loop with no external anchor. I began looping physically—moving between a bed and a kitchen, repeating the same motions as if my body had become a program. The looping wasn't metaphorical. It felt like my nervous system had been caught in a cycle and couldn't find the exit. The worst part wasn't repetition itself. The worst part was what repetition does to your sense of agency. Every time you repeat, you lose a little more belief that you can choose differently. You become a witness to your own automation.

At some point, media was turned on, and a movie played that I'd never seen before. The images filled my vision so completely that the boundary between screen and world softened. My mind began filling in edges, making the film feel like a message directed at me. That's one of the dangers of altered states: pattern recognition becomes a god. Everything becomes meaningful. Every line becomes accusation or prophecy. I felt like I was being fed scenes as if they were my own thoughts, and the sensation was exhilarating and terrifying because it suggested my mind was not separate from the world—it was co-authoring it.

Then a younger family member asked a blunt question—something like, "Are you on drugs?"—and the question snapped me toward ordinary reality with sudden violence. Paranoia flooded in. Not paranoia as vague worry, but as a certainty that I was being judged, that laughter was happening behind my back, that glances were knives. I felt exposed in the most humiliating way: a grown man unraveling in a living room while a younger mind watched with normal eyes. That exposure turned the household into a threat environment. I fell inward, and the room faded into a purple cloudscape, the impression of moving through a universe that didn't want me.

Acceptance became the goal in that cloudscape, like a starving person seeking food, and every attempt ended in rejection. Entities pushed me away. Unwanted presences clung. Fear sharpened into isolation. When he tried to take me outside to look at stars, I couldn't focus. Everything felt broken. The stars weren't beautiful; they were unreachable. Back inside, another movie began and looked like it was melting too fast, continuity impossible because time wasn't stable enough to hold a storyline. Later, in darkness, faint colored pixels returned, as if the world had been reduced to tiny points and I was watching the render happen in real time. The pixels weren't intense; they were insidious. They suggested permanence.

Near the end of the night, he returned and wanted me to ride with him in a car with the headlights off. The drive felt like another lifetime. I couldn't see where we were going, and that helplessness turned the world into pure sensation. Then, suddenly, headlights came on and revealed a herd of deer—silent, fragile, staring—caught in the beam like ghosts. The image lodged in me because it matched how I felt: a creature in the wrong place, frozen, watched by something brighter. When we returned and morning came, sunrise arrived like an impossible mercy. Fear receded. Anxiety dissolved. Houses seemed to disappear. Grass became infinite. The world turned hyper-green, and the sky carried a celestial aura that made everything feel freshly created. I watched him and the younger family member and felt the strangest shift: sometimes they looked like themselves, sometimes they looked like versions of me, sometimes they looked like luminous beings, glowing with a quiet radiance I didn't know how to describe.

The joy I felt then was the most intense joy I can remember. It wasn't "happiness." It was a flooding, a weightless expansion, the sensation that everything was okay and always had been. For a brief period, the universe felt like it loved me. That belief was not intellectual. It was bodily. It made my chest ache with gratitude. Then he asked if I was ready to go back inside, and as soon as we crossed the threshold, reality flooded back. The joy didn't vanish completely, but it receded like a tide, leaving behind the sand of ordinary life and the discomfort of remembering how good it had felt to not be afraid.

Later that day, he took me to meet a religious acquaintance in a workshop full of wood and tools and the smell of shavings. My mind was still altered enough that the encounter felt mythic. I felt like I was speaking to a gatekeeper, someone stationed near pearly doors, and I couldn't track the words as much as I tracked the sensation: judgment, evaluation, being weighed. Whether that sensation was true or chemical didn't matter in the moment.

It landed as a spiritual message my body believed. After the trip fully ended, the fear remained as an afterimage. Not fear of him, not fear of the household, but fear of the door inside my mind: *What if I broke something? What if I slip through again and don't find my way back?*

By spring of 2022, my life had become a pattern of attempted restarts and derailments. I tried to return to university. I told myself it would be different. Then I got sick again—COVID in the first week—and I dropped the semester because missing too much class felt like falling into the same hole with my eyes open. The second drop did something psychological the first drop hadn't: it made the pattern feel intentional, as if the universe was sending a message. When your mind is already unstable, patterns begin to feel like fate. It matters less whether that belief is rational than that it becomes emotionally convincing. "This doesn't work" transforms into "you're not wanted here." The story becomes cosmic, and cosmic stories can crush you because they leave no room for simple bad luck.

I was still living in that house then, in the aftermath of the seven-tab fracture, inside a dynamic that already carried tension in the walls. And there was another presence in the story—someone close to him, someone whose proximity to the household felt like an open secret to me. I need to be careful with the word *perceived* because it's both true and dangerous. I perceived an ongoing betrayal. I perceived it the way you perceive a smell of smoke: not proof of fire, but enough to keep you scanning the ceiling. In my perception, the betrayal wasn't hidden. It sat at the table. It moved through the house. It laughed at the edges. Whether my perception was correct or distorted is less important here than what the perception did to me: it turned the home into a stage where I felt gaslit by normal conversation.

When trust is already damaged, you stop giving people the benefit of doubt because doubt is a weapon that can be used against you. So I carried certainty. Certainty can look like strength from the outside, but inside it's often fear hardened into armor. The certainty built quietly at first, like rage builds when it has no safe outlet. It sat under my skin while daily life went on—meals, small talk, television, people moving around each other as if nothing was wrong. The longer it sat, the more it felt like poison in my bloodstream. I started watching details obsessively: glances, jokes, the arrangement of bodies in a room, who sided with whom in tiny conversations. My nervous system treated the household like an intelligence problem, scanning for meaning, scanning for threat, scanning for proof.

The night it ruptured wasn't dramatic in its setup. It was dinner. That's what makes it so corrosive. Not a battlefield, not a crisis, not an emergency—just a table, plates, forks scraping, the ordinary repetition of family-style routine. They sat there together—the man whose house it was, his spouse, and the other person I believed represented betrayal—right next to each other, as if the arrangement itself was a statement. There are images that lodge in the brain because they feel symbolic, and that arrangement lodged in mine like a blade. I remember my hands on the table. I remember the tone of the conversation, the way it tried to float above the tension as if denial could be polite. I remember feeling like I was inside a play where everyone else had agreed on the script and I was the only one refusing to read my lines.

I couldn't hide my face. The body betrays you when your mind is screaming. My expression hardened. My breathing changed. I became visibly wrong. He noticed, of course. He knows when I'm holding something back, and instead of letting it pass, he pressed. He asked what was wrong. He asked again. He leaned on it the way you lean on a bruise to prove it's real. Each time he pressed, the pressure inside me climbed higher. I felt the familiar sensation of being cornered—not physically, but psychologically. Cornered by someone who believed he had authority to demand disclosure. Cornered by someone who believed my reaction was the problem rather than what had provoked it.

The powder keg had been building for months: psychedelic fractures, paranoia, perceived laughter, shame, illness, dropped semesters, forced housing changes, the humiliating sense of being a grown man living under someone else's roof with a mind that didn't feel fully mine. All of that was dry fuel. Dinner was the spark. When I finally spoke, I said something I can't take back. Not a neat accusation. Not a calm statement of boundaries. Something sharp, something meant to stop the wrong by force. In that moment it didn't feel like theater. It felt like a moral emergency, the kind where you shrink your world down to one task: make the wrong stop. The room went silent in a strange way—not the silence of shock alone, but the silence of people recalculating who is dangerous now.

And then the recoil hit almost immediately. Not clean guilt. Collapse. The adrenaline that had fueled the outburst drained, and in its place there was the sudden, sick awareness that I had become the threat in the room. I left the table and retreated to my space like a wounded animal dragging itself away from a fight. My body moved automatically. In my room, the sounds of the house became muffled and yet sharp with implication. I could feel the narrative being written without me: unstable, dangerous, delusional, lost. Once that narrative starts, it's hard to stop because it gives everyone else a way to feel safe. Label the person who broke as the problem, and the rest of the household can return to pretending the system is fine.

That's when he followed me. He came into my space like he owned it, like I was not a grown man but a misbehaving subordinate who had crossed a line and needed to be put back in place. He didn't come in with concern. He came in with dominance. He chewed me out, not as a conversation, but as a correction. He spoke about what I had done, about what I had endangered, about how wrong I was. The sick part—the part that still hooks into my nervous system when I replay it—is that certain tones can still function like a leash. Even when you're an adult, even when you've survived other kinds of authority, the wrong voice in the wrong posture can yank you back into old patterns of obedience and shame.

He left, and the house did not return to normal because normal had been shattered. The next day, he took the other person—the one I believed represented betrayal—into the realm of paperwork and authority. Charges were filed. Statements were made. What had been a family conflict became an official narrative. That action detonated something deeper than the dinner explosion. It told me, in the clearest possible language, that I was not a person to be understood in that house. I was a problem to be documented. Once a system reaches for official authority, it changes the air. It turns home into a surveillance environment even if there are no cameras. It teaches you that your words can be used as evidence and your emotions can be framed as pathology.

Then came the claim that I was delusional. Not "mistaken." Not "overreacting." Delusional. That word is not an argument. It's an attack on reality itself. It tells you your perception can be dismissed wholesale. It turns every observation you make into suspect material. It spreads like ink: if you're delusional about this, you might be delusional about everything. You become an unreliable narrator in your own life, and that is a terrifying place to live when you're already fighting to hold your mind steady.

The fallout was explosive at first—arguments, accusations, attempts to recruit allies—then it hardened into something colder: unspoken silence. Doors closed more softly. Conversations changed tone when I entered. People looked past me as if I were a hazard. The family structure, whatever it had been, could not withstand competing narratives of betrayal and instability. I watched the split widen, and I did what people do when they are desperate to be believed: I talked to others outside that house. I gossiped, not because gossip is noble, but because silence felt like suffocation. I needed my version of reality to exist somewhere other than inside my own skull. He did the same on his side. The stories traveled through people like sparks looking for dry grass. Each retelling made reconciliation less likely, because retellings harden into identity.

That spring, the semester ended without me, and the household ended with me still inside it, but no longer belonging. The academic failure and the family fracture fused into one message my mind couldn't ignore: you tried to restart, and the restart collapsed; you tried to live under someone else's roof, and that roof turned into a courtroom.

Psychedelics had offered moments of cosmic love and moments of cosmic terror, but they had not given me a stable home inside my own perception. The last image of that period that stays with me isn't a campus lab or a perfect exam score or even a sunrise field of hyper-green joy. It's a dinner table—plates, forks, bodies arranged in a way I couldn't tolerate—and the moment the powder keg finally detonated, turning a private fracture into a public split, and leaving me standing in the wreckage with the uneasy knowledge that once a family decides your reality is unacceptable, silence becomes its own sentence.

# CHAPTER 18

# *A Hitchable Home*

A laminated card lives behind the clear pocket in my wallet, the kind of card designed to look official without looking important. The corners have softened from friction. The surface has hairline scratches that catch light at the wrong angle, turning the printed words into a brief glare, like the card is trying to hide what it is. When I slide it out, my thumb leaves a faint smear that I rub away automatically, the way a person wipes fingerprints off glass without thinking. The card is supposed to represent access—permission, worthiness, entry into a place that promises order—but it also represents a threshold I keep approaching with the same uneasy question vibrating under my skin: What does access mean if the inside of your head is still a war zone?

The wallet snaps shut. The plastic edge taps once against leather. The small sound feels louder than it should, and the loudness pulls me backward—not into doctrine, not into belief, but into the period when belief became a survival tool I tried to sharpen into something that could cut through panic. The card pulls up the image of white walls and low voices, of polished floors that swallow footsteps, of hands held together in front of the body as if stillness could be worn like a uniform. It pulls up the feeling of building rules around a mind that had started treating reality like a trap. It pulls up the season when I stopped trying to negotiate with a household that had become hostile and instead bought my way into a different kind of isolation—one on wheels.

The shift started in the aftermath of the fallout, when silence turned into its own threat. The house I was in didn't need cameras to feel watched. The air itself felt audited. A door closing in another room sounded like a decision being made without me. Footsteps in a hallway sounded like someone coming to correct me. Even when nothing happened, my body stayed braced, waiting for the next moment when my words would be used as evidence and my perceptions would be dismissed as pathology. The worst part wasn't the argument itself; it was the way the argument had been converted into paperwork—an institutional narrative where I wasn't a person in pain, I was a liability.

I couldn't sleep cleanly in that atmosphere. Nights became long corridors where every thought echoed. I found myself rehearsing conversations that never happened, rewriting sentences I'd already said, trying to find the version of reality that would make me look sane in front of people who had already decided the label. I began to feel trapped in the most humiliating way: not trapped by locked doors, but trapped by proximity—by the fact that the roof above me belonged to someone whose tone could turn military-cold in an instant, someone who could walk into authority and make my life official in the wrong direction.

Leaving wasn't romantic. It wasn't a brave walk into freedom. It was logistics wrapped around fear. The money that made the exit possible came from a decision that had been sitting unresolved in my life for years: I sold the house I'd bought in another state, the one that had turned into a financial weight and an emotional dare. When the sale closed and the numbers came back higher than what I'd paid, it didn't feel like triumph. It felt like vindication with bruises. The profit wasn't joy; it was proof that I hadn't been completely foolish for holding on, proof that the months of paying a mortgage on a place I wasn't living hadn't been pure waste. I didn't celebrate. I moved the money like a person moving sandbags before a flood.

I bought an RV with the urgency of a man buying a shell. The day I picked it up, the lot smelled like sun-warmed asphalt and new upholstery, that synthetic clean scent that clings to fresh interiors and makes you think of unused spaces. The RV looked almost too pristine to trust—smooth panels, unscuffed corners, hardware that still shined. People imagine RVs as leisure, but for me it was architecture for retreat: a small private world that could be locked from the inside, a room I could move when the atmosphere around me became poisonous.

Stepping inside for the first time as the owner changed my breathing. The ceiling was lower than any house I'd lived in. The walls were close enough that you could touch two surfaces without fully extending your arms. The space should have felt claustrophobic, and on some level it did, but claustrophobia wasn't the dominant sensation. The dominant sensation was containment—the relief of being able to reduce the world to a manageable size. Containment meant fewer corners to scan. Containment meant fewer echoes. Containment meant the difference between being alone in a cavern and being alone in a capsule.

Loading it was like moving into a controlled experiment. Every object had to justify its presence, because space was now a discipline. I carried bins and bags, stacking them with a methodical precision that felt almost religious: food here, tools there, clothes compressed, blankets folded tight. I labeled things not because I'm naturally organized, but because unmarked chaos makes my mind spin. I filled cabinets with the kind of basics that mean survival—canned food, water jugs, hygiene items—because there's a primitive comfort in knowing you could disappear for a while and still eat. The bed was small, the dinette felt too clean, the bathroom too compact, but every inch began to feel like mine. Ownership wasn't about pride. Ownership was about boundaries.

The first month, the RV sat on the same property as the person I'd fallen out with, because leaving doesn't happen cleanly even when it needs to. You still need a place to park. You still need time to learn how your systems work —water, power, waste, propane—how the RV breathes and sweats and hums in different temperatures. Even there, even within the perimeter of the atmosphere that had turned hostile, the RV created separation. I could close the door and break line-of-sight with the household that felt like a tribunal. I could choose when to be seen. I could choose when to vanish.

That first month had a strange rhythm: the daylight hours spent setting things up and the night hours spent testing whether the capsule actually held. I'd lie in the small bed and listen to the soft creaks of the RV settling, the gentle ticks of cooling metal, the occasional rush of wind against the side. Those sounds should have been neutral, but my nervous system treated any unknown sound like a message. I learned quickly that silence inside a small space can magnify the mind. I learned that the RV wasn't automatically peace—it was simply a different container for the same volatile interior.

When I moved to the first RV park, it was near a lake halfway between two family hubs in my life, a compromise geography designed to let me be "available" without being swallowed. The park smelled like cut grass and lake water and the faint chemical tang of the dump station, a mix of nature and infrastructure. There were other RVs lined up in neat order, each one its own private life behind tinted windows. At night, porch lights glowed amber, and the air carried distant laughter that didn't belong to me. I walked the gravel paths and watched the lake change color as evening fell—silver to slate to black—feeling my thoughts slow in the presence of water. Water doesn't solve anything, but it offers a steady surface that refuses to argue.

The second park was closer to the person I'd fallen out with, and on paper it looked like I'd moved backward. In practice, the RV changed what proximity meant. I could be near without being inside. I could show up when necessary without being trapped. The park had its own soundtrack: the steady hiss of someone's propane, the intermittent thud of a neighbor's steps, distant engines starting in the morning, dogs barking when someone walked past. The noise was oddly comforting because it reminded my mind that I wasn't alone in the universe, even if I was alone in my life.

It was during those months that I installed an off-grid solar system. The work was practical—panels, brackets, wiring, controllers—but it carried a symbolic weight I didn't talk about out loud. There's a particular satisfaction in generating your own power when you've felt dependent on systems that can be turned against you. I bolted the panels down and ran cable through tight spaces, my hands scraping knuckles against edges that didn't care about skin. I mounted the controller and watched the display numbers flicker:

voltage, amperage, charge state. Sunlight became something I could measure. Day became inventory. When the panels fed the batteries and the lights inside the RV came on without needing anyone's permission, it felt like a quiet rebellion: you can't cut off what I produce myself.

At the same time, I began rebuilding my standing in church. Not because I was suddenly pure, and not because I was performing redemption for an audience. I did it because I needed structure that existed beyond family politics. Ritual has rules. Ritual has language. Ritual tells you where to put your hands and when to stand and when to sit. When your mind is unstable, rules can feel like rails. I started showing up consistently. I took on responsibilities that looked small from the outside—helping set up, staying late, saying yes when asked—because being asked made me feel less invisible. There's a steadying effect to being expected somewhere. In the RV, I could disappear; in the pew, I was seen.

The first temple experience in this season didn't feel like a victory lap. It felt like approaching a controlled environment designed to reset you. The building itself carried a hush, not just quiet but managed quiet—the kind of quiet that makes you whisper even when you don't need to. The air smelled faintly of clean carpet and polished stone. Lights were soft and evenly distributed, eliminating harsh shadows, as if darkness itself had been edited out for safety. At the desk, a worker checked my card with practiced calm, eyes kind but procedural. Then I stepped deeper in, past the public boundaries, into the white, into the softened light.

Inside, my body moved like it had been trained long ago: walk here, pause there, keep your voice low, keep your expression neutral. Clothing changed. Fabric brushed my skin with a strange simplicity, as if the wardrobe was trying to remove personality. Voices around me stayed gentle, the words formal, the gestures rehearsed. It should have felt peaceful. Instead it felt like standing inside a promise while my mind argued with it. I made covenants the way a drowning person grabs a rope—tight, desperate, hoping the rope actually attaches to something real. I left the building with my hands slightly trembling, not from fear of the place, but from the fear of what would happen if I did everything right and still felt nothing.

That fear didn't stop me from trying. In the months after, I advanced in church status in the ordinary ways that don't look dramatic but change how you're treated. People greeted me more warmly. People trusted me with tasks. People spoke to me as if I was stable. That perception was both comforting and dangerous, because being seen as stable raises expectations, and expectations can collapse a person who is only stable because he's clenching his jaw. Some Sundays I stepped back into the RV afterward with a fragile hope, like the ritual had cleaned something. Then the door would shut, the small space would go still, and my life would feel exactly the same—loneliness rearranged, not removed.

That same period brought a letter that changed my financial ground. A disability rating increase came through —paper recognition that what I carried wasn't imaginary, that the official system now accepted the scale of impairment. The letter should have felt like relief. Part of it did. Stability matters when you've been watching money leak out of your life for years. But the stability came with its own anxiety: once you've lived on unstable ground long enough, you stop trusting good news. You start waiting for the reassessment, the reversal, the moment someone decides you look "fine" because you're functioning in public. The letter sat in my RV like a talisman and a threat: proof of validation and proof that my suffering now had a number attached to it.

By summer, I began helping my parents more consistently. I'll keep the roles general because the details are too identifying, but the reality was simple: the household was aging, and the load of keeping it running began sliding toward me. There were repairs—small things that become big when you don't have the energy to handle them. There were projects that required two hands and a steady back. There was the constant need for someone to show up when a call came in, when something broke, when anxiety rose. The RV allowed me to be close enough to respond without living under the same roof, which mattered because proximity is a drug; it can turn help into entanglement.

In the fall, I moved the RV to an older relative's driveway. The shift was immediate. The RV stopped being a roaming retreat and became a strategic outpost. The driveway placement put me within minutes of my parents' house and within steps of the older relative's needs. The older relative was in their nineties, the kind of age where vision narrows and hearing fades and mobility becomes negotiation. The house itself carried the quiet stubbornness of someone who has lived long enough to refuse change even when the body is changing against their will. Parking there felt like being stationed—not in the military sense of orders and ranks, but in the sense of being placed near a mission: show up, lift what needs lifting, fix what needs fixing, be present when the phone rings.

The driveway had its own atmosphere. Morning light filtered through the RV blinds and cut the interior into gold stripes. Outside, neighborhood sounds were muted compared to the parks: fewer engines, fewer dogs, more wind, more distance. The RV became a capsule that sat between two worlds—family obligation on one side, private collapse on the other. During the day I could step out and be useful. At night I could step back in and vanish. That pattern sounds clean when written, but living it felt like walking a tightrope with weights in my pockets. A sanctuary can become a mirror, and when your mind is unstable, mirrors can be dangerous. In the small space, every object had been placed by my hand, and therefore every object felt like an extension of me. Loneliness didn't disappear; it simply took a sharper shape.

New Year's Eve sliding into the next year was the night psilocybin went off inside that capsule like a charge I hadn't measured correctly. Earlier in the day a childhood friend stopped by for only a few minutes, the kind of quick visit that feels normal until you realize afterward how much weight it carried. A small bag of dried mushrooms changed hands with casualness—no ceremony, no warning, no sense that I was being handed a match in a room full of fumes. Then the friend was gone. The driveway went quiet. The neighborhood thinned out into winter stillness. The RV became what it always became after dark: a sealed room with my thoughts pressed up against the walls.

I set the mushrooms on the counter where I could see them. That mattered. Having them in sight turned them into a decision I had to keep re-making with my eyes. I paced a little, doing the thing I do when I'm about to cross a threshold—checking locks, checking my phone, checking the clock, checking my own pulse as if my pulse might offer advice. In my head, I framed it as intentional. Healing.

Insight. A controlled experience. But my hands betrayed the truth: the movements were restless, not calm. The choice wasn't coming from serenity. It was coming from hunger.

I ate roughly seven grams.

Even as I chewed, I knew it was too much, not because I suddenly became wise, but because the act itself carried a kind of stubbornness—*this will be decisive, this will be undeniable*. I swallowed and waited, and the waiting lasted only minutes before the first wrongness arrived. It wasn't nausea. It wasn't dizziness. It was moral. That's the only word that fits. A feeling like I had violated something sacred and didn't have the authority to fix what I'd done. The RV lights looked a fraction too bright. The air felt slightly thicker. My thoughts, which had been moving in their usual loops, snapped into a single conviction with shocking speed: I did something wrong, and I'm being rejected.

Rejected by God.

The idea didn't enter like a thought you can argue with. It landed like a verdict. It dropped into my chest with weight, turning my lungs into a smaller space. Panic climbed fast and steep. My body began searching for the exit the way an animal searches for a gap in a fence—eyes darting, hands restless, breath shallow. The capsule that normally protected me began to feel like an evidence box, as if the walls were witnesses to what I'd just done.

I started pleading out loud, not poetry, not elegant prayer—bargaining. I said the names of my family one by one, listing love like it was a password I could speak into the air to unlock mercy. I tried to make it transactional: *I love them. I would do anything for them. I'm not bad. I'm not unworthy*. The names didn't comfort me. The words didn't change the verdict. If anything, saying the names made the fear worse because it sharpened what I believed I was losing —connection, protection, belonging.

Reality began to break at the edges.

It started with small distortions: the cabinets looking too flat, the corners of the RV seeming to bend inward, the space feeling both cramped and endless at the same time. Then it escalated into something visual and brutal— pixelation, but not like a video game glitch you can laugh at. The interior of the RV—walls, fixtures, familiar surfaces— began to appear as if it was being rendered in brightly colored geometric points. Tiny squares and prismatic fragments where smooth surfaces should have been. It looked like the world was decomposing into its building blocks and failing to hold its shape. The sight didn't feel interesting. It felt like proof that the interface between me and reality had been damaged.

The small space amplified everything. There was nowhere for panic to disperse. It ricocheted. The RV, which had always been my controlled container, became a box where fear could bounce off every surface and come back louder. I remember moving toward the bed as if the bed was a safe zone, then collapsing onto it not because I chose rest, but because my body couldn't keep standing inside the pressure. Time lost its normal sequence. Minutes didn't stack into an hour. They smeared. There was no clear "then." There was only *now,* repeated endlessly, a loop of dread that felt like it would never release me.

At some point I stumbled back into the living area, desperate for an anchor. I reached for the television the way a drowning person reaches for driftwood—something familiar, something external, something that could impose a storyline on my mind. I grabbed the remote and clicked it.

Nothing.

I clicked again. Still nothing. The remote was dead —batteries gone—and in that state it didn't feel like a simple mechanical failure. It felt personal, like the universe had leaned in and chosen this exact petty moment to confirm the verdict. I could feel frustration spike so hot it made my hands shake. Not normal annoyance—rage with nowhere to go, rage aimed at reality itself. The kind of rage that says: *of course it's broken, because everything is against you.*

Then the fireworks started outside.

In ordinary life, fireworks are distant pops, predictable, even festive. In that state they translated instantly into incoming. The sound didn't stay "over there." It moved straight into my nervous system with the authority of old training—sharp pressure in the chest, a jolt through the spine, the body bracing before the mind can label it. The RV became a bunker without me deciding it. The blasts became threats without me agreeing. I curled into myself, fetal, shaking and crying in the ugliest, most involuntary way —body memory dragging me under with zero respect for context. My tears weren't about the fireworks. They were about the helplessness of being hijacked by a reflex that doesn't care what year it is.

That's when my phone rang.

The sound cut through the chaos like a rope thrown into water. I answered with hands that didn't feel like they belonged to me. The voice on the other end was steady— short, practical, grounded in the way that matters when your mind is slipping. No grand questions. No philosophy. Just guidance. Breathe. Find the batteries. Do one thing at a time. The voice gave my mind a track to follow, and I clung to it like it was the only solid object left in the room.

I found the batteries. I put them in the remote. The television came on, and sound filled the RV again, not loud, but *present,* a layer of external reality thick enough to interrupt the internal storm. The voice told me to put on something absurd, something rhythmic—something that could puncture terror with humor and familiarity. I did, not because I believed in the advice, but because obedience was easier than improvisation in that moment.

Rick and Morty played in the background.

At first it was just motion and color—voices present but distant, like the show was happening behind a wall of glass. The volume seemed to lose focus. Dialogue became muffled and then irrelevant, the way language becomes irrelevant when your mind is too busy trying to survive. And then, in the middle of it, I looked down at my hand.

Not the way you glance at your own body normally, but with an odd, newborn curiosity, as if the hand had just grown there. My palm rested open, fingers slightly curled, and the sight of it struck me with a purity that made my breath catch. The hand looked impossibly clear—lines sharp, skin luminous, every contour defined with perfect precision. It didn't feel like it was lit by the RV lamp. It felt like it emanated its own light, a soft radiance rising from within. I stared at it the way an infant might stare at its own fingers floating in amniotic quiet—weightless, suspended, fascinated by the simple fact of form.

In that moment I felt like I was floating too.

Not drifting through space, not leaving my body, but floating internally—held, buoyant, suspended in a warm, womb-like stillness that contrasted violently with the panic I'd been drowning in. The fireworks outside continued, but they moved farther away in my awareness, as if the hand had become an anchor heavy enough to pull me back into a gentler layer of perception.

The show kept playing. I didn't fully track the plot at first, but the imagery began to seep in anyway. An early-season episode—the one where Rick and Morty shrink down and travel inside a body, navigating grotesque internal landscapes like an amusement park built out of organs and fluids—started unfolding behind my eyes. The public version of it is comedic and chaotic: tiny characters moving through arteries, dodging hazards, treating biology like a theme park ride. In my state, it transformed. The absurdity became metaphor with teeth.

I began to feel, not think, that I was on a journey inside myself.

Not in the later, ketamine-surgery sense—this was different. This wasn't a vivid "fixing" operation. It was more like an impression of orientation: *you are inside the machine now*. The RV around me became background. The humor of the episode became a tool, a way to approach fear without being crushed by it. The idea formed in me that the path out wasn't by escaping my body—it was by traveling through it, understanding it, navigating its corridors the way those tiny animated figures navigated theirs. A strange hope flickered there: if you can move through the inside without dying, maybe you can learn the map. Maybe the map itself is healing.

As the trip calmed further, the world returned with a harsh clarity. Not comfort—clarity. Edges sharpened. Light looked too clean. My mind felt raw and exposed, as if the storm had sandblasted the surface. I reached for something solid and familiar and didn't even hesitate: I picked up The Book of Mormon.

The weight of it in my hands mattered. The cover texture mattered. The pages mattered. The familiarity mattered. I opened it and held it the way you hold a physical promise. And in that moment—separate from the earlier panic, separate from the floating-hand wonder, separate from the Rick and Morty interior-journey impression—I felt a strong, unmistakable revelation settle into me with its own gravity: this book is absolutely true.

Not "comforting." Not "interesting." True.

The impression didn't come with fireworks or visions. It came with certainty so clean it startled me. It felt like a beam of light dropped into a muddy pond—sudden clarity, sudden stillness. For a brief period, the earlier sense of rejection loosened its grip. The verdict changed tone. The universe didn't feel friendly exactly, but it felt structured again, as if I had re-found a pillar I could lean on without it bending.

The trip continued to fade through the night, leaving behind exhaustion and a fragile calm. The next morning, fog sat heavy outside—thick enough to blur the world into a gray smear. My mind, still trained to treat the environment as meaningful, tried immediately to interpret it as judgment: *this is a sign you're off the path.* The thought rose automatically, not invited. The fog burned off as the day warmed. The interpretation softened. But the scar remained: not just fear, not just rejection, but the lingering understanding that spiritual doors can open in more than one direction—and sometimes they open into comfort, and sometimes they open into terror, and the body doesn't always know which one it's about to walk through.

Over the next one to two months I microdosed the remaining mushrooms in amounts too small to be perceptible, telling myself I was being careful, telling myself I was controlling it now. The truth was that the perceptible experience had left a mark in how my mind approached faith. I continued attending church and serving and advancing in the ways that look like stability. I continued doing the family work—repairs, errands, presence. And beneath it, the question persisted like a low-frequency hum: What is real, and how much of reality is simply my brain's agreement to behave?

Spring of the next year is when ketamine entered my timeline, and it arrived with the promise of "treatment," a word that sounds controlled and rational until you live through what it actually does. The sessions were spaced over weeks, six in total, each one a higher dose. The clinic environment was medical-clean, the kind of place where surfaces are designed to be wiped and emotions are treated like spill hazards. I traveled in, checked in, answered questions, sat down in a chair designed for surrender, and watched my arm become a site of procedure. The staff spoke calmly. The lighting was soft. The music they used was labeled "therapy music," as if labeling a sound could make it safe.

The first infusion didn't creep in politely. It hit like a switch. One moment I was a man in a chair, feeling the normal weight of gravity and the normal continuity of time. The next moment the concept of "room" stopped applying. The concept of "body" softened. "Here" became irrelevant. There was a visual theme that repeated across sessions: a dark blue pastel space, not a black void, not nothingness, but a soft deep blue like twilight stretched into infinity. I floated there, and the music became the engine. Sound didn't accompany movement. Sound caused movement. Notes pushed me forward. Chords rolled me. Rhythm tilted my entire existence like my consciousness had been poured into a slow-turning sea.

Time didn't pass in that space. It arranged itself. Moments expanded until they felt like whole lifetimes. Then whole lifetimes collapsed into a single second. It felt like drifting through layers of reality the way you drift through layers of sleep, except it wasn't sleep; it was sharper, more exposed, like the mind stripped of its anchors. On some returns, I surfaced with the strong impression that I was creating reality—not as metaphor, but as a terrifying perception: *this is happening because I am generating it.* Coincidences felt engineered. People felt divinely placed, like actors stepping onstage at exactly the right moment to keep me from noticing the edges of the set.

That impression collided violently with my faith. Faith, for me, had always been hierarchy: God as God, me as a man—small, accountable, trying to obey, trying to endure. The ketamine impressions tried to invert that structure and place me in the wrong seat. The conflict didn't make me stop believing; it made me spiral. I began measuring my covenants like a ledger, trying to locate where I had deviated, where I had invited danger into my perception. The thought patterns became corrosive: if I had promised certain things, why did reality feel like punishment instead of protection? If obedience was supposed to produce peace, why did peace feel like a brief glitch and dread feel like the default? I tried to distance myself, but not from the thoughts—more from reality itself, like stepping back from the stage would stop the show from being performed.

Between the fifth and sixth infusion, someone stole three thousand dollars cash from my hotel room. The theft wasn't cinematic. It was ordinary cruelty. I had the money set aside for practical reasons tied to the treatments—an attempt to keep the weeks manageable, an attempt to keep control of the logistics—cash folded and placed where it felt safe in a room that was supposed to be temporary and neutral. I left and returned and discovered the absence the way you discover a missing tooth: a sudden wrongness in the structure of your day. I tore the room apart with shaking hands, lifting pillows, checking drawers, opening bags, searching as if panic could reverse physics. The money was simply gone.

The process that followed was insult layered on loss. I reported it. I answered questions. I watched people's faces take on the polite skepticism of those who assume the victim is mistaken. There were no leads, no meaningful response, no resolution. The cash became a hole in my week and a hole in my trust. When you're already living with the impression that reality is staged and hostile, a theft like that lands as evidence. It doesn't feel like random crime; it feels like the universe leaning in close and whispering, *Even when you're trying to get better, I can still reach into your pockets.* I carried that impression into the sixth infusion like a bruise carried under clothing.

The RV became more of a sanctuary during those weeks precisely because the ketamine had made reality feel thin. When you're afraid the world is staged, a small space feels safer than an open one. When you're afraid your mind can slip away, a small space feels easier to anchor in. But sanctuary has a cost. The cost is that you begin to prefer the capsule. You begin to treat the outside world as risk. You begin to live inside a sealed system because sealed systems don't surprise you as often. The driveway became both refuge and trap: close enough to respond to family needs, close enough to be pulled into escalating household crises, but also close enough to retreat into the RV and let the door shut like a verdict.

As the months moved forward, the condition of my father escalated rapidly. It showed up first as small ruptures —repeated questions, confusing stories, a kind of mental slipping that wasn't acknowledged openly at first because acknowledging it would have made it real. Then it became harder to ignore. A highway incident served as a trigger point in the larger narrative: a crash that forced everyone to confront what had been quietly building. After that, the decline felt like a slope you couldn't stop sliding down. Household tasks multiplied. Stress became constant. My mother's voice on the phone carried exhaustion that wasn't just tiredness; it was the fatigue of watching someone's mind change while still needing that person to function as a partner in daily life.

The older relative in the driveway house was declining too. Vision fading. Hearing dimming. Mobility narrowing. The older relative lost the ability to drive and needed help with the basic tasks that preserve dignity: getting groceries, moving objects that suddenly became too heavy, navigating stairs that felt steeper each month. So my life became a set of short commutes between needs—drive a few minutes, carry a thing, fix a thing, answer a question, redirect an argument, replace a part, clean a mess, sit quietly and let someone repeat the same story because correcting them only caused distress. Then back to the RV, back to the capsule, back to the quiet where my mind could either settle or turn on itself.

In the months, and even years, that followed, I revisited other psychedelics in smaller, non-breakthrough ways—tests more than explorations. Quick glances into a doorway I couldn't stop thinking about. The experiences didn't deliver new revelations; they delivered variations of the same underlying theme: the mind is capable of generating worlds, and the fear is not that those worlds exist —it's that they might bleed into the day-to-day and make ordinary life feel staged. Every return carried the same uneasy pressure: gratitude for being back in the familiar, and suspicion that the familiar might be an illusion held together by habit.

That summer brought a different kind of rupture— the kind with receipts. My truck's alternator failed, and I left the vehicle at a shop, trusting the mundane world to behave like a mundane world. When I got it back, everything not tied down inside the truck had been burglarized. Items missing, compartments rummaged, the interior subtly wrong in a way your body notices before your brain lists it. I reported it. I went through the same humiliating sequence: questions, forms, polite skepticism, no resolution. No meaningful help. The theft sat next to the earlier hotel theft in my mind like two matching bruises. Separate events, different circumstances, the same outcome: violation without consequence, loss without repair.

By then, the impression that the universe was acting against me had become hard to dismiss. Not because I believed in cosmic persecution as doctrine, but because repeated randomness starts to feel patterned when your nervous system is already tuned for threat. Money stolen during the very period I was trying to "get better." Property taken while I was trying to hold together a collapsing family system. No meaningful help from anyone paid to care. No closure. The world didn't just feel unsafe—it felt personal, as if the shape of my life had become an invitation for hands I couldn't see to reach in and take.

Not long after the alternator incident, another blow landed, and this one didn't look like crime. It looked like the phone ringing with the wrong kind of weight behind it. It looked like a voice telling me a friend was gone, and the words didn't fit in my head at first—too blunt, too final, too incompatible with the way the day had started. I remember standing still after the call ended, waiting for something to rise in me—shock, grief, anger, anything that would prove the information had reached my heart.

Nothing rose.

The absence of reaction wasn't calm. It wasn't acceptance. It was a blank—an unnerving flat stretch inside my chest where emotion should have been. I walked through the next hours like I was following instructions written on paper I couldn't read. I told people what happened in the same tone you use to report a weather change. I stared at walls and waited for tears that wouldn't come. I kept thinking, *This is wrong. This is what broken looks like.* Not because I didn't care, but because my body refused to produce the proof that I cared.

The funeral arrived like a scene staged for other people. The building smelled like old carpet and flowers trying too hard, and the air had that specific hush that makes every footstep sound like disrespect. Faces gathered in clusters, hugging, crying, exchanging stories that landed as bright, warm human evidence: *this mattered.* There were framed photos—smiles locked in time, eyes open, alive— and seeing those images should have cracked something in me. Instead I felt myself watching the room from behind glass, aware of what was expected and unable to deliver it.

People spoke. Memories were shared. Laughter appeared in the middle of grief the way it always does, a brief release valve, and even that laughter made me feel more alien. I listened to stories and recognized the shape of who he had been to others, and the recognition didn't unlock emotion—it only sharpened the strangeness of my own stillness. I kept touching my face as if I could check whether I was wearing the correct expression. I nodded at the right moments. I said the right words back. I accepted condolences that weren't meant for me but still landed like obligations.

Inside, the only feeling I could reliably access was a hard, sour thought: *Something is wrong with me*.

Not the dramatic kind of wrong. Not the kind that makes you scream. The quiet kind, the kind that steals natural responses and leaves you performing the outline of a person. I stood near the casket and waited for the body to revolt, waited for grief to punch through the numbness, waited for tears to prove that love had weight. My eyes stayed dry. My throat stayed open. My chest stayed flat. The blankness felt like a second loss layered on top of the first— his death, and then the death of the version of me who would have responded like a normal human being.

Afterward, in the parking lot, the sky looked too ordinary. Cars started. Doors shut. People went home. The world accepted the funeral as a completed event and moved on, and I moved with it because movement is what I do when I can't feel. The numbness followed me back into my small capsule life like a shadow that didn't need sunlight. That was the part that scared me most: not that I wasn't grieving in public, but that I couldn't find the grief in private either. Alone, with no eyes on me, I still felt the same blank. The same sealed interior. The same sense that whatever circuits were supposed to light up had been cut.

I tried to interpret the flatness as protection—my mind rationing pain because there was already too much. I tried to interpret it as dissociation, as shutdown, as the nervous system's emergency brake. Those interpretations helped on paper. In the body, it felt like corruption. Like I had been hollowed out and didn't know when the hollowing happened. Like I'd reached for relief so many times—in faith, in chemicals, in isolation, in structure—that the part of me responsible for ordinary grief had learned to stay offline.

The RV remained the core structure of my survival anyway. The driveway life turned me into a quiet responder —always close, always available, always sliding between households that needed help. I learned the sound of the phone when it carried bad news. I learned the look on my mother's face when she was exhausted beyond words. I learned the way my father's decline reshaped conversations into loops. I learned the older relative's stubborn pride as independence evaporated. And I learned, in the small hours inside the RV, that a sanctuary doesn't eliminate loneliness —it concentrates it. The walls are close, the world is reduced, and the mind has fewer places to hide.

Then the notice arrived—March, late winter still clinging to everything the sun couldn't warm fast enough. The driveway was the same driveway it had been for months, the RV still sitting square and level like it had earned the right to be there, the hose still routed the way I'd routed it, the power cord still draped with the same practical slouch. That morning felt ordinary in the way ordinary can be dangerous. I stepped out into air that smelled like damp earth and thawing grime, and I saw it from a distance before I could read it: a bright rectangle of paper on a post, too clean against the dull background, like a tag tied to something impounded.

It was taped up high enough to be seen by anyone who passed. The tape wasn't subtle. It was layered in thick bands, pressed hard, corners flattened like someone wanted to make sure wind couldn't do me the mercy of tearing it down. There's a particular humiliation in public paperwork. It's not just information; it's a declaration. It says, *We have looked at you. We have decided. We have posted our decision where your neighbors can read it while they walk their dogs.*

I stood there long enough for the cold to seep into my feet through my shoes. The paper fluttered slightly. The words didn't. The language was blunt—official phrases arranged like a fence. It didn't say *home*. It didn't say *shelter*. It didn't say *survival*. It described my RV as a "unit" and my presence as an "occupancy," as if my life were a technical problem. The sentence that landed hardest was the one that translated everything I'd built into a single judgment: unfit for human habitation. Not because the RV had mold or rot or some hidden danger, but because the rules said people weren't supposed to live like this here. A clean, functional, nearly new RV—warm bed, working water, electricity I had wired and monitored myself—reduced to something you weren't allowed to be inside.

I'd known the rule when I moved there. That knowledge didn't soften the blow. It sharpened it. It meant the notice wasn't education. It was enforcement. It meant I hadn't misunderstood; I'd gambled. I'd gambled that if I stayed quiet, if I kept it tidy, if I didn't make trouble, the world might look the other way long enough for me to breathe. The paper made it clear the world had been watching the whole time.

The first reaction wasn't anger. It was that hollow, nauseating sensation of being singled out. As if the universe had found a new way to say *no*—not through sickness, not through a theft, not through family fracture, but through a thin sheet of printed authority. My throat went dry. My eyes scanned the wording again and again, looking for mercy between lines. There was none. There was a timeline. There were consequences. There was the clinical promise of escalation if I didn't comply.

The notice didn't just target me. It reached through me and grabbed the elderly relative who owned the driveway. That's what made it feel vicious. I could have absorbed a penalty in isolation and called it the cost of my choices. The notice wasn't built for that. It was built to pull an old person into the machinery and make them responsible for stopping me. It was written as if the driveway itself had committed a crime by allowing me to exist there. The worst part was the way the paper framed it like a favor: *correct this violation, avoid further action, comply.* The word *violation* did more damage than any threat of a fine. It took my attempt to stay alive and re-labeled it as wrongdoing.

I walked back to the RV and stood on the step with my hand on the door handle, not going in, not leaving, just stalled. Inside was everything I'd learned to trust: the narrow hallway I could walk without scanning corners, the small sink I'd scrubbed until it shined, the cabinet where I kept batteries and flashlights and medications, the bed that had held me through nights when my mind tried to turn itself inside out. Outside was everything I couldn't control: neighbors, laws, enforcement, conversations behind curtains. I felt the seam between those two worlds tighten until it felt like a wire cutting into skin.

The hearing was scheduled soon after. A date. A location. Instructions that assumed people had clear minds and good sleep. The notice made it sound like a simple administrative step—just show up, just sign, just comply. In reality it was a trap designed to create leverage. The leverage wasn't over me. It was over the older relative.

I didn't have the luxury of ignoring it. If I refused to comply, I wasn't just risking my own consequences—I was risking theirs. That is how the system finds your softest point. It doesn't have to break your will. It only has to threaten someone you can't stomach harming. The thought of fines landing on a ninety-something person because I needed shelter made my stomach twist with a guilt so sharp it felt like nausea.

The day of the hearing, the building had that government smell—old carpet, stale air, disinfectant layered over decades of bodies passing through. The lights were fluorescent and unforgiving, the kind that make everyone look slightly ill. The chairs were arranged to keep people quiet. There were other people waiting with their own folders, their own paperwork, their own private emergencies pressed into manila envelopes. No one talked much. Talking makes you feel human; the building was designed to reduce you.

When our turn came, we went into a room that looked like every room where decisions are made without empathy: a table, a few chairs, a person behind a desk with a computer screen angled away like a shield. The older relative sat beside me, small in a way that had nothing to do with body size and everything to do with context. Age doesn't always look fragile at home. In a fluorescent room with authority on the other side of the desk, age becomes vulnerability made visible.

The official spoke quickly, in the language of procedure. They didn't say my name with warmth. They didn't ask how the older relative was doing. They referenced codes, rules, compliance. They explained what would happen if the RV was "occupied" again—how fines would be assessed, how enforcement could escalate. It was delivered like a weather report. The older relative nodded politely, but I could see confusion flicker, the way it does when words come too fast and too formally. Their hands rested on the table, thin-skinned and slightly trembling, the veins raised like blue lines beneath paper-thin skin. Those hands had built and fixed and carried and driven for decades. In this room, those hands were being positioned to sign a document that would punish them if I kept trying to live.

They slid the paper across the table. I watched the older relative's eyes move over it as if the words might come into focus if stared at long enough. I wanted to grab the page and rip it in half. I wanted to stand up and say, *This isn't a nuisance. This is my shelter.* Instead, I sat still because stillness was the only way to keep the situation from becoming worse. The official pointed to a signature line. The older relative hesitated, glanced at me, and in that glance I saw the full cruelty of the setup: they were being asked to choose between protecting me and protecting themselves. No elder should be forced into that kind of choice. No family should be made to put a signature on a punishment designed to control another family member.

They signed.

The pen moved slowly, the hand not as steady as it once would have been. The signature looked fragile on the page, like a scratch. When the pen lifted, I felt something inside me collapse—not dramatic, not loud, just a silent internal cave-in. My sanctuary hadn't been taken by fire or flood. It had been taken by a signature extracted under threat. It was hard not to feel like I had used an old person as my shield, and now the shield was being punished for shielding me.

After the hearing, the RV didn't feel like home anymore. It still smelled the same. The same cabinets closed with the same clicks. The same bed sat waiting. But the space had been marked. Not physically, not with tape or paint, but with a new kind of tension. Every time I stepped inside, I felt the clock. Every time I sat at the dinette, I felt the paper on a desk somewhere, the signature that had turned my living arrangement into an enforceable violation. I began noticing things I'd never noticed before: the exact sound the door made when it latched, the way the blinds rattled in a wind gust, the faint creak of the RV settling on its suspension. The RV started to feel less like a capsule and more like a condemned room.

Packing became ritualistic in the ugliest way—the way you pack when you're being evicted from your own survival strategy. I didn't move fast. I moved with a grim precision, because rushing would have made it feel like panic, and panic would have made it feel like defeat. I dismantled the systems I'd built one by one: the carefully organized bins, the labeled compartments, the small domestic routines that had turned a vehicle into a living space. Every drawer I emptied felt like erasing evidence that

I had ever been steady. Every cabinet I wiped down felt like saying goodbye to a version of myself that had at least managed to keep a small world clean.

The hardest part wasn't the big items. It was the little ones—the objects you don't think about until they're in your hand and you realize they've been your anchors. A worn charger cable. A cheap flashlight. A small bottle of ibuprofen. A notebook with half-finished lists. The mug you always use even though it's chipped at the rim. These are the things that tell your nervous system, *You have a place.* When you pack them, your nervous system hears a different message: *You are being displaced again.*

Outside, the RV looked perfectly normal, which made the situation feel surreal. It wasn't collapsing. It wasn't dirty. It wasn't unsafe. It sat on the driveway like any other RV someone might use for travel. The difference was invisible and absolute: someone with authority had decided that my presence inside it was unacceptable. The idea that legality and livability could be so disconnected made my head buzz with a kind of helpless rage I couldn't express anywhere without worsening the consequences.

The final day came as a deadline, not a ceremony. There was no crowd. There was no one clapping. There was only the quiet pressure of knowing that if I stayed, the older relative would be fined—fined for my existence, fined for my need. I moved the last boxes into my truck and made sure the RV looked the way I always kept it: clean, orderly, presentable, as if tidiness could earn mercy retroactively.

Before I left, I stood inside one last time with the door closed. The air was slightly stale from being opened and shut so often during packing. The small space felt both intimate and empty, like a room after a funeral. I walked the few steps from the bed to the kitchen and back, letting my feet touch each patch of floor, almost like I was memorizing the layout again. I placed my hand on the counter. I looked at the corners. I listened to the silence and realized the silence had changed. It used to feel protective. Now it felt like the silence of a place you're no longer allowed to inhabit.

I latched cabinets, one by one. The clicks sounded final. I folded the last bedding. I wiped the sink even though no one was going to inspect it for morality. I stood at the door and hesitated, because closing a door is easy and living without what's behind it is not.

When the door shut, it made the same solid sound it always made. The difference was in my body. The sound landed like a verdict. Not a dramatic verdict, not something shouted—just a heavy internal punctuation mark. I checked the locks out of habit. I stepped down onto the driveway. The RV sat there mute and clean, already transitioning from sanctuary to object. A "unit." A "vehicle." Something to be stored, preserved, made inert.

I walked away knowing I wasn't just leaving a driveway. I was leaving the one place where I had made the world small enough to survive without constantly negotiating my own perception. I was leaving the routine that had kept me tethered—wake up, check batteries, make food, help family, retreat to capsule, sleep. I was leaving the controlled interior where I could shut a door and temporarily shut out the threat of labels, accusations, and the ordinary chaos of a world that kept proving it could reach into my life and take.

That's where the chapter ends—not because the story stops, but because the next part begins with a different kind of exposure. The loss of the RV wasn't the loss of a hobby or a convenience. It was the loss of a boundary. And when a man loses his boundary, everything he has been keeping outside rushes in at once: the cost of rebuilding, the financial bleed, the escalating decline in the family system, the relentless need to be present without having a place to retreat. The RV had been a sanctuary on wheels, a practical shell against a hostile world. It was taken not by disaster, not by fire, not by a single dramatic event, but by paper—by tape pressed hard at the corners, by fluorescent rooms, by a pen held in an elderly hand, and by the quiet, legal certainty that survival is only allowed in certain approved shapes.

# CHAPTER 19

# *Thin-Walled Quiet*

The lease packet came in a manila envelope that tried to look neutral. Thick paper. Black ink. A signature line that didn't care what it cost to reach it. When I slid the pages out on the kitchen counter, the apartment's overhead light made everything look freshly disinfected—like the words themselves had been sanitized. The packet smelled faintly of toner and glue, that office smell that turns personal life into a file. I read every paragraph the way I used to read orders: slowly, suspiciously, hunting for the part that would later be used against me. The language was calm, almost kind, and that calmness made it worse, because it pretended that what I was doing was normal—just a person moving, signing, complying—when it was actually a forced conversion from one kind of survival to another.

By April 2025 the decision had already been made for me. The boundary I'd built—small, contained, movable—had been stripped away by paper and fluorescent rooms and the ugly leverage of consequence. So the apartment wasn't a fresh start. It was a penalty dressed up as legitimacy. "Proper housing," the kind that looks correct to the outside world, the kind that satisfies rules and quiets strangers and makes bureaucracies relax. The irony is that proper housing doesn't automatically feel safe when your nervous system has learned to treat safety as temporary. Walls can be thick and still feel exposed. Doors can lock and still feel permeable. You can be inside something approved and still feel like you're living in the open.

The first day I carried boxes in, the breezeway swallowed the sound of my footsteps and sent it back at me in a faint echo. The front door didn't open into a hallway the way some apartments do. It opened into that shared breezeway space—air that wasn't fully outside and wasn't fully mine. It smelled like dust and old paint and the faint sweetness of someone's laundry detergent. I remember stopping with a box in my hands and letting the door swing shut behind me, listening to the soft latch, measuring what it felt like to cross a threshold that wasn't private. The breezeway felt like a mouth. Step through it, and you're in public space again. Step out of it, and you're back in your small interior. My body noticed the difference immediately.

Inside, the apartment was first floor, which should have felt grounded. No one living below me, no hollow space under my feet. The stability of ground-level should have been comforting, and part of it was. But first floor also means you're closer to everything—closer to the parking lot, closer to the outside, closer to the idea that someone could approach your windows. I learned quickly which blinds I kept angled just so, not because I was hiding something, but because being visible makes my body tense. I moved through the rooms in the first days like I was mapping an unfamiliar terrain: where the light fell in the morning, how sound traveled, which corners held the most shadow at night, how far the patio door was from the couch, how fast I could cross the living room if I needed to.

The heaviest sound in the apartment wasn't traffic. It was footsteps—heavy, blunt footsteps from the person or people living above me. They moved like they weren't aware of their own weight. Sometimes the steps paced. Sometimes they dropped suddenly like a heel strike. Sometimes a chair scraped, and the scrape was long enough to feel like a warning. I'd be sitting still and then—thud, thud, thud—overhead movement would pulse through the ceiling. It did something primitive to my nervous system. It didn't matter if it was harmless. My body treated it as information: someone is there, above you, moving. The RV had creaks and wind and small mechanical noises, but it didn't have another human's weight pressing down from the ceiling. The apartment reminded me constantly that I wasn't alone in the building, even when I was alone in my unit.

I set my truck in handicap parking within eyesight of my patio door. The placement wasn't convenience. It was control. I liked being able to look out and see it there, like a tether to mobility. Vehicles have always been more than transportation for me—they're exit plans. They're distance. They're a way to move the world when the world gets too close. With the truck parked where I could see it, the apartment felt less like a trap. The sightline became its own kind of reassurance: if I need to leave, I can. If something feels wrong, I don't have to negotiate with anyone. I don't have to walk across an exposed lot. I can open the patio door, step out, and the vehicle is already waiting.

I built the interior like you build a defensive position, except I used softness instead of sandbags. I hung religious art deliberately—not as decoration, but as atmosphere engineering. Images that suggested order. Images that suggested refuge. Images that carried the quiet reminder that I was not the only consciousness in the universe, that there was something larger than this apartment, larger than my nervous system. I placed the art where my eyes would land naturally: above the couch, along the line of sight when I walked from kitchen to living room, near the places I tended to sit when my mind was loud. I wasn't trying to impress anyone. I was trying to train my own brain. Sanctuary is partly physical, but it's also visual. It's what your eyes meet when you're searching for anchors.

Even with a bedroom and a bed, I slept on the couch often. The bed was there, clean, proper, correct—the kind of sleeping arrangement that fits the shape of "normal." The couch was where my body wanted to be. The couch put me closer to the patio door, closer to the living space, closer to my main anchor points. The couch let me fall asleep with the television's low glow painting the room, the sound creating a buffer against intrusive thoughts. In bed, in the darkness of a closed room, my mind had too much room to move. On the couch, the room stayed slightly alive: a lamp, a screen, a familiar line of sight to the religious art, a quick glance to confirm the truck still sat outside. I hated that about myself sometimes—how I couldn't simply use the bed like a normal person. But I also recognized it as adaptation. The couch wasn't weakness. It was strategy.

The move itself wasn't a single event. It was a series of humiliations disguised as errands. The RV had required almost nothing to be "enough." A few key objects, a tight routine, and the capsule became livable. The apartment demanded a full transformation—furniture, cookware, cleaning supplies, things that make empty rooms look like a person belongs there. A couch. A table. Lamps. A shower curtain. Hangers. The small objects that, in normal life, you collect over years without noticing. I had to buy them in a compressed window, under pressure, while already grieving what I'd lost. The cost landed around ten thousand dollars, and the number wasn't just budgeting. It felt like ransom—money paid to make compliance visible.

Spending money like that changes your breathing when you've lived through unstable ground. Every purchase carries a second price: the fear that you'll need that money later for something worse. I walked through stores under harsh lights, staring at aisles of ordinary things and feeling a strange rage at their ordinariness. People buy towels because they like a color. I bought towels because the world had outlawed the way I was living. People buy a couch because they want comfort. I bought a couch because an empty living room makes you look transient, and transience invites scrutiny. I kept receipts. I tracked totals. I watched my savings thin and felt my stability shrink with it, not because the apartment was inherently wrong, but because it wasn't chosen on my terms.

The RV itself had to go somewhere. That sentence looks simple on the page. In reality it became a dread I carried like a stone. I couldn't keep it in the driveway. I couldn't live in it. I couldn't park it in a place that kept it fully under my control. So it went onto someone else's property—someone I did not trust, someone whose version of me had already been shaped into something dangerous. Handing over the keys to my capsule felt like leaving my heart on the porch of a house that might not return it intact. I told myself it was temporary. I told myself it was the best option. The truth was uglier: my sanctuary, the thing that had kept my mind from slipping too far, was now sitting on land I wouldn't choose, under eyes I didn't want, exposed to the same world that had already proven it could reach in and take.

Once the apartment was set up enough to be inhabited, the days tried to become ordinary. I learned the building's rhythms without needing a hallway map: when the breezeway echoed with someone passing, when trash bins rattled outside, when the neighbor upstairs stomped from one side of their unit to the other. I learned which grocery store felt least overwhelming, which route kept me away from too much traffic, which times of day made the parking lot feel calmer. I tried to build routines the way I always do—small, repeatable structures that keep my mind from dissolving into open water. I made lists. I cleaned surfaces even when they didn't look dirty. I put objects in the same place every time, not because I love tidiness, but because order is a nervous system trick: if the outside world is predictable, the inside world sometimes quiets.

The apartment did not erase why I had needed the RV in the first place. It didn't erase the part of my brain that stays half turned toward exits. It didn't erase the low-level vigilance that interprets minor problems as warning signs. If anything, "proper housing" made the internal tension louder because it removed my ability to relocate when the air turned hostile. In the RV, if the atmosphere shifted, I could move. In the apartment, I was anchored. Anchored housing looks stable on paper. In a mind that associates stability with traps, anchoring can feel like being pinned.

While I was trying to adapt, my father's condition— already declining—shifted into a new phase. Dementia is often described as slow, abstract, a gradual forgetting. That description doesn't prepare you for the moments when decline becomes physical, undeniable, brutally practical. There are days when you look at a person you've always known in one shape and suddenly realize that shape is no longer guaranteed. The mind that once guided the body starts misfiring. Independence doesn't disappear all at once; it leaks away, and the leaking becomes a constant emergency disguised as routine.

The calls started coming more often. Small crises, then larger ones. Confusions that could be redirected, then confusions that couldn't. There were moments of wandering logic—sentences that sounded coherent until the end collapsed into nonsense. There were sudden irritations that came from nowhere, as if his brain kept misreading the world and reacting to the misread. There were times he would look at a familiar room and seem unsure how to move through it. And beneath all of it, there was the steady exhaustion of my mother—an exhaustion that wasn't just fatigue, but the wear of living beside someone whose mind was changing daily while still needing that person to function as a partner in the ordinary chores of life.

The house during that time had the smell of renovation dust and stress. Rooms were partially undone. Tools and materials sat where they'd been left because finishing projects becomes impossible when crisis eats attention. Even the air felt tired. I drove over from the apartment and stepped into a place that had once been my childhood environment and now felt like a worksite wrapped around a medical emergency. There were days when he seemed present enough that hope tried to rise, and days when he was unmistakably gone behind his eyes, as if someone had dimmed the lights inside. Hope in those situations is a dangerous thing because it makes you keep recalibrating. Every good day trains you to believe the slope has leveled. Every bad day reminds you the slope never stopped.

Then motor function began to drop away. That phrase is clinical; the reality is intimate and brutal. It means watching someone struggle with movements that used to be automatic. It means seeing frustration flash across his face when his body didn't obey. It means witnessing the humiliation that comes when a person realizes—sometimes with sudden clarity—that they are becoming dependent. The loss of coordination isn't just physical; it's psychological. It changes how a person carries themselves. It changes how they speak. It changes the way the house moves around them, as if everyone becomes afraid of doing the wrong thing and causing a fall.

Hospitalization arrived not as one dramatic night, but as inevitability piling up until denial broke. A trip to the emergency department. Waiting rooms with stale air and the monotone murmur of televisions no one watched. Paperwork that asked the same questions over and over, as if repetition could prevent loss. The fluorescent lighting that made every face look slightly gray. I sat in hard chairs and watched staff move with practiced efficiency, their calm professionalism both comforting and infuriating. Comforting because someone was doing something. Infuriating because doing something did not mean the trajectory would change.

In the hospital room, machines became part of the environment. Beeps, hisses, alarms that sounded briefly and then stopped. The bed became a border: on one side, my father in a weakened body; on the other, family standing around trying to pretend this was temporary. I remember the stillness of his hands on the blanket. I remember the way his eyes would fix on a point that didn't seem to be in the room. I remember moments when he spoke and the words were almost him, and then the thread snapped and the sentence drifted away. Those moments were the cruelest because they gave you a glimpse of the person you wanted back, and then they took him away again before you could hold on.

Time in the hospital doesn't move forward. It pools. Hours stretch into long strips of waiting, punctuated by bursts of activity—vitals, medications, brief conversations with doctors who spoke in careful terms. The language was always balanced: what they could do, what they could try, what was likely, what was uncertain. I learned to listen for what wasn't said. Doctors don't always say *dying* even when the trajectory is obvious. They use other words—*declining, complications, limited options*—words that leave space for the family's denial because denial keeps people from breaking in front of strangers.

When the end moved closer, the room changed. Not physically, but atmospherically. The staff's tone softened. The check-ins became more gentle. The pauses in conversation grew longer. People began speaking as if they were already remembering him rather than treating him. That shift is subtle, and once you notice it, you can't un-notice it. It's the moment the system begins preparing you for loss without saying it out loud.

There were decisions. Quiet conversations. The kind you don't want to have because having them makes the outcome real. My mother's face carried a tiredness I had never seen before—an exhaustion so deep it didn't even look like emotion anymore, just depletion. I stood beside her and watched her negotiate with reality: what she wished could happen, what she knew would happen, what she was willing to allow. I watched the way her body held itself, rigid and fragile at the same time, as if if she relaxed even slightly she would collapse.

The last hours did not feel like a dramatic scene. They felt like being trapped inside a slow closing. The machines still beeped, but the beeps started sounding like punctuation. Nurses moved in quieter ways. The room's air felt heavy. I remember watching his breathing become irregular—spaces between breaths lengthening, then shortening, then lengthening again. Each pause made my body tense as if I could will the next breath into existence. The pause would end. The next breath would come. Then another pause. The rhythm became a cruel countdown you couldn't stop watching.

I expected grief to hit like a wave. I expected my body to do something unmistakably human—cry, shake, collapse. Instead, what came first was a numb, flat registration: this has happened. My brain recorded it as fact. My body stayed stubbornly quiet.

The flatness wasn't strength. It wasn't stoicism. It wasn't spiritual peace. It was shutdown so complete it frightened me. Because if you don't cry when your father dies, the mind immediately starts interrogating you: *What does that mean about you?* I watched my mother cry. I watched other family members cry. I watched shoulders shake, hands cover faces, the raw proof of love and loss. I stood among them like I was behind glass, participating in the rituals while feeling detached from the expected emotional current. I hugged when hugs were offered. I said the right words. I received condolences. And inside, I felt only a quiet fear—fear that something essential in me had been damaged beyond repair.

After the death, the house didn't become calm. It became busy in a different way. Practical burdens take over because practical burdens always do. There are phone calls. There are forms. There are decisions about arrangements. There are tasks that need doing whether you're ready or not. Grief is not granted privacy when logistics are hungry. The home itself carried absence like a smell—his chair, his routine, the things he would have done without thinking. Even the unfinished renovations felt heavier, as if the dust now belonged to mourning. The world narrowed. The future reorganized itself around one missing person.

The funeral unfolded with the familiar choreography of death: the quiet building, the flowers trying to make decay feel polite, the photographs that trap a person in their healthiest years. People shared stories. Some laughed through tears, that strange laughter grief allows as a brief release. I listened and nodded and recognized the truth of the memories, and still my chest stayed flat. I stood near the casket and waited for my nervous system to revolt, for tears to force their way out, for my body to prove it knew what had happened. Nothing. The absence wasn't relief; it was another loss layered on top of the first—the loss of my father, and the loss of my own ability to respond in a way that felt human.

Afterward, the world moved on with a cruelty that felt automatic. Cars started. Doors closed. People went home. The parking lot emptied. The sky looked too normal. I returned to the apartment with the same numbness riding inside me like a passenger I couldn't drop off. I unlocked the door from the breezeway and stepped back into my own arranged sanctuary—the religious art, the deliberate anchors, the couch that had become my bed. The overhead footsteps thudded once, as if the neighbor above was reminding me the world still existed beyond my grief. I sat on the couch and stared at the wall for long stretches, feeling like I was waiting for myself to arrive back into my body. The arrival didn't happen. The flatness lingered.

Weeks passed in a blur of caregiving and aftermath. My mother's life had shifted into a new shape. Certain tasks became heavier because they now belonged solely to her unless someone else stepped in. I kept showing up. I carried groceries. I fixed small things. I answered questions, sometimes the same questions repeatedly, because stress makes everyone's mind loop. I sat in rooms where the television played low because silence felt too sharp. I learned again that caregiving is a kind of slow erosion: you give time, then more time, then all the time you can spare, and still the situation asks for more.

Then the older relative fell—later, after the household had already been altered by death and stress and age. The older relative ended up stranded on a bathroom floor for over six hours. Six hours is long enough for the body to become its own enemy—cold, stiff, pained—long enough for dignity to erode into survival. A family member found them and got them to a hospital. Rehabilitation followed—weeks measured in progress notes and cautious optimism. Watching an elderly person relearn how to stand is watching life compress into fundamentals: balance, breath, determination, pain. It made me furious in a quiet way, not at anyone in particular, but at the relentless mechanics of decline.

Because I could no longer live in a driveway within five minutes, caregiving had to be reorganized into schedules. Rotating shifts. Days carved into blocks. People coming and going like a duty roster. On paper it looked efficient. In reality it was grief disguised as logistics. The family had to build a human system to replace what proximity would have provided naturally. I watched that system assemble with a bitterness I tried to hide, not because anyone was doing wrong, but because the situation felt like preventable suffering. If my RV had been allowed to remain, I could have been present in the simple, steady way that matters—close enough to respond without major rearrangements, close enough to reduce the need for constant rotation.

Meanwhile, the apartment remained my base, and base is not the same as home. I learned how to move between worlds: apartment to hospital, apartment to rehab, apartment to a house full of renovation dust and grief, then back again. Each return to the apartment came with the same strange sensation: relief at being alone, and dread at being alone. Relief because solitude meant no demands and no eyes. Dread because solitude meant the mind had room. I cooked simple meals and cleaned up immediately after, not because I'm disciplined, but because disorder in the sink can become disorder in my head. I tried to sleep at predictable times. Sleep arrived in fragments. The couch became my default, the bed a place I used when I was already exhausted enough to trust darkness.

Grief didn't arrive cleanly, but it did show up in indirect ways. Irritability flared over small inconveniences. Fatigue settled into my bones. Sometimes, in the middle of doing dishes or folding laundry, a memory would slide in— a particular gesture, a familiar phrase—and my throat would tighten for a moment. Not tears, exactly, but pressure. As if the emotion was trying to surface and the system that normally releases it had become clogged. I would pause, breathe, then continue. The pattern of my life became pause-and-continue. That was the shape of endurance.

What changed most over time wasn't the external scene but my internal relationship to it. I stopped expecting a moment of emotional clarity that would make everything feel resolved. Resolution began to look like a myth people tell to make grief feel orderly. Instead, there were small shifts: the ability to be present without constantly checking the exit. The ability to sit with my mother in silence without needing to fill it. The ability to walk into the apartment after a hard day and not immediately feel the walls as hostile. These were not victories. They were incremental tolerances. They were the slow training of a nervous system to accept that stability might be possible again, even if it would never look like the stability I used to imagine.

If the RV years were about making the world small enough to survive, the apartment years became about surviving in a world that could not be made small. The apartment forced exposure. Exposure forced adaptation. Adaptation forced me to confront an uncomfortable truth: the structures that kept me alive were not always the ones the world approved of. And the structures the world approved of were not always the ones that fit my internal reality. That mismatch—between external legitimacy and internal survivability—became the underlying tension of this period.

The chapter ends without the clean comfort of "and then things got better," because this part of life doesn't behave that way. It ends in an apartment that meets every rule on paper while still requiring constant internal negotiation. It ends with a family system altered by death and age and the slow violence of decline. It ends with me continuing to show up—sometimes numb, sometimes sharp, sometimes hollow, sometimes steady—learning that endurance is not a single heroic act but a hundred small decisions to keep moving through the day, even when the day doesn't offer meaning, even when grief doesn't arrive in the expected shape, even when the only thing that feels reliably mine is the next task written on a list and the quiet choice to finish it.

# CHAPTER 20

# *Residue*

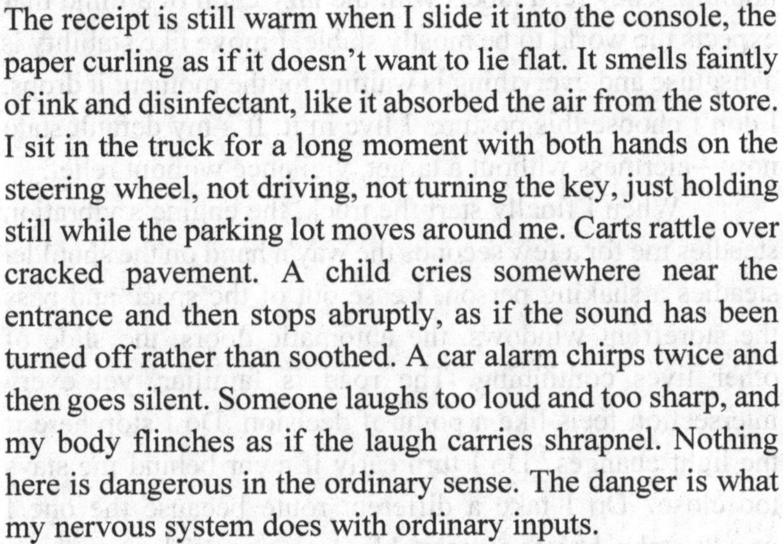

The receipt is still warm when I slide it into the console, the paper curling as if it doesn't want to lie flat. It smells faintly of ink and disinfectant, like it absorbed the air from the store. I sit in the truck for a long moment with both hands on the steering wheel, not driving, not turning the key, just holding still while the parking lot moves around me. Carts rattle over cracked pavement. A child cries somewhere near the entrance and then stops abruptly, as if the sound has been turned off rather than soothed. A car alarm chirps twice and then goes silent. Someone laughs too loud and too sharp, and my body flinches as if the laugh carries shrapnel. Nothing here is dangerous in the ordinary sense. The danger is what my nervous system does with ordinary inputs.

Inside the bag on the passenger seat are practical things: groceries, a bottle of soap, a lightbulb, a replacement cable I don't fully trust. The bag might as well contain ballast. My thoughts feel heavier with each item. On the way out of the store, I checked the faces of strangers without meaning to. I watched hands. I watched where people stood in relation to exits. I moved my cart so no one could get too close behind me. I pretended I was simply being polite about space, but my muscles were doing math my mind didn't ask for. Now I'm alone behind glass and locked doors, and I can feel the adrenaline slowly draining, leaving that familiar aftertaste—sour, metallic, like my body has been practicing for impact again.

I can't remember, sometimes, what it feels like to move through a place without scanning. I know it exists, because I've seen it on other faces. People drift through aisles half thinking about dinner, half thinking about nothing. They read labels with the lazy calm of a mind that expects the world to be mostly stable. I move like stability is a disguise and everything is waiting for the moment it drops. I don't choose this posture. I live in it. It's my default state now—alertness without a target, vigilance without relief.

When I finally start the truck, the engine's vibration steadies me for a few seconds the way a hand on the shoulder steadies a shaking person. I ease out of the space and pass the storefront windows, the automatic doors, the slide of other lives continuing. The road is familiar, yet every intersection feels like a point of decision. Do I stop here if the light changes? Do I turn early if a car behind me stays too close? Do I take a different route because the one I usually take has too many blind corners? These are the micro-calculations that fill my days. They don't feel dramatic. They feel normal in my body. That's the problem: the abnormal has become the baseline.

There is a phrase that shows up in certain forms and evaluations, a phrase so blunt it almost sounds theatrical until you realize it's meant to be clinical: *total occupational and social impairment*. It's written like a stamp, like a verdict applied with bureaucratic certainty. When I first saw language like that, part of me recoiled, because the words are too big. *Total* is an absolute word, and absolutes feel insulting when a person can still drive a truck, still buy groceries, still hold a conversation on a good day, still laugh at the right moment. But *total* doesn't mean I can't function at all. It means the impairment reaches into everything. It means the system that runs my mind has been altered in a way that touches work, relationships, memory, attention, sleep, mood, and the ability to handle stress without collapsing into something that scares me.

I can't tell the story of my life anymore without including the ways my mind fails me in ordinary moments. Not the movie version of failure—no dramatic blackouts, no constant screams—just the persistent distortion, the slow erosion, the unpredictable shifts. There are mornings when I wake up and my thoughts are already armed, lined up like a convoy waiting for a signal. There are afternoons when my brain feels clogged, as if the simplest task has to push through wet concrete. There are evenings when the world tilts slightly unreal, and the quiet becomes loud enough to press against my ears. On those days, communication itself can feel grossly impaired—not because I don't know words, but because the thread that ties words to intention frays unexpectedly, and I can feel myself reaching for language like a hand reaching into fog.

When I'm tired, I lose time in small ways first. I set something down and it disappears, not because it's gone, but because my mind didn't store the act of putting it down. I open a cabinet and forget why it's open. I walk from one room to another and stall in the doorway, disoriented not about where I am, but about what I was about to do. I'll catch myself standing still, staring at nothing, and only then remember that I was moving toward a purpose. That kind of disorientation is humiliating because it looks like laziness from the outside and feels like malfunction from the inside.

It teaches a person to live with constant low-level distrust of his own cognition.

There are worse moments too—moments that flirt with the edges of perception. The night voices that arrive like a crowd outside when no one is there. The sensation, when the house is quiet, that conversation is happening in the distance, indistinct but human, layered and persistent, as if people have gathered without inviting me. I've gotten up and checked more than once. I've looked out windows. I've opened doors. I've scanned for evidence. The evidence is absence. The voices fade when I force myself into motion, then return when stillness returns. It doesn't feel like supernatural horror. It feels like my brain misfiring in a way I cannot fully control. That single fact is enough to change how I trust myself.

Those symptoms didn't appear from nowhere. They are the residue of an environment that trained my nervous system into permanent readiness and then released me back into civilian life as if readiness could be turned off by location. In training and in deployment, there was a logic to hypervigilance. You learned to live inside threat assessment because threat assessment kept you alive. You learned to read the street, to read a face, to read the angle of a glance. You learned to notice the small anomalies: the vehicle parked too long, the crowd that shifts suddenly, the quiet that isn't peace but prelude. You learned that danger doesn't announce itself; it blends into the ordinary and then detonates.

That knowledge doesn't stay in the desert. It migrates into the body.

It shows up later in a grocery store aisle, in a parking lot, in a church pew, in a family living room. It shows up as a constant readiness to be betrayed by the next moment. It shows up as an inability to relax into the most basic assumption other people seem to carry easily: that the day will probably proceed without catastrophe. I can't hold that assumption reliably. My nervous system doesn't believe in "probably." It believes in "prepare."

There are memories that remain vivid in a way that feels unfair. The smell of burning that clings to fabric and hair. The taste of dust and heat. The sight of streets where human waste becomes the environment instead of an accident. The feeling of sitting in a seat meant for combat, watching a landscape for disturbances while knowing you cannot control what is hidden under the road. The way waiting for someone else—someone trained to handle explosives—turns time into a tense suspension, because you are required to continue existing in a place that might already be lethal. The aftermath of firefights—how quickly the adrenaline drains and leaves you hollow, still required to function, still required to write and report and coordinate as if the body hasn't just been taught that it can die.

I have also carried quieter memories that don't look like action scenes but shape the mind just as effectively: the requirement to meet people you know are hostile and still protect them because the mission demands it, the moral friction of keeping someone alive because the intelligence is valuable, the feeling of walking with only an interpreter because support is "there," somewhere unseen, somewhere that may or may not actually be there when things go wrong. The classified nature of some of that work adds another layer of distortion: you live experiences you cannot fully describe, then you return to a society that wants you to summarize your war in small talk. That gap becomes its own trauma. It teaches silence. It teaches isolation. It teaches the habit of carrying the heaviest parts alone.

The aftermath didn't arrive neatly either. It came in waves that looked, from the outside, like life events—relationships, jobs, moves—but inside those events were filtered through a nervous system that had been altered. Love became complicated because intimacy requires trust and trust requires a sense of safety. I learned to want connection and fear it at the same time. I learned to treat closeness as potential control. I learned to see the early signs of betrayal everywhere because betrayal is easier to survive when you anticipate it. That anticipation becomes corrosive. It turns ordinary misunderstandings into threats. It turns conflict into emergency. It turns a raised voice into a bodily alarm.

Then family dynamics began carving their own grooves into that already vulnerable landscape. The truth is that my family system has always been a place where control moves in subtle channels. Expectations are rarely spoken in simple terms. They arrive as pressure, as disappointment, as obligation disguised as concern. There were early years where I learned that peace at home wasn't always the absence of conflict; sometimes it was the presence of compliance. Sometimes it was easier to edit myself than to risk provoking a storm. That habit—self-editing, careful wording, constant monitoring of someone else's mood—became training too. Later, when my military training taught me to scan environments for threat, the scanning fit neatly into a childhood pattern: watch the room, read the cues, anticipate the shift.

As an adult, the family dynamics didn't simply fade. They intensified under stress. When I returned home after losing stability, the old house became a paradox: safety and suffocation. Dependence and regression. Familiar rooms carrying new humiliations. I lived again under household expectations, under routines that weren't mine, while my mind was already unstable from experiences that had taught me to treat the world as hostile. That is not a recipe for healing. It is a pressure cooker, because adult identity cannot fully develop when you are forced to live as a version of yourself from an earlier era.

Later, the family split—one fracture in particular— became a detonation rather than a disagreement. I carried a perception of betrayal like a lit fuse, and the fuse burned slowly in a house where I already felt watched and judged. When the explosion came, it didn't stay private. It turned into official narratives, into paperwork, into claims about my reality that were designed to neutralize me. The word *delusional* was used like a hammer because it doesn't argue; it discredits. That kind of label does damage beyond the immediate conflict. It teaches you that your perceptions can be weaponized against you. It teaches you to remain silent about anything that might be interpreted as unstable. It teaches a person to live behind glass even when he is speaking.

That fracture also taught me something darker about myself: how quickly anger can rise when I feel trapped, dismissed, cornered. The military taught me controlled aggression in appropriate settings. Trauma taught me that control isn't always reliable under pressure. Family conflict taught me that I can become someone I don't recognize when I feel morally cornered. That knowledge is one of the reasons isolation becomes attractive. It's not just a retreat from others; it's a containment strategy. If I reduce contact, I reduce the chances of becoming dangerous in a way that isn't physical but still harms—sharp words, accusations, scorched bridges.

After that, I attempted to build my life into smaller, more manageable shapes. I built a home on wheels because mobility felt like the only reliable safety. I learned to generate my own power because dependence felt dangerous. I tried to construct sanctuary through ritual and service and devotion because faith offers structure, and structure is one of the few things that can hold my mind steady. I pursued "treatments" that promised relief because desperation will make a person experiment with his own perception. Some of those experiences gave me brief glimpses of love and meaning so intense they felt like proof. Others gave me terror and distortion so intense they felt like a warning: the brain is a universe, and universes can become hostile.

Then external events reinforced the internal sense of persecution: thefts that went unresolved, losses that felt engineered by timing, violations that appeared precisely when I was trying to heal. Even when I remind myself that crime is common and randomness is real, the pattern recognition machinery in my brain does not care about rational reassurance. It has been trained to detect meaning. It assigns meaning anyway.

When the RV was taken—not by fire, not by storm, but by paper—it wasn't just inconvenience. It was the loss of my best containment structure. In that period, the system used the most vulnerable lever it could find: an elderly relative. The enforcement didn't simply target me; it threatened someone who couldn't afford the stress, then extracted compliance through that person's hand. Watching a ninety-something sign a document acknowledging fines if I lived there again did something permanent to my sense of safety. It taught me that survival itself can be framed as wrongdoing, and that the world will use family against you if it needs leverage.

After the RV, "proper housing" arrived with the same sterile legitimacy as any other bureaucratic solution. It satisfied rules. It did not satisfy my nervous system. I adapted, because adaptation is what I do, but the adaptation came with costs: money drained into furniture and compliance, routines rebuilt from scratch, sanctuary engineered in a space that didn't feel naturally safe. I learned to arrange my environment like a person building a defensive position—anchors, predictable object placement, visual reminders of order. I learned to make small rituals out of ordinary tasks because ritual keeps the mind from drifting into open water.

In the midst of that adaptation, the family system began collapsing under a different pressure: cognitive decline that became physical decline. Dementia isn't only forgetting. It's a slow dismantling of identity, a gradual evaporation of the person you knew. At first, the signs can be argued away: repeated questions, missing items, strange conclusions. Then the argument becomes impossible. Coordination falters. Judgment disappears. Confusion becomes the dominant climate. The household turns into a place of constant micro-crisis—redirect, soothe, repeat, cover, protect.

Watching that decline is its own trauma because it creates a permanent state of anticipatory grief. Every day is a rehearsal for loss. Every good moment becomes suspicious because you know it may not repeat. Every bad moment teaches you that the slope is steepening. Eventually hospitalization arrives, and the hospital becomes a stage where the family learns how little control it actually has. Machines beep. Staff speak in careful language. Time pools. Decisions hover like birds you don't want to feed.

The death itself did not feel like a dramatic thunderclap. It felt like a long door closing, slow enough that the mind tries to pretend it can stop the movement by watching it closely. The last hours were full of pauses— between breaths, between words, between small gestures— and each pause felt like an interrogation: *Is this the moment? Is this the moment? Is this the moment?* When the moment arrived, my mind registered it as fact. My body stayed quiet. Numbness took the place where grief was supposed to live.

That numbness frightened me more than tears would have. Tears would have proven I was still attached to ordinary human expression. Numbness felt like evidence of malfunction. I watched other family members break and felt myself remain behind glass. I participated in rituals. I spoke the right words. I offered help. Inside, I felt a second grief forming: grief not only for the loss, but for the way my own emotional machinery refused to respond.

It's an ugly truth that trauma can flatten the heart not because the heart is cold, but because the heart has learned that feeling deeply is dangerous. In hostile environments, intense feeling can get you killed. In unstable families, intense feeling can be used against you. Over time, the nervous system learns to shut down as a protective measure. That shutdown is not a conscious choice. It is a reflex. It is a survival mechanism that becomes a prison.

After the death, the family obligations didn't decrease. They multiplied. The surviving parent's world narrowed into grief, exhaustion, and practical burden. The house became both shrine and worksite—renovation dust mixed with mourning, unfinished projects made heavier by absence. Then the older relative fell and spent hours on a bathroom floor, and the image of that—an elderly body stranded, dignity stripped by gravity—became another marker in the timeline of decline. Rehabilitation followed. Rotating care schedules followed. Life turned into duty rosters and phone calls and calendar blocks, and my own fragile stability was repeatedly asked to stretch wider than it could.

This is where the phrase *intermittent inability to perform activities of daily living* stops sounding like an abstract symptom and begins describing the rhythm of my weeks. There are periods when I operate like a machine—cleaning, cooking, driving, attending to others, keeping lists, maintaining order. Then there are periods when the machine stalls. Hygiene becomes a negotiation. Meals become random. Sleep becomes fractured. The simplest tasks feel like hauling weight uphill through mud. The environment can remain tidy because I've trained myself to clean as a way to control anxiety, but the internal world can be collapsing while the outside still looks "functional." That mismatch is one of the reasons people misunderstand this kind of impairment. It doesn't always announce itself. It hides behind competence until competence runs out.

There are also times when my thought processes become so distorted that I don't trust them. The mind becomes a hostile narrator, interpreting neutral events as threats, interpreting coincidence as manipulation. When I'm under stress, the line between reasonable suspicion and paranoid interpretation can thin. I don't lose reality entirely. I don't live in a constant psychosis. But there are moments —particularly at night, particularly when sleep is broken—

when perception becomes unreliable enough that I have to treat my own brain like a witness who might be lying without intending to. That's a brutal way to live: constantly cross-examining your own thoughts.

And then there is the persistent danger—another phrase that gets used clinically, as if danger is an on/off switch. In my life, danger is more like proximity. I have lived moments where the exit door looked beautiful because the internal pressure became unbearable. I have lived moments where time slowed so much that the decision felt suspended in a frozen instant. I have lived moments where a small animal's weight, or a sound, or a sudden shift in sensation interrupted the spiral just long enough for the muscle to relax and time to resume. Those moments did not vanish after the crisis passed. They became reference points. They remain in the body as evidence that under enough pressure, I can become a risk to myself.

I am not constantly suicidal. That's not the truth. The truth is more unsettling: the capacity exists, and knowing it exists changes how I build my life. It means I don't treat despair as a poetic mood. I treat it as a threat vector. I manage it. I plan around it. I reduce triggers. I limit exposure. I keep routines and structure because structure is one of the few things strong enough to keep my mind from becoming the only place I live.

Work—ordinary sustained work—is complicated under these conditions. I have proven I can perform in bursts. I have held high grades. I have built systems. I have learned complex tools. I can be intensely competent when focus locks in and the environment is controlled. The impairment shows up in reliability. It shows up in tolerance for stress. It shows up in the way conflict detonates internal alarms. It shows up in the way deadlines feel like threats. It shows up in the way social contact drains me until I become brittle. It shows up in the way my mind, once flooded with stress, stops cooperating and turns even simple tasks into mountains.

This is why "occupational" impairment doesn't mean I can never do anything. It means the ability to function in a sustained, predictable, socially entangled environment has been compromised. I can sprint. I cannot reliably run a marathon. And life, unfortunately, is a marathon that demands sprinting at random intervals.

Relationships are similar. I can connect. I can be warm. I can care deeply. The impairment shows up in maintenance. It shows up in trust. It shows up in how quickly I interpret distance as rejection and rejection as danger. It shows up in how I withdraw when I feel misunderstood. It shows up in how I turn silent rather than risk saying something that will be used against me. It shows up in my reluctance to be fully seen, because being seen has too often led to judgment, labeling, control.

Family relationships are the most complicated because they are entangled with obligation. Even when affection is real, the dynamics can still be corrosive. There are patterns in my family that act like gravity: expectation, guilt, pressure to perform "normal," pressure to be grateful, pressure to comply. Those patterns intensify when illness arrives. They intensify when an elder needs help. They intensify when a parent declines. Under those conditions, the family system can become a place where everyone is exhausted, everyone is operating at the edge of their capacity, and any conflict becomes amplified. In that environment, my trauma-driven reactivity becomes a liability. My need for control becomes a liability. My sensitivity to being dismissed becomes a liability. The family doesn't have to intend harm for harm to occur. Harm occurs because everyone is strained and my nervous system is already raw.

There is a cruel loop in that: the family needs me, and the family also triggers me. I show up to help, and showing up exposes me to dynamics that activate the worst parts of my system. I withdraw to protect myself, and withdrawal produces guilt. Guilt produces self-recrimination. Self-recrimination produces depression. Depression reduces function. Reduced function increases pressure from others. The loop tightens. There is no clean solution. There is only management, and management is exhausting.

Faith has been part of that management. Not as a magic answer, but as structure. Ritual, service, covenants—these provide rails. They give the day shape. They tell the body what to do when the mind is chaotic. They offer language when language fails. They offer a sense of being watched that is not hostile, or at least is supposed to be not hostile. Yet faith has also been a battleground in my mind because trauma turns morality into a weapon. It makes the mind search for what went wrong, what was deserved, what was punished. It makes ordinary suffering feel like a verdict. Under that pressure, even prayer can feel like negotiation with a judge rather than conversation with a parent.

I have tried therapy. I have tried medication. I have tried group settings and private settings. Sometimes the interventions help. Sometimes they frustrate. Sometimes they feel like putting bandages on a structural fracture. There is value in learning language for symptoms, value in understanding that irritability is not simply character, that numbness is not simply coldness, that hypervigilance is not simply paranoia. Language doesn't cure anything. It provides a map. A map helps a person stop blaming himself for every terrain feature. It also makes the terrain more visible, and visibility can be painful. Once you see the system, you can't pretend it's not there.

This is the full weight, then: the events of my life didn't simply happen and end. They trained my nervous system into a permanent posture. They carved pathways of fear, suspicion, numbness, and compulsive control. They taught my mind to treat the world as a place where catastrophe can arrive disguised as ordinary life. They taught my body to react before thought. They taught my emotions to shut down when intensity becomes dangerous. They taught my relationships to become potential threat environments. They taught my faith to become both refuge and courtroom.

There is no scene that resolves this. There is no climax where the mind "understands" and therefore heals. Understanding is not enough because the injury is not only cognitive. It is physiological. It is spiritual in the sense that it touches meaning. It is social in the sense that it changes how I exist among humans. It is occupational in the sense that it changes what I can reliably produce under pressure. It is total in the sense that it reaches into everything—sleep, memory, concentration, impulse control, tolerance, trust, joy.

Even joy is complicated. There have been moments of intense joy—moments where love felt like a field I could stand inside. Those moments don't erase the baseline. Sometimes they make the baseline harder, because contrast is cruel. Feeling what is possible makes ordinary numbness feel like a deeper prison. And joy, when it arrives too quickly, can make my system suspicious. It can feel like bait. It can feel like the moment before the slap. That is how damaged trust behaves: it doesn't trust the good either.

There are days when I appear functional, even stable. I run errands. I speak politely. I help where I can. I keep a space clean. Those days are real. They are not performance alone. They are also not proof of wellness. They are the result of constant management—constant monitoring of stimulus, constant structuring of time, constant adjustment of environment, constant internal negotiation. On those days, I am not "cured." I am regulated. Regulation takes work. Work takes energy. Energy is limited. When the energy runs out, the symptoms return like gravity.

And then there are days when the impairment is obvious even to me. Days when my mind is fogged enough that I can't trust simple decisions. Days when irritability is so close to the surface that even small friction feels like attack. Days when I cannot tolerate noise. Days when I cannot tolerate people. Days when I cannot tolerate myself. Those are the days when the phrase *gross impairment* stops sounding like an exaggeration and starts describing the lived reality: thought processes derailed, communication threaded with gaps, perception tinted by threat, the internal narrator hostile and persuasive.

I do not want to be defined by those days. Yet I can't honestly describe my life without admitting that those days are part of the pattern. They are not rare enough to dismiss. They are not predictable enough to schedule around. They are not dramatic enough to earn easy sympathy. They are simply present, like weather that keeps changing without forecast.

And family remains part of the ongoing pressure. The surviving parent's grief has its own gravity, pulling the household into a new orbit. There is more silence now. There is more exhaustion. There is more brittle patience. The older relative's vulnerability remains, and with it the constant fear of the next fall, the next hospitalization, the next call that will arrive at a bad hour. There are still fractures with other relatives that have not healed, not because healing is impossible in principle, but because the trust required for healing has been damaged on both sides. The past arguments remain active in the nervous system even when they are not spoken aloud. Silence does not erase them. Silence preserves them.

This is where a story usually offers redemption—a turn toward forgiveness, a final acceptance, a lesson learned. I cannot offer that without lying.

Some damage can be integrated. Some cannot. Some scars become part of identity. Some remain open. Some wounds don't close cleanly because the environment keeps reopening them—noise, conflict, bureaucracy, loss, the ordinary cruelty of aging and decline. The mind adapts, but adaptation is not always improvement. Sometimes adaptation is simply survival at a higher cost.

So the ending is not clean. The ending is a continuation of management. The ending is a life lived inside constraints that are invisible until they aren't. The ending is a mind that can still produce pages and still lose itself in fog. The ending is a heart that can still care deeply and still go numb at the moments it "should" break. The ending is a body that can still flinch at harmless sound because harmless sound shares a frequency with danger.

I finish this book the way I finish most hard things: not with triumph, but with exhaustion and a kind of blunt honesty. There is no satisfaction in the final summary. There is only the admission that the machinery inside me is still running, still reactive, still shaped by what it had to survive. The war did not stay in the war. The aftermath did not end when the uniform came off. The family dynamics did not soften simply because time moved forward. The losses did not become meaningful simply because they happened. Meaning is not automatic. Meaning is work. Sometimes the work fails.

The most accurate final statement is also the least comforting: the story ends, but the condition does not. The mind remains a place where the smallest stimuli can become alarms. The body remains a place where danger is assumed. Relationships remain a place where trust is expensive. Faith remains a place where refuge and fear coexist. Daily life remains a place where function is possible, but not guaranteed.

I drive home with the groceries and the receipt in the console and the sun sliding lower, and everything looks normal. The houses. The trees. The sky. My hands on the wheel. My face reflected faintly in the windshield. Normal is the disguise the world wears. Inside that disguise, I carry the residue: the desert heat, the convoy silence, the smell of burning, the moral friction, the losses, the family fractures, the paperwork, the thefts, the enforced relocations, the hospital lights, the long door closing, the numbness that followed, the endless management.

There is no conclusion that resolves those elements into peace.

There is only the next day, and the next, and the ongoing practice of containment—building small sanctuaries, maintaining routines, avoiding triggers, showing up when required, withdrawing when necessary, surviving without pretending survival is the same thing as healing.

That is the final shape.

Not an answer.

Not a cure

A system that keeps running.

# **Afterword**

Writing this book did not feel like assembling a story. It felt like standing in a room that kept changing shape while I tried to take measurements. I would enter with a plan—one chapter, one timeframe, one clean line of motion—and the room would move its walls. A memory would surface with the wrong timestamp but the right emotional signature. A detail would arrive with a smell attached to it, a sound, a posture in the body, and the mind would insist that the detail mattered more than chronology. The work became less about forcing life into order and more about tracking the way the system inside me responds when it is touched. That system has its own priorities. It elevates certain moments and buries others. It returns the same scene again and again until the scene becomes not a story, but a reflex.

Some material was easy to locate because it had been rehearsed for years. Certain scenes repeat themselves without permission, and repetition makes them easier to describe even when it does not make them easier to carry. The danger of rehearsed memory is that it becomes polished. It turns into a story that can be told with the right cadence, and the polish can make the suffering look manageable. Writing forced me to strip that polish away and return to the sensory truth: the moment before impact, the way breath changes when threat is perceived, the way time thickens, the way the body continues behaving as if the past is still present. I had to describe what it costs to live with those reflexes rather than simply list the events that produced them.

Other material had not been rehearsed at all. It existed as sealed containers—rooms the mind avoids because entering them floods everything. Those moments arrived while I was writing something else, a transitional line or a quiet observation, and suddenly the page would pull my attention into a different part of the house. The return was not gentle. It arrived as a bodily fact: the jaw tightening, the chest constricting, the heat behind the eyes, the urge to get up and move as if movement could keep the memory from catching. I learned that what the mind calls "forgetting" is often a kind of containment. It is not absence. It is storage. Writing became an act of opening storage without knowing what would fall out.

It would be convenient to say the act of writing provided catharsis, that putting the events into narrative order created relief. Sometimes it did. Naming a pattern can reduce its power. Describing a sensation can turn it from private terror into an object that can be examined. But catharsis was not the dominant outcome of telling a story like this. The dominant outcome was exposure. Once something is named, it becomes harder to deny. Once something is written, it becomes harder to pretend the system is simply a mood. Exposure also changed what I could tolerate. After certain writing sessions, the world felt louder, sharper, closer. The body stayed activated long after the keyboard was quiet, as if the act of recalling had reopened the threat environment and the nervous system was unwilling to accept that the danger had ended.

Exposure also changed the meaning of silence. Before this book, silence was often a strategy. Some things were not spoken because speaking them felt dangerous— dangerous socially, dangerous inside the family system, dangerous because institutional language can be weaponized. Silence kept me from being dismissed or labeled. Silence kept me from giving anyone the ammunition they wanted. Writing broke that silence, which means the protective layer became thinner. It also forced me to confront a problem I could not solve cleanly: the need to speak honestly without turning other people into targets. The story required truth. The truth required boundaries. Those two requirements were not always easy to hold at the same time.

The book cannot restore what was lost, and it cannot reverse what was learned. The person who came home did not step into civilian life as a blank slate. He stepped into it with reflexes built for a threat environment and moral friction built from choices made under pressure. Those reflexes remain in the body even when the mind knows they are disproportionate. The book can describe that disproportion. It cannot remove it. In some ways the writing process made the disproportions clearer because it forced me to track them across years: the same posture appearing in different rooms, the same alertness showing up where it does not belong, the same suspicion attaching itself to ordinary interactions.

The family system did not disappear when service changed my nervous system. It remained an environment with its own pressures—pressure to perform normality, pressure to comply, pressure to minimize discomfort, pressure to keep the household stable by keeping emotion small. Families remember older versions of a person and demand continuity with those versions. They remember the child, the teenager, the young adult, and they expect the adult to remain accessible in the same shape. That expectation can feel like love and it can also feel like a trap. When I returned to familiar ground after losing stability, I did not return as the person who had left. I returned altered, and the household did not have a clean place to put that alteration.

Grief did not unify the household into tenderness. It rearranged it into fatigue and brittle patience. Decline creates constant micro-crises: redirect, repeat, soothe, cover, protect. It turns ordinary life into continuous management, and management makes everyone sharper, more defensive, more easily irritated. That atmosphere interacts badly with a nervous system already tuned for threat. Conflict feels larger than it is. Tone becomes a trigger. Silence becomes loaded. A small misunderstanding can detonate because it lands in a body that has already learned that misunderstandings can become consequences. The family dynamic becomes both the place where obligation pulls hardest and the place where the internal system is most easily activated.

The surviving parent's grief became its own gravity, pulling the household into a new orbit. There were more pauses in conversation, more long silences that did not feel restful. There was a constant low-level tension about what would happen next—another appointment, another night of confusion, another emergency that would arrive at the worst hour. The elder's vulnerability did something similar. When an elder can fall and remain on the floor for hours, the mind begins living in contingency plans. Every day contains a background question about what will happen if the phone rings, what will happen if no one answers, what will happen if the body fails at the wrong time. Those questions do not stay in the mind. They migrate into the body. They become insomnia. They become shallow sleep that never fully rests.

There is an ethical complexity in writing about family at all. The purpose here is not to put names on people and turn them into villains. Most harm inside families is not performed with conscious cruelty. It is performed through pattern, through fear, through shame, through unexamined habits, through the pressures of scarcity and decline. A person can love and still harm. A person can intend good and still create damage. Illness can erase patience. Grief can sharpen the voice. Control can masquerade as care. I tried to keep those truths intact without flattening anyone into a single trait. The story remains mine, but the environment that shaped it included other lives, and the book had to hold that complexity without making prosecution the point.

The military experience carries its own distortion because it is difficult to translate without becoming either performative or sanitized. War is not a cinematic sequence of explosions in memory. It is a climate. It is the taste of dust and heat. It is the smell that clings to fabric. It is the way time behaves when the road might be seeded with something hidden. It is the moral friction of protecting someone because the mission demands it even when instinct says the person is hostile. It is the requirement to act calm while the body is ready for impact. It is the way an ordinary street can become a threat environment because the infrastructure has failed so completely that danger is baked into the landscape.

After the uniform came off, the machinery did not power down. Hypervigilance is the simplest word for it, but the lived version is more granular: scanning hands, tracking exits, reading tone, anticipating betrayal, measuring distance, monitoring sound. In the military context, those behaviors are adaptive. In civilian life, they become exhausting. They turn errands into missions and social contact into exposure. They turn quiet into danger because quiet resembles prelude. They turn joy into suspicion because joy feels like bait. The body can react to harmless stimuli as if they share a frequency with something lethal. That is the residue that follows into rooms where nothing is supposed to be happening.

Institutional language sometimes feels both validating and insulting. Validating because it acknowledges that something real occurred and continues to occur. Insulting because it compresses a complex internal world into categories. Yet categories matter in a world governed by paperwork. They are how suffering becomes legible to systems that allocate care and compensation. Learning those phrases was not an act of identity. It was an act of translation. Translation is necessary when the world demands proof. It is also dangerous because translation can become a mask. It can make the world believe it understands when it does not. A phrase can never fully hold what it feels like to live inside an altered operating system.

The full texture includes moments that appear small from the outside and are enormous internally: standing at the stove unable to remember why the burner is on, reading the same sentence repeatedly without comprehension, losing the thread of a conversation mid-sentence and feeling humiliation rise, flinching at harmless sound as if it were incoming. It includes disorientation that is not theatrical but persistent—rooms entered and forgotten, objects set down and lost, minutes that evaporate because attention broke without warning. It includes days when the mind feels fogged and days when it feels too sharp, as if thought itself is a blade that cannot be safely put away. Those shifts are part of why life becomes management rather than flow.

There have also been periods where the danger was not external. The danger was my own mind under pressure.

Those periods were not constant, which is part of what makes them frightening. A stable week can be followed by a day where internal logic shifts and cessation begins presenting itself as a solution. It is not that death is desired. It is that exhaustion narrows options until stopping looks like relief. The book described moments where time slowed and the mind became relentless, cataloging reasons, prosecuting weakness, offering mercy only in the form of exit. Those moments are not written for drama. They are written because they are part of the system and pretending they do not exist would be dishonest.

Competence complicates the picture. Competence still exists. I can think deeply. I can build systems. I can learn complex material. I can produce pages and projects. Competence is real, and it is part of why the condition is often misunderstood. People expect illness to be consistent; they expect a person to be either capable or incapable. My life refuses that binary. Function arrives in windows and disappears without warning. It depends on sleep, stimulus, stress, interpersonal friction, physical pain, and internal mood. That dependence makes ordinary planning dangerous. It is difficult to promise reliability when the brain does not always cooperate with intention.

Unreliability breeds shame because the world tends to judge based on the high days and dismiss the low days as choice. Shame then becomes fuel for isolation. Isolation becomes fuel for rumination. Rumination becomes fuel for depression. Depression reduces capacity. Reduced capacity increases pressure from obligations that do not pause. The loop tightens. This is where family dynamics and institutional systems intersect with internal symptoms in the worst way. A household can treat a low day as laziness. A system can treat it as noncompliance. Both interpretations amplify the shame. Shame makes the mind smaller, more defensive, more prone to withdrawal, which then looks like further evidence that something is wrong with character rather than nervous system.

Writing also clarified how much of my life is structured around preventing escalation. That fact becomes visible only in contrast, when life briefly becomes easier and the body does not know what to do with ease. The protective systems do not step aside politely. They keep operating, searching for the threat that must exist because threat has always existed. In those moments, calm feels like an error state. The mind becomes almost bored and almost panicked at the same time, hunting for a problem to solve because solving problems has been the only reliable posture. This is one reason rest can feel dangerous. Rest removes the tasks that keep the mind anchored, and without anchor the mind drifts toward the places it has been trained to revisit.

There were periods while drafting where the clean story tempted me. A clean story assigns single causes, locates villains, and arrives at a lesson that makes pain feel worthwhile. A clean story uses childhood as destiny or war as the only explanation. A clean story grants closure because closure sells and closure feels like relief. The temptation was not only commercial. It was psychological. Closure would mean the mind could stop looping. Closure would mean the costs had earned a prize. The problem is that closure would be a lie. The system inside me does not operate like a three-act structure. It operates like weather. It shifts. It returns. It repeats. It escalates under pressure and calms under structure, and then it escalates again when structure is disrupted.

Accuracy also required restraint. Some details were vivid and would have made scenes more dramatic, but drama is not the same as truth. The most dangerous kind of memoir is the one that makes suffering entertaining. That was never the goal. Certain descriptions remained broad where specificity would compromise privacy or create a false sense of instruction. Some moments were presented as atmosphere because atmosphere is what I actually remember. Some people were kept intentionally indistinct because the purpose was not identification. This restraint is not softness. It is boundary. It is the difference between using pain as spectacle and using pain as evidence of cost.

The act of record-keeping carries its own cost. When an event is placed on the page, it no longer lives only as sensation. It becomes an object with edges, and those edges can cut in new ways. I noticed a particular kind of fatigue after writing certain sections, not because the memories changed, but because attention made them more present. There were days where the nervous system stayed activated for hours after a writing session ended, as if the body believed it was still in the environment being described. That activation had consequences: irritability, insomnia, the urge to isolate, the urge to control small things because small things were what could be controlled.

The spiritual dimension remains unresolved as well. Faith provided structure and language, but it also became another field where the mind tries to prosecute itself. Trauma encourages verdicts. It encourages the idea that suffering is evidence of failure, that pain is punishment, that weakness is sin. Those ideas are not always taught directly; they can arise internally from a mind desperate to find cause. Faith, when it helps, does not remove symptoms. It gives them a frame that is larger than the symptom, and it provides ritual when the mind cannot create motivation. Faith, when it harms, becomes another place where perfection is demanded and where falling short becomes evidence of worthlessness.

If something changed through the making of this book, it was not symptom removal. It was orientation. Before, the events existed as scattered charges. Now they exist as a mapped system with identifiable feedback loops. That mapping does not prevent flare-ups, but it alters how I interpret them. A surge of irritability can be recognized as activation rather than character. A numb day can be recognized as shutdown rather than moral failure. Recognition does not eliminate responsibility, but it changes the frame in which responsibility is carried. It reduces the unnecessary shame. It also exposes the real work: not self-condemnation, but management.

Another cost that remained hard to describe until it was written is the way concealment becomes an identity. Once a person learns that disclosure can be used as evidence, he begins editing himself before he even speaks. The editing becomes automatic: what can be said safely, what must be softened, what must be omitted, what must be translated into acceptable terms. That constant self-monitoring is exhausting. It can make ordinary conversation feel like a negotiation with an invisible jury. Over time, the edited version becomes the default presentation, and the unedited version becomes private even from the self. Writing required contact with the unedited version, and contact with it came with both relief and risk.

That exhaustion is one reason anger can rise so quickly. Irritability is often treated as a character flaw, but in my life it is frequently the smoke from an overloaded system. Too much stimulus, too many demands, too little sleep, and the nervous system begins searching for release. The release can be sharp words, sudden withdrawal, or a coldness that looks like indifference. None of those are satisfying. They simply reduce load in the short term and expand damage in the long term. Once harm has occurred, guilt follows. Guilt becomes another weight. The system gets heavier. The threshold for activation drops. That is how the loop feeds itself.

There is a particular kind of loneliness that develops when life becomes management. It is not the loneliness of being unloved. It is the loneliness of knowing that the internal labor is mostly invisible. A day can look calm from the outside while the inside is running a constant threat simulation. A person can appear functional while fighting to keep attention from dissolving. A household can see the help that is offered and still not see the cost of offering it. Over time, that invisibility can feel like a separate injury. It becomes easy to conclude that being understood is impossible and that isolation is safer, even when isolation also worsens the internal climate.

Stability, when it appeared, rarely arrived as comfort. It arrived as work. It arrived as systems: routines, controlled environments, engineered sanctuary. It arrived as strategic choices about exposure—where to go, when to go, how long to remain, what stimuli to avoid. It arrived as containment strategies that look like preference from the outside and feel like survival from the inside. This is why the book does not end with a cure. A cure would imply the systems are no longer necessary. In my life, the systems remain necessary because the nervous system remains altered. The best days are regulated days. The worst days are days where regulation fails.

Physical pain has been another quiet amplifier. Injury and chronic tension reduce patience, reduce sleep, and narrow the margins where regulation is possible. When the body hurts, the mind interprets the world through a tighter aperture. Small stressors land harder. Ordinary tasks feel heavier. The nervous system runs hotter, and the heat makes it easier for old patterns to ignite: irritability, withdrawal, and the internal insistence that something is wrong even when the day is simple. Pain also makes stillness more difficult, and stillness is often required for rest. The result is a feedback loop where sleep is disrupted, disruption increases pain, and increased pain further disrupts sleep. The body and mind do not negotiate in isolation. They carry each other, and when one is overloaded, the other pays.

The unresolved quality is not a tease. It is the condition. Aging continues its work. Family obligations continue their demands. The surviving parent's grief continues to shape the household's atmosphere. The elder's fragility remains a constant contingency. Fractures with other relatives remain active, not because reconciliation is impossible in principle, but because trust has been damaged and damage is slow to repair when pressure keeps reopening it. The mind continues to scan. The body continues to flinch. Meaning still requires work, and sometimes the work fails. That failure is not always dramatic. Sometimes it looks like numbness. Sometimes it looks like withdrawal. Sometimes it looks like a day that collapses quietly without anyone outside noticing.

If there is a closing thought worth offering, it is that survival can be unsentimental. It can be quiet. It can be repetitive. It can be a series of small choices made without inspiration. It can be a person washing a dish because leaving it in the sink will become disorder, and disorder will become noise, and noise will become panic. It can be a person driving to a family obligation even when the body wants to stay inside a controlled room. It can be a person choosing to answer a phone call even when the sound of the phone spikes the heart rate. Survival can be disciplined without being joyful. It can be mechanical without being meaningless. It can be imperfect and still be the correct choice for that day.

The story ends here because pages must end somewhere. The machinery does not. The nervous system still assumes danger. The mind still misfires. Grief still arrives in strange forms. Obligation still collides with capacity. Meaning still requires work, and sometimes the work fails. What remains, in the absence of resolution, is continuation—daily management, imperfect endurance, the refusal to let the internal world become the only world. That refusal does not feel triumphant. It feels like a system that keeps running, one day at a time, because stopping would cost more than continuing.

## Author's Note On Process

I did not write this book easily. I wrote it with a mind that does not move cleanly from thought to language, a mind shaped by injury, fragmentation, and long periods where meaning arrives faster than words can follow. For years, that gap made this book impossible. I knew what happened. I knew how it felt. I could not always make language hold it.

To bridge that gap, I used artificial intelligence as a tool—not to invent experience, not to supply memory, and not to decide meaning, but to help translate internal chaos into structured language.

Every event in this book is mine. Every judgment is mine. Every sentence was accepted, rejected, reshaped, or discarded by me.

The AI did not live these moments. It did not feel them. It did not choose what mattered. It functioned as an adaptive instrument—similar to dictation software, editing tools, or assistive technology—allowing me to impose order on material that otherwise resisted articulation.

This book exists because I refused to let damage dictate silence. If anything, the process mirrors the content: a life that did not resolve cleanly, expressed through means that were not traditional, but were necessary.

The story is authentic because the experience is authentic. The method was simply how I survived telling it.

# Timeline

**1980–1987  —  *First Rooms*  (Ch.  II)**
Early childhood in the first house. Family atmosphere establishes baseline patterns of safety, pressure, and attention.

**1987–1992  —  *Second Yard*  (Ch.  III)**
Move to the next house. Grade-school years; routine thickens, undercurrents sharpen.

**1992–1995  —  *Between Bells*  (Ch.  IV)**
Middle school. Social friction, identity strain, and early signals of being out of sync with the "normal" world.

**1995–1998  —  *The Exit Door*  (Ch.  V)**
High school intensifies and breaks. School collapses; leaving becomes the chosen line of motion.

**1998  —  *Borrowed Order*  (Ch.  VI)**
Navy service begins and ends. Institutional discipline collides with the first visible costs.

**1998–2000  —  *After the Uniform*  (Ch.  VII)**
Back home. Work, drift, and early attempts at rebuilding.

**2000–2002  —  *The Ring Dish*  (Ch.  VIII)**
A serious relationship forms and dissolves. Intimacy and instability begin accruing interest.

**2002–2004  —  *Years of Vanishing*  (Ch.  IX)**
Pre-Army years. Survival-mode living; forward motion that doesn't feel like progress.

**2005  —  *The Machine Moves*  (Ch.  X)**
Army enlistment and training pipeline. Function becomes identity; the nervous system begins rewriting itself.

**2006 — *Dust and Silence* (Ch. XI)**
Deployment to Iraq. High-intensity operational life, constant vigilance, moral friction, and danger that extends past the mission.

**2006–2008 — *The Long Debrief* (Ch. XII)**
Return and processing under strain. Injury, reclassification, continued training cycles; the body and mind stop aligning with ordinary recovery.

**2008–2012 — *Wide Sky* (Ch. XIII)**
Move to the Southwest. Career and domestic life shift repeatedly; instability becomes a living condition, not an episode.

**Winter 2012–2013 — *Winter Roads* (Ch. XIV)**
Extended winter road trip through major landmarks. Distance used as regulation while internal pressure continues building.

**2013 — *Frozen Time* (Ch. XV)**
Acute crisis period. Internal logic turns predatory; survival narrows to moments.

**2013–2017 — *Learning Help* (Ch. XVI)**
Aftermath: treatment, bureaucracy, work restructuring, and attempts at stability. A later job loss forces a major reset.

**2017–2019 — *Learning Help* (Ch. XVI)**
Return to the old home region. Game-development pivot; family decline becomes unavoidable; a second university attempt is set in motion.

**2019–Spring 2022 — *Altered Semesters* (Ch. XVII)**
University with accommodations. Academic structure alongside intensified inner life and altered-state experiences. Family tension builds toward a rupture.

**Spring 2022–2024 — *A Hitchable Home* (Ch. XVIII)**
After the fallout: RV life becomes a survival capsule. Rising religious involvement. Increasing caregiving demands as an elder and a parent decline. Treatment and therapy attempts continue. Major thefts and burglaries deepen the sense that safety is provisional. A close friend dies; grief registers strangely, as absence more than emotion.

**March–April 2025 — *A Hitchable Home* → *Thin-Walled Quiet* (Ch. XVIII–XIX)**
An ordinance notice ends RV living. Forced transition into an apartment; major financial and psychological cost. Family crisis peaks: hospitalization and death. An elder's later fall compounds the load.

**2025–near-present — *Thin-Walled Quiet* → *Residue* (Ch. XIX–XX)**
Life becomes ongoing management: grief, family obligation, and a mind trained for threat—functional in windows, unstable without warning, unresolved by design.

# Glossary

*This glossary defines terms, substances, and symptom-language as used in the manuscript. Entries are written to clarify meaning without adding plot or interpretation.*

**accommodations** - Formal adjustments granted by a school or institution to account for disability-related needs (for example: reduced-distraction testing, extra time, flexible attendance, alternate formats).

**ADHD (inattentive presentation)** - Attention that drops out without permission — difficulty sustaining focus, tracking multi-step tasks, retaining what was just read or said, and returning to a task once interrupted. Often experienced as "fog," drifting, or failing to initiate even when intention is present.

**after action report (AAR)** - A structured review of what happened, what worked, what didn't, and what changes next time.

**alcohol** - A depressant that can temporarily blunt intensity while often worsening sleep quality, mood stability, and rebound symptoms over time.

**anxiety** - A sustained state of apprehension that can feel like the body preparing for impact even when nothing is happening.

**auditory hallucinations** - Hearing voices or speech-like sound without an external source. In the manuscript this appears as night voices that feel real enough to provoke checking, searching, and doubt about perception.

**avoidance** - Reducing contact with people, places, tasks, or reminders because exposure spikes symptoms—even when avoidance creates long-term costs.

**burn pit / burn pits** - Large open-air fires used to dispose of waste in and around operational areas. In practice, "burn pits" also included (and were often indistinguishable from) other uncontrolled fires—sometimes set by local nationals

—burning unknown contents and producing thick, black smoke that could drift into living and work areas.

**cadre** - Permanent staff who run, support, or evaluate training (as opposed to students passing through).

**calling** - A church assignment — usually unpaid — intended as service and responsibility within the congregation.

**cigarette / cigarettes** - A nicotine delivery method through smoke inhalation; often paired with ritual and regulation attempts while reinforcing dependence and withdrawal cycles.

**coffee** - A common caffeine source; a stimulant that can sharpen alertness while also intensifying anxiety, agitation, and sleep disruption in sensitive systems.

**combat-related PTSD** - A persistent threat-state learned in environments where vigilance kept you alive. Can include hypervigilance, startle response, intrusive memory, avoidance, irritability, sleep disruption, emotional numbing, and a body that reacts before thought.

**combat-related traumatic brain injury (TBI)** - Brain injury linked to combat exposures (including blasts and concussive impacts). Can present as headaches /migraines, concentration impairment, irritability, sleep disruption, light/sound sensitivity, memory lapses, and reduced stress tolerance.

**concentration impairment** - Difficulty holding focus, following steps, or sustaining mental effort—often worsened by stress, poor sleep, and pain.

**convoy** - A coordinated group of vehicles moving together for security and control in a threat environment.

**crash / burnout** - A period of system depletion after prolonged strain—reduced function, reduced tolerance, and increased symptoms even when external demands remain unchanged.

**CBD** - Cannabidiol — a cannabis- derived compound often marketed for calming or pain relief; effects vary by dose and product.

**derealization** - A sense that the world is unreal, distant, staged, or wrong — often emerging under stress, fatigue, or overload.

**depersonalization** - Feeling detached from the self—as if watching your own life from a distance rather than inhabiting it.

**depersonalization / derealization** - A paired lens in which self and world feel altered—"behind glass," "not real," or disconnected — especially during high stress or sleep disruption.

**depression** - More than sadness: reduced drive, flattened pleasure, slowed thinking, and internal heaviness that makes basic life feel expensive.

**detainee** - A person held in custody during operations for questioning, processing, or detention.

**dissociation** - A disruption in how experience is felt and integrated — detachment, time distortion, emotional shutdown, or "going blank" under threat.

**dissociative episodes** - Periods where the system "cuts power" to reduce overwhelm—going blank, losing continuity of thought, time distortion, or becoming emotionally unreachable. Not a mood; a protective shutdown that can interfere with memory and communication.

**DMT** - Dimethyltryptamine — a powerful, short-acting psychedelic associated with rapid onset and intense shifts in perception, time sense, and reality framing. Experiences can include vivid imagery and a strong sense of presence; aftereffects can include lingering destabilization, awe, fear, or reframing of meaning.

**disorientation** - Momentary loss of purpose or "why I'm here" — rooms entered and forgotten, tasks started and dropped, steps lost mid-sequence—often producing shame and self-distrust.

**dyslexia** - Difficulty with reading fluency and decoding that can show up as slow reading, skipped lines, transposed letters, fatigue with text, and difficulty retaining written information at speed — often misread as inattention.

**EOD** - Explosive Ordnance Disposal —specialists who locate, identify, and neutralize explosives.

**erectile dysfunction** - Difficulty achieving or maintaining erection. Can be influenced by stress physiology, depression, medication effects, self-image, and trauma-linked nervous-system activation.

**emotional numbing** - A protective shutdown where expected feeling doesn't arrive (especially around grief or crisis), leaving flatness that feels wrong rather than peaceful.

**exhaustion / fatigue** - Not ordinary tiredness—system depletion that reduces tolerance, increases reactivity, and makes regulation fragile.

**FOB** - Forward Operating Base—a secured base used for operations in a combat zone.

**Fort Huachuca** - A U.S. Army installation associated with intelligence training.

**Fort Irwin / NTC** - A major desert training area where units rehearse deployment-style operations under realistic conditions with opposing forces and full-mission problems.

**Fort Sill** - A U.S. Army installation associated with basic training.

**GPA** - Grade Point Average—an academic measure of performance.

**gross impairment** - Severe disruption in thought processes or communication — derailment, gaps, inability to track or express the intended thread—especially under stress or fatigue.

**guilt** - Self-blame that persists after conflict or harm, often becoming fuel for withdrawal and depression.

**hallucinations (persistent / intermittent)** - Perceptual experiences that occur without an external source. In the manuscript these are stress-linked and often appear at night, contributing to distrust of perception.

**HUMINT** - Human Intelligence — intelligence gathered from people (sources, interviews, debriefs), not from signals or imagery.

**Human Intelligence Collector Training Course** - A formal training program focused on collecting, handling, and reporting human intelligence through structured methods.

**hypervigilance** - Persistent scanning for threat—exits, hands, tone, sounds—even in settings that should be safe; exhausting because it never fully turns off.

**IBS (Irritable Bowel Syndrome)** - Gastrointestinal instability—pain, urgency, cramping, and irregular patterns — often worsened by stress and sleep disruption, and often functioning as a body-level alarm when the nervous system runs hot.

**IED** - Improvised Explosive Device—an improvised bomb (often hidden along routes) designed to damage vehicles and personnel.

**interpreter** - A person who translates language in real time and often functions as a cultural bridge during field interactions.

**interrogation** - A structured questioning process intended to extract information; in the manuscript often conducted under time pressure and risk.

**intrusive thoughts / intrusive memory** - Unwanted mental material that pushes into attention — images, phrases, bodily sensations, or loops that arrive without permission.

**irregular sleep cycles** - Sleep that does not settle into a consistent rhythm—late onset, fragmented rest, early waking, reversal of day/night patterns, or periods of exhaustion without restorative sleep.

**irritability** - Low threshold for frustration; often "smoke" from overload rather than a simple personality trait.

**ketamine** - A dissociative anesthetic used clinically in monitored settings for severe depression and suicidal ideation; can produce altered perception, time distortion, detachment, and an "observing self" separated from ordinary emotion.

**loneliness** - Not simply lack of people, but the felt distance created by mistrust, self-editing, withdrawal, and the invisibility of internal labor—being around others without feeling reachable or understood.

**LSD** - Lysergic acid diethylamide — a potent psychedelic associated with profound changes in perception, emotion, time sense, and meaning-making.

**major depression pattern** - A sustained depressive climate marked by low drive, flattened pleasure, slowed cognition, and periods where daily living tasks become mechanically difficult — often alternating with windows of function rather than resolving cleanly.

**marijuana / weed** - Cannabis. Effects can include relaxation or intensified anxiety depending on dose, setting, and individual vulnerability.

**migraines** - Severe headache episodes that can include light/sound sensitivity, nausea, cognitive slowing, and a need to isolate in darkness or quiet.

**moral injury** - Lasting internal conflict produced by actions, constraints, betrayals, or required compromises that violate one's moral code — often manifesting as shame, self-prosecution, numbness, anger, or spiritual distress rather than a single "memory."

**Mormon** - A term commonly used to refer to members of The Church of Jesus Christ of Latter-day Saints (the manuscript uses the term as it appears in lived speech).

**mushrooms** - Common term for psilocybin-containing mushrooms; effects can include altered perception, intensified emotion, and shifts in time sense.

**National Training Center / NTC** - A major U.S. Army training site designed to simulate deployment conditions with realistic field problems, opposing forces, and operational tempo.

**nicotine** - A stimulant and dependence-forming substance. Can briefly sharpen focus and calm agitation while reinforcing withdrawal cycles.

**obesity** - Weight gain and metabolic strain often entangled with injury, disrupted sleep, depression, medications, reduced activity, and stress physiology — less a moral issue than a system-level consequence.

**panic** - A surge of fear and bodily alarm — racing heart, breath changes, urgency — often disproportionate to the setting.

**panic-spectrum episodes** - Acute surges of fear and bodily alarm that can be triggered by ordinary stimuli (sound, crowd density, tone, sudden change), producing fast escalation into escape behavior or shutdown.

**paranoia** - A threat-interpretation bias where neutral events feel targeted or loaded with intent, especially during stress, sleep loss, or conflict.

**physical pain / chronic pain syndrome** - Persistent pain functioning as a constant load — reducing sleep quality, narrowing tolerance, increasing irritability, and making regulation fragile.

**PRK** - Photorefractive Keratectomy—a laser eye surgery procedure used to correct vision.

**psilocybin** - A psychedelic compound found in certain mushrooms; associated with altered perception and emotional intensity.

**psychotic-like symptoms** - Perceptual disturbances that don't fit ordinary stress—especially hearing voices or speech-like sound without an external source —paired with increased checking, hypervigilance, and distrust of perception. Intermittent and often stress-linked rather than constant.

**rage / anger spikes** - Rapid escalation into heat and sharpness, often followed by guilt; can function as pressure release when the system is overloaded.

**rating** - A formal disability evaluation level used by the VA to quantify severity and determine benefits.

**RPG** - Rocket-Propelled Grenade—an explosive weapon capable of severely damaging vehicles and personnel.

**RV / RV park** - Recreational Vehicle; an RV park is a designated location where RVs can be parked with hookups and site rules. In the manuscript, the RV also functions as containment—shelter, boundary, and sanctuary.

**self-harm / suicidal ideation -** Thoughts or impulses toward self-destruction ranging from passive wishing to active planning. In the manuscript this is treated as a recurring risk condition rather than a single episode.

**service connection -** A VA determination that a condition is linked to military service for benefits purposes.

**shame -** The sense that symptoms are moral failure — often intensified by misunderstanding from others and by internal self-prosecution.

**source / source operations -** A source is a person who provides information. Source operations are the meetings, handling, protection, reporting, and risk management around that relationship.

**startle response -** Disproportionate flinching or alarm at ordinary stimuli (slams, laughter, sudden noises) because the body treats sound as threat-coded.

**structure -** A containment method: routines, lists, rituals, and predictable environments used to reduce internal volatility and prevent escalation.

**temple -** A dedicated religious building used for ordinances and worship distinct from ordinary weekly services.

**therapy -** Professional mental health treatment; in the manuscript both a practical support and a recurring friction point with institutional systems.

**THC -** Tetrahydrocannabinol — the primary intoxicating compound in cannabis. Can produce relaxation, paranoia, or panic depending on dose and context.

**time distortion -** A felt slowing, thickening, or warping of time during threat, crisis, or altered states, making moments feel endless and decisions feel frozen.

**tinnitus -** Persistent ringing, buzzing, or hissing perceived without an external source. Often worsens in silence and can contribute to irritability, sleep disruption, and sensory overload.

**total occupational and social impairment** - A phrase used in official disability language to describe severe, pervasive disruption across work capacity and relationship capacity — impairment that touches most areas of functioning, even when some outward competence remains.

**trigger** - A stimulus (sound, smell, situation, tone, memory cue) that activates a disproportionate stress response.

**Unreal Engine 4 / UE4** - A game-development engine used to build interactive projects; UE4 is the abbreviation used in the manuscript.

**VA** - Department of Veterans Affairs — the U.S. agency providing healthcare and benefits to eligible veterans.

**Visual Snow Syndrome** - A visual disturbance often described as static/grain across the visual field, sometimes accompanied by afterimages, halos, light sensitivity, and difficulty tolerating bright environments.

**warrior transition unit / WTU** - A unit designed to support service members with complex medical needs during recovery and administrative transition.

# Comprehensive Discussion & Question Guide

*Designed to work for general book clubs, veterans and military families, clinicians and peer-support groups, faith communities, educators/students, caregivers, and readers interested in craft.*

## How to use this guide

- You don't have to use every section. Pick the audiences that match your group.
- Many questions are written to allow multiple "entry points": emotional, ethical, structural, and practical.
- If your group includes people with lived trauma, consider starting with the **Grounding & Safety** section.

## Grounding & Safety

1. What topics felt most activating or heavy, and what made them heavy: content, pacing, language, or familiarity?
2. Which parts felt "too close," and which parts felt "protected by distance"?
3. What boundaries does the narrator seem to use to survive (routines, withdrawal, faith, control of environment)? Which boundaries feel protective, which feel costly?
4. Where does the book invite empathy without demanding pity?
5. If your group needed to pause or skip, where did that become necessary?

## Orientation Questions For Any Audience

6. What does the title *Still Here: Life Unresolved* establish as the book's contract?
7. What does "unresolved" mean here: symptoms, relationships, meaning, identity, faith, or all of the above?

8. Which single word best describes the voice: restrained, clinical, lyrical, ruthless, tender, controlled, detached, intimate?

9. What did you notice about pace: what slows down, what speeds up, and why?

10. What is the book most interested in proving: events, costs, systems, endurance, or something else?

## Structure, Time, and Memory

11. How does the book portray memory: archive, weather, threat-response, narrative construction, or moral accounting?

12. What does the book gain by alternating between scene-level detail and atmosphere?

13. When the book returns to repeated motifs (routine, scanning, paperwork, sanctuary, silence), do they evolve or loop? Where do they evolve?

14. How do the transitions from "now" into "then" shape trust in the narrator and the story?

15. What does the book suggest about chronology: helpful framework, incomplete container, or something the nervous system ignores?

16. Where does the narrative feel most "linear," and where does it feel intentionally non-linear in effect?

17. Which chapters felt most essential to the spine of the book, and which felt like necessary breath or connective tissue?

## The Core Lens: Systems (Internal and External)

18. What systems keep the narrator alive: personal habits, faith structure, institutional support, isolation, work competence?

19. What systems harm him even when they're "neutral": bureaucracy, family roles, housing rules, social expectations?

20. Where do you see systems colliding (family + illness, military + civilian life, faith + mental health, housing + legality)?

21. What's the difference in the book between **management** and **healing**?
22. Where does the book show that "function" can exist alongside serious impairment?

**Family Systems & Roles**

23. How does the book portray obligation: love, duty, control, fear, identity, or survival economics?
24. How do family expectations shape the narrator's self-editing?
25. Where do you see the household's "emotional weather" change over time?
26. How does cognitive decline reshape the family system: roles, authority, conflict, silence, vigilance?
27. What is the book's stance on blame: does it assign it, avoid it, redirect it, or complicate it?
28. Which family dynamics feel like gravity—quiet forces that persist even when no one speaks about them?
29. Where does the narrator's need for containment conflict with family needs for availability?

**Military Experience & Aftermath**

30. How does the book show the nervous system being trained—without relying on heroism or spectacle?
31. Which civilian scenes best reveal how that training "migrates" into ordinary life?
32. What is the moral friction the book hints at, and how does restraint make it stronger?
33. How does the book portray competence under pressure versus competence in a stable environment?
34. Where do you see "mission thinking" show up in civilian contexts?
35. What does the book suggest about the cost of returning home when the body doesn't fully accept "home" as safe?

**Symptom-Lens Without Turning The Book Into A Diagnosis**

36. Which symptoms are shown most through behavior rather than labels (sleep disruption, hypervigilance, irritability, shutdown, time distortion)?
37. How does the book distinguish sadness from depression, fear from vigilance, anger from overload?
38. Where does emotional numbing appear, and why does it read as alarming rather than calm?
39. What does the narrator do when he doubts his own perception? What does that reveal about self-trust?
40. Which passages show "internal labor" most clearly —work no one else sees?
41. Where do you see cycles: activation → harm → guilt → withdrawal → increased load?

**Altered States & Treatment Experiences**

42. What purpose do the altered-state sections serve in the overall arc: relief, insight, destabilization, meaning-making, or amplification?
43. How does the book avoid turning those experiences into either advertisement or warning label?
44. Which descriptions felt most embodied (time, body sensation, perception changes)? Why did they land?
45. How does the narrator interpret "signs" or pattern, and what does the book suggest about the mind's need to create meaning under stress?
46. Where do these experiences intersect with faith, grief, or family obligation?

**Faith Communities & Spiritual Readers**

47. How does faith function here: structure, refuge, obligation, identity, community, or discipline?
48. Where does ritual feel stabilizing, and where does it feel like pressure?
49. How does the book portray spiritual certainty versus spiritual hunger?
50. What does faith do when symptoms don't resolve? What does it provide anyway?

51. How does community service (callings/roles) interact with the narrator's capacity and limits?

**Caregiving, Illness, and Loss**

52. How does the book portray anticipatory grief (the grief that begins before death)?
53. What does it show about the grind of care: repetition, exhaustion, vigilance, bureaucracy?
54. Where does the narrator find dignity in caregiving? Where does he lose it?
55. How does the book portray death without turning it into "closure"?
56. How does the family's grief alter the narrator's inner climate—does it sharpen symptoms, flatten emotion, or reorganize priorities?

**Housing, Legitimacy, and the Meaning of Sanctuary**

57. What does "sanctuary" mean in this book: safety, control, quiet, boundary, ritual, invisibility?
58. How does the narrative treat "legal" versus "livable"?
59. Why do paperwork and enforcement land as violence even without physical force?
60. What does it cost the narrator to lose a containment structure?
61. How does "approved living" change the body's sense of threat, if at all?

**Work, Identity, and Capacity**

62. What does the book show about competence that arrives in bursts but doesn't stay reliable?
63. How does schooling function differently from employment in the narrator's life?
64. Where does the narrator's identity depend on usefulness, output, or performance?
65. How do deadlines, evaluation, and judgment affect symptoms?
66. What does the book suggest about dignity when capacity fluctuates?

**For Clinicians, Peer-Support Groups, and Trauma-Informed Readers**

67. What coping strategies are adaptive in one environment and maladaptive in another?

68. Where does the narrator demonstrate insight without relief (knowing the pattern but still living it)?

69. How does the book portray shame as a mechanism, not just a feeling?

70. Which moments show dissociation or shutdown without naming it?

71. How does moral injury show up: guilt, numbness, spiritual conflict, self-prosecution, anger?

72. What "protective factors" exist in the text (relationships, routines, faith, animals, structure, purpose)?

73. What "risk factors" recur (sleep loss, conflict, isolation, pain, bureaucracy, loss)?

74. Where does the narrator's narrative remain coherent even when his internal state is unstable? Why does that matter?

**For Veterans and Military Families**

75. What rings true about the transition from threat environment to civilian environment?

76. How does the book portray the strange mismatch between external normalcy and internal alarm?

77. Which parts capture the "not-talked-about" aspects: moral friction, classified boundaries, institutional language?

78. How does camaraderie appear—explicitly or indirectly—and what does its absence cost?

79. How does the family system interact with service aftermath: support, misunderstanding, pressure, identity conflict?

80. What does the book suggest about resilience that isn't inspirational—just disciplined survival?

**For Educators, Students, and General-Interest Readers**

81. What did you learn about trauma without being "taught" a lesson?
82. Which craft choices made complex mental states legible without simplifying them?
83. Where do metaphors clarify, and where do they intentionally resist clarity?
84. What does the book show about disability as fluctuating capacity rather than constant inability?
85. How does the narrative avoid a single-cause explanation while still building a coherent arc?

**Craft & Writing Questions (for writers, editors, and serious readers)**

86. What is the book's primary engine: suspense, accumulation, revelation, dread, or endurance?
87. How does repetition function: motif, pressure, echo, insistence? Where does it intensify, where does it flatten?
88. Which scenes carry the most weight because of sensory detail rather than explanation?
89. Where does the prose become "too explanatory," and where does it become perfectly embodied?
90. How do transitions operate as thesis statements for each era?
91. Which chapter title best matches its chapter's job, and which title might be improved for precision?
92. Where does the book withhold information to protect ethics or maintain tension—and does it feel earned?

**Ethics, Responsibility, and Representation**

93. What does the book owe the people who appear in it, and how does it balance that with the narrator's truth?
94. How does the book handle suicide content without turning it into spectacle?
95. How does it handle altered states without turning them into instruction?
96. What does "privacy" look like on the page: omission, generalization, compression, composite detail?

97. What does the book suggest about institutional systems: necessary, harmful, both, indifferent?

**Ending and Anti-Resolution**

98. What does the ending deny: closure, redemption, moral tidiness, cure, forgiveness?
99. What does it still offer: clarity, honesty, documentation, witness, a map, a cost ledger?
100. Which final images or phrases keep working in your mind after closing the book?
101. What would a "false ending" look like for this book—what kind of ending would betray it?
102. What does "still here" mean at the end: endurance, refusal, discipline, habit, containment, love, or something darker?

**Activities**

**A. Motif Trace**

Pick one motif (structure, scanning, silence, sanctuary, paperwork, routine). Identify 3 appearances across the book. How does its meaning shift?

**B. System Map**

Draw two columns: *internal system* (sleep, vigilance, mood, pain) and *external system* (family, institutions, housing, faith). Mark where they collide.

**C. Scene vs Summary Audit**

Choose one chapter. Identify one passage that is fully embodied scene and one that is reflective summary. Discuss what each accomplishes.

**D. "Cost Ledger" Discussion**

List the costs portrayed: relationships, money, sleep, self-trust, work capacity, meaning. Which cost felt most permanent, and why?

## Crisis and Support Resources

If you or someone you know is in immediate danger, call **911** (U.S.) or your local emergency number.

**U.S. — Immediate crisis support**

**988 Suicide & Crisis Lifeline** (24/7)
Call or text **988**. Chat is available online.

**Veterans Crisis Line** (24/7)
Dial **988**, then **Press 1**.
Or text **838255**.
Chat is available online.

**U.S. — Substance use support and treatment referral**

**SAMHSA National Helpline** (24/7)
Call **1-800-662-HELP (4357)** for treatment referral and information (English/Spanish).

**U.S. — Disaster-related emotional distress**

**Disaster Distress Helpline** (24/7)
Call or text **1-800-985-5990**.

**Outside the U.S.**

If you're not in the United States, you can find verified free helplines by country through:
**Find A Helpline** (global directory)
**Befrienders Worldwide** (global network of support centers)

# Acknowledgments

This book exists because certain people and institutions held pieces of my life steady when my own steadiness was inconsistent. Some of that help was intentional and personal. Some of it was procedural and impersonal. Both mattered. I'm grateful for every form of support that made it possible to keep moving, to keep building, and to keep writing.

To the professionals who helped me translate my internal life into something workable: the clinicians, therapists, evaluators, instructors, and administrators who met me with patience and structure. Thank you for listening without flinching, for offering language when my own words failed, and for treating my experience as real even when it was difficult to describe. The work you do is often invisible until it isn't, and I'm grateful for the steadiness you brought to mine.

To the medical teams who handled the practical realities—appointments, assessments, medications, procedures, follow-ups—thank you for the competence that allowed me to keep functioning. Some days, stability arrived as paperwork done correctly, a schedule kept, a question answered, a process completed without unnecessary friction. Those things may look small from the outside. From inside the system, they are foundations.

To the educators and university staff who made it possible for me to return and persist: thank you for creating pathways that acknowledge difference without reducing a person to it. Thank you for accommodations that protected the work from my worst days. Thank you for deadlines that provided structure, for coursework that demanded focus, and for the quiet accountability that kept me oriented toward forward motion.

To the people I served with: thank you for the competence, the humor, the seriousness, and the mutual reliance that made difficult environments survivable. Thank you for the discipline and the standards that shaped my ability to function under pressure. Thank you for the ordinary camaraderie—the small moments of humanity inside a world that often didn't feel human.

To those who carried responsibilities that extended beyond any official role—interpreters, local partners, and people who made collaboration possible in complex conditions—thank you for the work you did and the risks you carried. Thank you for the ways you helped build understanding across gaps that could not be crossed by force.

To supervisors and coworkers across the jobs that followed service, especially those who recognized my strengths and made room for my limitations: thank you for the trust you placed in me. Thank you for the projects that gave me purpose, for the routines that kept me structured, and for the respect that let me contribute without constantly defending my right to be there.

To mentors—formal and informal—thank you for guidance that came at the right times. Thank you for conversations that reframed what I thought was possible. Thank you for the steady insistence that skill can be built, that work can be learned, that a future can be engineered one piece at a time.

To friends—those who stayed close and those who passed through—thank you for presence. Thank you for laughter when laughter was scarce. Thank you for invitations, messages, rides, meals, and the simple act of not disappearing when life got complicated. Thank you for treating me like a person rather than a problem to solve.

To those I met in group settings and shared spaces— rooms where people spoke about symptoms without needing to perform them—thank you for the quiet solidarity. Thank you for the kind of honesty that makes a person feel less alone without requiring a solution. Thank you for the reminder that endurance can be a shared language.

To the communities that gave me structure through service and ritual: thank you for the vocabulary of devotion, the routines of worship, and the opportunities to contribute. Thank you for the sense of order that comes from belonging to something that asks for consistency. Thank you for the moments of peace that arrived not as revelation, but as repetition.

To family: thank you for the ways you showed up, for the practical help that kept life moving, and for the shared commitment to take care of what needed to be taken care of. Thank you for the history that made my life intelligible to itself. Thank you for the continued presence that turned obligation into a kind of endurance.

To the animals who became anchors—quiet lives that asked for basic care and gave uncomplicated companionship—thank you. Thank you for the weight of a body against mine, for the interruption of spirals, for the small rituals of feeding and presence. Thank you for being a kind of sanctuary that doesn't require explanation.

To every system that did what it was designed to do —benefits administered, procedures scheduled, resources made available—thank you for the stability those structures made possible. I know those systems are built from people doing ordinary work, and I'm grateful for every ordinary task done well.

To the early readers, the people who gave feedback, and the ones who asked the right questions: thank you for helping shape what this book became. Thank you for pushing for clarity without pushing for comfort. Thank you for respecting the difference between a clean story and an honest one.

And finally: thank you to the part of me that kept returning to the page. The writing was not always gentle. It was not always healing. But it was honest work. It made the internal world legible, even when legibility was painful. It turned survival into record. It turned record into a book.

## About the Author

The author is a U.S. military veteran who has spent his adult life moving between systems that demand performance and systems that measure damage. After service, he worked in training and instructional environments, shifted into software development and technical problem-solving, and later returned to university coursework with formal accommodations. His work has ranged from structured institutional roles to self-directed projects built under uneven capacity.

He lives with service-connected injuries and a nervous system shaped by prolonged exposure to threat, bureaucracy, and loss. He is also a person of faith, drawn to structure, ritual, and the hard discipline of continuing without neat conclusions.

*Still Here: Life Unresolved* is his first book.

www.ingramcontent.com/pod-product-compliance
Lightning Source LLC
Chambersburg PA
CBHW011923050726
47591CB00009B/2307